XML Internationalization and Localization

Yves Savourel

201 West 103rd Street, Indianapolis, Indiana 46290

XML Internationalization and Localization

Copyright © 2001 by Sams Publishing

International Standard Book Number: 0-672-32096-7

Library of Congress Catalog Card Number: 00-111800

Printed in the United States of America

First Printing: June 2001

04   03   02   01   4   3   2   1

Trademarks

All terms mentioned in this book that are known to be trademarks or service marks have been appropriately capitalized. Sams Publishing cannot attest to the accuracy of this information. Use of a term in this book should not be regarded as affecting the validity of any trademark or service mark.

XML (eXtensible Markup Language) is a generic term used by MIT, INRIA, and Keio on behalf of the World Wide Web Consortium (W3C®).

Photoshop is a registered trademark of Adobe Systems Incorporated. Déjà Vu is a trademark of Atril. System3 is a trademark of GlobalSight Corporation. OpenTag is a registered trademark of International Language Engineering Corporation. Flash is a registered trademark of Macromedia. TMX and TBX are registered trademarks of the Localisation Industry Standards Association. SQL Server and Windows are registered trademarks of Microsoft Corporation. OmniMark is a trademark of OmniMark Technologies. Rainbow and Horizon are trademarks of RWS Group LLC. SDLX and SDLWebFlow are trademarks of SDL International. Transit is a trademark of STAR. Translator's Workbench is a trademark of TRADOS Gmbh.

Warning and Disclaimer

EXECUTIVE EDITOR
Michael Stephens

ACQUISITIONS EDITOR
Carol Ackerman

DEVELOPMENT AND TECHNICAL EDITOR
Ultan Ó Broin

MANAGING EDITOR
Matt Purcell

PROJECT EDITORS
Natalie F. Harris
Sheila Schroeder

COPY EDITOR
Cynthia Fields

INDEXER
Eric Schroeder

PROOFREADER
Matt Wynalda

TEAM COORDINATOR
Lynne Williams

MEDIA DEVELOPER
Dan Scherf

INTERIOR DESIGNER
Dan Armstrong

COVER DESIGNER
Alan Clements

PAGE LAYOUT
Mark Walchle

Overview

Contents

About the Author

Yves Savourel has been involved in internationalization and localization for more than a decade: first at International Language Engineering (ILE), then at Sykes Enterprises, and now at the RWS Group. His first localization project was WordStar version 7 in six languages and in IBM Assembler. Too lazy to deal with the tedious work of resizing strings manually, Yves wrote a utility to do it. This led to more tools, and ultimately the creation of the R&D group at ILE.

While giving software internationalization classes and providing consulting, Yves' main focus has always been on developing tools and solutions for localization processes. SGML and XML have been part of these developments. Yves is one of the creators of the OpenTag format and technical co-chair of the OSCAR group at LISA for TMX. He is also part of the recent development of XLIFF and other XML-related initiatives for internationalization and localization.

Yves is a native of Brittany. He lived in France, Africa, and on islands in the Indian Ocean before settling in Boulder, Colorado. He is still a traveler at heart, and takes every opportunity to learn about different cultures and see new horizons, whether they are peaceful Burmese villages on the banks of the Kwai River or hectic business parks in Silicon Valley.

Dedication

To Amity

Acknowledgments

Many people have influenced the writing of this book through their support, their guidance, or their comments. They have not simply made the book better: They have made it possible.

Yves Lang—From the misty Inca ruins of Machu Pichu to the scorching Australian desert, from the rainy fjords of New Zealand to the blue lagoons of Bora-Bora, and from the slopes of the Himalayas to the deep forests of Borneo, he shared many adventures with me and always encouraged my dreams of writing.

Bernard Gateau—In a Parisian café, a warm spring morning many years ago, he took a chance and hired me as a localization engineer despite my complete inexperience, and without even asking if I could speak English. He has been a visionary entrepreneur and one of the main pioneers of the localization industry. I, like many others, owe him a lot.

Ultan Ó Broin, who did the technical editing of this book, patiently corrected many errors and suggested many changes. Richard Ishida, who is at the origin of many ideas and provided helpful notes, and Shigemichi Yazawa, whose solid knowledge of XML, deep understanding of internationalization, and good advice is always so useful (Chapters 7 and 8 are their work as much as mine). Christian Lieske, who managed to make his numerous comments not only extremely pertinent but also fun to read. Brooks Kline, for his suggestions and help with so many details from making graphics to setting up Oracle. Clove Lynch, whose sharp eyes found various inconsistencies and mistakes.

This book is also the work of many people at Sams who have spent long hours to produce the pages you are perusing now. Michael Stephens, Carol Ackerman, Natalie Harris, Sheila Schroeder, Cynthia Fields (thanks for making my poor English readable), Matt Wynalda, Lynne Williams, Vicki Harding, Katie Robinson, and all the other people who have contributed were patient, understanding, and much more than helpful. Thanks to Laurel Wagers from Multilingual Computing & Technology for putting me in touch with them.

Many thanks should also go to the people who helped one way or another in specific parts of the book: Susan McCormick, Daniel Brockmann, Alan Melby, David Pooley, Laurent Romary, Barb Schnell, and Carlos Villar. Thanks also to RWS for letting me take the time to work on this book.

These pages contain text in various languages. Many people were kind enough to spend some of their free time to provide me with these translations. Thanks to the staff at RWS and WorldPoint (many languages); Yishak Woldemariam Tedla, Daniel Yacob, and Menasse Zaudou (Amahric and Tigrigna); Sherri Zhu (Chinese); Dena Bugel-Shundra (Hebrew); Elisabeth Naiman (German); Jack Cain (Inuktitut); Shigemichi Yazawa, and Yusuke Kirimoto (Japanese); Signe Rirdance and John Freivalds (Latvian); Darek Krol (Polish); Sergei Mouraviev and Sergei Rodinov (Russian); Nalinrat Krittiyanont Guba (Thai); Milen Epik (Turkish); and others who helped in the translations.

In addition to those who helped me write this book, there are also the people who made XML and Unicode in the first place. They deserve much more than the few lines here:

Jon Bosak, Bert Bos, Tim Bray, James Clark, Mark Davis, Michael Everson, Asmus Freytag, Rick Jelliffe, John Jenkins, Chris Lilley, Eve Malher, Mike Ksar, David Ragett, and many others have been instrumental in the making of XML and Unicode. Martin Dürst, Richard Ishida, Tex Texin, Michel Suignard, Misha Wolf, François Yergeau, and their colleagues in the W3C Internationalization Working Group have made multilingual XML possible.

These people are the true dreamers and makers of Unicode and XML. They are not only highly knowledgeable but also incredibly responsive and helpful. By patiently explaining the intricacies of these standards to many like you and me, they have given us the powerful communication means that XML and Unicode are. Today and in the future, the Egyptian executive looking up quotes on his cell phone, the Russian student surfing the Web, or the Chinese manager querying his inventory might not know how much they owe to the people who worked on the construction of these standards. I do, and, frankly, I think we should name streets and avenues after them.

Whatever experience you accumulate and can use when writing a book comes from the people you have worked with through the years. I was very lucky the past decade to work with a number of outstanding people, and without them I certainly would not know much more now than when I started.

The ILE R&D Crew: Darlene Baze, Bill Brotherton, Milen Epik, Jim Hargrave, Thierry Sourbier, Shigemichi Yazawa, and its other members and associates throughout the years: Chris Anderson, Mark Brissenden, Chris Cowperthwait, Sue Gallup, Nalinrat Krittiyanont Guba, Clove Lynch, Walter Smith, and Debbie Wilcox. I learned much from them, and must thank them for the good habits they forced me to take, and for letting me, from time to time, "hold the world" in our meetings.

I have also been fortunate to be part of a few special interest groups in which the knowledgeable participants helped me understand the problems related to localization with XML.

One of these groups is the OSCAR committee, especially Denise Baldwin, Robert Barnary, Scott Bennett, Mustafa Borçbakan, Henri Broekmate, Sarah Caroll, Gerard Cattin des Bois, Daniel Grasmick, Etienne Kroger, Ben Martin, Alan Melby, Nikolai Puntikov, Enda McDonnell, David Pooley, Franz Rau, Russ Rolfe, Ann-Loy Searle, Mark Son-Bell, Cornelis Van Der Laan, Logan Wright, and the initiators of ITS: Steven Forth, Richard Ishida, Jörg Schütz, and Jorden Woods.

Another group is the XLIFF group, dedicated and so easy to work with, especially John Corrigan, Fiona Ebbs, Tony Jewtushenko, Milan Karásek, Mark Levins, Matthew Lovatt, Enda McDonnell, John Reid, and Peter Reynolds.

These people proved that competitors could build something together for the good of the industry. Much of the progress you have seen in localization in recent years came from them. I learned a great deal working at their side, not only about technologies but also about listening and learning from another's opinion.

Thanks also to the people with whom, in various circumstances, I worked on XML-related topics: Peter Cheeseman, Malcolm Ishida, Steve Peterson, Christian Sestier, and Jussi Sipola.

And, finally, thanks to the staff of Old-Chicago at Boulder, who put up with me during many long evenings when I was drafting and editing these pages. They kept my plate and glass full, and—when it was needed to keep me sane—made me, for a few hours, forget everything about XML internationalization and localization.

Tell Us What You Think!

As the reader of this book, *you* are our most important critic and commentator. We value your opinion and want to know what we're doing right, what we could do better, what areas you'd like to see us publish in, and any other words of wisdom you're willing to pass our way.

As an executive editor for Sams, I welcome your comments. You can fax, e-mail, or write me directly to let me know what you did or didn't like about this book—as well as what we can do to make our books stronger.

Please note that I cannot help you with technical problems related to the topic of this book, and that due to the high volume of mail I receive, I might not be able to reply to every message.

When you write, please be sure to include this book's title and author as well as your name and phone or fax number. I will carefully review your comments and share them with the author and editors who worked on the book.

Fax: 317-581-4770

E-mail: feedback@samspublishing.com

Mail: Michael Stephens
            Sams
            201 West 103rd Street
            Indianapolis, IN 46290 USA

Foreword

When Isaac Newton wrote "Principia," his language of choice was Latin rather than his mother tongue of English. This befitted both the period and the educated readership of the era during which he lived. Newton was already aware of a principle that many of today's businesses have accepted only recently: Technical information is only informative if the intended audience can read it. The globalization of most industries today has resulted in a great diversity of people who need access to technical information. Material authored in one language might need to be made available in over 30 languages. To keep companies moving at the accelerated pace to which they have grown accustomed, this goal must be achieved in the shortest possible time and at the lowest possible cost.

Within the last 15 years, a whole new industry has flourished to make technical information available in the native language of the reader, regardless of the language of origin. This new activity has been labeled "localization" because it puts material into the language of local users around the world. Its most fundamental precept is that translation is but one of a slew of processes needed to transform information, both content (text) and presentation (tagging), into an equivalent message in a foreign language.

In the last few years, the increased need for immediacy of multilingual versions and, simultaneously, the mounting pressure for cost containment have forced the localization industry to look for new solutions. It is clear that any successful localization activity requires the support of a dedicated localization tools development team. Lacking any development antecedents, this endeavor had to be started from scratch. Some unique talents were needed to make it happen.

It took someone with an unusually broad vision of the world and an acute understanding of the technical challenges of localization to pull together solutions to a problem of such multidisciplinary dimensions. With degrees in history, geography, and computer sciences, Yves Savourel was that person. When I asked him to join us at ILE Corporation in 1990, I knew he would be able to help with our ongoing development of localization tools. I had no inkling of the absolutely innovative thinking he would apply to problems which themselves were barely visible on the localization horizon.

XML Internationalization and Localization is the result of eleven years of Yves' conceptualization and development of localization tools. In a way, these years have been one long, enormously fruitful brainstorming session, with seeds sown and new ideas grafted onto the old in a long continuum. Yves' dedication to localization tools development, together with the universality of XML and Unicode, finally bring a compilation of practical solutions for using XML to create truly internationalized formats. The book also explains how best to apply XML in various localization solutions. The outcome is improved text portability across internationalization and localization tools, across content management solutions and visualization environments, and across localization suppliers.

XML Internationalization and Localization provides the most complete information and up-to-date technologies for implementing truly multilingual and portable text-handling solutions. And it is written in English, not in Latin.

Bernard Gateau
Founder of International Language Engineering

Here is a book from someone who really knows what he is talking about, and knows how to say it. Yves has a firm grasp of the technical aspects of XML development, which he complements with a wealth of experience in the field of localisation. The writing style is extremely clear—accessible to people unfamiliar with internationalisation issues, but never tedious to those who are. The book is also well equipped with useful examples, and ranges impressively over the whole subject area. Globalisation of technology and products has never been more topical, so whether you are an XML developer, producer, or localizer this remarkable work should be on your bookshelf.

Richard Ishida
Internationalisation Consultant
W3C, Unicode, and LISA contributor

Introduction

The sun, high in a sky spotted with massive clouds, heats the heavy air charged with humidity: Borneo, the big island under the tropics, north of Papua New Guinea. Here, far from Western civilization, computers and screens, I'm looking forward to a real vacation. No running water or air conditioning; just the sky, the trees, the mud, and the wilderness. Our longboat is plodding steadily through the latté-colored waters of the Sukau River between the dense vegetation of the banks. The low humming of the engine is almost covered by the noise of the forest.

We reach a place where we have to slow down: A knot of half-submerged trunks is blocking the channel. Our boatman grabs his long pole and slowly guides the canoe through the obstacle.

Suddenly a strange chirping sound pierces the droning of the jungle. While I'm wondering what bird could make such an annoying sound, the boatman reaches to the stack of clothes piled at his feet, brings a little black box up to his ear, and starts talking in Malay. So much for being far from technology! He tucks the cell phone between his shoulder and his ear and resumes guiding the boat through the flow, just like a Silicon Valley commuter weaving his car through rush-hour traffic.

I can't understand what he is saying, but he looks excited. He smiles at us. I forget the intrusion of the cell phone; I even like it now: Maybe someone from the camp has spotted some interesting birds or animals on the way back and, warned in time, we will be at the right place at the right moment to see them. I listen more intently, and suddenly catch a word: "Internet." No, that can't be right. For a few wild seconds I hold on to the improbable hope that it is, by some strange coincidence, the local name of a subspecies of proboscis monkey or white-crested hornbill. No such luck: after hearing the words "server" and "ISP," I must face the truth: Ahmed, our friendly boatman, has a dark side—he is also a Webmaster.

Many months later, I was hiking under the high canopy of the Amazon forest on a muddy trail leading to an ox-bow lake to watch piranhas. Between brief stops to point out tarantula burrows and rare birds' nests, Hernando, our young Peruvian guide, was chatting eagerly…about his HTML classes at school, and the latest Web technology.

Then, not long ago, while walking in the packed and colorful streets of Jahipur, in Radjasthan, I couldn't help but observe the numerous signs that advertised Internet outlets. Kriss, our ever-smiling Indian guide, noticed and started to talk with great enthusiasm about his other job: the dot-com enterprise he was starting up.

Have no doubt, the Internet reaches everywhere, bringing changes and opening new horizons. It has caught on in the most remote parts of our world. It touches every culture and takes root in countless cities and villages. It brings changes wherever it is. Some we can already notice, some we cannot yet even fathom.

At the heart of this planet-wide system is the data: transferred, displayed, translated, parsed, stored, searched, indexed—always changing and always expanding.

As technologies adapt to the new dimension, XML is used more and more. As the content grows to new domains, English is used less and less.

Tomorrow, or even probably as you read this, Ahmed, Hernando, and Kriss will create data in their own languages: Malay, Spanish, and Hindi, and store it in XML documents. Along with them, many people will try to access the newly reachable markets, building repositories and XML-based systems where content must be adapted to different languages and cultures.

The purpose of this book is to help you, the reader, understand what it takes to build these XML-enabled systems and put the methods in place to localize your data more efficiently.

Who Should Read This Book?

This book is aimed at computer professionals working with XML content in multiple languages and anyone who wants to learn how to create XML vocabularies that can be seamlessly localized.

Other people who should read this book are the localization professionals. First, they might want to improve their knowledge of internationalization of XML and how to streamline the process of translating XML content. Second, XML is now used more and more in the localization process, regardless of whether the project has XML components.

Database architects who work with XML can also use many sections of this book. So can multilingual Web site developers and people involved in content management.

Organization

The book is divided into twenty chapters. You do not have to read them sequentially but can pick and choose whatever topic is appropriate to your current interest. However, having a good understanding of the second chapter, "Character Representation," will help anywhere in the book.

Chapter 1, "Globalization with XML," sets the stage for internationalization and localization from the viewpoint of markup languages. It also presents the main challenges brought either by XML or by the languages.

Part I—Enabling XML Material

Chapter 2, "Character Representation," explains how characters and encoding-related issues are treated in XML documents.

Chapter 3, "Miscellaneous Tagging," presents a selection of specific text properties that can be used in any documents and for which XML offers special constructs.

Chapter 4, "Coding the Presentation," offers an overview of the internationalization issues for the basic aspects of DSSSL, CSS, and XSL.

Chapter 5, "Special Aspects of Rendering," elaborates on the use of style sheets for more specific aspects of rendering: bi-directional display, vertical writing, ruby text, sorting, combined text, and so forth.

Chapter 6, "XML Conversion," discusses additional ways to transform XML documents through the use of custom-made scripts or programs that create different types of outputs.

Part II—Preparing XML for Localization

Chapter 7, "Creating Internationalized Document Types," shows how to create new XML vocabularies more suited for localization and how to efficiently identify the different localization-related properties of the elements and attributes of XML vocabularies.

Chapter 8, "Writing Internationalized Documents," shows how to author XML documents with localization in mind and how to represent localization-related properties within the documents when this cannot be done at the document type level.

Chapter 9, "Automated References," takes you through the different means you can utilize to reuse text in XML documents, whether the source is in another XML document or in a different format.

Chapter 10, "Segmentation," addresses one of the most problematic topics of translation tools and reuse: how the text to translate is broken down.

Chapter 11, "Mixed Data," talks about the various types of data XML containers can use: scripts, raw text, binary information, and so forth. It also looks at how XML fragments can be encapsulated in various container formats.

Chapter 12, "XML and Databases," discusses how databases use XML for exchange and publishing mechanisms and how XML fits into database structures.

Part III—Localizing XML Material

Chapter 13, "Localization Kits," describes the kind of information needed to successfully start a localization project with XML: what to provide to the localizer, what to expect back, and so forth.

Chapter 14, "XML-Enabled Translation Tools," presents an overview of the different commercial translation tools relative to their support of XML.

Chapter 15, "Online Translation," extends the tools review to the online portals and various ASP solutions that offer support for localizing XML data.

Chapter 16, "Using XML to Localize," shows different ways you can take advantage of the benefits of XML documents to localize other types of data, and how to prepare any XML documents for translation.

Chapter 17, "Text Extraction," presents the different aspects linked to storing localizable data extracted from various native formats. It discusses OpenTag and the XML Localisation Interchange File Format (XLIFF).

Chapter 18, "TMX," discusses the Translation Memory eXchange format.

Chapter 19, "Terminology Exchange," describes TBX, the TermBase eXchange format.

Chapter 20, "Conclusion," summarizes the main aspects of internationalization and localization for XML projects.

Conventions

Hexadecimal values in the text are prefixed with the two characters `0x`. For example, `0xA1` is the hexadecimal notation for 161. In source code samples, they are noted according to the relevant syntax for the given format of the sample.

UCS (Universal Character Set) characters are often rendered as `U+` and the corresponding code in hexadecimal. For example, `U+03A9` is the code point of the character 'Ω'. All UCS values refer to Unicode version 3.1, unless stated otherwise.

UCS character names are noted in capitals and monospace font. The names are the ones defined in Unicode version 3.1. For example, `U+03A9` is `GREEK CAPITAL LETTER OMEGA`.

A UTR (Unicode Technical Report) is a technical work done by the Unicode Consortium. All UTRs are available online at `http://www.unicode.org/unicode/reports/trNNN` where `NNN` is the UTR number.

An RFC (Request For Comments) is the result of works carried out by the IETF (Internet Engineering Task Force). Each RFC has a unique number and is considered the specification for a given subject. Most RFCs are available online at `http://www.ietf.org/rfc/rfcNNN.txt` where `NNN` is the RFC number.

For simplification, the Web-related examples given in this book do not always follow the recommendations for accessibility provided by the W3C. However, you are encouraged to follow these guidelines for your own material. You can find more information about the Web Accessibility Initiative at `http://www.w3.org/WAI`.

When a line of code is too long to fit on one line in the book, it is broken at a convenient place and continued on the next line. A code continuation character (↪) precedes the continuation of a line of code.

Appendix A is a glossary of the main terms used in the book.

Globalization with XML

In This Chapter:

Internationalization is the process of developing a product in such a way that it works with data in different languages and can be adapted to various target markets without engineering changes.

Localization is the subsequent process of translating and adapting a product to a given market's cultural conventions.

The global strategy for any given product or service must include at least an internationalization part and almost always some localization. With the growing role XML plays in the management of data, it has become a significant component in both areas.

Although documentation and Web sites remain obviously important domains for XML applications, the utilization of the markup language goes beyond that today. You can now see XML formats for user interfaces, data transfer layers, repository format, database export/import mechanisms, graphics, and many other applications.

In addition, XML is increasingly used during the localization process itself, regardless of whether the projects have XML components.

This chapter provides a close look at what are called markup languages, at what internationalization and localization mean and their importance in the development cycle of a product, and at some of the challenges XML material and languages offer.

Markup Languages

The term *markup language* covers two main notions that are often confused. A good understanding of these concepts can go a long way toward clarifying their respective issues.

- **Metalanguages**—A metalanguage is a set of syntactic rules that can be used to describe different formats. Examples of metalanguages are SGML and XML. With these two metalanguages the description of a format is usually done through a DTD (Document Type Definition).
- **Document Types**—The second aspect of markup languages is the document type: a format devised to serve a specific purpose. You can see it as an application written in one of the metalanguages. Examples of such applications are TEI, HTML, OpenTag, XSL, and MARTIF. In XML context, document types are often called *vocabularies*.

Figure 1.1 illustrates this framework: Both metalanguages are used to define different document types.

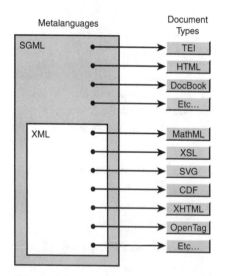

FIGURE 1.1

The relationships between markup languages.

SGML (Standard Generalized Markup Language) was created in the mid '70s and became an ISO standard (ISO 8879) in 1984. As the importance of the Internet grew during the last decade, it became clear that a lighter and less complex version of SGML would be very useful. Several initiatives of simplified SGML were sketched:

SGML-Lite, PFSGML (Poor-Folk's SGML), SO (SGML Online), or MGML (Minimal Generalized Markup Language) are some of them. All these efforts finally resulted in the emergence of XML.

XML, or eXtensible Markup Language, is an international standard developed by the World Wide Web Consortium (W3C). The version 1.0 specifications were released in February 1998, and a second edition of version 1.0 was published in October 2000. One of the big differences between SGML and XML is that an XML document is not necessarily associated with a DTD: You can parse XML files without knowledge of how the elements are structured. This simplifies greatly the development of XML-enabled tools.

On the document types side, some formats are more known than others: For example, HTML (Hypertext Markup Language) is widely used. Although it is merely a document type like any other, it is often mistakenly presented as a sibling of SGML or XML.

The recent XHTML specification is the W3C's recommendation for the latest version of HTML. XHTML is an XML application, just as HTML was an SGML one.

Key Components of the Development Cycle

Internationalization and localization are key parts of the development cycle of your product or service. They should be clearly identified as important components of the production process.

The different areas where internationalization and localization are needed in the project must be clearly identified and the relevant personnel should be assigned to them. Someone must *own* these aspects of the project and they should be taken into account in your schedules and budgets.

Make no mistake: Failure to think about localization ahead of time and to take the necessary steps to develop an internationalized product will always have financial consequences later. This is true not only for software applications, but also for documentation, Web sites, help systems, or any other component of your product.

Three areas of action are involved in internationalization or localization:

- **Development and authoring**—How the source material is created and updated.
- **Pre- and post-processing of the content**—How the localizable parts are routed, leveraged, tested, and adjusted in any ways before or after translation.
- **Linguistic work**—How the content is translated, edited, and proofed and also how the terminology is established, maintained, and verified.

Figure 1.2 shows the interactions of these three different areas. Obviously, the various tasks are often tightly related. For example, establishing the terminology is likely to occur during the development, or some of the pre-processing can be taken care of at the development stage by implementing appropriate methodology or using dedicated tools.

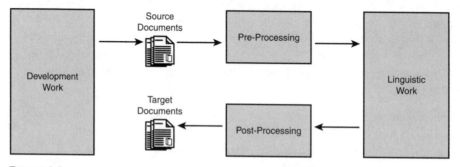

FIGURE 1.2

The relationships of the three main areas of multilingual content development.

The work can be done by different departments within the same organization, or by different vendors. As a general rule, the fewer the steps between the linguistic work and the authoring, the less costly the localization will be.

Regardless of whether you use external resources to do part or all of these tasks, the same guidelines apply.

Internationalization

Often, internationalization is seen as an activity related to software engineering: making sure double-byte strings are handled properly, that all translatable text is externalized, and so forth. In reality, internationalization goes much beyond those simple tasks and affects every single piece of your projects. For example, preparing for localization is closely tied to content development. Keep in mind that the biggest chunk of your budget will almost always be the cost linked to documentation. That is where you can realize substantial savings if you optimize the source material and the process to take into account its multilingual nature.

Internationalizing your project involves two sequential activities: enabling and preparing for localization.

Enabling

The most important facet of internationalization is to make sure the data contained in your document can be processed correctly regardless of its language or the script it uses.

In XML this means your vocabulary has elements describing the intent rather than the rendering, that localizable content is easily identified and lends itself well to the use of translation tools and surrounding processes.

If you are doing any transformation or rendering of the data, any templates and style sheets you might use take into account locale-specific requirements.

The following list enumerates some of the aspects you should be able to address after enabling is done:

- Text with extended characters (that is, non-ASCII characters) can be rendered appropriately, including ligatures, composite characters, writing direction, and so forth.
- Users can input text in different languages correctly and the result is processed and stored without corruptions.
- Numbered lists are generated with the correct digits.
- Ordered lists or tables are sorted according to the rules specific to the locale.
- The different languages in multilingual documents are identified properly and consistently.
- Text is wrapped adequately even if the language does not use spaces to separate words.
- The content can be searched or indexed correctly regardless of its language.
- Any automated text, such as quotation marks or captions, is generated according to the locale of the text.
- Numbers, dates, and time are formatted according to the rules used for the given locale.
- Whenever possible you use a system of IDs that will make the reuse of previously translated content easy.
- Whenever it makes sense you use XML features to reduce the repetitions of translatable parts. For example, you could use external entities for frequently used well-defined paragraphs. Do not go overboard though.
- Formatting is marked up in a generic way and different locale-specific styles can be applied easily.

Thanks to the work of many people at the W3C, XML is already enabled: It uses ISO-10646/Unicode, provides all the mechanisms to identify languages and encodings, and offers all the mechanisms necessary to handle non-Roman languages.

Nevertheless, you still must make sure these mechanisms are used correctly to create XML documents that can be seamlessly localized.

Preparing for Localization

The second aspect of internationalization, which assumes that enabling has been done already, is to make sure that your content can be localized without modification of its structural core or its setup.

In addition, you want to ensure that the work can be done with the maximum efficiency to lower costs and obtain rapid turnaround time.

The following list enumerates some of the aspects to address:

- Non-translatable parts within translatable documents are easily identifiable.
- Terminology is established and maintained.
- Any special requirements, such as maximum length or forced use of a subset of characters, are documented.
- The list of components that need to be localized is created and updated, and you have a process to assemble these components into a Localization Kit.
- You have methods in place to test the localized versions of your XML data. Any automated testing procedure can be used on translated data as well.
- Any modifications of the content of the source language that is done automatically can be reproduced for the target language as well (for example, creation of an index).
- The directory structure of your data takes into account the localized components.
- You have designated people responsible for the support of the localization process, for answering questions, for dispatching feedback from the localizer to the developers and authors, and so forth.

All these details can make a significant difference when localization occurs. Always keep in mind that ultimately the complexity of your source material will be multiplied by the number of target languages.

Localization

After your material has been internationalized and is ready, you can move to the localization stage.

Whether the localization is done by a localization vendor or not, the process involves very similar steps. The complexity and details of the process obviously depend largely on the type of XML documents to work on, but it usually involves, in one form or another, the following activities:

- Analysis
- Preparation
- Translation and Editing
- Post-processing
- Verification and QA

In some cases, for example with online translation or working from a content-management system, the steps will be more integrated.

More in-depth discussions on the different methods to translate XML files are in Chapters 13, "Localization Kits," 14, "XML-Enabled Translation Tools," 15, "Online Translation," and 16, "Using XML to Localize." The following notes are a simple summary of a possible scenario.

Analysis

After receiving the source material, the first thing a localizer usually does is to verify it. In the case of XML files this means to make sure they are at least well formed. If the files come with a DTD or a schema, you probably want to make sure they are also valid.

Hopefully the localizer has already had a sample of the XML files (that is, at the bid stage), knows what to expect, and has a solution for the localization process.

During this phase, the project is scoped, word counts and other statistical data are gathered, and a timetable can be set up.

Preparation

Preparation is about packaging the files for the linguists. A project seldom comes with XML documents only; in many cases work must be done to prepare the translation for entities, files, graphics, and other additional source files.

If the source XML documents are for one reason or another not supported by the tools, they might have to be pre-processed into a different format, for example extracted into a temporary format such as XLIFF (XML Localisation Interchange File Format) or RTF, where the translatable text is separated from the markup codes.

Preparation can also involve generating leveraged files or preparing translation
memories, as well as putting together reference material such as glossaries or
assembling context information.

This is also one of the times when people involved with the product in the target
markets should be included: They provide approval of the terminology, evaluation of
the stylistic guidelines for the translation, and other information specific to the targeted
audience.

Translation and Editing

After they are packaged, the files are given to the linguists. The translation and editing
is often done by contractors working off-site, so usually some level of coordination as
well as FTP, e-mails, or other communications means are involved.

Regardless of what tool is used for translation, having a way to see the preview output
of the XML source goes a long way in helping the linguists to provide a good quality
translation.

If any translation memories are available, tools can be used to re-cycle interactively the
segments of text that have already been translated.

Post-Processing

When the main linguistic steps are completed, the translated material comes back to
whomever prepared it and any post-processing work is done if it is necessary (that is,
reverting from the format used for translation back to the original XML).

Verification and QA

Depending on the type of XML material (documents, UI, help, database files, and so
forth), the verification phase might be involved. For example, in some cases, linguists
would look again at the translated text in the running environment that was not
reproducible during translation and editing. In others, the files would be processed to
generate various outputs that would be proofed.

Then, after a final quality assurance step, the deliverable XML files are ready to be sent
back to the production stage.

XML Challenges

XML is flexible and offers a clear set of construction rules. A growing number of
parsers and enabled tools are now available, and a flourishing companion technology

(for example, XSL, XPath, or XLink) is rapidly growing. All this has made XML an ideal medium with which to manipulate, store, transport, and exchange all sorts of data, not only on the Internet, but in any environment.

Types of Data

XML is used in a broad range of areas: for example, as a system to store your documentation, as a repository for corporate data, or as an interface for applications. Table 1.1 shows a few examples of XML applications.

TABLE 1.1

A Few Examples of XML Applications

Document Type	Domain of Application
SOAP	Capsule to transfer data and executable code across different systems
XHTML	Online documents served up over the Internet
XUL	Language to describe user interface: menus, dialog boxes, forms, and so forth
VoiceXML	Programming language for voice systems
SVG	Coding of text and vector-based graphics
TMX	Interchange format for translation memories
XML Query	Language to query Web documents
Open eBook	Format for electronic book presentation
XTM	Topic maps description
Wf-XML	Language to exchange information between workflow management systems
OMF	Weather observation definition format
CML	Markup language for chemical data

In addition to new formats created since XML has become available, many older SGML content types are now adapted to be XML applications. In localization this diversity of vocabularies comes with its share of problems: Each type of document raises different kinds of challenges.

Patchwork Documents

One of the most powerful features offered by XML is the namespaces mechanism. It enables you to mix elements of different vocabularies within the same document.

For example, Listing 1.1 shows a document that uses three different namespaces. The main one is a catalog entry for which the namespace URI is `urn:MacMillan:Sams:Catalog_v1`. The document includes a `<number>` element borrowed from a different vocabulary (identified as `urn:gov:book:isbn`) as well as some HTML markup (mapped to `http://www.w3.org/TR/REC-html40`).

LISTING 1.1

`Namespaces1.xml`—Example of a Document with Elements from Different Document Types

```
<?xml version="1.0" ?>
<book xmlns="urn:MacMillan:Sams:Catalog_v1"
      xmlns:isbn="urn:gov:book:isbn"
      xmlns:html="http://www.w3.org/TR/REC-html40">
 <title>XML Internationalization and Localization</title>
 <isbn:number>0-672-32096-7</isbn:number>
 <orig-lang>en-us<orig-lang>
 <descr>
  <html:P>
   A practical guide on how to <html:I>internationalize</html:I> and
   <html:I>localize</html:I> XML applications.
  </html:P>
 </descr>
</book>
```

This system provides the opportunity to reuse in your own vocabulary markups that already have been defined. It brings, in some regards, an "object-oriented" dimension to XML.

When localizing such documents, you must make sure that tools support namespaces correctly. The only part that is fixed in the namespace syntax is the URI to which the prefix is mapped. In the example the prefixes `isbn` and `html` could have been named anything else, they are just a shorthand notation.

Another issue appears when leveraging translation. Because the element notation can vary depending on the context, the tags that are within translation memory segments can appear different while they are really identical. This can prevent exact matches from being found when they should.

For instance, the previous document could be also coded as shown in Listing 1.2 and the description text ends up with a different syntax for the same HTML tags.

LISTING 1.2

`Namespaces2.xml`—An Alternate Notation

```xml
<?xml version="1.0" ?>
<book xmlns="urn:MacMillan:Sams:Catalog_v1"
      xmlns:isbn="urn:gov:book:isbn">
 <title>XML Internationalization and Localization</title>
 <isbn:number>0-672-32096-7</isbn:number>
 <orig-lang>en-us</orig-lang>
 <descr>
  <P xmlns:html="http://www.w3.org/TR/REC-html40">
   A practical guide on how to <I>internationalize</I> and
   <I>localize</I> XML applications.
  </P>
 </descr>
</book>
```

The same problem arises when the prefixes are named differently in separate documents. Note that this can happen only if the documents are not validated against a DTD where unique prefixes would be declared.

The simplest way to solve these cases is to implement leveraging methods that truly abstract the way they store information about inline codes.

On-Demand Documents

New ways to view documents came with the Internet. Rather than being considered final outputs, documents are often built on-the-fly, when requested by a user. Maintaining and updating the information can be done much more efficiently.

The first problem from a localization

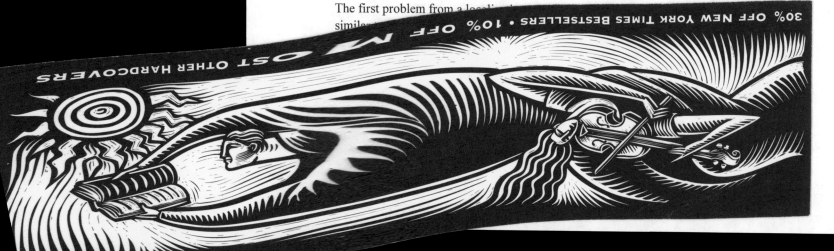

The second issue is that the boundaries between data content and code content become very fuzzy: Embedded scripts in different languages, queries, external references and many other code-related statements can be found between paragraphs of simple text. In some cases (for example, XSL or VoiceXML), it is difficult to decide whether a file should be treated as a source code file or a text document.

Here again the tools and methods must be adjusted to deal with the wide breadth of domains where XML is used and the different types of content it stores.

Single-Source Documents

An aspect related to on-demand documents is the capability to use the same source to generate different outputs, for example a dynamic Web page, a PDF file, and an online help topic.

In this scenario the translators might have to deal with several partial or nonexistent contexts.

On the authoring side the design and organization for multiple outputs are often quite complex and should absolutely include thoughts about the localized versions of the different generated materials. Whatever steps are used to create the final outputs must be reproducible, without any addition, for all targeted languages. An oversight of this issue is most likely to increase the cost of the localization.

Language Challenges

Now that we have seen the main steps involved in globalization and what type of material we will have to implement them, it is time to look at the different challenges that the use of different languages brings.

Languages are usually divided by families: sets of different branches that have evolved from a main original root. In the world of computing, languages are most often grouped based on rendering properties that are required for each language: what character sets they use, writing direction, and so forth. Some present only a few difficulties whereas others offer more difficult and unique problems.

Beyond the problems of rendering text, many additional issues make each language special: grammatical rules for gender, accord of the adjectives, noun and verb inflexions, cultural issues for graphics, abbreviations, collation, and so forth.

Character Sets

There are different ways to represent speech in a written form: Alphabets, ideographs, and syllabic notations are the main ones.

An alphabet is a finite set of characters (letters), combined to form the representation of sounds or grammatical information (for example, the Latin, or Roman, alphabet). In some cases each letter can have different forms depending on the context (its position in the word, the previous or next letter, the semantic, and so forth). Uppercase and lowercase are examples of such forms, but some scripts like Arabic go beyond that and use even more forms.

Syllabic notations are also widely used. In a syllabary each character represents the sound of a syllable (for instance, Hangul for Korean, the Canadian Aboriginal Syllabics for Inuktitut, or Hiragana and Katakana for Japanese). Some scripts mix the alphabetic and phonetic mechanisms.

Characters in an ideograph-based script represent concepts. The *Hanzi* ideographs (called *Kanji* in Japanese and *Hanja* in Korean) are the most commonly known example of such a writing system. They are unified and called *Han* characters in Unicode.

Some languages use only one script; others utilize several. Japanese uses four systems. For example, the word *Nihongo* ("Japanese" in Japanese) can be written different ways, as shown in Table 1.2.

TABLE 1.2

Possible Ways to Write the Word "Japanese" in Japanese

Representation	Script
日本語	Kanji (ideographs)
にほんご	Hiragana (phonetic)
ニホンゴ	Katakana (phonetic, normally used to represent non-Japanese words)
Nihongo	Romaji (transliteration in Latin alphabet)

This illustrates how complex a language can be for computing.

The digital representation of these various systems leads to different ways of storing the text. The association between the different sets of characters and their computer binary representations is called *encoding* and their implementation can be rather complex at times.

Punctuation and Marks

Punctuation signs also vary from one language to the other. In addition, some scripts use marks that have no equivalent in the Latin script.

Some languages also have additional punctuation signs. For example, Spanish uses an additional mark, an inverted question mark, at the beginning of interrogative sentences: "¿Que hora es?".

Table 1.3 lists a few examples of punctuation and marks.

TABLE 1.3

Examples of Punctuation and Marks in Various Scripts

Script	Symbols
Georgian	paragraph separator ': '
Armenian	exclamation mark ''', comma ''', question mark ''', full stop ': '
Arabic	comma '،', semicolon '؛', question mark '؟', percent sign '٪', ornate left parenthesis '﴾', ornate right parenthesis '﴿'
Thai	bullet '๏', ellipsis 'ๆ', section ending 'ๆ' (*Angkhankhu*), chapter ending '๛' (*Khomut*)
Greek	question mark ';'
French	left quotation mark '«', right quotation mark '»'
Ethiopic	wordspace '፡', full stop '።', comma '፣', semicolon '፤', question mark '፧', paragraph separator '፨'
Spanish	inverted question mark '¿', inverted exclamation mark '¡'
Chinese, Japanese	comma '、', period '。', ditto mark ' 〃 '
Tibetan	brackets '࿒' (*Gug rtags gyon* mark) and '࿓' (*Gug rtags gyas* mark), list enumerator '༖', topic separator '༈'

Word Separation

The use of spaces to separate words, which might look like an obvious thing to many, is not the way all languages work. Some languages, such as Amharic, use other characters to separate words.

In other cases, such as in Chinese, Korean, Japanese, and Thai, you don't separate words at all. For an example, see the following sentence in Thai:

เราจะบริหารและจัดการเว็บไซต์เป็นภาษาต่างๆเพื่อให้สามารถใช้ได้ไปทั่วโลก.

Finally, you can find languages in which spaces occur within a word. In classical Mongolian for instance, grammatical suffixes are added to the stem word separated by a narrow space, whereas another type of space separator can occur before final vowels.

As you can imagine, such properties will have a direct impact on how to handle wrapping, justification, searches, parsing, and many other aspects of text processing.

Digits

Noticeable differences between writing systems are also found in the representation of numbers.

Whereas the *Western digit* (borrowed from Arabic) is by far the most used digit system, it's not the only one. The *Arabic digits* come in two collections called *Arabic-Indic digits* and *Eastern Arabic digits* (used in Urdu and Farsi, for example). These were borrowed from India, where there are almost as many digit sets as there are scripts. In addition, Thai, Ethiopic, Khmer, Tibetan, Lao, Mongolian, and many other scripts have different digits. Most of them are listed in Table 1.4.

TABLE 1.4

Different Sets of Digits in Different Scripts

Script	*Digits*									
Western	0	1	2	3	4	5	6	7	8	9
Arabic-Indic	٠	١	٢	٣	٤	٥	٦	٧	٨	٩
Eastern Arabic	٠	١	٢	٣	۴	۵	۶	٧	٨	٩
Bengali	০	১	২	৩	৪	৫	৬	৭	৮	৯
Devanagari	०	१	२	३	४	५	६	७	८	९
Lao	໐	໑	໒	໓	໔	໕	໖	໗	໘	໙
Gurmukhi	੦	੧	੨	੩	੪	੫	੬	੭	੮	੯
Gujarati	૦	૧	૨	૩	૪	૫	૬	૭	૮	૯
Oriya	୦	୧	୨	୩	୪	୫	୬	୭	୮	୯
Telugu	౦	౧	౨	౩	౪	౫	౬	౭	౮	౯
Kannada	೦	೧	೨	೩	೪	೫	೬	೭	೮	೯
Malayalam	൦	൧	൨	൩	൪	൫	൬	൭	൮	൯
Tibetan	༠	༡	༢	༣	༤	༥	༦	༧	༨	༩
Thai	๐	๑	๒	๓	๔	๕	๖	๗	๘	๙

In addition to differences in digits, some scripts can use different numeric systems altogether. For example, Ethiopic has its own numeric system, as presented in Table 1.5.

TABLE 1.5

Ethiopic Numerals

Western	1	2	3	4	5	6	7	8	9
Ethiopic	፩	፪	፫	፬	፭	፮	፯	፰	፱
Western	10	20	30	40	50	60	70	80	90
Ethiopic	፲	፳	፴	፵	፶	፷	፸	፹	፺
Western	100	10000							
Ethiopic	፻	፼							

Chinese-based scripts usually use Western digits but also have their own set of numerals. However, in some cases accounting numbers, yet another set of numerals, are also used. Accounting numbers help to minimize the possibilities of misinterpretation or forgery. They are presented in Table 1.6.

TABLE 1.6

The Chinese Accounting Numerals

Western	0	1	2	3	4	5	6	7	8	9
Accounting	零	壹	貳	參	肆	伍	陸	柒	捌	玖
Western	10	100	1,000		10,000		100,000,000			
Accounting	拾	佰	仟		萬		億			
Western	1,000,000,000,000									
Accounting	兆									

In all cases, keep in mind that Western digits are often used, even for languages that have their own set.

Use of the correct digits is not only part of the translation of the text, it can also affect the way XML documents are rendered. For instance, the engines generating numbered lists should make provision for different types of notations.

Decimal and group separators are also different per language, and so is the way that numbers are grouped: by hundreds, by thousands, and so forth.

Writing Direction

One fundamental difference you can find in some scripts is the direction in which the text is written.

Semitic languages such as Arabic and Hebrew are displayed from right to left, top to bottom. Because they often include left-to-right runs of text or number as well, they are called *bi-directional* languages. Figure 1.3 illustrates this with a Hebrew text that includes two runs of ASCII characters.

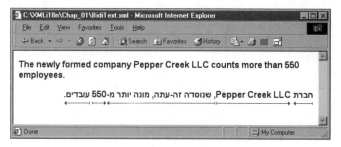

FIGURE 1.3

Bi-directional text is a mix of left-to-right and right-to-left runs of text.

Other languages, such as Urdu, Farsi, Pashto, Dhivehi, and Syriac have also adopted the Arabic writing system or scripts derived from it.

East Asian languages such as Chinese, Korean, and Japanese are traditionally written from top to bottom, with columns running from right to left. The left-to-right horizontal writing is also now commonly used.

All these variations require rendering mechanisms very different from the one used for the Roman script.

Formatting Styles

Typography choices vary from one script to another. For example, when Westerners use bold text, a Chinese or Japanese author may prefer a different method of emphasis such as dots or accent-like symbols above or below each character. The use of italics might be less appropriate in some scripts, and using uppercase to emphasize a term is impossible in non-case scripts.

Different types of layout are also used: East Asian languages can sometimes have combined characters or lines within the same row. In Arabic, justification is done with elongated connecting lines between letters (the *Kashida*), whereas some languages use wider spacing between characters and others use extra space between words.

Character Shapes

Some scripts have characteristics that are unknown or rarely used in the Latin script and offer interesting challenges. One such characteristic is multiform characters.

For instance, in Arabic, each letter does not have an upper- and lowercase form, but rather several forms depending on its location: isolated, initial, in-between, or final.

Another example is Greek, in which the letter sigma has two forms in lowercase: 'σ' and, when in terminal position, 'ς'. In uppercase both forms are converted to a unique shape: 'Σ'.

Sort Order and Case

Any presentation of a set of data must, at some point, be ordered. The mechanisms used at that time, such as collation and folding, are highly locale specific.

Languages that use ideographic-based scripts have various ways to order their characters: by phonetic, by stroke count, by radical, and so forth.

Many scripts use non–Latin-based alphabets, syllabaries, or a mixture of both. Even the languages that use the Roman alphabet such as Danish, English, and German have different ways to order it. A few examples:

- In Danish and Norwegian, 'æ' comes after 'z'', 'ø' after 'æ', and 'å' after 'ø'.
- In Swedish and Finnish, 'ü' is equivalent to 'y', 'w' is equivalent to 'v', 'å' comes after 'z', 'ä' after 'å', and 'ö' after 'ä'.
- In German 'ae', is equivalent to 'ä' that comes after 'a', 'oe' is equivalent to 'ö' that comes after 'o', 'ue' is equivalent to 'ü' that comes after 'u', and 'ß' is equivalent to 'ss'.
- In Icelandic 'ð' comes after 'd', and 'þ' after 'z'.
- In Lithuanian 'y' is equivalent to 'i'.

Related to sort order are the conventions for uppercasing and lowercasing. Although some scripts do not have such distinction, others possess very specific rules. Here are some examples:

- The German 'ß' is uppercased to 'SS'.
- The ligature 'ij' is capitalized 'IJ' in Dutch whereas it is transformed to 'Ij' in Croatian.
- In Japanese the character '—' (U+30FC) indicates a prolonged sound for the preceding character. It changes the sorting order depending on the vowel.
- Turkish uses two letters 'i' and 'ı' that uppercase respectively to 'İ' and 'I'. This is a case in which the usual conversion rule for the ASCII characters 'i' and 'I' does not apply.

Date and Time Formatting

In addition to differences in calendars, time and dates are represented in various ways across the world: 12-hour versus 24-hour formats; the order in which month, day, and year are presented; the characters used as separators; which day is the first day of the week; and many other details make this category of information often difficult to render in a neutral fashion.

Summary

In this chapter we have drawn a brief overview of internationalization and localization. Truly integrating these two activities as part of your project development cycle is vital to ensure costs savings.

XML brings many challenges for localization: for example, lack of context when translating, processing of composite files, and the fuzzy border between source code and source document. Tools must be adapted for these issues.

A simple overview of some of the challenges brought by the use of different languages shows that although XML itself is usually well prepared for handling most languages, implementation of XML tools must follow as well.

References

The books and Web sites in the following list are some places to look for additional information about internationalization and localization methodologies, as well as the XML basics.

Nadine Kano, 1995, *Developing International Software for Windows 95 and Windows NT.* Microsoft Press. ISBN 1-55615-840-8.

Bert Esslink, 2000, *A Practical Guide to Localization.* John Benjamins B.V., ISBN 1-58811-006-0.

Apple Computer Inc., 1992, *Guide to Macintosh Software Localization.* Addison Wesley Longman, ISBN 020-1608561.

Charles Goldfarb and Paul Prescod, 2000, *The XML Handbook.* Prentice Hall, ISBN 1-850-32211-2.

Microsoft, 1993, *The GUI Guide: International Terminology for the Windows Interface.* Microsoft Press.

The XML Cover Pages: `http://www.oasis-open.org/cover/xml.html`

XML architecture: `http://www.w3.org/XML`

Enabling XML Material

PART

I

Character Representation

In This Chapter:

Any document is made of a collection of characters. Each character must have a digital representation. The mechanism to define which digital representation corresponds to which character is probably one of the least understood aspects of internationalization: the encoding of character sets.

Character Set Encoding

First, we need to define more clearly the different components that play a role in this mechanism. One of the problems is that the definitions vary according to which standards authority you are referring. The following are probably not the best, but they are intended to be simple.

A *character* is the smallest component of written language that has a semantic value. Examples of characters are letters, ideographs (for example, Chinese characters), punctuation marks, digits, mathematic symbols, diacritical marks, and so on.

A *character set* is a group of characters without associated numerical values. An example of a character set is the Latin alphabet; another one is *Zhùyin fúhào*, also known as *Bopomofo* (ㄅㄆㄇㄈ), the collection of Chinese phonetic symbols; another the Cyrillic alphabet.

Coded character sets are character sets in which each character is associated with a scalar value: a *code point*. For example, in ASCII the uppercase letter 'A' has the value 65, the lowercase letter 'z' has the value 122, and so forth. Unicode, for example, is a coded character set.

A coded character set is meant to be *encoded*: converted into a digital representation so that the characters can be serialized in files, databases, or strings. This is done through a *character encoding scheme*, often simply called *encoding*. The encoding method maps each character value to a given sequence of bytes.

In many cases the encoding is just a direct projection of the scalar values, and there is no real distinction between the coded character set and its serialized representation. For example, in ISO 8859-1 (Latin 1), the character 'A' (code point 65) is encoded as a byte 0x41 (1000001 in binary), and the character 'á' (code point 225) is encoded as a byte 0xE1 (11100001 in binary). Those two bit sequences are direct computer representations of 65 and 225. This is illustrated in Figure 2.1.

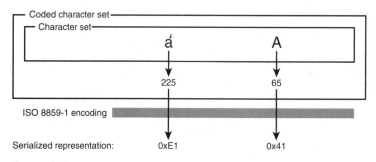

FIGURE 2.1

Direct encoding of the ISO 8859-1 *character set; the serialization is a direct representation of the code points.*

In other cases, however, the encoding method is more complex. For instance, in UTF-8, an encoding of Unicode, the character 'á' (225) is encoded as two bytes: 0xC3 and 0xA1. Some encoding methods are used on several character sets, such as EUC (Extended Unix Code). Others are unique to a given character set, like the GBK encoding for the GBK character set (Simplified Chinese). Figure 2.2 illustrates UTF-8 encoding of the Unicode character set.

In XML, the character set to use is ISO/IEC 10646. You have the choice of using UTF-8, UTF-16, or UTF-32 for its encoding.

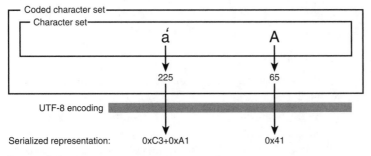

FIGURE 2.2

UTF-8 *encoding of the Unicode character set. In* UTF-8, *ASCII characters are encoded in a single byte, and extended characters use two or more bytes.*

Encoding XML Documents

The last decade has seen the creation of two large character sets: ISO/IEC 10646 and Unicode. The first is defined and maintained by ISO and the second by the Unicode Consortium. Fortunately, both groups realized the need to synchronize their efforts and since 1991 have worked on a common character repertoire. Each organization still publishes its own standard, and they sometimes use different terminology, but they are closely coordinating any further extensions.

This synchronization started at version 1.1 of Unicode, which matched ISO/IEC 10646:1993. The latest version of Unicode is 3.1, which corresponds to ISO/IEC 10646:2000.

The XML specifications generally use the ISO/IEC 10646 terminology. In the rest of this book we will refer to this repertoire of characters as *UCS (Universal Character Set)*, the term used by ISO/IEC 10646 and in the W3C documents. For our purposes, we can consider Unicode and ISO/IEC 10646 as a single character set.

In XML, the range of allowed characters is defined as follows (parsed characters, not encoded bytes):

```
Char ::= #x9 | #xA | #xD | [#x20-#xD7FF] | [#xE000-#xFFFD] |
         [#x10000-#x10FFFF]
```

As you can see, XML does not include the characters in the surrogate blocks and excludes the code points 0xFFFE and 0xFFFF.

In the allowed ranges, there are several characters whose use is strongly discouraged. These are listed in Table 2.1, where the Description column gives the reason for their exclusion.

TABLE 2.1	
Characters Allowed But Not Suitable to Use in XML	
Characters	*Description*
U+2028 and U+2029	Line and paragraph separators (conflict with markup, use markup instead).
U+202A to U+202E	Bidirectional embedding controls (conflict with markup, use markup instead).
U+206A and U+206B	Activate/inhibit symmetric swapping marks (deprecated).
U+206C and U+206D	Activate/inhibit Arabic form shaping (deprecated).
U+206E and U+206F	Activate/inhibit national digit shapes (deprecated).
U+FFF9 to U+FFFB	Interlinear annotation marks (conflict with markup, use Ruby markup instead).
U+FFFC	Object replacement character (use of markup is preferred).
U+E000 to U+F8FF	Private Use Area (lack of interoperability).
U+E0000 to U+E007F	Language Tags (Use xml:lang instead).

In addition, the use of compatibility characters is not recommended. Compatibility characters (characters above U+F8FF and below U+FFFE) include, for example, the Arabic Presentation Forms (U+FB50 to U+FDFF and U+FE70 to U+FEFF), the Hangul Compatibility Jamo (U+3130 to U+318F), and the Halfwidth and Fullwidth Forms (U+FF00 to U+FFEF).

For more information about using Unicode in XML see the W3C technical note at http://www.w3.org/TR/unicode-xml.

Surrogates

As the development of UCS progressed, it became clear that a pure 16-bit character repertoire would not be enough to define all the symbols needed. The surrogates were created to solve this problem.

A *surrogate pair* is a coded character representation for a single abstract character that consists of a sequence of two code points. The first is called *low-surrogate*, the second *high-surrogate*.

Surrogate pairs work a lot like double-bytes: The range U+D800 to U+DBFF is reserved for low-surrogates and the range U+DC00 to U+DFFF for high-surrogates. There is no overlap between both surrogate ranges and none between surrogates and the other Unicode values. Therefore, you can always know what type of character you are processing when accessing a string randomly.

When processed, the pair should be seen as a single character (also called a *supplementary character*) with a code point between 0x100000 and 0x10FFFF (also called a *supplementary code point*) that is a 31-bit scalar value S defined by the formula in Listing 2.1, where H is the high-surrogate and L the low-surrogate.

LISTING 2.1

Conversion of a Surrogate Pair H,L into a Scalar Value S

```
S = ( H - 0xD800 ) * 0x400 + ( L - 0xDC00 ) + 0x10000
```

The reverse mapping, from a scalar value S to its corresponding high- and low-surrogates H and L, is shown in Listing 2.2.

LISTING 2.2

Conversion from a Scalar Value S to Its Corresponding High-Surrogate H and Low-Surrogate L

```
H = ( S - 0x10000 ) / 0x400 + 0xD800
L = ( S - 0x10000 ) mod 0x400 + 0xDC00
```

This mechanism allows you to access more than one million extra characters above the 65,535 code points of the 16-bit Unicode.

Note that a portion of the surrogate pairs is user-defined and, like the characters in the Private Use Area, should be avoided in XML. A surrogate pair is user-defined when its low-surrogate value is between U+DB80 and U+DBFF.

Unicode 3.1 introduced 44,946 characters coded above U+FFFF.

The Universal Character Set

UCS supports most of the languages currently used with computers. Version 3.1 of Unicode (corresponding to ISO/IEC-10646-1:2000) was released at the end of March 2001. It assigns a total of 94,140 code points and allows for more than 100,000 user-defined characters (Private Use Area).

UCS is organized in blocks grouped by symbol collections and scripts.

A *script* is the set of characters needed to write a given set of languages. For instance, the Canadian Aboriginal Syllabics script is used to write the Inuktitut, Athapascan, and Algonquian languages. The Latin script is used for English, French, Hawaiian,

German, Hausa, and many other languages. Cyrillic is used for Russian, Bulgarian, Ukrainian, and others.

Some languages use several scripts. For example, Japanese uses the Kanji, Hiragana, Katakana, and Romaji (Latin) scripts. On the other hand, some scripts are unique to a given language, such as Hangul for Korean.

You can find a descriptive list of the scripts and symbol collections that Unicode 3.1 supports in Appendix C, "Scripts in UCS."

A parsed XML document must be in UCS, but there are different options for its encoding. The XML specifications require XML processors to support UTF-8 and UTF-16. In addition, XML tool providers are encouraged to support other encodings of UCS or other character sets, although it is not a requirement.

UTF-16

UTF-16 (UCS/Unicode Transformation Format, 16-bit encoding form) is a 16-bit encoding of UCS. Each UCS code point up to U+FFFF is encoded as a single 16-bit value. As we have already seen, the code points above U+FFFF are represented as pairs of 16-bit values (the high- and low-surrogates).

Listing 2.3 shows the hexadecimal representation of the XML document in UTF-16 displayed in Figure 2.3. The octets representing the text are in bold. Keep in mind that all characters are represented by a 16-bit code—even the Latin letters that could fit in 7-bit code. When the text is composed only of ASCII characters, the file is twice as large as its equivalent in ASCII.

LISTING 2.3

HexaUTF16.xml—Hexadecimal View of File Encoded in UTF-16

```
FF-FE 3C-00 3F-00 78-00 6D-00 6C-00 20-00 76-00
65-00 72-00 73-00 69-00 6F-00 6E-00 3D-00 22-00
31-00 2E-00 30-00 22-00 20-00 3F-00 3E-00 0D-00
0A-00 3C-00 64-00 6F-00 63-00 3E-00 0D-00 0A-00
20-00 3C-00 74-00 65-00 78-00 74-00 3E-00 50-00
72-00 E9-00 66-00 E9-00 72-00 65-00 6E-00 63-00
65-00 73-00 3C-00 2F-00 74-00 65-00 78-00 74-00
3E-00 0D-00 0A-00 3C-00 2F-00 64-00 6F-00 63-00
3E-00 0D-00 0A-00
```

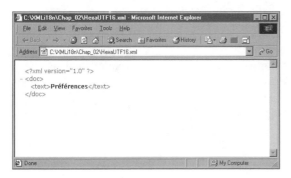

FIGURE 2.3

Display of the UTF-16 *XML document shown in Listing 2.3.*

The document starts with a code 0xFEFF, the Byte-Order-Mark, or *BOM*. The BOM is a special interpretation of the ZERO WIDTH NON-BREAK SPACE character. It serves basically as a peacekeeper in the never-ending conflict between big-endians and little-endians.

> **NOTE:**   The terms *big-endian* and *little-endian* come from a paper written by Danny Cohen in 1980, "Holy Wars and a Plea for Peace," in which he compared the technical disagreement to the fierce difference that broke apart the Lilliputian society in Swift's *Gulliver's Travels*. The Big-Endian reformist party followed an imperial decree stipulating that hard-boiled eggs should be opened at their big end, while the more traditional Little-Endian supporters, backed up by the neighboring Blefuscudian Empire, wanted to keep cracking the eggs at the little end. Both parties claimed to follow the precepts of the great prophet Lustrog, who wrote that "All true believers shall break their eggs at the convenient end."

Here the problem is not about whether a hard-boiled egg should be cracked at the big end or the little one, but whether the most significant byte (MSB) of the character values is stored first (big-endian, also called *network byte order*) or last (little-endian).

Some processor architectures, such as IBM-360, Motorola, and RISC, use the first option. Others, such as Intel or Vax, have opted for the second method. The BOM enables you to do two things:

- First, to detect whether the document is a UTF-16 file. This assertion is based on the fact that the odds that any other type of file starts with either 0xFFFE or 0xFEFF are very low.
- Second, to identify the type of byte order used: big-endian or little-endian. With that information, the XML processor can tell whether to swap the 8-bit groups.

The file presented in Listing 2.3 is little-endian, because it starts with FF-FE, not FE-FF.

The following text shows the word "Gulliver" in both UTF-16BE (big-endian) and UTF-16LE (little-endian):

```
    Text:        G     u     l     l     i     v     e     r
UTF-16BE:   FE FF 00 45 00 75 00 6C 00 6C 00 69 00 76 00 65 00 72
UTF-16LE:   FF FE 45 00 75 00 6C 00 6C 00 69 00 76 00 65 00 72 00
```

If the Byte-Order-Mark were not present at the beginning of the UTF-16 file, the tools, geared to support one method or the other, could possibly read each character with the incorrect byte order. This would lead to an output such as that in Figure 2.4. As you can see, when it comes to character encoding, Lilliputian details can have Brobdingnagian consequences.

FIGURE 2.4

The word "Gulliver" encoded in UTF-16 little-endian, but interpreted as big-endian.

If no BOM code is present at the top of the file, the XML parsers should assume the file is in UTF-8, the multibyte alternative to UTF-16.

UTF-8

UTF-8 (UCS/Unicode Transformation Format, 8-bit encoding form) is a multibyte 8-bit encoding in which each Unicode scalar value is mapped to a sequence of one to four bytes.

One of the main advantages of UTF-8 is its compatibility with ASCII. If no extended characters are present, there is no difference between the document encoded in ASCII and the one encoded in UTF-8.

Listing 2.4 shows an XML file with the words "Downloadable Resources" in Inuktitut, the language spoken by the Inuit in the Arctic Canadian territory of Nunavut. Inuktitut can be represented using the Canadian Aboriginal Syllabics script introduced in Unicode version 3.0 (code points U+1400 to U+167F). You can see in Figure 2.5 that the translation "ᑎᑎᕋᕐᓐᓇᕈᑎᓕᐅᕐᕕᖓᑕ ᓇᑭᖕᖓᕐᓂᖏᑦ" (*titirarunnarutiliurvingita nakinngaarningit*) is made of two words of, respectively, fourteen and seven syllabic characters. In UTF-8, each of these characters is transformed into a sequence of three bytes, while the punctuation and XML notation, both in ASCII, are encoded with single bytes.

LISTING 2.4

UTF8.xml—XML Document Encoded in UTF-8 (Displayed as if Encoded in windows-1252)

```
<?xml version="1.0" ?>
<doc>
  <text>á'□á'□á•‹á•ˆá"□á"‡á•ˆá'□á"•á□…á•□á••á-□á'• á"‡á'-á™¶á•□á",
➥á-□á'¦.</text>
</doc>
```

FIGURE 2.5

The rendering of the UTF-8 document from Listing 2.4.

Another strong point of UTF-8 is that you can convert a UTF-8 string to the Unicode 16-bit scalar values using a simple algorithm that does not require any time-consuming lookup operations. You can find the source code for the conversion of the different UTF encodings on the Unicode Consortium Web site at http://www.unicode.org.

At this point, you may wonder which encoding is preferred. The answer is easy: It depends on the context.

> **NOTE:** In `UTF-8`, because we are already working at the byte level, the byte order has no effect. However, a `UTF-8` file may start with a Byte-Order-Mark. This simply enables it to distinguish `UTF-8` from other UTF encodings.
>
> Some applications, such as the versions of WordPad and Notepad shipped with Windows 2000, add the BOM at the beginning of the file. Others, such as Word 2000, do not. Therefore, depending on which application you are using, you may find the BOM treated as such or as a normal `ZERO WIDTH NON-BREAK SPACE` included in the text.

In `UTF-16` the representation of all characters, including the basic Latin letters, will always take 16 bits instead of 8. Therefore, an XML document with only English text would be twice as large as the same document in `UTF-8`, where there is no difference from ASCII for the first 128 code points.

On the other hand, when the document contains a lot of non-ASCII characters, especially non-Latin extended characters, `UTF-8` takes more room.

In XML, where tags are almost always in ASCII characters, the trade-off is usually in favor of `UTF-8`.

Other Encodings

XML documents can be serialized using encodings other than `UTF-16` and `UTF-8`, and encodings for character sets other than UCS (although once parsed the characters must be in UCS values). If you choose to encode you documents differently, you must specify the encoding in the initial XML declaration, and the XML processor must be able to execute the conversion to UCS.

The most-used alternative code sets are those of the ISO 8859 family, as well as `EUC-JP`, `Shift_JIS` (Japanese), `Big5` (Traditional Chinese), `GB2312` (Simplified Chinese), `KS_C_5061_1987` (Korean), and a few others. See Table 2.2 for a more detailed list.

The Internet Assigned Numbers Authority (IANA) is responsible for the maintenance of the different values for the encoding declarations (called *charsets* by the IANA). There are about 200 of them registered.

TABLE 2.2	
Selected Charset Identifiers	
Identifier	*Description*
UTF-8	UCS/Unicode Transformation Format 8-bit encoding form
UTF-16	UCS/Unicode Transformation Format 16-bit encoding form
ISO-8859-1	ISO Latin 1, (also known as "ANSI"), Western European languages
ISO-8859-2	ISO Latin 2, Eastern European languages
windows-1252	Windows codepage 1252, Western European languages
Shift_JIS	Shift JIS, Japanese
EUC-JP	EUC Japanese (Unix systems)
TIS-650	Thai standard
Big5	Traditional Chinese

You can also see a larger list in Appendix B, "Encoding Declarations," and the latest and complete list of charset designators is available online at http://www.iana.org/assignments/character-sets.

> **NOTE:** The windows-1252 code set is used quite a lot in the Windows realm and needs a few comments:
>
> It is a very common mistake to assume windows-1252 is the same thing as the ANSI code set (ISO-8859-1, also known as Latin-1). The Windows codepage defines 34 extra characters in addition to the ones defined by ISO-8859-1. Examples include
>
> ‡ at code point 135 (U+2021, DOUBLE DAGGER),
> Œ at code point 140 (U+0152, LATIN CAPITAL LIGATURE OE),
> ™ at code point 153 (U+2122, TRADEMARK SIGN),
> … at code point 133 (U+2026, HORIZONTAL ELLIPSIS),
> and so forth.
>
> Some authoring tools automatically use and output windows-1252 characters but give ISO-8859-1 as the encoding identifier, creating problems when other tools read the characters specific to windows-1252.
>
> Note also that some of the Windows fonts, such as Courier or MS Sans Serif, do not have glyphs for these 34 extra characters, even on the latest versions of the operating system.

The way you encode your document should have no effect on how it will be processed. For instance, Listing 2.5 shows a file encoded in Shift_JIS. Listing 2.6 shows the same document encoded as UTF-8. Both will be rendered the same way, as shown in Figure 2.6.

LISTING 2.5

Ja_ShiftJIS.xml—XML Encoding Shift_JIS (Displayed as if It Were windows-1252)

```
<?xml version="1.0" encoding="Shift_JIS" ?>
<doc>
 <header>ff□[f^□\'¢‰»fefNfmf□fW□[(SGML/XML)</header>
 <para>RWS Group,í□AŽŸ,Ì,æ,¤,É□L"í,ÈSGML/XMLfT□[frfX,ð'ñ‹Ÿ,µ,Ä,¢,
➥Ü,·□B</para>
 <list>
  <item>Šù'¶,Ì•¶□',Ìf□□[fJfŠf[□[fVf‡f"</item>
  <item>Šù'¶,Ìff□[f^Œ`Ž®(FrameMaker□AWord□AOracle,È,Ç),ÆSGML/XML
➥Œ`Ž®ŠÔ,Ì•ÏŠ·</item>
  <item>frfWflfX,É□‡,Á,½□V,µ,¢SGML/XMLfAfvfŠfP□[fVf‡f",Ì□ì□¬
➥(DTD□Af}f‹f`fŠf"fKf‹ fA□[fLfefNf`ff□AŽ©"®f□□[fNftf□□[,È,Ç)</item>
  <item>Šù'¶,ÌSGML/XML•¶□',©,ç-|-ó,³,ê,½fefLfXfg,ÌŽg—p</item>
 </list>
</doc>
```

LISTING 2.6

Ja_UTF8.xml—XML Encoding UTF-8 (Displayed as if It Were windows-1252)

```
<?xml version="1.0" ?>
<doc>
 <header>ãf‡ãf¼ã,¿æ§‹é€ åŒ–ãf†ã,¯ãfŽãf-ã,¸ãf¼(SGML/XML)</header>
 <para>RWS Groupã□¯ã€□æ¬¡ã□®ã,ˆã□†ã□«å°fç¯„ã□ªSGML/XML
➥ã,µãf¼ãf"ã,¹ã,'æ□□ä¾›ã□—ã□¦ã□„ã□¾ã□™ã€,</para>
 <list>
  <item>æ—¢å-˜ã□®æ-‡æ›¸ã□®ãf-ãf¼ã,«ãfªã,¼ãf¼ã,·ãf§ãf³</item>
  <item>æ—¢å-˜ã□®ãf‡ãf¼ã,¿å½¢å¼□(FrameMakerã€□Wordã€□Oracleã□ªã□©)
➥ã□¨SGML/XMLå½¢å¼□é-"ã□®å¤‰æ□›</item>
  <item>ãf"ã,¸ãf□ã,¹ã□«å□ˆã□£ã□Ÿæ-°ã□—ã□„SGML/XMLã,¢ãf—ãfªã,±ãf¼ã,·
➥ãf§ãf³ã□®ä½œæˆ□(DTDã€□ãfžãf«ãf□ãfªãf³ã,¬ãf« ã,¢ãf¼ã,-ãf†ã,
➥¯ãf□ãf£ã€□è‡ªå‹•ãf¯ãf¼ã,¯ãf•ãf-ãf¼ã□ªã□©)</item>
  <item>æ—¢å-˜ã□®SGML/XMLæ-‡æ›¸ã□‹ã,‰ç¿»è¨³ã□•ã,Œã□Ÿãf†ã,-ã,¹ãfˆã□®
➥ä½¿ç"¨</item>
 </list>
</doc>
```

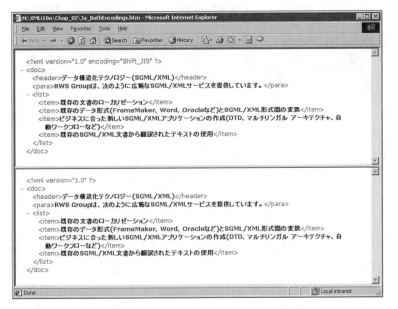

FIGURE 2.6

`Shift_JIS` *and* `UTF-8` *files shown together.*

Conversion Issues

Converting back and forth between UCS and other code sets can be tricky. The following paragraphs discuss some potential problems.

Macintosh Arabic code set has duplicated code points that work in pairs for the left-to-right and right-to-left ASCII characters. Some legacy data may use these codes instead of a single set of symbols mapped to different glyphs by the rendering engine. As was already mentioned, the use of compatibility characters is not recommended with XML. You may want to consider modifying legacy data at the same time you migrate to XML-based systems.

Another conversion issue is the Japanese encodings. Vendors often have slight differences in the character sets they support. For instance, `cp952`, the Microsoft implementation of `Shift_JIS`, counts more entries than the set defined by the Unicode Consortium. The NEC user-defined characters are included in some implementations and not in others.

There are also about 20 code points that have different mapping, depending on which encoding implementation you are using to convert to and from UCS.

TABLE 2.3

Characters with Potential Problems with Japanese Encodings

UCS Code	UCS Name
U+005C	REVERSE SOLIDUS
U+007E	TILDE
U+00A2	CENT SIGN
U+00A3	POUND SIGN
U+00A5	YEN SIGN
U+00AC	NOT SIGN
U+2014	EM DASH
U+2015	HORIZONTAL BAR
U+2016	DOUBLE VERTICAL LINE
U+2225	PARALLEL TO
U+301C	WAVE DASH
U+FF0D	FULLWIDTH HYPHENS-MINUS
U+FF3C	FULLWIDTH REVERSE SOLIDUS
U+FF5E	FULLWIDTH TILDE
U+FFE0	FULLWIDTH CENT SIGN
U+FFE1	FULLWIDTH POUND SIGN
U+FFE2	FULLWIDTH NOT SIGN
U+FFE3	FULLWIDTH MACRON
U+FFE4	FULLWIDTH BROKEN BAR
U+FFE5	FULLWIDTH YEN SIGN

One solution is to use numeric character references instead of the raw characters. Those notations do not depend on the encoding of the XML document, but are directly mapped to the correct UCS scalar values.

Some work is currently ongoing at the W3C to address the problems specific to Japanese. You can find the complete proposal for the XML Japanese Profile at `http://www.w3.org/TR/japanese-xml`.

Conversion Tools

A number of tools, sometimes called *transcoders*, support the conversion from one encoding to another. The main problem is that they seldom have support for XML and numeric character references.

The Academia Sinica (`http://www.ascc.net/xml`) offers various utilities such as xml-tcs, derived from the Bell Labs tcs tool, or GLUE.

There is also native2ascii, a utility that comes with the Java Development Kit. It is not specifically designed for XML but offers a wide choice of encodings. For more details, see the tool documentation at `http://java.sun.com/j2se/1.3/docs/tooldocs/solaris/native2ascii.html`.

Another possibility is to use Rainbow, a free toolbox of localization utilities. It offers an encoding conversion function and supports XML documents. Figure 2.7 shows the dialog box for this conversion function. The list of the encodings supported does not include every possible one, but covers quite a few of them. While Rainbow is a Windows application, it uses its own conversion libraries and works correctly regardless of whether you have language support installed. Rainbow can be downloaded at `http://www.opentag.com`.

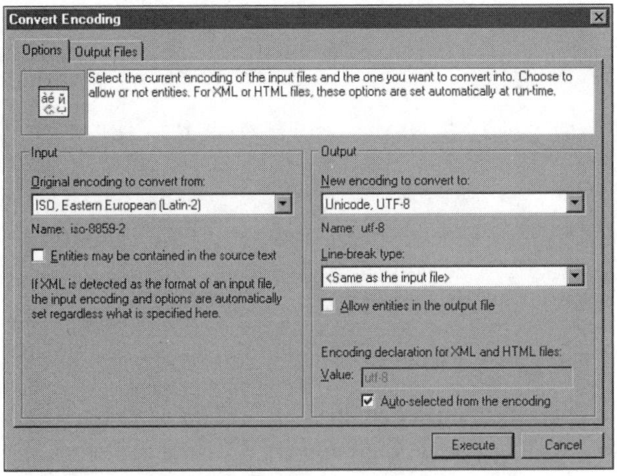

FIGURE 2.7

Option dialog box for the encoding conversion function of Rainbow.

Encoding in XHTML

The same principles described for any XML document apply to XHTML files as well. You must specify the encoding attribute in the XML declaration. In addition, for backward compatibility, the XHTML specifications also recommend including the `http-equiv` charset statement in an initial `<meta>` element, as shown in Listing 2.7.

LISTING 2.7

`XHTML_zh-cn.htm`—A Simplified Chinese XHTML File Encoded in `GB2312`

```
<?xml version="1.0" encoding="GB2312" ?>
<!DOCTYPE html
 PUBLIC "-//W3C//DTD XHTML 1.0 Strict//EN"
 "DTD/xhtml1-strict.dtd" >
<html xmlns="http://www.w3.org/1999/xhtml">
 <head>
  <meta type="http-equiv" value="charset=GB2312"/>
 </head>
<body>
 <h3>数据结构技术(SGML/XML)</h3>
 <p>RWS Group提供广泛的SGML(标准通用置标语言)和XML(扩展式置标语言)
➥服务，其中包括：</p>
 <ul>
  <li>译制现有文献</li>
  <li>将SGML/XML转换为若干种现有数据格式(例如FrameMaker, Word 和 Oracle)
➥或将这些数据格式转换为 SGML/XML</li>

<li>创建新的SGML/XML应用程序，以适合您的业务环境(例如DTD、多语体系和自动工作流程)
➥</li>
 </ul>
 <p>RWS Group懂得这些数据结构技术的重要性，并致力于协助客户做好这项技术的国际化和地
➥方化工作。</p>
 </body>
</html>
```

The values for the `http-equiv` charset parameter are the same as for the XML
encoding declaration. If the two encoding instructions are present but contradictory, the
encoding of the XML declaration takes precedence.

Escaped Characters Representation

When a character cannot be represented in the encoding of the XML document, you
can use a numeric character reference or a character entity to encode it. For example,
when the document is using the code set `ISO-8859-1` and you need to include the
trademark character, which is not included in Latin-1, you can use `&#x2122;` instead.

Numeric Character References

Each numeric character reference (NCR) provides a UCS value in either decimal or hexadecimal notation, as defined below:

```
NumCharRef ::= '&#' [0-9]+ ';' | '&#x' [0-9a-fA-F]+ ';'
```

For instance, `&#8482;` is the trademark symbol in decimal and `&#x2122;` in hexadecimal. The hexadecimal notation is used more often by far.

Any character can be represented with its numerical character reference, including the ASCII characters.

If you need to represent a surrogate value (a UCS code point above `0xFFFF`) with an NCR, keep in mind that it needs to be coded in a single character reference, not both high- and low-surrogate values. In other words, if you need to include the surrogate pair `<U+D800,U+DF0C>` (the `OLD ITALIC LETTER EM`) in your document, you apply the formula we saw in Listing 2.1 and use the notation `&#x1030C;` (or `&#66316;` in decimal). The notation `&#xD800;&#xDF0C;` is not legal.

A numeric character reference can be converted back and forth to a UCS scalar value without a lookup table. It also does not require a definition as does a character entity.

Character Entities

Character entities are parsed entities that map UCS characters. They are defined as follows

```
CharEnt ::= '&' EntName ';'
```

where `EntName` is the name of a predefined entity or an entity defined in the DTD associated with the XML document. You can also define the entities at the top of the XML document itself. For example, Listing 2.8 shows how to declare an entity named `&aWithRingAndAcute;` that corresponds to the UCS code point `U+01FB` and how to use it later within your XML content. Figure 2.8 is a rendering of this entity declaration.

LISTING 2.8

`Entity.xml`—Entity Declaration and Use

```
<?xml version="1.0"?>
 <!DOCTYPE doc [
 <!ATTLIST style id ID #REQUIRED>
 <!ENTITY aWithRingAndAcute "&#x01fb;">
 ]>
<?xml-stylesheet href="#sample" type="text/css"?>
```

LISTING 2.8   CONTINUED

```
<doc>
 <style id="sample"><!-- doc { display: block; }
  p { display: block; font: 2em, Arial, sans-serif; } -->
 </style>
 <p>&aWithRingAndAcute; is a character 'a' with ring and acute.</p>
</doc>
```

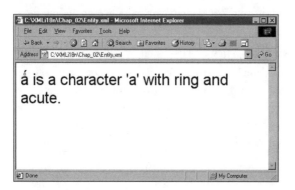

FIGURE 2.8

Rendering of Listing 2.8. The character 'a' with a ring and an acute is coded as a user-defined entity.

There are five predefined entities: &, <, >, ', and ", corresponding respectively to the ampersand, less-than, greater-than, apostrophe, and double-quote characters. You can use these entities even when the XML document has no corresponding declarations. All other entities must be declared.

From an interoperability viewpoint, it is better to use numeric character references rather than character entities. Some versions of different browsers or other XML tools do not always support all character entities correctly.

Using either numeric character references or character entities could lead to a few practical problems. For instance, executing a search or global replacement of text may be more difficult if you use tools that are not XML enabled.

The best way to encode an XML document is always to use UTF-8, where all characters except the special escaped ones can be encoded as raw values, not NCRs.

> **NOTE:** Keep in mind that entities are not limited to characters. They can be used as placeholders for repetitive runs of text, such as product names, references, and so forth.
>
> This could be a way to introduce the concept of variables in your documents, such as using an entity for the name or the version of a product. However, this should be used with prudence because it might make the work of the translator more difficult by hiding some of the context (for instance, whether the entity corresponds to a masculine or feminine noun). The use of entities in this context is discussed in Chapter 9, "Automated References."

Mixing Scripts

In some cases you may have to represent several languages using different scripts. In such occurrences, you have two options: Either use an encoding that supports all the scripts or use an encoding that supports one or more of the scripts and use numeric character references for the text in the remaining scripts.

The first solution with UTF-8 or UTF-16 is the most efficient because both encodings will support most of the scripts used today in computing.

Listing 2.9 shows an XML document with text in various languages that use different scripts including Roman, Kanji, Ethiopic, Cyrillic, and Thai. The document is encoded in UTF-16.

LISTING 2.9

MultiLang.xml—An XML File with the Same Sentence in Various Languages

---

```
<?xml version='1.0' ?>
<?xml-stylesheet href="#sample" type="text/css"?>
<doc>
 <style id="sample"><!-- doc {display: block}
 p {display: block; margin-bottom: 0.5em; }
 p.bidi {direction: rtl; } --> </style>
 <p xml:lang="ja">Japanese:
➥弊社ではどんなウェブサイトもあらゆる言語にグローバル化し、管理致します。</p>
 <p xml:lang="es">Spanish: Internacionalizamos y gestionamos cualquier
➥página web en cualquier idioma.</p>
```

LISTING 2.9   CONTINUED

```
<p xml:lang="th">Thai: เราจะบริหารและจัดการเว็บไซต์เป็นถษาต่างๆเพื่อให้สามารถ
ใช้ได้ไปทั่วโลก.</p>
<p xml:lang="tr">Turkish: Herhangi bir dildeki Web Sitesini
küreselleştirecek ve yöneteceğiz.</p>
<p xml:lang="iu">Inuktitut: ᐃᓄᒃᑎᑑᖕᖑᖅᑐᖅᑕᐅᓪᓕᖅ ᑕᒪᐃᓐᓄᑦ ᑕᐸᖅᑐᒋᔭᒃᓴᖅ.</p>
<p xml:lang="en">English: We will globalize and manage any Web site in
any language.</p>
<p class="bidi" xml:lang="ar">Arabic:
سنقوم بعولمة وإدارة أي موقع على الشبكة العالمية بأية لغة. </p>
<p xml:lang="ko">Korean: 저희는 어떠한 언어로 씌어진 웹사이트라도 세계화하고
관리할 수 있습니다.</p>
<p xml:lang="sv">Swedish: Vi erbjuder globalisering och hantering av
webbplatser på alla språk.</p>
<p xml:lang="ti">Tigrigna: ንኹን ቄብሳይት ብንኹነ ቋንቋ ዓለም ዓቀፋዊ ጌርና ናዳሎ ኢና፦.</p>
<p xml:lang="ru">Russian: Мы выполним глобализацию и поддержку любого
Web-узла на любом языке.</p>
<p xml:lang="zh-tw">Traditional Chinese:
我們可以將您的網站地方化爲任何語種並且爲您管理。</p>
<p xml:lang="am">Amahric: ግንኛውንም ድረ ገጽ በግንኛውም ቋንቋ አዘጋጅተን ዓለም አቀፋዊ
እናደርጋለን፦.</p>
<p xml:lang="zh-cn">Simplified Chinese:
我们将用任何语言全球化和管理任何网站。</p>
<p xml:lang="lv">Latvian: Mēs globalizēsim un pārvaldīsim jebkuru
Web vietu jebkurā valodā.</p>
</doc>
```

If you have the proper fonts and rendering engines installed on your machine, the XML processor will show the different scripts correctly, as in Figure 2.9.

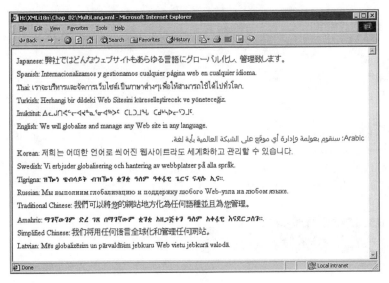

FIGURE 2.9

Rendering of text in multiple scripts.

Non-ASCII Element and Attribute Names

A direct effect of XML support for the large repertoire of UCS is that not only the content of the document but also the names of elements and attributes can have extended characters.

For example, as shown in Listing 2.10, you could use element and attribute names in Simplified Chinese rather than English.

LISTING 2.10

`ZHTags.xml`—An XML Document Using Chinese Element and Attribute Names

```
<?xml version="1.0" ?>
<书籍>
 <封面>
  <汇集>The Lord of the Rings</汇集>
  <标题>The Return of the King</标题>
  <作者>J.R.R. Tolkien</作者>
 </封面>
 <章节 数="1">
  <头注>Minas Tirith</头注>
```

LISTING 2.10   CONTINUED

```
 <段落识别 id="A34B">Pippin looked out from the shelter of Gandalf's
➥cloak.</段落识别>
 </章节>
</书籍>
```

If you choose to use extended characters in tag names, be aware that not all XML tools
will support it correctly. Most tools have been tested to handle UCS characters for the
data, but not for the tags. A robust XML processor should handle both without a
problem. Figure 2.10 shows the document in Internet Explorer 5.5.

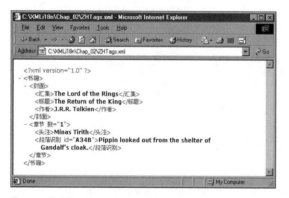

FIGURE 2.10

An XML document with Chinese element and attribute names, viewed in Internet Explorer 5.5.

Element and attribute names in non-ASCII characters are still rare. However, because
there is nothing in XML that would prevent their use, we should see some increase
of it.

A SOAP document is a good example of a place where you may find a vocabulary with
tag names in a language other than English. The purpose of SOAP (Simple Object
Access Protocol) is to exchange objects and data between applications. The data
encapsulated in a SOAP envelope contain XML tags over which the receiving
application has no control. They could include element or attribute names with
extended characters.

URIs Representation

XML documents often use uniform resource identifiers (URIs) to specify URLs in
links, to define namespaces, and so forth. URIs are defined by RFC2396 and amended

by RFC2732. They are based on a subset of the ASCII repertoire, so there is no direct way to represent extended characters in a URI. However, you can use the same escape mechanism as for the reserved ASCII characters.

The W3C and the IETF (Internet Engineering Task Force) are working on a more inclusive specification of URIs, but those recommendations are only at a draft stage at the time this is being written. Make sure you verify the latest specifications at the W3C site. Meanwhile, you can follow the guidelines already defined for creating an Internationalized URI (IURI), which is discussed in the following section.

Internationalized URIs

An *IURI (Internationalized URI)* is defined as an extension of a URI and is created by following these steps:

1. The characters are represented using the UCS repertoire and, if necessary, must be normalized (see the section "Character Normalization," which follows).
2. The string is encoded in UTF-8.
3. Each byte of each `UTF-8` sequence is escaped in the form `%HH`, where `HH` is the hexadecimal value of the byte.

The following are several examples of imaginary URIs with extended characters and their corresponding coded forms:

```
urn:FranceTéléCom-Schémas:FactureDirecte.v2
urn:FranceT%C3%A9l%C3%A9Com-Sch%C3%A9mas:FactureDirecte.v2

http://www.Работа.bg
http://www.%D0%A0%D0%B0%D0%B1%D0%BE%D1%82%D0%B0.bg

ftp://ftp.polyu.edu.hk/圖書館/書123/
ftp://ftp.polyu.edu.hk/%E5%9C%96%E6%9B%B8%E9%A4%A8/%E6%9B%B8123/

http://www.ᓄᓇᕗᑦ.ca
http://www.%E1%93%84%E1%93%87%E1%95%97%E1%92%BB%E1%92%A5.ca
```

In theory, you should be able to leave the URI in its normal form in the XML document, but in practice, for now, it is strongly recommended that you escape it yourself rather than relying on the XML processor to make the conversion for you.

Album is a freeware Windows tool that includes a function for converting non-coded URIs to their escaped form (and conversely), using the Clipboard. Album intercepts the Copy command, performs the conversion, and replaces the Clipboard content with the escaped sequence so it's available for the next Paste command. You can download Album at `http://www.opentag.com`.

If you need to implement the IURI mechanism in your own applications, you can use the source code samples provided by the W3C. Perl and Java examples are available at `http://www.w3.org/International/O-URL-code.html`.

Character Normalization

Using UCS does not solve all problems and brings a few of its own as well. One of the powerful mechanisms of Unicode is its character composition feature. You dispose of a number of non-spacing symbols that can be used in conjunction with other characters to compose graphemes.

> **NOTE:** A grapheme is a unique character, or a group of characters that represents a phoneme. For example: the character LATIN CAPITAL LETTER C (U+0043) and the character COMBINING CEDILLA (U+0327) put together make the grapheme Ç.
>
> A phoneme is a unit of the phonetic system of a language that corresponds to a set of similar speech sounds that are perceived as a single distinctive sound. For example, in French, both graphemes Ç and S correspond to the phoneme \s\.

The composition method is used, for example, to represent Vietnamese. The Latin-based script used to write Vietnamese is called *Quốc ngữ*. It uses the basic Roman alphabet, plus 7 additional base characters with accents (14 if you count the uppercase and lowercase variants). In addition, there are 5 tone marks that can appear with pretty much any base character. This makes up for quite a few graphemes that are not always precomposed. The character composition method allows these variations to be built easily.

Listing 2.11 shows an XML document with the Vietnamese names of some of the accents used with *Quốc ngữ*. Each name is written twice—first with the precomposed character, then decomposed into its base character and combining marks. The NCR notation is used so that you can see the UCS code point values. The rendering of the document is shown in Figure 2.11.

LISTING 2.11

`Vietnamese.xml`—Precomposed and Combining Forms of Some Vietnamese Characters

```
<?xml version="1.0" ?>
<?xml-stylesheet href="#default" type="text/css"?>
<file>
 <style id="default"><!--
  file {display: block}
  para {display: block; margin-bottom:1em; font-size:18pt; } -->
 </style>
 <para>'Huy&#x1EC1;n' or 'Huye&#x302;&#x300;n'</para>
 <para>'S&#x1EB3;c' or 'Sa&#x306;&#x309;c'</para>
 <para>'N&#x1EB7;ng' or 'Na&#x323;&#x306;ng'</para>
</file>
```

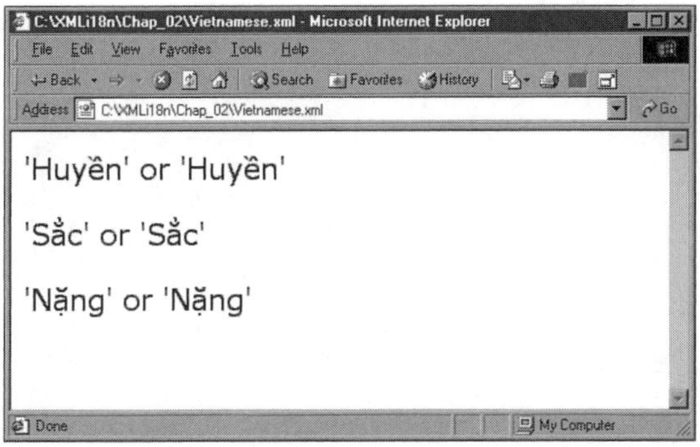

FIGURE 2.11

Rendering of the different forms of Vietnamese characters from Listing 2.11.

Korean is another language in which character combination is frequent. There, all the Hangul syllable blocks, which make up most of the characters used, can be precomposed or decomposed in basic forms called *jamo*.

For example, the word 무료 is made of two Hangul blocks (U+BB34 and U+B8CC) that can be decomposed in four jamo characters: ㅁㅜㄹㅛ (U+1106 with U+116E and U+1105 with U+116D). When collating Korean text that includes a mixture of precomposed and decomposed forms, one solution is to decompose all precomposed blocks into conjoining jamo before comparing.

Character composition is very useful and allows the representation of practically any alphabet-based character, as long as you have the relevant set of base letters and non-spacing diacritical marks. However, it also brings a problem.

The Problem

Accented characters used in many languages, such as á or ú, can be represented as combining characters, but they also have specific code points for their precomposed forms. This form is often the one used most.

Depending on the tools you are using to enter or convert your XML data, you may have identical characters represented one way or the other. This is not a problem as far as rendering is concerned, but it may be a problem when processing the data for sorting, searching, indexing, and so forth.

For example, Figure 2.12 displays the rendering of an XML file in which the character U+1EBE (LATIN CAPITAL LETTER E WITH CIRCUMFLEX AND ACUTE) is created three different ways.

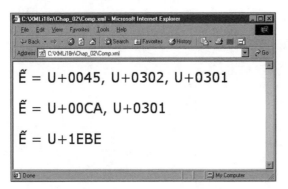

FIGURE 2.12

An XML document with three different forms to encode the same grapheme.

To solve this problem, you want to use the same form for all the characters that have different variations.

The Solution: The Normalized Form

The W3C *Character Model* defines the normalized form of character representation for XML. It is still a working draft at the time this book is being written (http://www.w3.org/TR/charmod). Make sure to verify the latest updates.

To be normalized, an XML document should pass the following requirements:

- All escaped characters that are not syntactically relevant and that are not needed because of the limitation of the encoding used are replaced by the actual characters.

- The text is in Unicode Canonical Composition (Normalization Form C) according to the Unicode Technical Report 15.
- The text does not contain any of the characters considered unsuitable for XML (see Table 2.1).

The Unicode Consortium provides mapping tables to indicate how characters can be decomposed or combined. There are four forms of normalization. They are explained in detail in the Unicode Technical Report #15, "Unicode Normalization Forms," available at http://www.unicode.org/unicode/reports/tr15.

In some cases, such as for Hangul blocks to jamo forms in Korean, the decomposition can be done by applying an algorithm. However, most of the time you have to rely on the information listed in the Unicode character database. The latest version of the database (UnicodeData-Latest.txt) is available at ftp://ftp.unicode.org/Public/UNIDATA.

Note also that in XML the need for a normalized form goes beyond the characters. Two XML documents can be semantically identical but have syntactic differences other than the way they are encoded.

Charlint

The W3C has made available a Perl utility to normalize UTF-8 files. The tool, written by Martin Dürst, is called Charlint (also known as Charlie). Any UTF-8 file (XML document or any other format) can be processed by Charlint and normalized.

The examples in Listings 2.12 and 2.13 show how our XML document looks before and after being processed by Charlint.

LISTING 2.12

Comp.xml—An XML File Before Normalization

```
<?xml version="1.0" ?>
<?xml-stylesheet href="#default" type="text/css"?>
<file>
 <style id="default"><!--
  file {display: block}
  para {display: block; margin-bottom:1em; font-size:22pt; } -->
 </style>
 <para>E&#x0302;&#x0301; = U+0045, U+0302, U+0301</para>
 <para>&#x00CA;&#x0301; = U+00CA, U+0301</para>
 <para>&#x1EBE; = U+1EBE</para>
</file>
```

The command line to run Charlint is rather simple. Note the use of -n to correctly read the NCRs and -N to output NCRs instead of raw UTF-8.

```
C:\XMLi18n\Chap_02>perl charlint.pl -n -N < Comp.xml > Comp2.xml
```

The output generated by Charlint standardizes the different forms of the same character into the precomposed one.

LISTING 2.13

Comp2.xml—The XML File After Normalization

```
<?xml version="1.0" ?>
<?xml-stylesheet href="#default" type="text/css"?>
<file>
 <style id="default"><!--
  file {display: block}
  para {display: block; margin-bottom:1em; font-size:22pt; } -->
 </style>
 <para>&#x1EBE; = U+0045, U+0302, U+0301</para>
 <para>&#x1EBE; = U+00CA, U+0301</para>
 <para>&#x1EBE; = U+1EBE</para>
</file>
```

You can download the Charlint utility from the W3C Web site at http://www.w3.org/International/charlint.

Summary

In this chapter we have seen the different ways characters can be represented and how the encoding methods used must be declared.

The character set of XML is ISO/IEC 10646. UTF-16 and UTF-8 are its default encodings. However, you can use the encoding declaration in the XML prolog if you want to use other code sets. The list of relevant encoding names is maintained by the IANA.

If a character cannot be coded in its raw form, XML offers an efficient mechanism to represent it: numeric character references (NCRs). You can also use character entities, especially the few predefined ones corresponding to the symbols escaped most often.

In some cases, when processing XML text, you may want to use a canonical form of each character to make valid comparison possible. The Charlint utility enables you to create UTF-8 XML documents with normalized characters.

References

Much information in this chapter refers to the work done by the Unicode Consortium, the W3C, and the IETF. These documents are online at the addresses in the following list. The document identified as a draft is still a work in progress at the time of this book's publication. Be sure you get the latest information.

XML 1.0 specifications: `http://www.w3.org/TR/REC-xml`

XML Internationalization working group: `http://www.w3.org/International`

XHTML 1.0 specifications: `http://www.w3.org/TR/xhtml1`

Unicode and XML: `http://www.w3.org/TR/unicode-xml`

(draft) WWW Character model: `http://www.w3.org/TR/charmod`

Unicode Normalization Forms (UTR15): `http://www.unicode.org/unicode/reports/tr15`

IANA charsets: `http://www.iana.org/assignments/character-sets`

URI definition: `http://www.ietf.org/rfc/rfc2396.txt`

URI definition amendment: `http://www.ietf.org/rfc/rfc2732.txt`

# CHAPTER 3

Miscellaneous Tagging

In This Chapter:

Several text properties are common to all types of XML documents, regardless of their final purpose. These characteristics occur so frequently that the various XML standards often include special provisions for them.

These properties cover the following challenges:

- **How to identify the language of the content**—For example, how to distinguish a paragraph in German from one in Czech.
- **How to handle white spaces**—Basically, how to note the difference between spaces that are meant to make the structure of the document more readable (spaces such as indentations and empty lines), and the ones that are meaningful.
- **How to represent date and time information**—In our case especially, how to display this information both from locale-specific and from locale-neutral viewpoints.

Language Settings

To address language identification, XML provides a default attribute to specify the language of any element: `xml:lang`. In many respects this attribute can also be seen as a *locale*.

A locale is, roughly, the combination of a language and a region. The classic example is the difference between French, the language, and the two locales: French for France, and Canadian French (Québécois). Many other examples exist: the various flavors of Spanish, Brazilian versus Portuguese, and so forth.

In addition to linguistic differences, the locale also often indicates possible variations on how to process data: Currency, numbers, date/time formatting, sorting, and character uppercasing and lowercasing are some of the locale-specific areas.

Sometimes the locale even goes beyond and points to deeper differences such as the type of writing system (for example, Classical Mongolian versus Cyrillic Mongolian, or Azerbaijani Arabic versus Azerbaijani Cyrillic).

> **NOTE:** A good example of a language where differences are clear between locales is Spanish.
>
> Spanish is spoken in many countries and therefore comes in many different varieties. When localizing for a specific market you must decide which flavor you need.
>
> For example, Spaniards use "*utilidades*" for "*utility programs,*" Argentines use "*utilitiarios,*" and Mexicans use "*utilerías.*" Another example is the term "*computer.*" Spaniards use the word "*ordenador*" but all Latin Americans use "*computadora*" instead. Such discrepancies cause a few dilemmas when you want to have only one Spanish translation for all markets.
>
> To reduce costs, companies often try to use a "neutral" or "international" Spanish. This is an artificial creation, as is "Latin American Spanish."
>
> Finally, to avoid confusion, you might want to refer to the Spanish spoken in Spain as "Iberian Spanish" rather than "Castilian Spanish," the term "*Castellano*" being often used in South America to refer to the Spanish spoken there.

When defining your own XML vocabulary, you should use `xml:lang` as your attribute to specify the locale information, rather than come up with your own attribute. There are a couple of good reasons for this.

First, `xml:lang` will be understood immediately by any XML user. And second, it will allow you to take advantage of interoperability among the various XML-related technologies such as XSL or CSS.

If you use a DTD to specify your format, `xml:lang` must still be declared, just as with any other attribute. For example:

```
<!ATTLIST p
 xml:lang NMTOKEN #IMPLIED >
```

Language Codes

The values of the `xml:lang` attribute should conform to the language tags defined in the XML specifications, as shown in Listing 3.1.

LISTING 3.1

Definition of the Value for the `xml:lang` **Attribute**

```
LangValue   ::= Langcode ('-' Subcode)*
Langcode    ::= ISO639Code | IanaCode | UserCode
ISO639Code  ::= ([a-z] | [A-Z]) ([a-z] | [A-Z])
IanaCode    ::= ('i' | 'I') '-' ([a-z] | [A-Z])+
UserCode    ::= ('x' | 'X') '-' ([a-z] | [A-Z])+
Subcode     ::= ([a-z] | [A-Z])+
```

In addition, according to RFC1766, the part on the right of the `'-'` can be up to 8 characters long.

Currently the language codes use ISO 639 2-letter codes, but as of January 2001, RFC1766 has been superseded by RFC3066, which introduces the use of ISO 639 3-letter codes.

According to this last RFC, if a language can be identified with both types of code, the 2-letter code must be used. The 3-letter codes should be used only for representing languages that do not have 2-letter codes. For example, the code for Korean must always be `ko` and never `kor`.

In addition, there are 2 types of 3-letter codes: Terminology and Bibliography. Currently none of the languages that should be using a 3-letter code have a discrepancy between the Terminology form and the Bibliography form. If such a conflict occurs in the future, the Terminology code should be used.

Finally, if a language has both an ISO code and an IANA code, the ISO code must be used.

TABLE 3.1

Use of ISO Codes

Languages	639-1	639-2/T	639-2/B	xml:lang
French	fr	fra	fre	fr
German	de	deu	ger	de
Manipuri		mni	mni	mni
Navajo	nv	nav	nav	nv

> **NOTE:** Normally, attribute values in XML are case sensitive. However, for simplification purposes and to match the RFC3066 standard, the values of the `xml:lang` attribute are not case sensitive. For example, the four values "`pt-BR`", "`PT-BR`", "`pt-br`", and "`PT-br`" (Brazilian Portuguese) are considered identical.
>
> Usually the language code is represented in lowercase and the country code in uppercase, but this is not a rule.

User-Defined Codes

In some cases the list of variant codes you can build from the predefined language and region codes is not enough.

For instance, as we have seen already, you might have to localize a document in two types of Spanish: one for the audience in Spain (Iberian Spanish) and the other for the Latin American market. The first should be coded "`es-ES`", or simply "`es`" because Spain is the default country for Spanish. For the second, however, no country code corresponds to "Latin America." To solve this you can create your own locale codes as defined by `UserCode` in Listing 3.1. For example, you could use something such as "`x-es-LatAm`" for your Latin-American Spanish document.

A special kind of user-defined code exists: the one registered to the IANA. Most of them start with the prefix `i-`. The list of these language tags is updated regularly and you can find it at `http://www.iana.org/assignments/languages`.

> **NOTE:** Be aware that some localization tools might be programmed to handle only 4-letter codes, and might not be able to process IANA or user-defined codes correctly.

For a detailed list of language codes, see Appendix D.

Multilingual Documents

As you saw in Chapter 2, "Character Representation," one characteristic of XML is its capability to handle content in different languages when necessary.

For example, as shown in Listing 3.2, a SOAP data file could store description of an item in several languages.

LISTING 3.2

Soap1.xml—SOAP Envelope with Multilingual Entries

```
<!-- SOAP excerpt -->
<Envelope
 xmlns="http://schemas.xmlsoap.org/soap/envelope/"
 encodingStyle="http://schemas.xmlsoap.org/soap/envelope/">
 <Body>
  <d:GetItem xmlns:d="uri:myData" xml:lang="en">
   <d:PartNum>NCD-67543</d:PartNum>
   <d:InStock>5</d:InStock>
   <d:Desc>Manual water pump</d:Desc>
   <d:Desc xml:lang="fr">Pompe à eau manuelle</d:Desc>
   <d:Desc xml:lang="ja">手動ウォーター・ポンプ</d:Desc>
  </d:GetItem>
 </Body>
</Envelope>
```

The default language from the `<d:GetItem>` element level is set to en (English). The child elements inherit the property, so the first `<d:Desc>` element does not need to repeat the attribute. However, because the second one contains the description in French, you need to override the default `xml:lang` attribute.

Always keep in mind that XML element and attribute names can have non-ASCII characters as well. In such occurrences, the language specifications work the same. Listing 3.3 shows the same SOAP envelope, but this time with the user data marked up with a Russian vocabulary. The data are identical and the `xml:lang` mechanism is expected to behave the same: It applies to the content, not to the tags.

LISTING 3.3

Soap2.xml—SOAP Envelope with Multilingual Entries and Some Non-ASCII Elements

```
<!-- SOAP excerpt -->
<Envelope
 xmlns="http://schemas.xmlsoap.org/soap/envelope/"
 encodingStyle="http://schemas.xmlsoap.org/soap/envelope/">
 <Body>
  <д:ДостатьОбъект
➥xmlns:д="uri:%D0%9C%D0%BE%D0%B8%D0%94%D0%B0%D0%BD%D0%BD%D1%8B%D0%B5"
➥xml:lang="en">
```

LISTING 3.3   CONTINUED

```
  <д:НомерОбъекта>NCD-67543</д:НомерОбъекта>
  <д:ВНаличии>5</д:ВНаличии>
  <д:Описание>Manual water pump</д:Описание>
  <д:Описание xml:lang="fr">Pompe à eau manuelle</д:Описание>
  <д:Описание xml:lang="ja">手動ウォーター・ポンプ</д:Описание>
  </д:ДостатьОбъект>
 </Body>
</Envelope>
```

Note the value of the `xmlns` attribute: The namespace prefix `д` is associated to a URI reference (МоиДанные), but here the URI has already been coded into its UTF-8/escaped form as described in Chapter 2.

The `lang` Attribute in XHTML

For historical reasons, in addition to `xml:lang`, XHTML also allows the attribute `lang` to specify language switch. Both have exactly the same significance.

In case the same element has both `xml:lang` and `lang` with two different values, `xml:lang` takes precedence over `lang`.

> **NOTE:** Using `xml:lang` or `lang` has no direct impact on the way the text is rendered. For example, specifying a paragraph as Arabic does not trigger right-to-left display. You must use the style sheets and the various internationalization elements and attributes such as `<bdo>`, `<dir>`, and `<ruby>` for XHTML to indicate to the user-agent how the text should be displayed.
>
> However, take into account that language is important in some cases: for example, to select an appropriate font. If a document is encoded in UTF-8 or UTF-16, there is no easy way to distinguish Chinese from Japanese, because most ideographs have been unified.

The `lang()` Function in XPath

XPath is the language used in various XML applications to specify a "path notation" that allows you to navigate through the hierarchical structure of any XML document. It is also used to test whether the node of a document instance matches a given pattern. XPath is used, for example, in conjunction with XPointer and XSLT.

XPath designers have wisely provided a function to match languages: `lang()`.

The function uses the `xml:lang` attribute to match a given parameter. This is very useful because, following the XML specifications, the function is not case sensitive and allows you to match a language value very simply.

When you specify only a language code rather than a locale code (for example, `en` versus `en-GB`), the function returns true for any attributes where the first part of its value matches the argument. The separator between both parts of the value is '-'. Consider the following XSL statement:

```
<xsl:for-each select="lang('es')">
```

When this command is used on the XML document shown in Listing 3.4, it will return true for all the following elements:

```
<p xml:lang="es">Spanish text</p>
<p xml:lang="ES">Spanish text</p>
<p xml:lang="es-ES">Iberian Spanish text</p>
<p xml:lang='es-mx'>Mexican Spanish text</p>
```

LISTING 3.4

`Spanish.xml`— Multilingual Document with Different Spanish Flavors

```
<?xml version="1.0" ?>
<document>
 <p xml:lang="es">Spanish text</p>
 <p xml:lang="fr">French text</p>
 <p xml:lang="ES">Spanish text</p>
 <p xml:lang="CA-es">Catalan text</p>
 <p xml:lang="es-ES">Iberian Spanish text</p>
 <p xml:lang="es-mx">Mexican Spanish text</p>
</document>
```

Keep in mind that not all XSL processors support all XSL features yet. The `lang()` function is not supported in all browsers, for example.

Space Handling

Although internationalization is often about separating the presentation information from the content, a few instances exist where the presentation parameters must be known by the tools for a more efficient translation. One of them is the information about how to handle white spaces.

White spaces are defined as spaces, tabs, carriage returns, and line-feeds:

```
WS ::= (#x20 | #x9 | #xD | #xA)+
```

You will notice that other "space"-like characters such as NO-BREAK SPACE (U+00A0), IDEOGRAPHIC SPACE (U+3000), EM SPACE (U+2003), THIN SPACE (U+2009), EN QUAD (U+2000), and so forth are not included in the white space list. They are treated just like regular characters as far as XML processors are concerned.

As for the language, XML defines a special attribute to indicate how white spaces should be handled in a given element set: xml:space.

The attribute can have two values: default or preserve. The first one lets the XML processor behave as its default mechanism is set, whereas the second one indicates that all white spaces must be preserved and passed without transformation.

If you use a DTD to specify your format, xml:space must be declared, just as any other attribute:

```
<!ATTLIST SourceCode
 xml:space (default|preserve) 'preserve' >
```

or

```
<!ATTLIST pre
 xml:space (preserve) #FIXED 'preserve'>
```

Always keep in mind that xml:space is an indicator for the parser, not the rendering engine, although some rendering engines are taking it into consideration (such as Adobe's SVG viewer).

Localization tools should take into account the presence of xml:space when extracting content. It is the best indicator to specify whether the white spaces of a run of text should be left alone. This information should be carried during the translation.

Listing 3.5 shows an XML file where the element <cmdline> contains preformatted text, while the multiple spaces in the <p> element should be reduced to a single blank.

LISTING 3.5

Spaces1.xml—Usage of the xml:space **Attribute**

```
<?xml version="1.0" ?>
<doc>
 <cmdline id="1" xml:space="preserve">Command line:
-x       run the tool with option x
-f[name] specify [name] for font</cmdline>
```

LISTING 3.5 CONTINUED

```
<p id="2">Text where
any  set of white spaces  is reduced to 1.</p>
</doc>
```

XHTML

The XHTML specifications add a few clauses to the handling of white spaces.

In addition to line-breaks, tabulations, and space, the characters FORM FEED (U+000C) and ZERO WIDTH SPACE (U+200B) must also be treated as white spaces.

Leading and trailing white spaces in block elements should be removed unless the xml:space attribute is set to preserve. In other words, the following XHTML fragments are identical to one another.

```
<p> This  is an example  </p>

<p>
This is  an

example
</p>

<p>This is an example</p>
```

CSS

When rendering is involved, you can use the white-space property of CSS to specify how the preformatting should be handled. The values available are normal, pre, nowrap, and inherit.

If you take the document shown in Listing 3.5 and apply to it the style sheet displayed in Listing 3.6, you can see in Figure 3.1 that the rendering of the <cmdline> is done correctly.

LISTING 3.6

Spaces3.css—Style Sheet used to Display Figure 3.1

```
doc {
 display: block;
 margin-top: 10px; margin-left: 10px;
}
```

LISTING 3.6   CONTINUED

```
p {
 display: block;
 margin-bottom: 10px;
}

cmdline {
 display: block;
 margin-bottom: 10px;
 white-space: pre; font-family: "Courier New";
}
```

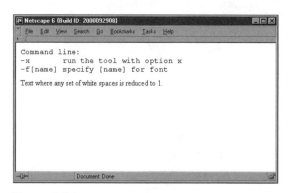

FIGURE 3.1

Rendering of white spaces with the white-space *CSS attribute in Navigator 6.*

Note that the same example would not work with Internet Explorer 5.5, which does not support the white-space property correctly yet (version 5.5.4522.1800, with SP1).

Date and Time Representation

As is true for any software application, XML documents should store date and time information in a locale-independent manner or with enough information about what locale was used to format it.

Time stamps will become more and more important as distributed applications across several time zones will increase the complexity of synchronizing tasks.

One challenge with XML is that documents can be used for a wide range of applications and can serve many different purposes. Ideally, storing date/time information as a number would be the best way to proceed: The correct formatting could be applied at rendering time. However, this is practical only if you process the documents with your own application, such as SOAP.

In many cases, you will have XML documents in which the user will interact directly with the file, without the benefit of a reformatting of the content. In such occurrences, the date/time must be directly readable by the user.

ISO Format

As always, the best way to implement locale-specific information is to use existing standards when possible. ISO offers a wide palette of standardized representations for date, time, duration, and intervals in the ISO 8601:1988 specifications.

Each application can have different requirements and you should pick the format that best fits the type of information you need to represent.

As an example, you can look at the TMX format. This XML standard for translation memory exchange uses several attributes related to date/time information: changedate, creationdate, and lastusagedate. All three of them use the same format:

YYYYMMDDThhmmssZ

For instance, the string 20000811T133402Z represents August 11, 2000 at 1:34 p.m. 2 seconds, in UTC.

Listing 3.8 presents a short TMX document (just one entry: a software string in English and Esperanto) generated by a translation memory utility that demonstrates how the different attributes are used.

LISTING 3.8

Date_Time.tmx—TMX Document with the Three Date/Time Attributes

```
<?xml version="1.0" ?>
<!DOCTYPE tmx SYSTEM "tmx12.dtd">
<tmx xmlns="http://www.lisa.org/tmx" version="1.2">
 <header creationtool="Rainbow"
    creationtoolversion="2.00-1"
    datatype="PlainText"
    segtype="sentence"
    adminlang="en-US"
    srclang="en-US"
    o-tmf="Rainbow"
    creationdate="20000101T163812Z"
    creationid="YvesS"
```

LISTING 3.8   CONTINUED

```
      changedate="20000314T023401Z"
      changeid="Amity"
      o-encoding="iso-8859-3">
  </header>
  <body>
  <tu tuid="0001"
    datatype="Text"
    usagecount="2"
    lastusagedate="20000314T023401Z">
   <tuv lang="EN"
     creationdate="20000212T153400Z">
   <seg>Search for PATTERN in each FILE or standard input.</seg>
   </tuv>
   <tuv lang="EO"
     creationdate="20000309T021145Z"
     changedate="20000314T023401Z">
   <seg>Serĉi pri ŜABLONO en ĉiu DOSIERO aŭ la normala enigo.</seg>
   </tuv>
  </tu>
  </body>
</tmx>
```

When developing a new schema or porting an XML DTD to a schema definition, you
might want to take advantage of the predefined types for date and time. The XML
Schema offers a collection of predefined types for date, time, duration, and intervals.

For example, the three date/time-related attributes we have seen in TMX would be of
the type `timeInstant`, as in the excerpt below:

```
<attribute name='lastusagedate' type='timeInstant' use='optional'/>
<attribute name='creationdate' type='timeInstant' use='optional'/>
<attribute name='changedate' type='timeInstant' use='optional'/>
```

Summary

In this chapter we have seen three types of information often encountered in XML
documents. Make sure you address them when developing your own XML schema or
when writing localization tools.

First, use `xml:lang` to indicate the different locales within your documents.

Second, make sure preformatted blocks of text are clearly indicated to the XML parser, so that tools can carry on that information during translation and avoid unnecessary reformatting. The attribute `xml:space` is a good way to do this.

Third, for any date or time related attribute, use one of the forms of the ISO 8601:1988 standard, or a locale-independent raw numerical value if no human is meant to read the XML document.

References

The following is a list of some online reference documents. Make sure you get the latest information.

ISO 639-2, Language Codes (Library of Congress Network Development & MARC Standards Office): `http://lcweb.loc.gov/standards/iso639-2`

ISO 3166 country codes (ISO 3166 Maintenance Agency): `http://www.din.de/gremien/nas/nabd/iso3166ma/index.html`

IANA Language Tags: `http://www.iana.org/assignments/languages`

RFC1766, Tags for the Identification of Languages: `http://www.ietf.org/rfc/rfc1766.txt`

RFC3066, Tags for the Identification of Languages: `http://www.ietf.org/rfc/rfc3066.txt`

White spaces in XML: `http://www.w3.org/TR/REC-xml#sec-white-space`

White spaces in XHTML: `http://www.w3.org/TR/xhtml1/#uaconf`

XML Schema Part 2: Datatypes: `http://www.w3.org/TR/xmlschema-2`

ISO 9801:1988 Date and Time Formats (International Organization for Standardization): `http://www.iso.ch`

# CHAPTER 4

Coding the Presentation

In This Chapter:

One fundamental aspect of XML is to separate the structure of a document from its presentation. Granted, this is not always put into practice: XHTML is a good example of an XML application where many formatting properties are embedded into the elements and attributes. But overall, as tools support and authors understand XML principles better, this separation will become more and more visible.

Separating the structure from the presentation is especially crucial in XML solutions designed to store documents that will be converted into various display formats.

The organization and the structure of the documents are clearly implemented through the tags themselves. The rendering and layout are achieved through the use of style sheets, or by converting the XML data to different output formats that can be displayed later on.

This chapter and the next one will discuss the language-related issues of three main technologies closely related (by chronological order): DSSSL, CSS, and XSL. This chapter addresses the general aspects of the presentation mechanisms such as character representation, fonts, translatable text, and so forth. Chapter 5, "Special Aspects of Rendering," will take on more specific topics such as writing directions, sorting, and ruby text. The more customized methods to generate output from XML are discussed in Chapter 6, "XML Conversion."

The first option, DSSSL (pronounced "*deesel*") is the *Document Style Semantics and Specifications Language*. It is an ISO standard (ISO/IEC 10179) created for SGML. Because XML is derived from SGML, you can, in many cases, use DSSSL to format XML documents.

The second choice is CSS, the *Cascading Style Sheet* model. It was originally created for HTML files, but you can use it as well with XML documents. It's probably the most used of the three solutions for the time being.

A third option, XSL, the *Extensible Style Sheet Language*, has been developed to provide transformation and formatting capabilities to XML. Only the first part of XSL, the transformation, is fully defined at this time. As the specifications are finalized and implemented, XSL will become an important component of the XML palette of tools for the future.

Document Style Semantics and Specifications Language

DSSSL realizes the rendering of XML documents through conversion to an output format such as HTML, MIF, RTF, or other formats. DSSSL is a forerunner to CSS and XSL. Both mechanisms borrow much from it and have adopted many of its constructs and principles. Because DSSSL is much less used with XML than CSS and XSL, we will only talk briefly about it here.

DSSSL is composed of a *Style Language* and a *Transformation Language*. The Style Language allows you to specify the kind of formatting to be applied to the various parts of the document. The Transformation Language allows you to define how to convert the original document to another SGML application or to a different format.

Several implementations of DSSSL processors exist. The most commonly used is probably OpenJade, a public domain program based on James Clark's Jade application. It is maintained by the OpenJade team and available at `http://www.netfolder.com/DSSSL`.

Encoding and Character Representation

Because DSSSL files are also SGML documents, they can use the same encoding declaration and character representation as any other SGML documents.

Note that if you are using OpenJade, it ignores the `SP_CHARSET_FIXED` and `SP_SYSTEM_CHARSET` environment variables. It utilizes only the `SP_ENCODING` variable, which you can also specify using the `-b` parameter.

Localizable Properties

DSSSL files can include translatable text. For example the `(literal )` function enables you to generate text from the style sheet. You need to make sure instruction blocks using it are identified and can be selected on a per-language basis.

Listing 4.1 shows an excerpt of a DSSSL style sheet where the <name> and <partnum> elements of the XML input document will be preceded with corresponding labels.

`Sample.dsl`—The `(literal )` Function Used in DSSSL

```
<!doctype style-sheet PUBLIC "-//Netfolder//DTD DSSSL library//EN" >
(root
    (make scroll
        (process-children)
    )
)
(element inventory
    (make paragraph
        start-indent: 30pt
        font-family-name: "Times New Roman"
        font-size: 12pt
        font-weight: 'medium
        space-after: 10pt
        (process-matching-children "item")
        (process-matching-children "name")
        (process-matching-children "partnum")
    )
)
(element item
    (make paragraph
        font-family-name: "Courier New"
        font-size: 12pt
    )
)
(element name
    (make paragraph
        (literal "Nom de l'article : ")
        (process-children)
    )
)
(element partnum
    (make paragraph
        (literal "Num&eacute;ro d'inventaire : ")
        (process-children)
    )
)
```

Overall, DSSSL is a very powerful way to render XML source into multiple types of output. On the down side, its notation, similar to LISP's, and its complexity can deter a few from using it with XML.

Cascading Style Sheets

The Cascading Style Sheet mechanism (CSS) has been in place for some time. The first drafts were done as early as 1994. The first edition of the CSS1 specifications was released on December 17, 1996. The second level, CSS2, became a W3C recommendation on May 12, 1998. The third level, CSS3, is currently at the Working Draft stage. As its history shows, CSS was originally targeted for HTML, but its scope has been adjusted since to encompass XML as well.

In XML, as a general rule, you use a style sheet defined in a separate file and link it to the document with the traditional `xml-stylesheet` processing instruction:

```
<?xml version="1.0" ?>
<?xml-stylesheet type="text/css" href="filename.css" ?>
...etc...
```

It can also be a good idea to split your style sheets in two parts: one file with the general formatting rules and another with the locale-specific rules.

You call the locale-specific file from the XML document and can change it when the document is localized. The locale-specific CSS file can embed the generic style sheet, common to all languages, using an `@import` rule. Figure 4.1 shows how such a setup would work with two XML documents in, for example, both English and Russian.

In the English and Russian documents, the style sheet links would be declared respectively:

```
<?xml-stylesheet type="text/css" href="en-Specific.css" ?>
```

and

```
<?xml-stylesheet type="text/css" href="ru-Specific.css" ?>
```

although both locale-specific style sheets would include the following rule:

```
@import "Common.css";
```

The same mechanism could also be set to work with filenames identical for all locales, but from locale-specific directories.

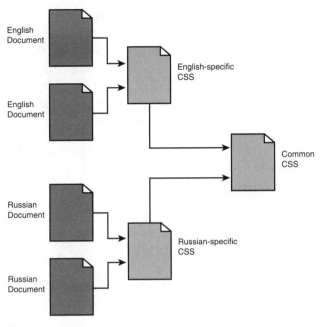

FIGURE 4.1

Relationships between the style sheets and the documents.

Encoding and Character Representation

Because style sheets can include translatable text as well as names of elements, fonts, or other items in any languages, you must be able to have the files in the appropriate encoding.

The CSS2 specifications provide the following rules to determine the encoding of a file (in order of priority):

1. By an HTTP `charset` parameter in a `Content-Type` field.
2. By an `@charset` rule.
3. By the mechanisms of the language of the referencing document. For example, in XHTML, the `charset` attribute of the `<link>` element.

The first option does not apply all the time because XML and CSS are not always used through HTTP protocol. The third option can prove difficult to maintain if you have to deal with a large set of documents.

To ensure the CSS parsers recognize encodings correctly, make sure to use the
`@charset` statement at the top of the CSS files. As shown in Listing 4.2, it should be
placed before any other character. The parameter values are the same as for the XML
encoding declaration (see Appendix B, "Encoding Declarations," for a detailed list).
However, because there is no standard requirement as which encodings must be
supported by the CSS processors, you want to make sure to pick an encoding after
trying it with the various engines with which your documents will be processed.

LISTING 4.2

`Charset.css`—Using the `@charset` Statement in a CSS File

```
@charset "iso-8859-1";
@import "Common.css";

device:before {
 content: "Périphérique : ";
 font-weight: bold
}
params:before {
 content: "Paramètres : ";
 font-weight: bold
}
```

Characters that are not in the character set of the file can be coded in hexadecimal
notation with a leading backslash (\HH notation). For example: \A is line-feed, \C6 is
'Æ', \985 is 'অ' and so forth. Listing 4.3 demonstrates how to use the notation.

LISTING 4.3

`HexaNotation.css`—Using Hexadecimal Notations in a CSS File

```
/* All extended characters are in hexadecimal notation: no need
   to specify an encoding. */
@import "Common.css";

device:before {
 content: "P\E9 riph\E9 rique\A0 :\A0";
 font-weight: bold
}
params:before {
 content: "Param\E8 tres\A0 :\A0";
 font-weight: bold
}
```

If a digit or a letter immediately follows the hexadecimal escaped character, you need to make sure the processor knows where to separate them. For instance, in the string R&D if you need to escape the & the resulting string R\26D would be confusing: Is the escaped character U+026D ('ɭ') or U+0026 ('&')?

To work around this problem, you need to either add a trailing space after the escaped character (for example, R&\26 D), or to pad the hexadecimal value to 6 digits (for example, R\000026D). Both notations will be interpreted as R&D.

Note that any space character just after the hexadecimal character will be treated as a separator: R\000026D and R\000026 D will be both interpreted as R&D.

Note also that two consecutive characters in hexadecimal notation do not need a space separator: \26\26 is the same as \26 \26.

Fonts

The proper selection of fonts is an important aspect of correctly rendering XML documents that can include a large number of UCS characters. CSS dedicates two main mechanisms to deal with fonts: font specification and font selection (including a font matching algorithm).

Font Specification

Seven properties describe a font. All matching mechanisms are based on this information.

The font-family property specifies a prioritized list of font families that should be used to display the text. For example, the following lines specify to use Arial first, then, if the characters to display are not available in Arial, use NunacomU, and if that font is not available or does not support the relevant characters, fall back to any serif font available.

```
para {
  font-family: Arial, NunacomU, serif;
}
```

If you need to specify a font name that includes characters not supported by the encoding the CSS file uses (declared with the @charset rule), you can use the \HH notation already mentioned.

The other properties (font-style, font-variant, font-weight, font-stretch, font-size, and font-size-adjust) may also need to be adapted for the translated files.

The font-size-adjust parameter is especially useful to make sure text that uses fonts other than the first choice font keeps a proportionate size. Each font has an x-height value: the higher the value, the more legible the text is at smaller sizes. Therefore, when you fall back to a font that has a smaller x-height value than the first choice font, using the same font-size results in less legible text. The font-size-adjust property provides a way to correct the size actually used.

For example: Let's say the first choice font is Verdana, which has an aspect value of 0.58, and the fall-back font is Times New Roman, which has an aspect value of 0.46. If your original font-size is 12px, the corrected font size when using Times New Roman would be 12 * (0.58 / 0.46) = 15.13px. Aspect values on bicameral fonts are based on the size of the lowercase characters.

Font Selection

The @font-face descriptions provide a way to extend the font database of the user agent. When localizing, you must make sure to verify if any @font-face rule appears in the style sheet and change or adapt it to the localized documents.

In an @font-face definition block, the unicode-range descriptor is useful to indicate to the user agent what range of characters the font supports. This prevents the user agent from checking or downloading a font that does not include the glyphs for the characters in the document.

The value used a wild-character based syntax. The Table 4.1 shows a few examples.

TABLE 4.1

Examples of Values for the unicode-range Property

Value	Description
U+A9	One character: the Copyright sign
U+900-97F	From U+0900 to U+097F: the Devanagari script
U+104?	From U+1040 to U+104F: the digits for the Myanmar script
U+00??	From U+0000 to U+00FF: the Latin-1 range

Listing 4.4 shows an example of an @font-face rule in a style sheet: The root element <doc> uses a font called GF Zemen Unicode. The font characteristics are declared at the top of the file. Here those characteristics are limited to the URL and the range of characters the font supports.

LISTING 4.4

FontFace.css—Example of Font Declaration

```
@font-face {
  font-family: "GF Zemen Unicode";
```

LISTING 4.4   CONTINUED

```
src: url("ftp://ftp.ethiopic.org/pub/fonts/TrueType/gfzemenu.ttf");
unicode-range: U+00?? U+1200-137F; /* Latin-1 and Ethiopic */
}
doc {
 font-family: "GF Zemen Unicode";
}
/* etc... */
```

Some applications can have various implementation problems when selecting fonts. You always want to test the rendering with the various localized texts.

For example, in Internet Explorer 5.5, raster fonts will not always select the specified font for extended characters, even if that font is available and supports the characters to display. A text that looks just fine in English when translated can produce characters of different physical size for the same `point-size`. Listing 4.5 shows an example of an XML document with the two types of fonts used on two identical texts.

LISTING 4.5

Fonts.xml—A Simple Set of Characters

```
<?xml version="1.0" encoding="iso-8859-1" ?>
<?xml-stylesheet type="text/css" href="Fonts.css"?>
<doc>
 <para>aaaaa</para>
 <para>aáaâa</para>
 <para class="tt">aaaaa</para>
 <para class="tt">aáaâa</para>
</doc>
```

The style sheet used is shown in Listing 4.6. It is a simple style sheet: The default class uses `Courier`, whereas the "tt" class uses `Courier New`. The first font is a raster font, whereas the second is true-type.

LISTING 4.6

Fonts.css—Style Sheet with Two Different Fonts to Display Identical Paragraphs

```
doc {
 display: block;
 margin-top: 15px; margin-left: 10px;
```

LISTING 4.6   CONTINUED

```
}
para {
 display: block;
 margin-bottom: 10px;
 font-size: 1.5em;
 font-family: Courier;
}
para.tt {
 display: block;
 margin-bottom: 10px;
 font-size: 1.5em;
 font-family: "Courier New";
}
```

Figure 4.2 displays the corresponding rendering with Internet Explorer 5.5. As you can see, the accented characters of the text using the raster font have mismatched character height, while the text associated to the true-type font displays correctly.

It seems that the browser behaves differently depending on the unit used for the font-size property: The same style sheet with 12pt instead of 1.5em will result in a perfectly correct display of the extended characters. Another possible solution is to add a font-size-adjust property to correct the problem. Another solution is to use Courier New directly.

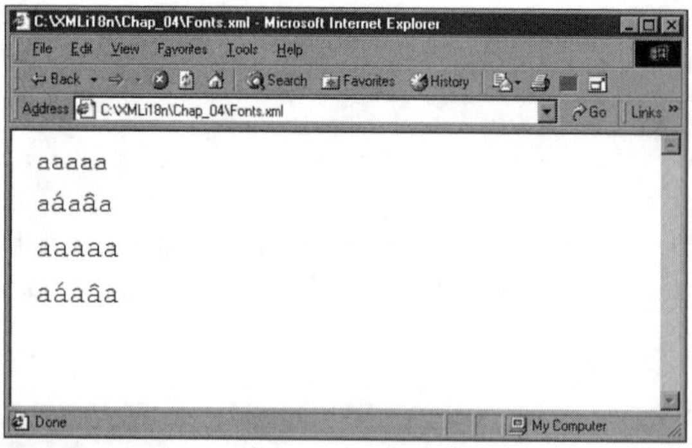

FIGURE 4.2
Extended characters with different height.

Figure 4.3 displays the same file with the same style sheet in Navigator 6. Here all characters are sized proportionally. Here it seems that the application uses Courier New for all characters, even when Courier is specified.

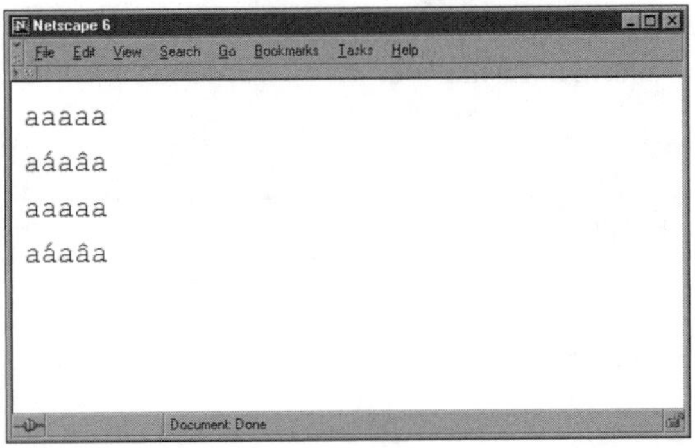

FIGURE 4.3

Extended characters with the same height.

The behaviors illustrated here are related to Internet Explorer and Navigator implementations, but it underlines an important point. Do not assume that, once translated and including non-ASCII characters, the text will behave the same way as before localization. This is especially true in the manipulation of font-related parameters.

To avoid unpleasant surprises, you probably want to try your style sheets with a few paragraphs with pseudo-translated text.

Locale-Specific Properties

In addition to font selection and description, the CSS files have various properties that may need to be translated or modified.

The content Property

The value of the content property is a string that is displayed during rendering. It is used to generate automated text. For instance, Listing 4.7 shows a document with a <note> element that should be displayed after a label reading Warning!. The label is not included in the document.

LISTING 4.7

Note.xml—A <note> Element to Render with Generated Text

```
<?xml version="1.0" ?>
<?xml-stylesheet type="text/css" href="Note.css"?>
<doc>
 <p>This is a simple paragraph of text.</p>
 <note>This is the text of a very important note.</note>
</doc>
```

The text `Warning!` (followed by two non-breaking spaces) is generated from the style sheet, using the `content` property, as shown in Listing 4.8.

LISTING 4.8

`Note.css`—Use of the `content` Property

```
doc {
 display: block;
 margin-top: 15px; margin-left: 10px;
}
p {
 display: block;
 margin-bottom: 20px;
}
note:before {
 content: "Warning!\a0\a0";
 font-weight: bold;
}
note {
 border: solid red;
 padding: 5px 5px 5px 5px;
 margin-bottom: 20px;
}
```

Figure 4.4 displays the resulting output in Netscape 6.

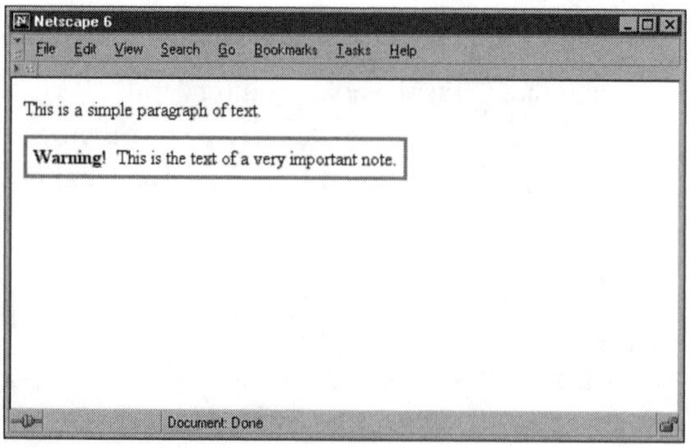

FIGURE 4.4

Generated text with the content *property.*

With any text that is the result of a run-time composition, you must be very careful with the way pieces of text are concatenated: Do not break up phrases and beware of potential grammatical issues. Many languages accord the adjectives depending on the gender of the subject: Separating those two components is, to say the least, risky when it comes to translation.

The `quotes` Property

Another type of automated text that may need to be adapted for each language is the quotation mark. The `quotes` property enables you to define which character or string will be used to open and close quotes at different embedded levels.

In case the quote is in a language different from its surrounding text, it is usually customary to use the quote style of the surrounding text, not the one of the quote itself.

The definition is done in two parts: First specifying the different characters to use with the `quotes` property and then specifying that quotes need to be generated before and after the relevant element (here <qo>), using the `content` property. For this last part, CSS offers the `open-quote` and `close-quote` keywords to refer to whatever has been defined in the `quotes` properties. Listing 4.9 shows an example of this.

LISTING 4.9

`Quotes.css`—Definition of Quotation Marks

```
body {
 display: block;
 margin: 15px 15px 15px 15px;
}
p {
 display: block;
 margin-bottom: 10px;
}
qo {
 display: inline;
}
 qo:before { content: open-quote; }
 qo:after { content: close-quote; }

/* Locale-specific marks: */

[lang|='en'] > * { /* English */
 quotes: "\201C" "\201D";
}
[lang|='fr'] > * { /* French (guillemets) */
 quotes: "\AB\A0" "\A0\BB";
}
[lang|='fi'] > * { /* Finnish (same direction) */
```

LISTING 4.9 **CONTINUED**

```
quotes: "\201D" "\201D";
}
[lang|='de'] > * { /* German */
 quotes: "\201E" "\201C";
}
[lang|='ja'] > * { /* Japanese */
 quotes: "\300C" "\300D";
}
[lang|='nl'] > * { /* Dutch */
 quotes: "\2018" "\2019";
}
[lang|='pl'] > * { /* Polish */
 quotes: "\201E" "\201D";
}
```

For each language, a rule using the "child of" connector sets the values for the `quotes` property. This is to ensure that the style of the quote follows the rules for the language of the parent element in which `<qo>` is embedded.

> **NOTE:** The version of Netscape 6 used when creating these examples did not recognize the `xml:lang` attribute to identify languages, and the `:lang` pseudo-class did not work either. To work around the problem we are using here a simple `lang` attribute and the `[lang|='<value>']` selector.

Listing 4.10 is an example of an XML document where the `<qo>` element is used with various language settings. It also includes a quote within a quote for two different languages.

LISTING 4.10

`Quotes.xml`—Example of a Document with Quotation Marks in Different Language Contexts

```
<?xml version="1.0" encoding="iso-8859-1" ?>
<?xml-stylesheet type="text/css" href="Quotes.css"?>
<doc>
 <body>
  <p lang="en">English text with <qo>English quoted text</qo>.</p>
  <p lang="fr">Text en Français avec <qo>English quoted text</qo>.</p>
```

LISTING 4.10 CONTINUED

```
 <p lang="fr">Text en Français avec <qo lang="en">
➥English quoted text containing a <qo>quote</qo> itself</qo>.</p>
 <p lang="fi"><qo>Quotes</qo> in Finnish.</p>
 <p lang="pl"><qo>Quotes</qo> in Polish.</p>
 <p lang="ja"><qo>Quotes</qo> in Japanese.</p>
 <p lang="de"><qo>Quotes</qo> in German.</p>
 <p lang="nl"><qo>Quotes</qo> in Dutch.</p>
</body>
</doc>
```

Figure 4.5 displays the result in Netscape 6, after the style sheet has been applied.

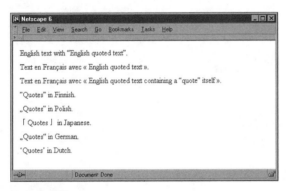

FIGURE 4.5

Use of the quote *property.*

Numbering

Among the different types of generated text CSS offers, lists and counters provide a powerful method to create collections of numbered items. The manner to enumerate items can vary from one language to the other: different numbering systems, various digit sets or alphabets, and so forth.

Listing 4.11 shows a style sheet with the definitions for a <numlist> element that contains one or more <item> elements. Each <item> element is numbered depending on a given style set with the list-style-type property.

LISTING 4.11

`Lists.css`—Style Sheet for Numbered Lists

```css
body {
 display: block;
 margin: 15px 15px 15px 15px;
}
b {
 font-weight: bold;
}
numlist {
 display: block;
 margin-left: 45px;
 margin-bottom: 5px;
 list-style-type: decimal;
 counter-reset: item;
}
numlist item {
 display: list-item;
}
numlist  {
   content: counter(item);
   counter-increment: item;
}

numlist[class='type1'] {
 list-style-type: upper-roman;
}
numlist[class='type2'] {
 list-style-type: hiragana;
}
numlist[class='type3'] {
 list-style-type: hiragana-iroha;
}
numlist[class='type4'] {
 list-style-type: lower-greek;
}
```

In our example, which goes with the XML document shown in Listing 4.12, we use a `class` attribute to select which type of sequence should be used. In real situations you would set the numbering style depending on the locale of the text.

LISTING 4.12

`Lists.xml`—Example of Lists in XML

```xml
<?xml version="1.0" encoding="iso-8859-1" ?>
<?xml-stylesheet type="text/css" href="Lists.css"?>
<doc>
 <body>
  <numlist><b>Decimal</b>
   <item>First item.</item>
   <item>Second item.</item>
   <item>Third item.</item>
  </numlist>
  <numlist class="type1"><b>Roman Uppercase</b>
   <item>First item.</item>
   <item>Second item.</item>
   <item>Third item.</item>
  </numlist>
  <numlist class="type2"><b>Hiragana</b>
   <item>First item.</item>
   <item>Second item.</item>
   <item>Third item.</item>
  </numlist>
  <numlist class="type3"><b>Hiragana "iroha"</b>
   <item>First item.</item>
   <item>Second item.</item>
   <item>Third item.</item>
  </numlist>
  <numlist class="type4"><b>Greek</b>
   <item>First item.</item>
   <item>Second item.</item>
   <item>Third item.</item>
  </numlist>
 </body>
</doc>
```

Figure 4.6 displays the rendering of the XML document.

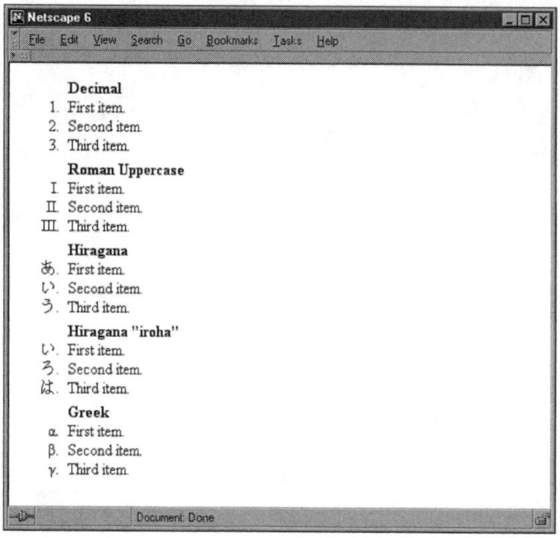

FIGURE 4.6

Use of the list-style-type *property.*

Table 4.2 shows the values possible for the list-style-type property as far as numbering is concerned. The same values can be used with the counter() function when you are utilizing the counter-increment property.

TABLE 4.2

Possible Values for the list-style-type Property for Numbers

Value	Description	First Ten Increments
decimal	Decimal ASCII	1, 2, 3, 4, 5, 6, 7, 8, 9, 10...
decimal-leading-zero	Decimal with leading zero	01, 02, 03, 04, 05, 06, 07, 08, 09, 10...
lower-roman	Roman lowercase	i, ii, iii, iv, v, vi, vii, viii, ix, x...
upper-roman	Roman uppercase	I, II, III, IV, V, VI, VII, VIII, IX, X...
lower-greek	Greek alphabet	α, β, γ, δ, ε, ζ, η, θ, ι, κ...
lower-alpha	Latin alphabet lowercase	a, b, c, d, e, f, g, h, i, j...
lower-latin	Latin alphabet lowercase	a, b, c, d, e, f, g, h, i, j...
upper-alpha	Latin alphabet uppercase	A, B, C, D, E, F, G, H, I, J...
upper-latin	Latin alphabet uppercase	A, B, C, D, E, F, G, H, I, J...

TABLE 4.2	CONTINUED	
Value	*Description*	*First Ten Increments*
hebrew	Traditional Hebrew numbering	'א, 'ב, 'ג, 'ד, 'ה, 'ו, 'ז, 'ח, 'ט, 'י...
armenian	Armenian alphabet	Ա, Բ, Գ, Դ, Ե, Զ, Է, Ը, Թ, Ժ...
georgian	Georgian old uppercase alphabet	Ⴀ, Ⴁ, Ⴂ, Ⴃ, Ⴄ, Ⴅ, Ⴆ, Ⴇ, Ⴈ, Ⴉ
cjk-ideographic	Ideographic numbers	一, 二, 三, 四, 五, 六, 七, 八, 九, 十...
hiragana	Hiragana	あ, い, う, え, お, か, き, く, け, こ...
hiragana-iroha	Hiragana, "iroha" order	い, ろ, は, に, ほ, へ, と, ち, り, ぬ...
katakana	Katakana	ア, イ, ウ, エ, オ, カ, キ, ク, ケ, コ...
katakana-iroha	Katakana, "iroha" order	イ, ロ, ハ, ニ, ホ, ヘ, ト, チ, リ, ヌ...

If you need to generate other types of numbering, for instance using Thai digits, CSS does not have any mechanism to do this. You could then move to XSL, which provides such an option.

The text-transform Property

The last locale-dependent property is text-transform. It provides the capability to modify the original text of the XML document into its corresponding capitalized, uppercased, or lowercased variation. The locale used to execute the transformation is one of the elements to which the property is applied.

Listing 4.13 presents a simple style sheet where three classes for <para> are defined to activate the different values of the text-transform property.

LISTING 4.13

TextTransform.css—Applying the text-transform Property

```
doc {
 margin: 15px 15px 15px 15px;
}
para {
 display: block;
 margin-bottom: 10px;
}
para[class="cap"] {
```

LISTING 4.13 CONTINUED

```
text-transform: capitalize;
}
para[class="upper"] {
 text-transform: uppercase;
}
para[class="lower"] {
 text-transform: lowercase;
}
```

Listing 4.14 shows the different runs of text to modify. Note some interesting characters: The 'ß' is German should be converted into 'SS'. The Turkish 'ı' and 'i' should become 'I' and 'İ', and conversely when lowercased. The letters ' d ', ' e ', and ' f ' are fullwidth forms of the ASCII characters and should be converted into the equivalent fullwidth uppercases.

LISTING 4.14

`TextTransform.xml`—Original Text Before the `text-transform` Property Is Applied

```
<?xml version="1.0" ?>
<?xml-stylesheet type="text/css" href="TextTransform.css"?>
<doc>
 <para class="lower">Text that has been lowercased.</para>
 <para class="upper">Text that has been uppercased.</para>
 <para class="cap">Text that has been capitalized.</para>
 <para class="upper" xml:lang="de">Uppercased German: ß, ü, ä.</para>
 <para class="upper" xml:lang="tr">Uppercased Turkish: ı and i</para>
 <para class="lower" xml:lang="tr">Lowercased Turkish: I and İ</para>
 <para class="upper">Various uppercasings: ě, ẵ, ặ, ẫ, ợ, dz, Dz, ʌ, ю, њ, d,
↪ e, f.</para>
</doc>
```

Figure 4.7 displays the results with Netscape 6. It illustrates some of the possible problems linked to internationalization issues and `text-transform`. There are two errors: the 'i' and 'I' in Turkish have not been converted to 'İ' and 'ı'. This is most likely because, as we have seen already, the rendering engine does not properly identify the language. The `text-transform` property offers an attractive way to implement some rendering issues, for example having the title capitalized in some output while displayed as a simple sentence in others. However, these casing changes are completely dependent on the locales (especially capitalization rules) and implementations rarely provide an accurate transformation for all languages. You should use this property only with great care. In the current draft version of XSL this property is actually deprecated.

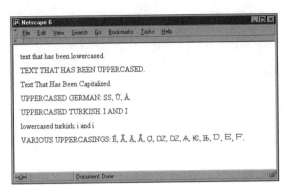

FIGURE 4.7

Rendering of the text modified with `text-transform.`

Extensible Style Sheet Language

The Extensible Style Sheet Language has been created for XML with the experience drawn from DSSSL and CSS. Like DSSSL, XSL is composed of two parts: a transformation mechanism called *XSL Transformation (XSLT)*, and a formatting language responsible to apply display and layout properties to the objects created using XSLT. The formatting part of XSL is referred to as *XSL Formatting Objects (XSL-FO)*.

As of now, not all parts of XSL are final recommendations. XSLT is, as well as XPath, the powerful common language to describe matches in XML documents used in XSL. XSL-FO, on the other hand, is still at the drafting stage.

Encoding and Character Representation

XSL files are XML documents, and use the standard XML methods to declare encoding and represent characters as does any other XML document. Refer to Chapter 2, "Character Representation," for detailed information.

Transformation (XSLT)

In addition to being rendered by various user agents such as browsers, XML documents are also very often utilized as a storage structure from where various parts are taken to a different format. A very powerful way to carry out this operation is the XSL Transformation mechanism.

Based on XSL style sheets, XSLT templates allow you to create various types of outputs. For example, Listing 4.15 shows an XML document. We can use XSLT templates to create various HTML representations of it.

LISTING 4.15

`Discours.xml`—Original XML Document with the Data to Transform

```
<?xml version="1.0" encoding="iso-8859-1" ?>
<?xml-stylesheet type="text/xsl" href="Excerpts.xsl"?>
<document xml:lang="fr">
 <info>
  <title>Discours de la méthode</title>
  <author>René Descartes</author>
  <intro xml:lang="en">The four main rules to solve a problem or thing
➥using logic. Excerpt from "Discours de la méthode" Édition Victor
➥Cousin Paris, 1824.</intro>
 </info>
 <list>
  <item>
   <para>Le premier étoit de <emph>ne recevoir jamais aucune chose pour
➥vraie que je ne la connusse évidemment être telle</emph>; c'est-à-dire,
➥d'éviter soigneusement la précipitation et la prévention, et de ne
➥comprendre rien de plus en mes jugements que ce qui se présenteroit si
➥clairement et si distinctement à mon esprit, que je n'eusse aucune
➥occasion de le mettre en doute.</para>
  </item>
  <item>
   <para>Le second, de <emph>diviser chacune des difficultés que
➥j'examinerois, en autant de parcelles qu'il se pourroit</emph>, et
➥qu'il seroit requis pour les mieux résoudre.</para>
  </item>
  <item>
   <para>Le troisième, de <emph>conduire par ordre mes pensées</emph>,
➥en commençant par les objets les plus simples et les plus aisés à
➥connoître, pour monter peu à peu comme par degrés jusques à la
➥connoissance des plus composés, et supposant même de l'ordre entre ceux
➥qui ne se précèdent point naturellement les uns les autres.</para>
  </item>
  <item>
   <para>Et le dernier, de faire partout des dénombrements si entiers et
➥des revues si générales, que je fusse assuré de <emph>ne rien
➥omettre</emph>.</para>
```

LISTING 4.15 **CONTINUED**

```
  </item>
 </list>
</document>
```

The XSL template itself (see Listing 4.16) is an XML document with mixed data: XSL elements to specify what elements to get from the original document and markup of the target format where the data should be inserted. The output file is created inside the first `<xsl:template>` block, and then the `<xsl:apply-templates/>` triggers the templates matching the various elements inside the `<document>` element recursively. The last template matches the text content of any element (`match="text()"` attribute) and displays it.

LISTING 4.16

`Excerpts.xsl`—XSLT Template

```
<?xml version="1.0" ?>
<xsl:stylesheet xmlns:xsl="http://www.w3.org/TR/WD-xsl">

 <xsl:template match="/">
  <HTML>
   <BODY>
    <xsl:for-each select="document">
     <xsl:apply-templates/>
    </xsl:for-each>
   </BODY>
  </HTML>
 </xsl:template>

 <xsl:template match="info">
  <TABLE BORDER="1" WIDTH="100%" CELLPADDING="5"
   CELLSPACING="0" BGCOLOR="navajowhite">
   <xsl:apply-templates/>
  </TABLE>
 </xsl:template>

 <xsl:template match="title">
  <TR><TD ALIGN="top">Title:</TD>
  <TD><B><xsl:apply-templates/></B></TD></TR>
 </xsl:template>
```

LISTING 4.16   CONTINUED

```
<xsl:template match="author">
 <TR><TD ALIGN="top">Author:</TD>
 <TD><B><xsl:apply-templates/></B></TD></TR>
</xsl:template>

<xsl:template match="intro">
 <TR><TD VALIGN="top">Introduction:</TD><TD><I><xsl:apply-templates/>
➥</I></TD></TR>
</xsl:template>

<xsl:template match="list">
 <UL><xsl:apply-templates/></UL>
</xsl:template>

<xsl:template match="item">
 <LI><xsl:apply-templates/></LI>
</xsl:template>

<xsl:template match="para">
 <P><xsl:apply-templates/></P>
</xsl:template>

<xsl:template
match="emph"><B><xsl:apply-templates/></B></xsl:template>

<xsl:template match="text()"><xsl:value-of/></xsl:template>

</xsl:stylesheet>
```

Figure 4.8 displays the resulting HTML output. You could easily modify the XSLT template to change the rendering or what elements are shown.

As with CSS, you can have sections of the template that should be localized as well. In Figure 4.8 these are the three table labels: Title:, Author:, and Introduction:. If the amount of text is large, you may want to have locale-specific templates. But if only a few labels need translation, you may be able to use one of the automatic reference mechanisms we will discuss later in Chapter 9, "Automated References." Here, using external entities would be efficient.

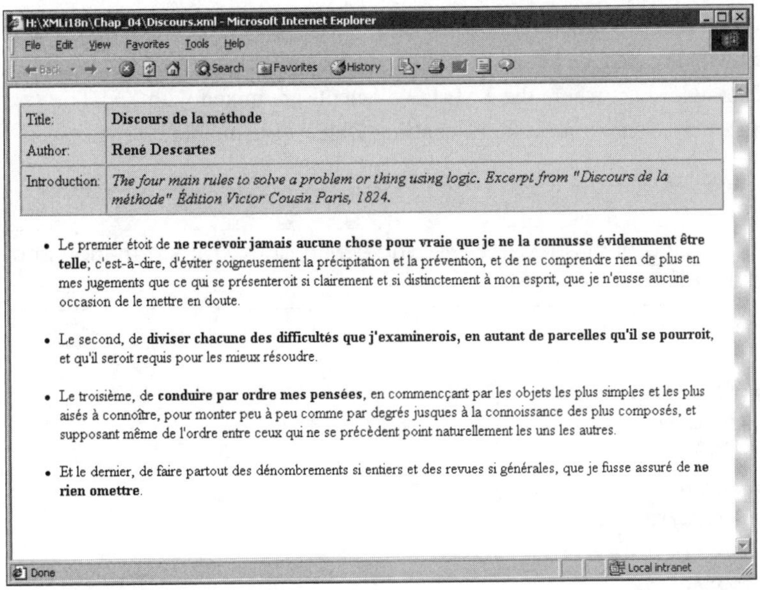

FIGURE 4.8

Rendering the initial XML document through the XSL template.

If you need to include language-specific template blocks, the XPath function `lang()` provides a way to match against the `xml:lang` attribute, as we have seen in Chapter 3, "Miscellaneous Tagging."

For example, you could easily generate different types of formatting for the `<emph>` element, depending on the language of the text. Italic, for instance, does not always make sense when it comes to onscreen display of Asian scripts such as Japanese or Traditional Chinese. In those two cases the use of accent marks above each emphasized character could be a better choice. The international layout specification for both CSS3 and XSL style sheets provides a means to do this through the `font-emphasize-style` property. In Simplified Chinese the same marks would be used below the characters and the `font-emphasize-position` offers a way to specify it.

Formatting Object (XSL-FO)

The Formatting Objects mechanism of XSL is still being defined. However, you can already see that it borrows many of its concepts from CSS and DSSSL. Most of its properties are defined as being the same as for CSS, or slightly modified.

The main difference is in the structure: how the information specifying the formatting is directly mixed with the XSLT elements, using namespaces. Listing 4.17 shows an excerpt of an XSL style sheet where the XSL-FO elements are mixed with XSLT elements to generate a given output. The Formatting Objects are in bold.

LISTING 4.17

`FObjects.xsl`—Excerpt of an XSL Style Sheet with Both Transformation and Formatting Object Elements

```
<xsl:template name="mainfooter">
 <fo:block
  font-family="Helvetica"
  font-weight="normal"
  font-size="10pt"
  padding-top="22mm"
  padding-left="10mm">
  <xsl:text>Page </xsl:text>
  <fo:page-number/>
  <xsl:text> / </xsl:text>
  <xsl:value-of select="title"/>
 </fo:block>
</xsl:template>
```

The current draft of XSL-FO already defines a wide range of internationalization features. They will allow you to control the layout of your text at an extremely detailed level. Describing these properties and how they work calls for a specific book on the subject, far more than we can include here. We will only point out a few properties, not in CSS2, or with different behaviors.

One new feature is the capability to specify properties related to hyphenations, line breaking, justifications, and so forth.

The `country` and `language` properties specify which locale-specific rules to apply to a `fo:block` or `fo:character` object. The `script` property goes one level deeper to allow indicating what script is used, for example, to make a difference among Hiragana, Katakana, or Kanji in Japanese.

The values for the script property are the four letter codes defined by ISO 15924 (currently a draft). Table 4.3 shows some of these codes. Each code has also a corresponding numeric identifier in a given range, for example: 100–199 are for right-to-left alphabetic scripts, 200–299 for left-to-right alphabetic scripts, 300–399 for Brahmi-derived scripts, 400–499 for syllabic scripts, 500–599 for ideographic scripts, and so forth.

TABLE 4.3

Some of the Script Codes of ISO 15924

Code	ID	Description
Arab	160	Arabic
Bopo	285	Bopomofo
Cans	440	Canadian aboriginal syllabics
Cyrl	220	Cyrillic
Deva	315	Devanagari
Hang	286	Hangul
Hani	500	Han ideographs
Hebr	125	Hebrew
Hira	410	Hiragana
Kana	411	Katakana
Latg	215	Latin, Gaelic variant
Latn	216	Latin
Taml	346	Tamil
Thaa	170	Thanaa
Thai	352	Thai
Tibt	330	Tibetan

Hyphenation is controlled by several properties: The `hyphenate` property specifies whether the object can be hyphenated if necessary. The `hyphenation-character` property defines which UCS character to use to mark the hyphenation. The minimum number of characters in a word after the hyphenation can be defined by `hyphenation-push-character-count`, and the minimum number of characters before is specified by `hyphenation-remain-character-count`.

In many aspects, future XSL-FO and CSS updates will make both styling mechanisms much richer in internationally related features than most desktop publishing packages. For example, provisions are available for *kumimoji* characters, for *warichu* lines, for *ruby* text, and so forth. However, keep in mind that the tools usually lack behind as far as implementation is concerned. Always check that the rendering engines you are using fulfill the subset of properties that you are utilizing for the different locales that you are targeting.

Summary

In this chapter we have looked at the basic mechanisms of three of the main methods to present XML documents: DSSSL, CSS, and XSL. All these methods have much in common and often use identical constructs. They all support UCS characters. They all provide font selection as well as automatically generated text. DSSSL is not often used with XML, but it has had a deep impact by inspiring most of CSS and XSL. Although these two powerful languages already allow for plenty of flexibility in rendering XML documents, the upcoming internationalization additions will boost their capabilities even more.

References

Most of the information in this chapter refers to the work done by the W3C, ISO, and the OpenJade team. These documents are online as shown in the following list. The documents identified as drafts are still works in progress at the time of this book's publication. Make sure you get the latest information.

DSSSL (The XML Cover Pages): `http://www.oasis-open.org/cover/dsssl.html`

DSSSL specification: `ftp://ftp.ornl.gov/pub/sgml/WG8/DSSSL`

DSSSL-O specifications: `http://www.ibiblio.org/pub/sun-info/standards/dsssl/dssslo/do960816.htm`

OpenJade DSSSL processor: `http://www.netfolder.com/DSSSL`

CSS1 Specifications: `http://www.w3.org/TR/REC-CSS1`

CSS2 Specifications: `http://www.w3.org/TR/REC-CSS2`

(draft) CSS3 Specifications: `http://www.w3.org/TR/css3-text`

(draft) XSL Specifications: `http://www.w3.org/TR/xsl`

XSLT Specifications: `http://www.w3.org/TR/xslt`

XPath Specifications: `http://www.w3.org/TR/xpath`

CHAPTER 5

Special Aspects of Rendering

In This Chapter:

- Writing Directions   101
- Text Layout   106
- Context Shaping   109
- Text Wrapping   110
- Sorting   112

This chapter looks at a few specific issues of rendering that pertain more directly to internationalization. Most are related to how the text is organized: writing direction, character layout, contextual shaping, and text wrapping. In addition, the chapter looks at the problems of ordering XML elements.

Writing Directions

Modern world languages use three main types of writing systems. These are (in no specific order)

- **Horizontal from left to right**—The lines running from top to bottom
- **Horizontal from right to left**—The lines running from top to bottom
- **Vertical from top to bottom**—The columns running from right to left

A few additional variations are also used, but they are only relevant for a very small set of more rare scripts. For example, *Boustrophedon* runs alternatively from left to right then right to left every other line (literally "like turning with an ox when plowing"). Thankfully for the software developers, this system is only used in extinct languages.

There is no need to talk about the first system (horizontal, left to right) because it is the most commonly used across languages, and computer programs have no problem dealing with it. Displaying text according the two other methods, however, requires special rendering engines. Text written right to left is used in scripts such as Hebrew, Arabic, Syriac, and Thaana, whereas Chinese, Japanese, and Korean utilize vertical writing, as well as horizontal.

Bi-Directional Text

The scripts that are written right to left are called *bi-directional* scripts. The reason is that the sentences are often interspersed with runs of left-to-right text—for example, foreign words, quotations, symbols, and numbers.

The rules to render bi-directional text are outlined in the Unicode Technical Report 9. They are quite complex and non-trivial to implement. This is typically done at the operating system level and you need to make sure you are running your applications on a *bidi-enabled* system.

There are no specific constructs in XML to specify that the data stored in a document should be represented as bi-directional text. It is a rendering issue and therefore should be coded at the rendering level (in other words, in the style sheets). CSS2 and XSL offer an initial set of properties that allow you to indicate bi-directional text: the `direction` and `unicode-bidi` properties. Additional properties are under development in CSS3.

Listing 5.1 shows several sets of left-to-right and right-to-left words. The first are represented by "abc", and the second by the three initial letters of the Hebrew alphabet: Alef ('א'), Bet ('ב'), and Gimel ('ג'). A number is attached to each word to indicate its position in the sequence.

In the XML document, as with any file, the text is always entered in its *logical order*. In the example, to make the logical order more visible the Hebrew words are represented in numeric character references rather than raw text. The Hebrew words are therefore coded `&#x5D0;&#x5D1;&#x5D2;`.

Two elements (`<Rtl>` and `<Ltr>`) are used to separate the text parts according to their main content: Paragraphs with mostly Hebrew words are included in `<Rtl>` elements, and paragraphs with mostly English text are inside `<Ltr>` blocks. Within each paragraph you can have insertions of words going the direction opposite to the default one. In addition, an inline element, `<RtlQuote>`, has been defined to permit the insertion of right-to-left phrases within left-to-right paragraphs.

LISTING 5.1

Bidi_Text.xml—Bi-Directional Text

```
<?xml version="1.0" ?>
<?xml-stylesheet type="text/css" href="Bidi_Text.css"?>
<Doc>
 <Rtl>
  <Para>&#x5D0;&#x5D1;&#x5D2;1 &#x5D0;&#x5D1;&#x5D2;2 abc3
↪&#x5D0;&#x5D1;&#x5D2;4 &#x5D0;&#x5D1;&#x5D2;5</Para>
```

LISTING 5.1 CONTINUED

```
 <Para>&#x5D0;&#x5D1;&#x5D2;6 <Emph>&#x5D0;&#x5D1;&#x5D2;7</Emph>
↪&#x5D0;&#x5D1;&#x5D2;8</Para>
 </Rtl>
 <Ltr>
  <Para>abc9 abc10 abc11 &#x5D0;&#x5D1;&#x5D2;12
↪&#x5D0;&#x5D1;&#x5D2;13</Para>
  <Para>abc14 abc15 &#x5D0;&#x5D1;&#x5D2;16</Para>
  <Para>abc17 <RtlQuote>&#x5D0;&#x5D1;&#x5D2;18 abc19 abc20
↪&#x5D0;&#x5D1;&#x5D2;21</RtlQuote>
    abc22 &#x5D0;&#x5D1;&#x5D2;23</Para>
 </Ltr>
</Doc>
```

Listing 5.2 shows the style sheet that goes with the XML sample file, and Figure 5.1 displays the corresponding rendering with Internet Explorer.

LISTING 5.2

`Bidi_Text.css`—Style Sheet for Bi-Directional Rendering

```
/* Bidi Specific */
Rtl, RtlQuote {
 direction: rtl; unicode-bidi: embed;
}
Ltr {
 direction: ltr; unicode-bidi: embed;
}

/* General */
Doc, Rtl, Ltr, Para {
 display: block; font-size: 1.2em;
}
RtlQuote {
 display: inline;
 text-decoration: underline;
}
Emph {
 display: inline;
 font-weight: bold;
}
```

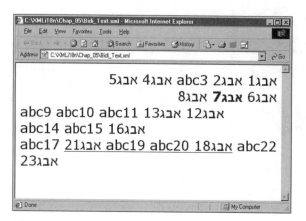

FIGURE 5.1

Display of bi-directional text within Internet Explorer 5.5.

Some XML rendering engines will display part of the bi-directional text correctly by detecting that some runs of characters have a right-to-left property. For example, if you remove the two first entries of our previous style sheet, Internet Explorer will still display some of the text correctly, as shown in Figure 5.2. However, this default behavior is limited and cannot work in cases such as for the `<RtlQuote>` element.

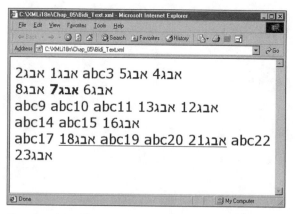

FIGURE 5.2

Default behavior for bi-directional text within Internet Explorer 5.5.

Vertical Writing

The third writing system you are likely to come across is vertical writing. It is used in Chinese, Japanese, and Korean in literature, newspapers, and various other media. The horizontal left-to-right system is often utilized in computers and technical documents.

In some cases, both methods coexist on the same pages. Listing 5.3 gives an example of these two methods.

The CSS3 specifications handle vertical writing through the `writing-mode` property.

LISTING 5.3

`Vertical.svg`—Vertical and Horizontal Text in an SVG Document

```
<?xml version="1.0" ?>
<svg width="330" height="330" viewbox="0 0 330 330">
 <g style="font-family:'MS Song';
    font-size:24;">
  <text x="300" y="30" style="writing-mode: tb;"
  >これは縦書きの例です。</text>
  <text x="20" y="26" style="writing-mode: rl;"
  >これは横書きの例です。</text>
 </g>
</svg>
```

Figure 5.3 shows the rendering of the file by the Adobe SVG viewer plug-in running with Internet Explorer.

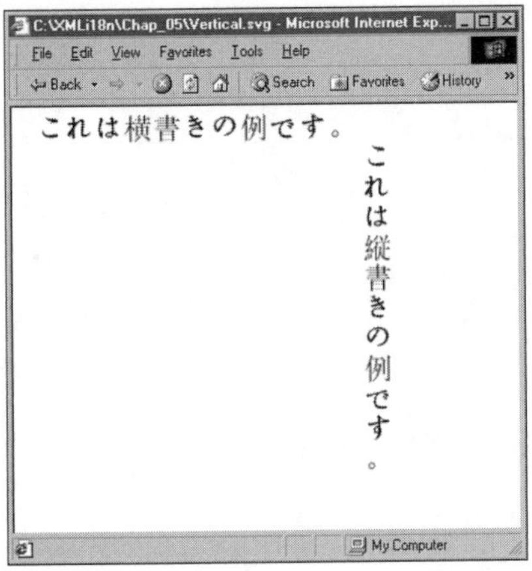

FIGURE 5.3

Rendering of horizontal and vertical text by the SVG viewer from Adobe.

Text Layout

In addition to writing direction, variations exist in the way some scripts arrange characters and how they use different formatting styles. Here again, this is a rendering issue, not directly related to XML. Although some of these features have already been addressed, many others are being added to CSS3 and XSL.

Ruby Text

The term *Ruby* designates a sequence of annotation text that is placed close to a base text. It is used, for example, to indicate the pronunciation of the base text in Japanese and Chinese.

As with XHTML, the Ruby module, defined by the W3C, can be used in your own vocabulary. A Ruby block is enclosed in a `<ruby>` element. Inside, the base text is delimited by the `<rb>` element, while the Ruby text is inside the `<rt>` element.

The module also allows for a fallback mechanism in case your processor does not support Ruby display: the `<rp>` element allows you to bracket the Ruby text between parentheses. The content of that element is not displayed if the Ruby text is correctly handled. In the example shown in Listing 5.4, the same Japanese text for "Information processing" is rendered twice: without and with the `<rp>` additions.

LISTING 5.4

`Ruby_Text.htm`—Ruby Text in XHTML

```
<?xml version="1.0" ?>
<!DOCTYPE html
 PUBLIC "-//W3C//DTD XHTML 1.0 Strict//EN"
 "http://www.w3.org/TR/xhtml1/DTD/xhtml1-strict.dtd">
<html xmlns="http://www.w3.org/1999/xhtml" xml:lang="en">
 <head>
  <title>Ruby Sample</title>
 </head>
 <body>
  <p>Information processing</p>
  <p xml:lang="ja">
   <ruby><rb>情報処理</rb><rt>じょうほうしょり</rt></ruby>
  </p>
  <p xml:lang="ja">
   <ruby><rb>情報処理</rb><rp>(</rp><rt>じょうほうしょり</rt><rp>)</rp>
➥</ruby>
  </p>
 </body>
</html>
```

Figure 5.4 shows the rendering of the sample file in Internet Explorer where it is supported, and Figure 5.5 displays the same file with Netscape 6 where it is not yet supported.

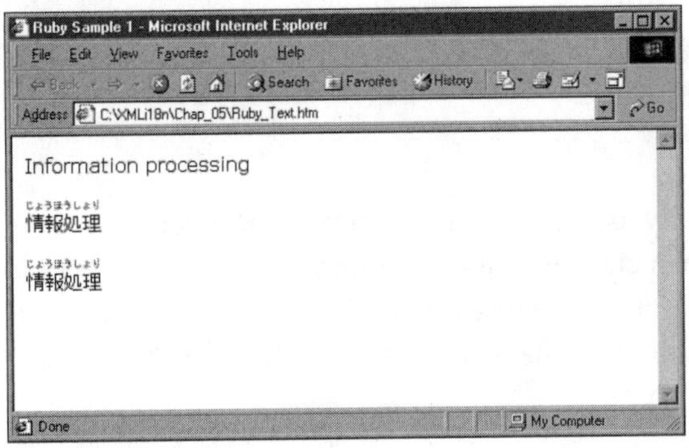

FIGURE 5.4

Display of Ruby text with Internet Explorer 5.5.

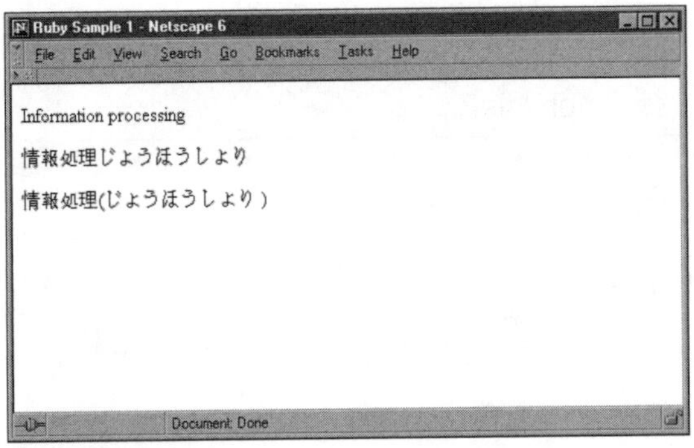

FIGURE 5.5

Display of Ruby text with Netscape 6.

The third level of CSS, currently still under development, integrates additional properties to control even better the rendering of Ruby text.

Combining Text

Another special layout, specific to Japanese this time, is the grouping of characters in blocks (*Kumimoji*) or inline annotations (*Warichu*) as shown in Figure 5.6. In CSS3 and XSL, this feature is controlled by the combine-text property with its value set respectively either to letters or lines.

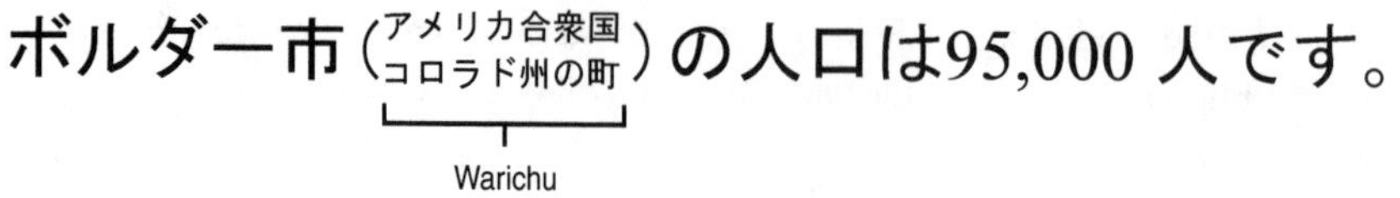

ボルダー市 (アメリカ合衆国 コロラド州の町) の人口は95,000 人です。

Warichu

FIGURE 5.6

Example of combining text in Warichu format.

Emphasis Styles

Alphabet-based writing systems usually use bold or italic to emphasize a portion of text. Scripts based on ideographic characters often use other means. For example, in Japanese you can add a mark above each glyph (*boten*) to make it stand out. Traditional Chinese does the same, whereas Simplified Chinese uses a mark below the characters.

In CSS3 and XSL, such typographical style is offered through the `font-emphasis-style` and `font-emphasis-position` properties. Listings 5.5 and 5.6 show a sample XML document that uses these properties. The rendering is displayed in Figure 5.7.

LISTING 5.5

`Boten.xml`—Example of Japanese Emphasis

```
<?xml version="1.0" ?>
<?xml-stylesheet type="text/css" href="Boten.css"?>
<Doc>
  <Para><Emph>強調</Emph>という言葉は重要です。</Para>
</Doc>
```

LISTING 5.6

`Boten.css`—CSS Properties for Font Emphasis

```
Doc, Para {
 display: block;
 font-size: 2em;
 margin-top: 50px;
}
Emph {
 display: inline;
 font-emphasis-style: accent;
 font-emphasis-position: above;
}
```

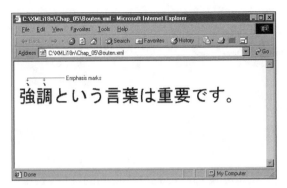

FIGURE 5.7

Asian emphasis marks. Note that these CSS properties are part of CSS3 and are not yet supported by most rendering engines. The marks on this screen shot have been added manually for demonstration purposes.

> **NOTE:** This is a good illustration of how the vocabulary should be about structure and not formatting. An element `<bold>` would be misleading whereas an element named, for example, `<emphasis>` would be more explicit.
>
> The name of an element should describe the function, not the implementation of the function. It should remind one of the intent, not the rendering of the intent. This is important because it helps authors and developers to think in an internationalization-minded fashion.

Context Shaping

As we have seen already, some languages use letters that have different forms depending on their position in the word or their preceding and following characters. Arabic is a good example.

Although UCS provides precomposed forms to represent different variants of many characters, you want to make sure *not* to use these characters in your documents. Context shaping, like writing direction, falls under the responsibility of the rendering engine, not the medium used for storage.

Figure 5.8 displays a character ARABIC LETTER AIN (U+0639) and its four different forms. Your text stores the same code point in all cases, but the rendering engine will pick a different glyph, depending on the context.

Isolated   Initial   Median   Final

FIGURE 5.8

Example of different forms for the same Arabic character.

Text Wrapping

Many scripts do not use spaces to separate words. Consequently, such runs of text are not able to wrap according to Roman-oriented algorithms.

In Thai, for example, a space usually denotes the end of a sentence, whereas the words within the sentences are not delimited by any character, as shown in Listing 5.7.

LISTING 5.7

`Wrapping_Thai.xml`—**Example of a Thai Sentence Without Spaces Between Words**

```
<?xml version="1.0" ?>
<?xml-stylesheet type="text/css" href="Wrapping_Thai.css"?>
<Data>
  <Entry>เลือกแหล่งกระดาษที่มีกระดาษที่ท่านต้องการใช้</Entry>
</Data>
```

Some rendering engines are Thai-enabled and, based on the class to which each character belongs and on rather elaborate word-breaking rules and dictionary lookup, they provide a correct wrapping for Thai text. Figure 5.9 shows the example displayed with Internet Explorer.

UCS offers a special character for the cases when the application does not support Thai word-breaking. The character ZERO WIDTH SPACE (U+200B) in a string indicates to the rendering engine that if a line break is needed, it could be done at that position. No physical space is displayed for that character. This solution is far from perfect, however: First, your rendering engine must support the ZERO WIDTH SPACE correctly and second, you must enter the markers in the text.

FIGURE 5.9

Wrapping of Thai text with Internet Explorer 5.5.

The same method could be used to provide line-break opportunities in a Chinese or Japanese text, both of which also do not use many white spaces. However, this is rarely needed: Due to their ideograph-based nature, these languages have simple rules for breaking lines. They define a list of characters that should not end a wrapped line or column, as well as a list of characters that should not start a line or a column. In addition, a few characters are allowed to hang outside the right or bottom margin.

Tables 5.1–5.3 enumerate the rules. Note that the small kana are obviously specific to Japanese rules.

TABLE 5.1

Characters That Should not End a Wrapped Line or Column

#	(U+0023)	#	(U+FF03)	$	(U+0028)	$	(U+FF04)
(	(U+0024)	(	(U+FF08)	@	(U+0040)	@	(U+FF20)
[	(U+005B)	[	(U+FF3B)	\	(U+005C)	＼	(U+FF3C)
{	(U+007B)	{	(U+FF5B)	‘	(U+2018)	“	(U+201C)
〈	(U+3008)	《	(U+300A)	「	(U+300C)	「	(U+FF62)
『	(U+300E)	【	(U+3010)	〔	(U+3014)	￡	(U+FFE1)
¥	(U+00A5)	￥	(U+FFE5)	§	(U+00A7)	〒	(U+3012)

TABLE 5.2

Characters That Should not Start a Wrapped Line or Column

゛	(U+309B)	゜	(U+309C)	゜	(U+FF9F)	!	(U+0021)
!	(U+FF01)	%	(U+0025)	%	(U+FF05)	)	(U+0029)

TABLE 5.2 CONTINUED

）	(U+FF09)	，	(U+002C)	，	(U+FF0C)	、	(U+3001)
、	(U+FF64)	．	(U+002E)	．	(U+FF0E)	。	(U+3002)
。	(U+FF61)	：	(U+003A)	：	(U+FF1A)	；	(U+003B)
；	(U+FF1B)	？	(U+003F)	？	(U+FF1F)	］	(U+005D)
］	(U+FF3D)	｝	(U+007D)	'	(U+2019)	"	(U+201D)
′	(U+2032)	″	(U+2033)	〉	(U+3009)	》	(U+300B)
」	(U+300D)	｣	(U+FF63)	』	(U+300F)	】	(U+3011)
〕	(U+3015)	¢	(U+FFE0)	°	(U+00B0)	・	(U+30FB)
・	(U+FF65)	‰	(U+2030)	℃	(U+2103)	℉	(U+2109)
あ	(U+3041)	ァ	(U+30A1)	ｱ	(U+FF67)	い	(U+3043)
ィ	(U+30A3)	ｨ	(U+FF68)	う	(U+3045)	ゥ	(U+30A5)
ｩ	(U+FF69)	ェ	(U+30A7)	ｪ	(U+FF6A)	お	(U+3049)
ォ	(U+30A9)	ｫ	(U+FF6B)	ヵ	(U+30F5)	ヶ	(U+30F6)
っ	(U+3063)	ッ	(U+30C3)	ｯ	(U+FF6F)	や	(U+3083)
ャ	(U+30E3)	ｬ	(U+FF6C)	ゅ	(U+3085)	ュ	(U+30E5)
ｭ	(U+FF6D)	ょ	(U+3087)	ョ	(U+30E7)	ｮ	(U+FF6E)
ゎ	(U+308E)	ヮ	(U+30EE)	々	(U+3005)	ゝ	(U+309D)
ゞ	(U+309E)	ー	(U+30FC)	ヽ	(U+30FD)	ヾ	(U+30FE)
ｰ	(U+FF70)	ﾞ	(U+FF9E)				

TABLE 5.3

Characters That Can Extend Past the Right or Bottom Margin

，	(U+002C)	，	(U+FF0C)	、	(U+3001)	、	(U+FF64)
．	(U+002E)	．	(U+FF0E)	。	(U+3002)	。	(U+FF61)

Sorting

When working with XML documents generated from a database, you can easily use the collation capabilities of the database to order your output. But in many other cases you might have to re-order the different items of a block of XML elements (for example, in a list).

XSL offers a dedicated method to achieve this: `<xsl:sort/>`. The element is called inside the `<xsl:apply-templates>` elements, in the sequence in which you want your different selections to be organized.

The attribute order can be set to either ascending or descending. If no order is specified then ascending is the default. The example in Listing 5.8 illustrates this: The entries are arranged by last names in ascending order. Then, if several entries have the same last name, they will be ordered according the first names, but this time in descending order.

LISTING 5.8

Sorting.xsl—Example of XSL Sort

```
<?xml version="1.0" ?>
<xsl:stylesheet xmlns:xsl="http://www.w3.org/1999/XSL/Transform"
 version="1.0">

<xsl:template match="/">
 <HTML>
  <BODY>
   <xsl:apply-templates/>
  </BODY>
 </HTML>
</xsl:template>

<xsl:template match="data">
 <TABLE BORDER="1" WIDTH="100%" CELLPADDING="5"
  CELLSPACING="0">
 <TR BGCOLOR="Indigo">
   <TD><FONT COLOR="White"><B>Family Name (ascending)</B></FONT></TD>
   <TD><FONT COLOR="White"><B>Given Name (descending)</B></FONT></TD>
 </TR>
  <xsl:apply-templates select="entry">
   <xsl:sort order="ascending" select="name/family-name"/>
   <xsl:sort order="descending" select="name/given-name"/>
  </xsl:apply-templates>
 </TABLE>
</xsl:template>

<xsl:template match="entry">
 <TR>
  <TD BGCOLOR="MediumTurquoise">
   <xsl:value-of select="name/family-name"/>
  </TD>
  <TD BGCOLOR="Khaki">
   <xsl:value-of select="name/given-name"/>
  </TD>
```

LISTING 5.8   CONTINUED

```
  </TR>
 </xsl:template>

</xsl:stylesheet>
```

When you apply the template to the XML document shown in Listing 5.9, you get the ordered table displayed in Figure 5.10.

LISTING 5.9

`Sorting.xml`—Data Sample to Sort

```
<?xml version="1.0" ?>
<?xml-stylesheet type="text/xsl" href="Sorting.xsl" ?>
<data>
 <entry><name>
   <given-name>Cari</given-name>
   <family-name>Smith</family-name>
  </name></entry>
 <entry><name>
   <given-name>Anny</given-name>
   <family-name>Smith</family-name>
  </name></entry>
 <entry><name>
   <given-name>Martin</given-name>
   <family-name>Auburn</family-name>
  </name></entry>
 <entry><name>
   <given-name>Alfred</given-name>
   <family-name>Albertson</family-name>
  </name></entry>
 <entry><name>
   <given-name>John</given-name>
   <family-name>Smith</family-name>
  </name></entry>
</data>
```

The `<xsl:sort/>` element provides a `lang` attribute that allows you to specify the language rules to use for each sequence. Again, make sure to test your XSL processor to see whether the language attribute is supported. This is not always the case.

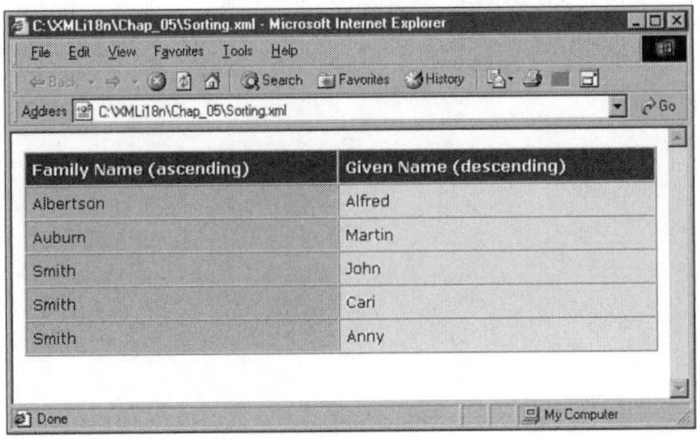

FIGURE **5.10**

Result of the sort function of XSL viewed in Internet Explorer.

Summary

In this chapter we have seen some of the ways special aspects of rendering can be addressed for XML documents. The upcoming CSS level 3 and XSL-FO provide a very complete range of properties addressing international layout characteristics. These properties often go far beyond what some traditional desktop publishing applications offer.

References

Much of the information in this chapter refers to the work done by the W3C or the Unicode Consortium. These documents are online as listed at the URLs below. The documents identified as drafts are still works in progress at the time of this book's publication. Make sure you get the latest information.

Unicode Bi-Directional Algorithm: `http://www.unicode.org/unicode/reports/tr9`

CSS1 Specifications: `http://www.w3.org/TR/REC-CSS1`

CSS2 Specifications: `http://www.w3.org/TR/REC-CSS2`

(draft) CSS3 Specifications: `http://www.w3.org/TR/css3-text`

(draft) Ruby Text: `http://www.w3.org/TR/ruby`

(draft) XSL Specifications: `http://www.w3.org/TR/xsl`

(draft) XSLT 1.1 Specifications: `http://www.w3.org/TR/xslt11`

# CHAPTER 6

XML Conversion

In This Chapter:

The previous two chapters discussed internationalization aspects of rendering XML documents through CSS and XSL. Despite the powerful range of functions that these two technologies offer, sometimes it is not enough to enable the creation of complex output. You must go one step further and write programs or scripts to generate these more complex types of output.

Microsoft Rich Text Format (RTF) files, Data files for macromedia Flash, binary output, and firmware data are some examples of such complex formats.

Parsing XML Documents

The conversion from XML to one of these formats first requires that you have an XML parser.

This topic goes far beyond the scope of this book and extensive literature exists about XML parsers. The two kinds of parsers are DOM (Document Object Model) parsers and SAX (Simple API for XML) parsers.

A DOM parser has the complete input document loaded in memory in a tree structure, where the document is broken down by nodes. DOM offers the advantage of easily accessing any part of the document at any time. You can insert, delete, modify, and rearrange the document in any form.

The main drawback of DOM is that it can be quite memory-consuming if the document is large and has a complex structure. It is also often slower than a SAX parser.

On the other hand, SAX is event-driven: The program defines handler functions that are triggered when an element, a character, or any other part of the XML document is read. Its memory trace is usually much smaller than for DOM, but it is also a sequential access: You must keep track of any inherited values passed from parent elements to their children, for example.

Both methods have advantages and disadvantages. A growing number of XML libraries are available for many different programming and scripting languages that offer both interfaces.

The .NET platform of Microsoft also offers an XML interface that is easy to use. Java provides numerous XML parsers and has a specific API for interfacing with them.

You can use a program specially written to do the conversion. For example, a choice of C/C++ or Java XML parsers could provide the core of the reader module while you could provide the writing routines.

Perl also has its own XML parser. Additionally, you can use specialized scripting languages such as OmniMark to do the rendering.

In some cases you might have to split your process into different steps to accommodate the different tools used. For instance, one might do the format transformation while another might perform the code set conversion. If you use Perl to generate an output file where characters need to be in an encoding not easily generated with Perl, you can create a temporary output where all extended characters are in the form \uHHHH (where HHHH is the Unicode code point of the character), and then use the Java utility native2ascii to convert the temporary output to raw characters.

Conversion Issues

A methodical analysis of the output can help you to isolate each potential problem from the viewpoint of internationalization:

- Verify what encoding needs to be used for the different locales in the output format.
- Verify that any encoding declarations, font definitions, and so forth are set appropriately.
- Check the notation of extended characters (many formats require some sort of escaped form for non-ASCII characters).
- Check what characters need to be escaped and what format needs to be used. For multibyte encoding, also make sure any ASCII-like byte value is escaped if necessary.
- Separate any locale-specific, hard-coded data to external templates so new languages can be added without modifying the conversion tool.

- Look for any internationalization-specific features of the output format that could be mapped to your XML structure (support for Ruby text, vertical and bi-directional writing, and so forth).

The more difficult problem to solve is usually the conversion of the characters from `UTF-16` (and sometimes `UTF-8`) to the encoding and notation used by the output format.

The Java `String` class offers the `getBytes()` method to perform this type of conversion. Other languages can also provide conversion routines through system APIs such as `WideCharToMultiByte()` in Windows, or libraries like ICU (International Components for Unicode) from IBM. (For more information about ICU, see `http//oss.software.ibm.com/icu`.)

We will use a sample program to illustrate two conversion scenarios: XML to RTF and XML to Flash. The tool, XML Converter, is a standard MFC application. It consists of a main dialog box that provides a simple edit box where you can enter an XML document, and another edit box where the result of the conversion is generated. This result is also automatically saved in a file you can view by clicking the **View File** button.

Clicking the appropriate button triggers the conversions. You can also select the output encoding to use for the conversion. Obviously you want to use appropriate encoding for the language of the XML document and the type of output format.

On the parser side, the program uses the Microsoft MSXML engine to parse the XML document. It creates a DOM tree where you can access the different nodes as needed.

Converting XML to RTF

RTF is a Microsoft format used mostly with Word. It has become an important standard in exchanging documentation files in general, and it is often one of the best ways to port a document to Word.

A powerful aspect of RTF is its support for multilingual text: Any language supported by your versions of Windows and Word can be represented in RTF.

In an RTF file, extended characters are usually represented as escaped sequences in the form `\'HH`, where `HH` is the hexadecimal value of the byte. If the encoding is double-byte then two escaped characters are used. For example:

```
"Été"    =   "\'c9 t\'e9"
"日本語"   =   "\'93\'fa\'96\'7b\'8c\'ea
```

The latest version of RTF has introduced the support of Unicode characters as well. The control word `\uDDD` enables you to specify any UCS character. The `DDD` value is the *decimal code point* of the UCS character. This value can be signed or unsigned. For instance, the character U+672C (本) is coded \u26412, and the character U+8A9E (語) is coded either \u-30050 or \u35486. Not all RTF readers support both notations, so you need to test the one that is appropriate for your specific environment.

In addition to the \uDDD control word, you should also offer a fallback solution for the RTF readers not supporting Unicode. This is done by outputting the bytes for the corresponding conversion to the relevant Windows code page. The control word \ucN indicates how many bytes are expected after the \uDDD entry, so the readers that support Unicode can skip over these characters. For example:

```
"日本語"  =  "{\uc2\u26085\'93\'fa\u26412\'96\'7b\u35486\'8c\'ea}
```

Note that, in some versions of Word, the \uDDD control word does not work when the sequence appears in a footnote.

The sample program uses the Windows API WideCharToMultiByte() to convert the UCS characters provided by the DOM interface into the selected Windows encoding.

If a character is not supported in the output encoding, it will be replaced by the closest corresponding ASCII character (for example 'a' for 'á'), or by a question mark (or \'3f if no close ASCII character can be found. If the RTF reader used to open the file is enabled for Unicode, it will use the \uDDD control words and skip the question marks, but an older application will display question marks.

Our sample application handles the conversion from XML to RTF in two functions. The first one is the OnConvertToRTF() method of the dialog box class, shown in Listing 6.1.

LISTING 6.1

XmlConverterDlg.cpp—OnConvertToRTF Function

```
void CXmlConverterDlg::OnConvertToRTF()
{
    CString              csOut;
    CString              csTmp;
    CString              csRtf;
    CString              csHeader;
    _bstr_t              bsText;
    BSTR                 bsTmp;
    wstring              wsText;
    wstring              wsTmp;
    _variant_t           varOut((bool)TRUE);
    IXMLDOMDocumentPtr    pDoc;
```

LISTING 6.1　CONTINUED

```
IXMLDOMNodeListPtr     pNodeList;
IXMLDOMNodePtr         pNode;
UINT                   unCodePage = GetCodePage();

csHeader =
"{\\rtf1\\ansi\\ansicpg1252\\uc1\\deff0\\deflang1033{\\fonttbl"
"{\\f0\\fswiss\\fcharset0\\fprq2 Arial Unicode MS Western;}"
"{\\f1\\fswiss\\fcharset238\\fprq2 Arial Unicode MS CE;}"
"{\\f2\\fswiss\\fcharset204\\fprq2 Arial Unicode MS Cyr;}"
"{\\f3\\fswiss\\fcharset161\\fprq2 Arial Unicode MS Greek;}"
"{\\f4\\fswiss\\fcharset162\\fprq2 Arial Unicode MS Tur;}"
"{\\f5\\fbidi \\fswiss\\fcharset177\\fprq2 Arial Unicode MS
➥ (Hebrew);}}";


m_edXML.GetWindowText(csTmp);

try
{
    TESTHR(CoInitialize(NULL));
    TESTHR(pDoc.CreateInstance("msxml2.domdocument"));

    varOut = pDoc->loadXML(_bstr_t(csTmp));
    if ((bool)varOut == FALSE)
    {
        throw(0);
    }
    csOut = csHeader;
    pNodeList = pDoc->getElementsByTagName("p");

    pNode = pNodeList->nextNode();
    while ( pNode != NULL )
    {
        TESTHR(pNode->get_text(&bsTmp));
        wsText = bsTmp;

        ConvertXMLStringToRTF(wsText, csRtf, unCodePage);
        csTmp = "{\\f0 ";
        csTmp += csRtf;
        csTmp += "\\par }";
        csOut += csTmp;
```

LISTING 6.1   CONTINUED

```
            pNode = pNodeList->nextNode();
        }

        csOut += "}";
    }
    catch (...)
    {
        csOut.LoadString(IDC_ERR_INVALIDDOC);
    }

    m_edRTF.SetWindowText(csOut);

    WriteFile(0);

    pNode = NULL;
    pNodeList = NULL;
    pDoc = NULL;
    CoUninitialize();
}
```

The text of the XML edit box is set to a variable and then passed to the `loadXML()` method of the DOM object.

The string that will contain the output is first set with a default RTF header. This header essentially defines styles and fonts that will be used in the file. In a real situation, you might need to make this parameter locale-specific and provide different templates for each language.

Our converter outputs only the content of all `<p>` elements. To get the list of them, we use the `getElementsByTagName()` method of the parser. This returns a list of nodes we can loop through.

For each `<p>` element, we convert the content from 16-bit UCS characters to the RTF text format. This is done through a call to the `ConvertXMLStringToRTF()` routine. Additional RTF-specific layout such as font and paragraph information is added around the converted string. Separating the text conversion allows for the handling of any inline codes separately (bold, italic, and so forth).

The `ConvertXMLStringToRTF()` function displayed in Listing 6.2 converts the text to the appropriate RTF encoding and character format.

LISTING 6.2

`XmlConverterDlg.cpp`—`ConvertXMLStringToRTF` **Function**

```cpp
void ConvertXMLStringToRTF
(
   wstring&            p_rwsText,
   CString&            p_rsOutput,
   const UINT          p_unCodePage
)
{
#define LBUF 30

   wstring             wsTmp;
   char                szBuf[LBUF];
   CString             csFmt;
   int                 nLen;


   p_rsOutput = "";

   for ( int i=0; i<p_rwsText.length(); i++ )
   {
      wsTmp = p_rwsText.at(i);

      if ( wsTmp[0] < 128 )
      {
         // ASCII: we can cast
         switch ( wsTmp[0] )
         {
            case L'\\':
               p_rsOutput += "\\\\";
               continue;

            case L'{':
               p_rsOutput += "\\{";
               continue;

            case L'}':
               p_rsOutput += "\\}";
               continue;

            default:
               p_rsOutput += (char)wsTmp[0];
```

LISTING 6.2   CONTINUED

```
                continue;
        }
    }


    // Else: non-ASCII
    WideCharToMultiByte(p_unCodePage, 0,
        (LPCWSTR)wsTmp.c_str(), 2,
        (LPSTR)szBuf, LBUF, NULL, NULL);

    if ( (nLen = strlen(szBuf)) < 2 )
    {
        // One byte
        csFmt.Format("\\u%d \\'%x", wsTmp[0], (unsigned char)szBuf[0]);
        p_rsOutput += csFmt;
    }
    else
    {
        // More than one byte
        csFmt.Format("{\\uc%d\\u%d", nLen, wsTmp[0]);
        p_rsOutput += csFmt;
        for ( int j=0; j<nLen; j++ )
        {
            csFmt.Format("\\'%x", (unsigned char)szBuf[j]);
            p_rsOutput += csFmt;
        }
        p_rsOutput += "}";
    }


}


#undef LBUF
}
```

To convert the XML string, the function loops through each character and escapes any escapable characters. Extended characters are converted from UTF-16 to the code set selected in the dialog box. If the converted character uses more than a single byte, the routine outputs it with a \ucN statement; otherwise, it uses the \uc1 defined in the header.

Figure 6.1 shows an example of conversion. The XML document contains two paragraphs that use some of the characters we have already used. You can enter them in any encoding you want as long as you specify the correct XML declaration. Here the encoding is `windows-1252` and the Japanese text uses numeric character references.

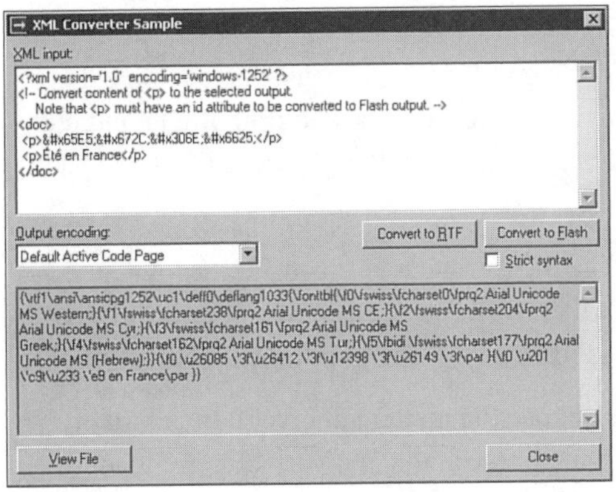

FIGURE 6.1

Conversion from XML to RTF.

Because all the XML text is converted to 1252 in RTF, the Japanese raw characters will be replaced with question marks, but the `\uDDD` codes will enable the reader to interpret the file properly, as shown in Figure 6.2.

FIGURE 6.2

RTF result opened in Word.

Depending on the languages you are converting, you might need to use other RTF control words to set alternate fonts, bi-directional properties, and so forth; however, the principles are the same.

Converting XML to Flash

Macromedia Flash is a popular application used to create animated graphic objects (called *movies*) you can use on Web pages.

Flash movies have always been time-consuming to localize because there is no easy way to access the translatable text of a movie. In addition, the solution of copying and pasting the translation presents some challenges when dealing with text in a code page different from the system code page.

One way to ease the process is to externalize the translatable text using the dynamic text property of the symbols, and to assign them variables. These variables can be set with values taken from a remote file using the `loadVariablesNum()` method.

For example, as shown in Figure 6.3, you can use the method at level 0 in the main frame of the movie. This is executed when the frame starts, the variables are loaded, and the external text is inserted in the movie.

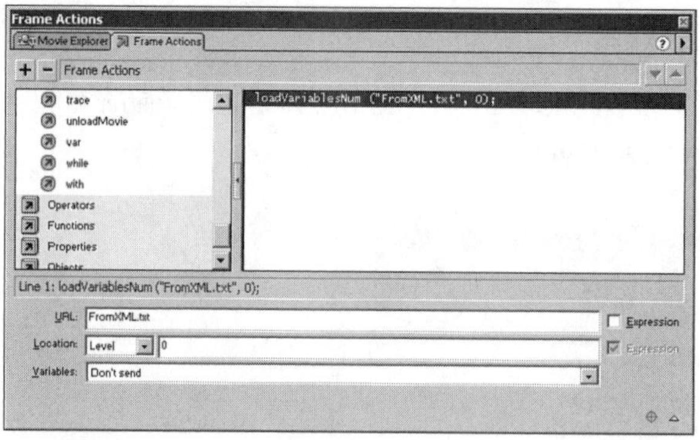

FIGURE 6.3

Using dynamic text loaded from an external file in Flash.

This technique works but requires the external file to be in a format that, to say the least, does not lend itself very well to localization. For example, to set the following three variables

```
varHome = "Home";
varMap  = "Site Map";
varRD   = "Research & Development";
```

the text file must contain a single line formatted as follows:

```
varHome=Home&varMap=Site+Map&varRD=Research+%26+Development
```

The text must be in one line, each `variable=value` pair should be separated by a character `&`, the spaces must be replaced by the character `+`, and all extended characters (and some ASCII characters, such as the `+` and the `&`) must be escaped into the `%HH` form where `HH` is the hexadecimal value for the given character. Some quick tests show that not all of this seems to be absolutely necessary; for example, using spaces instead of `+` characters does not generate incorrect text. The syntax seems to be the one used for URIs, but Flash documentation is rather vague and does not offer a comprehensive specification.

Regardless of the details of the syntax, if the original file for storing the text is an XML document, you can easily convert it to the Flash text file format.

The conversion is implemented in the `OnConvertToFlash()` function of the dialog class, as shown in Listing 6.3. You can either use the strict syntax (following the specifications exactly), or not (using the simplest notation that seems to work).

LISTING 6.3

`XmlConverterDlg.cpp`—`OnConvertToFlash` **Function**

```
void CXmlConverterDlg::OnConvertToFlash()
{
    CString                     csOut;
    CString                     csTmp;
    CString                     csFlash;
    _bstr_t                     bsText;
    BSTR                        bsTmp;
    wstring                     wsText;
    wstring                     wsTmp;
    _variant_t                  varOut((bool)TRUE);
    IXMLDOMDocumentPtr          pDoc;
    IXMLDOMNodeListPtr          pNodeList;
    IXMLDOMNodePtr              pNode;
    IXMLDOMNodePtr              pNode2;
    IXMLDOMNamedNodeMapPtr      pNamedNodeMap;
    UINT                        unCodePage = GetCodePage();
    BOOL                        bStrict = (m_chkStrictSyntax.GetCheck() ==
1);

    m_edXML.GetWindowText(csTmp);

    try
    {
```

LISTING 6.3 CONTINUED

```cpp
TESTHR(CoInitialize(NULL));
TESTHR(pDoc.CreateInstance("msxml2.domdocument"));

varOut = pDoc->loadXML(_bstr_t(csTmp));
if ((bool)varOut == FALSE)
{
   throw(0);
}
csOut = "";
pNodeList = pDoc->getElementsByTagName("p");

TESTHR(pNode = pNodeList->nextNode());
while ( pNode != NULL )
{
   TESTHR(pNode->get_attributes(&pNamedNodeMap));
   pNode2 = pNamedNodeMap->getNamedItem("id");
   if ( pNode2 == NULL )
   {
      pNode = pNodeList->nextNode();
      continue;
   }
   else
   {
      // Get ID value
      TESTHR(pNode2->get_text(&bsTmp));
      wsText = bsTmp;
      csTmp = "";
      for ( int i=0; i<wsText.length(); i++ )
      {
         csTmp += (char)wsText[i];
      }
      csTmp += '=';
   }

   TESTHR(pNode->get_text(&bsTmp));
   wsText = bsTmp;

   ConvertXMLStringToFlash(wsText, csFlash, unCodePage, bStrict);
   csTmp += csFlash;
   csTmp += "&"; // End of variable
   csOut += csTmp;
   pNode = pNodeList->nextNode();
```

LISTING 6.3   CONTINUED

```
        }

    }
    catch (...)
    {
        csOut.LoadString(IDC_ERR_INVALIDDOC);
    }

    m_edRTF.SetWindowText(csOut);

    WriteFile(1);

    pNode2 = NULL;
    pNode = NULL;
    pNamedNodeMap = NULL;
    pNodeList = NULL;
    pDoc = NULL;
    CoUninitialize();

}
```

The function works the same as for RTF except for the output creation. Because the Flash file will need both a variable name and a value for each <p> element, the application expects a unique ID for each of them; this is stored in the id attribute. The conversion of the id value to the variable name assumes the names are in ASCII for simplicity.

The conversion of the text itself is done in the ConvertXMLStringToFlash() function, shown in Listing 6.4.

LISTING 6.4

XmlConverterDlg.cpp—ConvertXMLStringToFlash **Function**

```
void ConvertXMLStringToFlash
(
    wstring&            p_rwsText,
    CString&            p_rsOutput,
    const UINT          p_unCodePage,
    const BOOL          p_bStrict
)
{
```

LISTING 6.4   CONTINUED

```
#define LBUF 30

    wstring              wsTmp;
    char                 szBuf[LBUF];
    CString              csFmt;
    int                  nLen;


    p_rsOutput = "";

    for ( int i=0; i<p_rwsText.length(); i++ )
    {
        wsTmp = p_rwsText.at(i);

        if ( wsTmp[0] < 128 )
        {
            // ASCII: we can cast
            switch ( wsTmp[0] )
            {
                case L' ':
                    if ( p_bStrict ) p_rsOutput += '+';
                    else p_rsOutput += ' ';
                    continue;

                case L'+':
                case L'/':
                case L'?':
                case L'&':
                case L'%':
                case L'*':
                    csFmt.Format("%%%x", (char)wsTmp[0]);
                    p_rsOutput += csFmt;
                    continue;

                default:
                    if ( wsTmp[0] < 32 )
                    {
                        // Control characters
                        csFmt.Format("%%%x", (char)wsTmp[0]);
                        p_rsOutput += csFmt;
                        continue;
                    }
```

LISTING **6.4**   CONTINUED

```
            p_rsOutput += (char)wsTmp[0];
            continue;
        }
    }


    // Else: non-ASCII
    WideCharToMultiByte(p_unCodePage, 0,
        (LPCWSTR)wsTmp.c_str(), 2,
        (LPSTR)szBuf, LBUF, NULL, NULL);


    nLen = strlen(szBuf);
    for ( int j=0; j<nLen; j++ )
    {
        if ( p_bStrict )
        {
            csFmt.Format("%%%x", (unsigned char)szBuf[j]);
            p_rsOutput += csFmt;
        }
        else
        {
            if ( szBuf[j] < 128 )
            {
                // ASCII-like bytes
                switch ( szBuf[j] )
                {
                    case L'+':
                    case L'/':
                    case L'?':
                    case L'&':
                    case L'%':
                    case L'*':
                        csFmt.Format("%%%x", (char)szBuf[j]);
                        p_rsOutput += csFmt;
                        break;

                    default:
                        p_rsOutput += (char)szBuf[j];
                        continue;
                }
            }
            else
            {
```

LISTING 6.4   CONTINUED

```
                csFmt.Format("%%%x", (unsigned char)szBuf[j]);
                p_rsOutput += csFmt;
            }
        }
    }
}

#undef LBUF
}
```

The routine escapes any extended character or reserved ASCII character to the %HH format. In addition, when the flag requiring a strict syntax is set, spaces are converted to + characters. Extended characters are converted the same way as for RTF, and the resulting bytes are escaped if necessary.

Figure 6.4 shows an example of conversion to Flash. The Flash movie used as an example has three variables: varIntro, btnMap, and btnHome, so the XML input should have three <p> elements corresponding to these IDs in order to work correctly. Here the text is in Polish, which is not a Latin-1 language; therefore, the fonts in the Flash movie should be set accordingly.

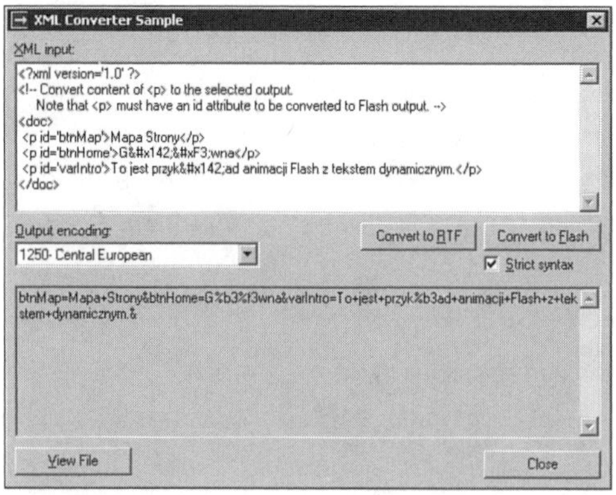

FIGURE 6.4

Conversion from XML to Flash.

When you click the **View File** button after a conversion to Flash, instead of opening the FromXML.txt file it generated, the program opens an HTML page with a Flash movie that uses the dynamic variables. You can then see your text directly displayed in the movie, as shown in Figure 6.5.

FIGURE 6.5

A Flash movie after the dynamic text has been updated with the latest output of the sample program.

Keep in mind that using this method to translate Flash text still depends on the limitations Flash has with regard to encoding support.

Summary

Converting XML documents to complex output formats can be done using many different languages and tools. Most programming and scripting languages now offer XML parsers and libraries that give you a wide range of choices for implementing conversion utilities.

More and more high-end applications also offer XML import/export solutions. For example, using the dedicated features of FrameMaker+SGML is probably a more efficient way to connect your XML data with FrameMarker than is developing your own converter from XML to MIF (Maker Interchange Format). However, many applications do not offer the extensive multilingual support that XML provides. For example, a solution may work well with Latin-1 languages such as English, but it may break down when the content is in Russian, Czech, or Korean.

As usual, testing early on with pseudotranslated files can give early warnings on the locale-specific problems your conversion process can conceal.

Preparing XML for Localization

PART II

In This Part:

# CHAPTER 7

Creating Internationalized Document Types

In This Chapter:

- Design Guidelines   137
- Localization Properties Definition   148

Beyond the built-in support that XML and related technologies offer for internationalization, you must consider several aspects when developing a new document type that will store translatable text. This chapter presents the guidelines to create XML document types that are more easily localized and can save cost and time in the long run.

In addition, there is much information pertaining to localization that neither DTDs nor schemas offer a standard way to define (for example, whether the content of an element or the value of an attribute is translatable). It is crucial that you know this type of property, along with many others, during the localization process. We will see how this can be specified.

At the end of 2000, an initiative to work on these issues and other XML-related aspects of internationalization and localization was started. The ITS (Internationalization Tag Sets) project is now part of a larger framework that is still being defined. Most of the topics discussed in this chapter and in Chapter 8, "Writing Internationalized Documents," should be addressed by ITS. You can find more information about ITS and participate in its work at `http://groups.yahoo.com/group/lisa-its`.

Design Guidelines

The first step in working with your own XML format is to define a document type. From an internationalization viewpoint, various guidelines must be conformed to. An excellent reading for this topic is Richard Ishida's paper "Localisation Considerations in DTD Design." You can see it at `http://www.xerox-emea.com/globaldesign/dtds.htm`. This section discusses many of the points made in that original paper.

Note also that one of the deliverables of the ITS project is a set of guidelines for creating XML content types. At the present time no draft has been published, but when the material is made available it will probably be more complete than this chapter.

Meanwhile, when creating a new document type for data that will be translated, you should consider, at least, the following rules:

- Use unique identifiers for translatable elements.
- Integrate language declarations using `xml:lang`.
- Think twice before using multilingual documents.
- Identify requirements for white space.
- Provide a mechanism for inserting localization properties within the content.
- Avoid translatable text in attribute values.
- Avoid conditional situations for translatable items.
- Do not use infinite naming schemes.
- Identify content referring to external sources.
- Avoid presentation-oriented names for elements and attributes.

Each of these aspects is discussed in more detail in the following paragraphs.

Unique Identifiers

A unique identifier for each non-inline element that has translatable content is extremely useful. This enables more flexibility, accuracy, and efficiency when leveraging; for example, you can reuse translation with IDs rather than recycling it with text match. Identifiers can also be used as links between documents.

Using IDs for some inline elements might be useful as well. Examples include quotations, references to UI text, and so forth.

If you use a DTD you might want to utilize the ID type to define any attribute that is an identifier. However, keep in mind that ID type does not allow the first character of the value to be a digit. For example, if `myId` is of type ID, the syntax `<p myId="1">` is incorrect whereas `<p myId="id1">` and `<p myId"_1">` are correct.

Note also that currently only a few authoring tools support automated handling of IDs. For instance, when copying and pasting XML fragments that have data with unique IDs, these attributes must be reset to avoid duplication.

Using identifiers that are globally unique (versus those that are unique within the document) is usually better because it will solve any duplication issues. This can be done, for example, by using a date/time stamp with a user string or a machine ID prefix.

Language Declaration

Indicating the language in which the content of a document is written is important. It allows you to choose a more appropriate style for rendering, for example to apply different algorithms when the text is processed for indexing, and to correctly format locale-dependent data such as time, date, and numbers.

As you have seen in previous chapters, XML offers a standard attribute to identify languages: `xml:lang`. There is no need to come up with your own; use the standard. Several XML-related technologies such as CSS or XPath have built-in functions to take advantage of it. For more details on how to use `xml:lang`, see Chapter 3, "Miscellaneous Tagging."

Make sure to provide the `xml:lang` attribute for all elements that have locale-sensitive content, including multimedia and graphical elements.

Multilingual Documents

There are two types of multilingual documents. The difference between them is whether the multilingual aspect happens at the content level (a single content including data in different languages) or at the structural level (the same content stored in different languages).

At the content level, the text is multilingual because the content uses several languages at the same time. The content is in a main language and includes fragments of text in others. When translated into another main language, the fragments will still exist. An example is a page describing a product with a legal note in two or three languages. Another example is code samples left in the source language.

When the difference is at the structural level, the same content exists in different languages. The same document could be stored in two separate instances. The fact that it is multilingual has nothing to do with the content, but is an architectural decision. Such a document can obviously also have multilingual data at the content level at the same time.

From an XML viewpoint there are no major issues with storing different language instances in the same document. The W3C Internationalization group has done an excellent job to make sure it is possible. The problems are from a localization viewpoint.

Multilingual files are never easy to handle. This is especially true for updates, when the documents contain several languages but the source language is the newest one and the others need to be updated. In this case, each language must be translated and edited by a different linguist. The unique file must be sent to different people, and then their work must be reintegrated into a single file. The benefit of having a single file is lost during translation, and the need to reconstruct the single file afterward takes time, augments cost, and increases the risks for mistakes.

If you decide to have multiple language instances in the same document and use IDs, remember that an attribute of ID type must be unique in the document. The following syntax, while well formed, is not valid:

```
<para id="id1" xml:lang="en">Text of the first paragraph.</para>
<para id="id1" xml:lang="fr">Texte du premier paragraphe.</para>
```

You could try to use a composite ID instead:

```
<para id="id1-en">Text of the first paragraph.</para>
<para id="id1-fr">Texte du premier paragraphe.</para>
```

But then you lose the use of `xml:lang` and its corresponding functionalities. If you use both, you have duplicate information.

The best approach is to add a level in the structure of the document. Wherever a text item appears, provide an extra element that contains the variant of each language. The attributes global to the item can be left at the item level, and any language-specific attribute goes at the variant level:

```
<para id="id1">
 <var xml:lang="en">Text of the first paragraph.</var>
 <var xml:lang="fr">Texte du premier paragraphe.</var>
</para>
```

Be careful when considering true multilingual documents because currently their drawbacks usually override their advantages. If the author opens the document in an editor not designed to work with multilingual files and does a global search and replace in one language, it will probably affect the text in the other languages as well.

Storing the content in a database and offering source language and one of the target languages at once is useful, but it is different. In that case the bilingual document is generated on purpose; after the target language has been updated you need only the target language to merge the text back into its repository.

XML is a very powerful mechanism for translation tools, as the use of formats such as OpenTag, TMX, XLIFF, and many proprietary XML applications shows. But those formats are intended to be used with specialized tools for a specific purpose. More powerful authoring applications may change the situation in the future, but for now multilingual documents (in the sense of storing different language instances in the same file) are not often a good solution for documentation, online help, or messages.

White Spaces

XML white spaces are normally left untouched by XML processing tools and are either collapsed or preserved as necessary when they are rendered.

XML provides a standard attribute, `xml:space`, which can be set to `preserve` to indicate that the white spaces inside a given element must be left alone. However, not specifying this attribute does not mean the white spaces can be collapsed.

The localization process changes the text; therefore, the knowledge of whether the white spaces are ultimately significant is very important. Because this cannot always be determined from the XML document, it should be done through a different mechanism. The localization properties definition document, discussed later in this chapter, might be a good solution for this.

Many translation tools that support XML have a tendency, based on HTML behavior, to collapse spaces. If the content of some elements is sensitive to white spaces, make sure that information is provided to the localizer.

Inline Localization Properties

The content of a document often has parts of translatable text that have specific requirements. For example, in the following fragment, the term "World Wide Web Consortium" is not to be translated.

```
<p>The XML specification is maintained by the World Wide Web
↪Consortium.</p>
```

This can be described with localization properties inside the document:

```
<p>The XML specification is maintained by the <span translate="no">World
↪Wide Web Consortium</span>.</p>
```

Such properties can be useful at the attribute level as well. For instance, the string for a software or firmware interface could have length restrictions and be coded as follows:

```
<panel id="grid34" xml:space="preserve">
 <msg id="s1">  Carbon:</p>
 <msg id="s2">  Oxygen:</p>
 <msg id="s3"> Hydrogen:</p>
</panel>
```

The length restriction information could be carried with the text as follows:

```
<panel id="grid34" xml:space="preserve" maxwidth="10">
 <msg id="s1">  Carbon:</p>
 <msg id="s2">  Oxygen:</p>
```

```
<msg id="s3"> Hydrogen:</p>
</panel>
```

The principle is to offer localization-specific information within the text so that it can be modified easily by the author and is readily accessible at translation time.

Chapter 8 discusses in detail how to implement such metadata. When designing your document type, make sure it has provisions to integrate this localization-specific markup.

Attribute Values

Several problems relate to using attributes that have translatable values.

First, it is quite difficult to specify localization information for attributes. Although the content of an element can be marked up by a specialized inline tag or flagged by specific attributes, the value of an attribute cannot easily be assigned metadata.

A second issue occurs if you are using ID-based mechanisms for leveraging translation. Because the attribute itself cannot have an explicit ID, the tools must implement extra features to work around it: They can use the name of the attribute prefixed by the ID of its element to get a unique identifier. For example, the fragment

```
<special-deal id="a1" title="The Migration">2 weeks all-inclusive to see
↪the herds migration in the Serengeti plain.</special-deal>
```

when prepared for leveraging would give you

```
  id: a1
data: 2 weeks all-inclusive to see the herds migration in the Serengeti
↪plain.
  id: a1-title
data: The Migration
```

But this extra feature might not always be implemented by all the tools.

A third problem is that white spaces are treated differently in an attribute value than in an element content. Here again, translation tools are usually not very well tuned to handle these differences.

A fourth reason to avoid translatable text in attributes is the way some translation tools deal with segmentation of subsegments. Consider for instance the following XHTML fragment:

```
<p>Click <a href="start.xml" title="Start Now!">here</a> to start.</p>
```

Some tools process it as a single segment

```
Segment 1: Click [code]Start Now![code]here[code] to start.
```

and some tools process it as two separate segments:

```
Segment 1: Click [code]here[code] to start.
Segment 2: Start Now!
```

This causes translation problems, loss of leveraging in some situations, incompatibility when exchanging translation memories, and so forth.

Finally, in some circumstances, you can have problems with the scope of the xml:lang attribute. By rule it applies to the content of the element where it appears and to all the attributes of that same element, regardless of their positions relative to the xml:lang attribute.

In some cases you might want to set the language of the element content but not the language of an attribute value. For example, an application might use the following fragment to display text in different languages but keep the text of the title attribute in English:

```
<item title="Example in German" xml:lang="de">
 Der Gipfel des Berges funkelt.
</item>
<item title="Example in Latin" xml:lang="la">
 Cacumen montis lucescit.
</item>
```

The attribute xml:lang is necessary because XSL templates, CSS styles, or other mechanisms might need to use it to apply specific actions or styles. However, using it incorrectly flags the English text of title as German or Latin.

Using an element for the title would solve the problem by allowing a different definition of the locale for both contents.

```
<item>
 <title xml:lang="en">Example in German</title>
 <para xml:lang="de">Der Gipfel des Berges funkelt.</para>
</entry>
<item>
 <title xml:lang="en">Example in Latin"</title>
 <para xml:lang="la">Cacumen montis lucescit.</para>
</item>
```

You want to be aware of translatable attributes in the XML schemes used by database systems. Often, when exporting or querying tables, an element represents the row level and an attribute represents each field. Most of the time there is a way to change the structure of the output, but it can require some additional work on top of the default XML export or query capabilities.

Conditional Translation

When defining the structure of your document type, avoid using elements that will have content for which the translation properties depend on the value of an attribute, the content of a parent or sibling element, or any other combination.

The UIML document shown in Listing 7.1 illustrates this.

LISTING 7.1

`ConditionalTrans.xml`—Document Where Translatable Elements Are Conditional

```xml
<?xml version="1.0" ?>
<uiml>
 <interface>
  <structure>
   <part name="Main">
    <part name="Component1" class="Component1Class"/>
   </part>
  </structure>
  <style>
   <property part-name="Main" name="rendering">Main</property>
   <property part-name="Main" name="content">Sample UI</property>
   <property part-name="Component1" name="rendering">Text</property>
   <property part-name="Component1" name="content">Some text to
➥translate.</property>
  </style>
 </interface>
 <peers>
  <presentation name="VoiceXML">
   <component name="Main" map-to="vxml:form"/>
   <component name="Text" map-to="vxml:block">
    <attribute name="content" map-to="PCDATA"/>
   </component>
  </presentation>
  <presentation name="WML">
   <component name="Main" map-to="wml:card">
    <attribute name="content" map-to="wml:card.title"/>
```

LISTING 7.1   CONTINUED

```
  </component>
  <component name="Text" map-to="wml:p">
   <attribute name="content" map-to="PCDATA"/>
  </component>
 </presentation>
</peers>
</uiml>
```

UIML (User Interface Markup Language) is a content type used to describe interfaces in a generic way so that rendering engines can transform a single source document into various outputs. The `<interface>` element describes the UI components, and the `<peers>` element contains the mapping to different outputs. In our example we have one output to VoiceXML, as displayed in Listing 7.2, and another output to WML (Wireless Markup Language), as shown in Listing 7.3 and Figure 7.1.

LISTING 7.2

`VoiceXMLOutput.vxml`—Output for VoiceXML

```
<?xml version="1.0" ?>
<vxml>
 <form>
  <block>Some text to translate.</block>
 </form>
</vxml>
```

LISTING 7.3

`WMLOutput.wml`—Output for WML

```
<?xml version="1.0" ?>
<wml>
 <card title="Sample UI">
  <p>Some text to translate.</p>
 </card>
</wml>
```

FIGURE 7.1

Corresponding display of the WML document.

The translatable text in the UIML document is stored inside the `<property>` elements that have the attribute `name` set to `content`. The content of the `<property>` elements that have their attribute `name` set to `rendering` should not be modified or the references made to them later in the document will become invalid.

Currently, with most localization tools you will not be able to specify whether `<property>` is translatable based on the value of `name`. This leads to some additional preparation of the files, and a higher risk to alter data that must remain untouched. Note that some preprocessing of the original document using XSLT may help in such situations.

Infinite Naming Scheme

The following rule might appear very basic, but it is still worth mentioning because it has been known to be broken.

Some XML documents are used without DTDs or schema, in contexts where they are never validated. As long as they are well formed, nothing is wrong. However, from a localization viewpoint, you also want such a format to use a finite set of element and attribute names. For example, the following XML fragment is not easy to deal with when translation time comes:

```
<message100>Root path:</message100>
<message101>Display Options<message101>
<message105>Threshold = </message105>
```

Creating element or attribute names that are dynamically generated might prevent the use of many XML tools (whether related to localization or not). For example, it would be difficult to define a DTD for such a document.

Instead, use an attribute to store the variable part of the identifier, as shown in the following code:

```
<message id="100">Root path:</message>
<message id="101">Display Options<message>
<message id="105">Threshold = </message>
```

Even if the identifier is of CDATA type rather than ID type, this notation is better than having tag names combined with variable parts such as identifiers.

External Source

If the content of an element or part of it is really a copy of something generated in a different file (XML or not), it is useful to distinguish that part from the rest of the content. This applies, for example, to references to user interface text, to citations coming from other documents, and so forth.

Some mechanisms such as XLink can be used to automatically refresh the content from the original source file. You can find a more detailed discussion of this in Chapter 9, "Automated References."

Even if you are not using any special automated function to generate content from external sources, it is always a good thing to have the reference delimited by a specific tag and, when possible, a pointer to the location of the original source text. With such information in place, tools can run validation or extraction programs that will help the verification of the consistency between the source text and its references. For example, consider the following code:

```
<p id="a123">Select the <ui id="ID_FILE_START">Start</ui> option from the
➡<ui id="ID_MAIN_FILE">File</ui> menu.</p>
```

Both `Start` and `File` can be checked against the original user-interface resources, even if no system is used to dynamically link them to the original file.

Naming of Elements and Attributes

The names of the elements and attributes do not directly affect the degree of readiness for localization of a document type, but they do have an effect on the way the users perceive the corresponding documents and handle them.

Appropriate names can make a difference in the general understanding of internation-alization. It helps to raise the level of awareness for some localization issues.

Elements describe the structure of a document, not how it will ultimately be displayed. However, it is still not unusual to see presentation-related names given to elements that actually have a logical meaning. For instance, the following paragraph uses <bold> to encapsulate an important word:

```
<par>This text is <bold>important</bold>.</par>
```

It would be better to use a name pertaining to the function of the tag rather than to how you think it will be rendered.

```
<par>This text is <emphasis>important</emphasis>.</par>
```

When translated into another language, the <bold> tag might have to be mapped to a completely different style to adapt the rendering to the style requirements of the new language.

In addition, a presentation element can apply to different contents in the source docu-ment, but once it is translated, each type of content might need a different type of pres-entation. Mixing the functions of the element in the document and how its content will be presented makes it difficult to automate and incorporate modifications that might be needed to adjust the presentation to the new style.

Localization Properties Definition

When you develop your document type, you need to maintain an auxiliary document that details the different localization properties associated with each element and/or attribute.

This document will be a precious reference to the localizer when preparing the source material for translation or doing estimations.

We will first look at what information is needed, and then describe some of the possi-ble strategies to define this information in a standardized document.

Requirements

Properties can be grouped by type. Most can apply to both elements and attributes, but some make sense only for elements.

For simplicity in this section the term *item* is used to mean both element and attribute.

Localization Actions

The most important property to specify is what localization action should be applied to each item: Make no change at all, translate, resize (for coordinates or position), redirect (for URL, references, and so forth), or modify in some way (font name, font size, style, and so forth).

Data Type

Because some documents might not always follow the guidelines and embed non-XML data, and because some special types of data need to be embedded, it is important to have a way to indicate that the content of an item might need to be parsed with a specific filter.

For example, a filter can indicate that an `onclick` attribute in XHTML should be parsed as a script and not as normal text, or that the content of a `<linkref>` element in some document type is a URI and might need to be converted to its Internationalized URI form.

Edition Properties

Some inline elements are subject to modification or deletion during translation. For example, a tag marking emphasis might need to be removed, whereas an index marker would need to move with its associated terms. In other cases an inline element might have to be split in two because the text initially in one sequence is divided into several sequences in the translated text.

Unique ID

The name of any attribute that is used as an ID for a given element is important information to give to the translation tools. This can be used for leveraging, automated maintenance of IDs, and so forth.

Text Size

Some items might have specific constraints in the number of characters or bytes that can be used. A maximum width as well as a minimum one might be useful for UI-type text. In some cases the restriction can apply to a block of text where white spaces are significant, and where the lines must have a given length. A specific number of lines or a specific height might also be required. The translated text would need to be reformatted according to these criteria. In addition, you might also have a limitation in the total size of the text block; for example, if the application that uses the XML document has a built-in buffer limit. Note that some of these properties are already part of XLIFF and it makes sense to provide a way to define them at the document type level, so XLIFF filters can take advantage of them. See Chapter 17, "Text Extraction," for more details on XLIFF.

Allowed Characters

Some content can be restricted to a given set of characters for different reasons: The target system has only limited font capabilities, the text is a filename or a URL, and so forth. ASCII only, characters allowed in a DOS pathname, a Macintosh pathname, characters allowed in a non-escaped URI, halfwidth Katakana only, uppercase only, and fullwidth characters only are some of the possible values for this property.

Segmentation

Text must be translated into meaningful segments: Some elements are considered inline (they are part of the text content), whereas some others are structural and mark breaks in the text continuity. For instance, in SVG, the `<text>` element is structural and the `<tspan>` element is inline.

In some circumstances, inline elements mark the logical end of a segment, or an embedded new segment. A `<quote>` element, for example, could indicate a new segment within the original one.

Terminology

The capability to specify terms within the source content is of great interest for many utilities. It facilitates various functions such as terminology validation, creation of glossaries, and indexing.

Implementations

Proprietary formats have already been developed. At least two of them are XML applications. Examples of the Analysis file used by SDLX can be found in Chapter 14, "XML-Enabled Translation Tools." Samples of the Rule file used with System 3 are listed in Chapter 15, "Online Translation."

These formats illustrate different approaches, but also show how similar these types of proprietary data are. It is clear that a single common format would make life much easier for everybody, and could be shared by both authoring and translation products.

One of the most important aspects of the file is how the scope of a property is described. If it is limited to an element and the attributes inside that element, it is difficult to address the cases where the values of the properties depend on conditions set outside the given element. For example, in the XML document shown in Listing 7.4, only the word "Overview" is translatable. This document type does not follow all the rules for a good internationalization, but it is not an exception, so the definition document must be able to address even cases like this.

LISTING 7.4

`Conditions.xml`—Conditional Translatable Text

```
<?xml version="1.0" ?>
<page>
 <entry class="topic" level="1">
  <param type="descr">Overview</param>
  <param type="source">overview.xml</param>
 </entry>
 <entry class="button">
  <param type="action">open(windows1)</param>
  <param type="descr">bold; pushlike;</param>
  <param type="source">openBtn.png</param>
 </entry>
</page>
```

The condition here is that the content of the `<param>` element is translatable only if its `type` attribute is set to `desc` and if the `class` attribute of its parent element is set to `topic`.

XPath is an XML-related technology that can code such an expression. With XPath, the condition would be coded as follows:

```
//entry[@class="topic"]/param[@type="desc"]
```

This is, for example, the way the System 3 Rule file works.

However, there are drawbacks in using XPath. It forces, more or less, any tool that utilizes the definition file to use an XML parser with XPath support. Such libraries are available in the open source community, but using XPath does narrow the flexibility that developers will have when implementing their applications.

Using XPath also makes the use of SAX-based parsers difficult. SAX (Simple API for XML) follows an event-driven model and processes an XML document sequentially, usually with a small memory footprint. Because most XPath implementations must have the whole XML document loaded into memory, this favors a DOM-based approach. DOM (Document Object Model) processes the whole file, building a tree, and then gives access to the different parts of the file through its nodes.

Although this is not usually a problem for small to medium-size XML documents, the DOM approach works less efficiently with large XML files. This is where the bias of XML shows. Designed originally for the Web, its use has now reached areas that have nothing to do with the Internet, and where the same assumptions cannot always be made. This should not be too much of an issue, but it is still something to keep in mind.

A second important aspect of the definition document is the capability to specify a default behavior for the items that are not otherwise defined. This gives the author more flexibility: You can define a generic rule and exceptions to it rather than list all different behaviors.

Finally, it might be wise to allow the definition for several document types in the same file. This can be handy when the user interface of a tool is limited or offers only to pick one definition file per batch process: You can still process instances of different document types at once, rather than having to group the input files by formats.

At present, there is no standard format for this localization properties definition file. The ITS project will very likely define one at some point.

Meanwhile, we can define one that could already be useful because it clearly formalizes the properties. The one presented here has been inspired by the discussions in the ITS Group, the Analysis file of SDLX, and the Rule file of System 3.

Table 7.1 defines the syntax for the localization properties themselves, and Table 7.2 lists some additional useful attributes.

TABLE 7.1

Localization Properties

Attribute	Values
localize	**no**—The data should be exactly the same after localization.
	yes—The data might need to be modified for the localized version. Its datatype indicates the type of modification to do.
	inherit—The value is inherited from the property of the parent element or from the default.
datatype	**[text]**—The data is in a data type different from the main one. [text] indicates that type. For example, javascript would indicate data in JavaScript.
	@[attribute-name]—Same as preceding, but this time the type of data is indicated in the attribute [attribute-name].
ws-collapsible (elements only)	**yes**—The white spaces in the element can be collapsed.
	no—The white spaces in the element cannot be collapsed.
	inherit—The value is inherited from the property of the parent element, or from the default.

TABLE 7.1 CONTINUED	
Attribute	*Values*
moveable (elements only)	**yes**—The element can be moved anywhere within its parent.
	no—The element should remain where it is relative to the other inline elements.
removable (elements only)	**yes**—The element can be removed.
	no—The element cannot be removed.
clonable (elements only)	**yes**—The original element can be replicated somewhere within the parent element. For example, a single sequence of original text can be split into several sequences with the same formatting.
	no—The element cannot be replicated.
addable (elements only)	**[idrefs]**—List of identifiers corresponding to the `<addable-element/>` elements that can be added for this element.
unique (elements only)	**[attribute-name]**—The element uses the attribute [attribute-name] as unique ID.
unit	**char**—The `maxwidth`, `minwidth`, `maxheight`, and `minheight` values are expressed in characters.
	pixel—The `maxwidth`, `minwidth`, `maxheight`, and `minheight` values are expressed in pixels.
	byte—The `maxwidth`, `minwidth`, `maxheight`, and `minheight` values are expressed in bytes.
	point—The `maxwidth`, `minwidth`, `maxheight`, and `minheight` values are expressed in points.
maxwidth	**[number]**—The data cannot be more than [number] units wide.
minwidth	**[number]**—The data cannot be less than [number] units wide.
maxheight	**[number]**—The data cannot be more than [number] units high.
minheight	**[number]**—The data cannot be less than [number] units high.
maxsize	**[number]**—The data cannot have more than [number] bytes total (including any possible line breaks).

TABLE 7.1 CONTINUED

Attribute	Values
charclass	**[unicode-range]**—The data can contain only characters that are included in the set defined by the [Unicode-range] expression. This expression follows the same rules as the `unicode-range` attribute of the CSS2 specifications. (See `http://www.w3.org/TR/REC-CSS2/fonts.html#dataqual` for details.)
inline (elements only)	**yes**—The element is an inline element (an element in mixed content).
	no—The element is a structural element. The end of the element also marks the end of a segment.
	subflow—The element delimits a subflow within a structural element.
term	**yes**—The element is a glossary term.
	no—The element is not a glossary term.
word-break (elements only)	**yes**—The element is a word delimiter.
	no—The element is not a word delimeter.

TABLE 7.2

Other Attributes

Attribute	Values
version	Version of the localization properties definition format (used by `<locprop>`)
root	Name of the root element for the content type associated to the set of rules (used by `<rules>`)
name	Descriptive name of a set of rules (used by `<rules>`)
namespace-uri	URI associated with a set of rules (used by `<rules>`)
id	Unique identifier for the given addable element (used by `<addable-element/>`)
name	Name of the given addable element (used by `<addable-element/>`)
type	Type of element (bold, italic, and so forth) (used by `<addable-element/>`)

TABLE 7.2	CONTINUED
Attribute	*Values*
attributes	Text of the optional attribute(s) for an addable element (used by `<addable-element/>`)
item	XPath expression pointing to the element or the attribute for which the rule applies (used by `<rule/>`)

The structure of a localization properties document is shown in Listing 7.5.

LISTING 7.5

`LocProp.dtd`—Localization Properties DTD

```
<!ELEMENT locprop (rules)+ >
<!ATTLIST locprop
    version        CDATA                   #FIXED "1.0" >


<!ELEMENT rules (element-defaults, attribute-defaults, addable-element*,
➥rule*) >
<!ATTLIST rules
    root           NMTOKEN                 #REQUIRED
    name           CDATA                   #IMPLIED
    namespace-uri  CDATA                   #IMPLIED
>


<!ELEMENT element-defaults EMPTY >
<!ATTLIST element-defaults
    localize       (yes|no|inherit)        #REQUIRED
    datatype       CDATA                   #IMPLIED
    ws-collapsible (yes|no|inherit)        "no"
    moveable       (yes|no)                "no"
    removable      (yes|no)                "no"
    cloneable      (yes|no)                "no"
    addable        IDREFS                  #IMPLIED
    unit           (char|pixel|byte|point) "char"
    maxwidth       NMTOKEN                 #IMPLIED
    minwidth       NMTOKEN                 #IMPLIED
    maxheight      NMTOKEN                 #IMPLIED
    minheight      NMTOKEN                 #IMPLIED
    maxsize        NMTOKEN                 #IMPLIED
    charclass      CDATA                   #IMPLIED
```

LISTING 7.5   CONTINUED

```
    inline          (yes|no|subflow)        "no"
    unique          CDATA                   #IMPLIED
    term            (yes|no)                "no"
    word-break      (yes|no)                "no"
>

<!ELEMENT attribute-defaults EMPTY >
<!ATTLIST attribute-defaults
    localize        (yes|no|inherit)        #REQUIRED
    datatype        CDATA                   #IMPLIED
    unit            (char|pixel|byte|point) "char"
    maxwidth        NMTOKEN                 #IMPLIED
    minwidth        NMTOKEN                 #IMPLIED
    maxheight       NMTOKEN                 #IMPLIED
    minheight       NMTOKEN                 #IMPLIED
    maxsize         NMTOKEN                 #IMPLIED
    charclass       CDATA              .    #IMPLIED
    term            (yes|no)                "no"
>

<!ELEMENT addable-element EMPTY >
<!ATTLIST addable-element
    id              ID                      #REQUIRED
    name            NMTOKEN                 #REQUIRED
    type            CDATA                   #IMPLIED
    attributes      CDATA                   #IMPLIED
>

<!ELEMENT rule EMPTY >
<!ATTLIST rule
    item            CDATA                   #REQUIRED
    localize        (yes|no|inherit)        "inherit"
    datatype        CDATA                   #IMPLIED
    ws-collapsible  (yes|no|inherit)        "inherit"
    moveable        (yes|no)                #IMPLIED
    removable       (yes|no)                #IMPLIED
    cloneable       (yes|no)                #IMPLIED
    addable         IDREFS                  #IMPLIED
    unit            (char|pixel|byte|point) #IMPLIED
    maxwidth        NMTOKEN                 #IMPLIED
    minwidth        NMTOKEN                 #IMPLIED
    maxheight       NMTOKEN                 #IMPLIED
```

LISTING 7.5   CONTINUED

```
    minheight       NMTOKEN                    #IMPLIED
    maxsize         NMTOKEN                    #IMPLIED
    charclass       CDATA                      #IMPLIED
    inline          (yes|no|subflow)           #IMPLIED
    unique          CDATA                      #IMPLIED
    term            (yes|no)                   #IMPLIED
    word-break      (yes|no)                   #IMPLIED
>
```

The definition file for this DTD would be as shown in Listing 7.6. The only translatable part is the name of each set of rules.

LISTING 7.6

`LocProp.lpd`—Localization Properties for `LocProp.dtd`

```
<?xml version="1.0" ?>
<locprop version="0.1">
 <rules root="locprop"
        name="Localization Properties Definition Format" >
  <element-defaults localize="no" />
  <attribute-defaults localize="no"/>
  <rule item="//rules@name" localize="yes"/>
  <rule item="//addable-element@name" localize="yes"/>
 </rules>
```

You can see that this system enables you to describe document types that do not always adhere to the guidelines. For example, localization properties for the UIML format discussed earlier (refer to Listing 7.1) can be assigned without problems, as displayed in Listing 7.7.

LISTING 7.7

`UIML.lpd`—Localization Properties for UIML

```
<?xml version="1.0" ?>
<locprop version="0.1">
 <rules name="UIML 2.0"
  root="uiml" >
  <element-defaults localize="no" />
  <attribute-defaults localize="no"/>
```

LISTING 7.7   CONTINUED

```
<rule item='//style/properties[@name="content"]' localize="yes"/>
</rules>
</locprop>
```

Rainbow

Rainbow, the localization toolbox mentioned in several chapters, offers a utility to generate localization properties definition files. To run it, start Rainbow, select **Localization Properties Definitions** from the **Tools** menu, and then select the command **XML
Document Types**. An editor opens and you can create or modify definition files from
there.

This Rainbow utility is temporary because no official format is defined yet. The application will be updated as the ITS group works out the final specifications. Rainbow's
XML Document Type Localization Properties dialog box is shown in Figure 7.2.

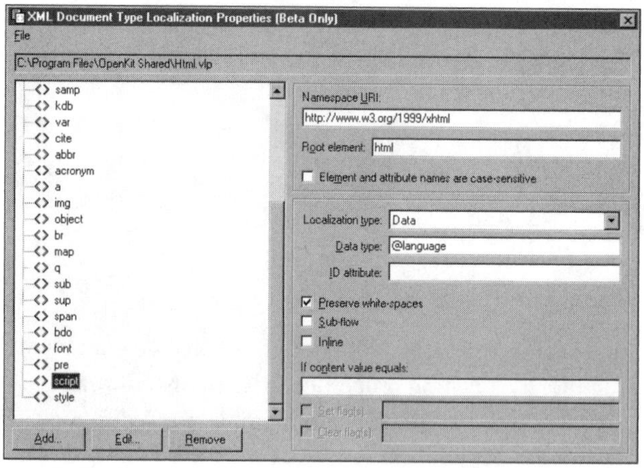

FIGURE 7.2
Rainbow's editor for Localization Properties Definition files.

Summary

When creating a new document type, follow the guidelines described in the first section of this chapter. Then provide the localizer with a clear description of your document type from a localization viewpoint: whether an element or an attribute is
translatable, what elements are inline, what elements or attributes have special requirements, and so forth. There is no standard way to present such information today,

but you can take inspiration from the localization properties definition format described here.

Keep in mind that not all localization properties can be defined at the document-type level. Some properties must be embedded inside the documents along with the data to which they refer. The next chapter discusses this, and offers some guidelines for authoring with internationalization in mind.

# CHAPTER 8

Writing Internationalized Documents

In This Chapter:

Even if the document type you are using has been developed with internationalization in mind, you will want to apply additional rules when authoring your documents. This chapter looks at a few guidelines that can make a significant difference when the documents come to the localization stage.

One method is the use of localization-related metadata along with the content to translate. The second part of the chapter discusses what localization properties are needed at the document level and how to implement them.

Authoring Guidelines

Although most of the rules outlined here apply to the documents created manually, they are also relevant when the files are generated from a database or from an application. These rules are as follows:

- Select the appropriate encoding.
- Use external files to include non-XML content.
- Use double quotes for translatable attributes.
- Use entities wisely.
- Write with content, not layout, in mind.
- Insert localization properties and comments within the content.

Each of these aspects is discussed in more detail in the following paragraphs.

Encoding

If you need to use non-ASCII characters, you can set the document to use an encoding that supports these characters. There is no need to use numeric character references if you can avoid it. A number of editors and authoring systems now support UTF-16 and UTF-8. If you do not work with one of them, use the relevant ISO, Windows, or

Macintosh code set specifically to the script you work with. For more details on which languages use which encoding see Appendix D, "Language Codes."

The use of the XML declaration is not mandatory; however, there is no reason not to use it. By default an XML document is in UTF-8 or, if the file starts with a Byte-Order-Mark, in UTF-16. Even though documents encoded in UTF-8 or UTF-16 do not require an encoding declaration, it is a good practice to use one systematically.

```
<?xml version='1.0' encoding='utf-8' ?>
```

UCS characters can sometimes be coded in different ways by using combining characters. For example:

```
á = U+00E1 (precomposed character)
á = U+0061 + U+0301 (sequence of base and combining characters)
```

The use of combining characters is rare in European languages, but it occurs more frequently in languages such as Vietnamese. Make sure that your document always uses a consistent notation. Mixing the use of precomposed and combining characters for the same letter or symbol will affect searching, indexing, translation memory matching, and other text-based functions.

Refer to Chapter 2, "Character Representation," for more details on encodings and related topics.

Non-XML Content

Some XML documents might have to contain non-XML sections, for example a script or a cascading style sheet. Whenever possible, use separate files for storing these blocks of data, and include them in your documents using processing instructions, XInclude, XLink, or similar mechanisms.

Because these data are in different formats, they may have to go through different localization processes. Separating them from the main XML body at the source can save a lot of time for the localizer, make the process safer, and ultimately result in better quality.

Double-Quoted Attributes

Try to avoid using translatable attributes, but in some cases you might not have a choice. In such cases, it is best to favor the use of double quotes to enclose the value rather than single quotes. The single quote character is the same as the ASCII apostrophe character, which is used quite often in many languages. Using single quotes would force any apostrophe inside the value to be escaped, whereas it can remain unescaped if the value is delimited by double quotes.

This is not a critical issue, but a detail that can facilitate readability and can be helpful when executing various tasks in the document using non-XML tools (for example, for a search and replace).

Entities

An entity is a predefined content that is mapped to a name. This name is then used anywhere in the document in place of the content it represents. In many respects, entities are very similar to the C/C++ `#define` statements.

Formats such as HTML used to offer character entities (for example `&aacute;` for the character á) to represent characters that did not exist in the code set of the document. There is no need for such entities in XML; simply use an encoding that supports the characters you need, as previously described.

The type of text you might want to map to entities is the one you share across documents; for example, product names, version numbers, repetitive sentences, and so forth. Be careful to always define blocks of text that make sense, not partial sentences or isolated words. For instance, many languages have adjectives or pronouns that depend on the gender and number of the noun.

You can also use entities to define styles. If for some reason you cannot use a style sheet and must set styles in various places in you documents, using a set of entities will help when the localizer adapts the styles for the new language. For example, instead of replacing a font name in many different locations, only a single change would be necessary.

Keep in mind that not all tools will deal with entities very well. Translation of entities may require extra steps. Also keep in mind that entities can be a problem when you want to reuse the translation with another document where the entities are not defined. As a general rule, do not use entities too much. In some cases they can be useful, but do not try to build some smart mechanism of dynamic content based on entities: It will most likely fail to work for the translated documents.

Writing for Content

Keep in mind that XML documents are about structure, not presentation.

First of all, when it is possible, use style sheets rather than embedding style and layout information within the text. CSS or XSL style sheets can be included in XML documents with the following processing instructions:

```
<?xml-stylesheet type="text/xsl" href="filename.xsl"?>
```

```
<?xml-stylesheet type="text/css" href="filename.css"?>
```

If, for some reason, you must implement presentation-related components inside a document, you still want to keep them to a minimum and avoid any side effects they could have on the translation.

For example, if you need to display a title in two lines in an XHTML page and use two elements for this, as shown in the following code, it will affect the way the sentence is segmented during translation:

```
<h1>Fourth Annual Meeting of</h1>
<h1>The Friends of The Moon</h1>
```

Instead, use a `<br/>` element. Although this is still not very elegant and breaks the rule to write for content rather than presentation, at least the integrity of the segment is preserved.

```
<h1>Fourth Annual Meeting of <br/>The Friends of The Moon</h1>
```

Beyond being helpful during localization, writing with content in mind rather than presentation has some benefits for your source language as well. These benefits include more consistency and an easier way to change the style.

Inserting Localization Properties and Comments

One of the most effective ways to help the translators is to provide them with context. By using localization notes you can improve the quality of the translation and reduce the volume of questions you will get from the linguists.

Such notes could be coded as standard XML comments, but it is better to have a dedicated element for this purpose. Tools can recognize such an element and present it more efficiently to the translators. In addition, having the notes stored in an element avoids any deletion that can happen with comments.

Some of the notes can be requirements, or types of information universally used. These can be more formalized and included as localization properties at the document level: for example, runs of text not to translate, restrictions in the length of an element, and so forth.

In some circumstances the XML documents can be generated from a database. If this is the case, make sure any localization property is stored in one or more dedicated fields, or generated from the field definition itself (for example, set a maximum width based on the size of the field).

The next section discusses in detail how to include localization properties in your documents.

Localization Properties Markup

The markup of properties can be done for both the XML content and the non-XML data that can be included in the documents.

Markup of Properties Within XML Documents

The best way to integrate a standard specialized markup in your own documents is to use namespaces.

As for the Localization Properties Definition, the ITS Project is slated to provide a standard set of tags for marking up localization properties within any XML content. The implementation described here is based on some of the preliminary discussions.

The properties necessary in a document are a subset of the ones that are available at the document type level. They are listed in Table 8.1.

TABLE 8.1

Localization Properties for a Document

Attribute	Values
localize	**no**—The data should be exactly the same after localization.
	yes—The data might need to be modified for the localized version. Its `datatype` indicates the type of modification to do.
datatype	**[text]**—The data is in a data type different from the main one. [text] indicates that type. For example, `javascript` would indicate data in JavaScript.
	@[attribute-name]—Same as preceding, but this time the type of data is indicated in the attribute [attribute-name].
unit	**char**—The `maxwidth`, `minwidth`, `maxheight`, and `minheight` values are expressed in characters.
	pixel—The `maxwidth`, `minwidth`, `maxheight`, and `minheight` values are expressed in pixels.
	byte—The `maxwidth`, `minwidth`, `maxheight`, and `minheight` values are expressed in bytes.
	point—The `maxwidth`, `minwidth`, `maxheight`, and `minheight` values are expressed in points.

TABLE 8.1 **CONTINUED**	
Attribute	*Values*
maxwidth	**[number]**—The data cannot be more than [number] units wide.
minwidth	**[number]**—The data cannot be less than [number] units wide.
maxheight	**[number]**—The data cannot be more than [number] units high.
minheight	**[number]**—The data cannot be less than [number] units high.
maxsize	**[number]**—The data cannot have more than [number] total bytes (including any possible line breaks).
charclass	**[unicode-range]**—The data can contain only characters that are included in the set defined by the [Unicode-range] expression. This expression follows the same rules as the unicode-range attribute of the CSS2 specifications. (See http://www.w3.org/TR/REC-CSS2/fonts.html#dataqual for details.)
term	**yes**—The element is a glossary term.
	no—The element is not a glossary term.
id	**[Identifier]**—In some cases, you might have to use document types that have no ID mechanism defined, and therefore you might not be able to use IDs for translatable elements. This attribute can be used as a fallback solution.

By using the namespace mechanism offered by XML, you can assign these properties to the content of the document in different ways:

- As attributes in any elements of the original document type.
- As attributes of a <loc:span> element that applies to a block of content, rather than the content of a single element.

In addition, a <loc:note> element, dedicated to localization-specific annotations, can also offer a better communication between the authors and the translators. This is a good way to carry information such as acronyms or term definitions, context descriptions, or requirements that cannot be expressed in another way.

To use the specialized namespace in you documents, make sure to declare its namespace. For example:

```
<?xml version="1.0" ?>
<myFormat xmlns:loc="urn:Localization-Properties">
...
   <!-- any localization properties can be used with the loc: prefix -->
...
</myFormat>
```

If you are using a DTD to validate your documents, you also need to declare the localization properties in the DTD.

First, declare the namespace:

```
<!ATTLIST myFormat
  xmlns:loc        CDATA        #FIXED "urn:Localization-Properties"
  ...
>
```

Then, you can simply include the declarations displayed in Listing 8.1.

LISTING 8.1

`LocProp.mod`—DTD Module for Localization Properties

```
<!ELEMENT loc:span ANY >
<!ATTLIST loc:span
    localize        (yes|no)                #IMPLIED
    datatype        CDATA                   #IMPLIED
    unit            (char|pixel|byte|point) #IMPLIED
    maxwidth        NMTOKEN                 #IMPLIED
    minwidth        NMTOKEN                 #IMPLIED
    maxheight       NMTOKEN                 #IMPLIED
    minheight       NMTOKEN                 #IMPLIED
    maxsize         NMTOKEN                 #IMPLIED
    charclass       CDATA                   #IMPLIED
    term            (yes|no)                #IMPLIED
>

<!ELEMENT loc:note (#PCDATA) >
<!ATTLIST loc:note
    from            CDATA                   #IMPLIED
    type            (normal|warning)        "normal"
>
```

Furthermore, any localization properties attribute that can be used in an element of the original DTD must be defined as well. For example:

```
<!ELEMENT title - - (#PCDATA) -(%head.misc;) -- document title -->
<!ATTLIST title %i18n;
                loc:id CDATA #IMPLIED >
```

After the namespace is declared, and if necessary the DTD is updated, using the properties is a simple matter of inserting them in the body of the document when needed.

Using `loc:id`

The `loc:id` attribute can be used as a fallback solution when you need an identifier for an element that has no attribute for that purpose.

For example, XHTML offers an `id` attribute for most elements. However, the `<title>` element is not among them. If you are using a localization process that relies on IDs, you can work around this problem by using the `loc:id` attribute, as shown in Listing 8.2.

LISTING 8.2

`LocIDSample.html`—Use of the Localization ID as a Fallback Solution

```
<?xml version="1.0" encoding="UTF-8"?>
<html xmlns="http://www.w3.org/1999/xhtml"
      xmlns:loc="urn:Localization-Properties"
 xml:lang="de" lang="de" >
 <head>
  <title loc:id="t1">Über PepperCreek LLC</title>
 </head>
 <body>
  <p id="t2">Unsere Firma in Japan ist auf technische Übersetzungen
➥spezialisiert, insbesondere auf dem Gebiet des gewerblichen
➥Rechtsschutzes.</p>
 </body>
</html>
```

As for use of the XML namespace method, if the attributes and elements are not defined in the DTD of the corresponding base document type, the document cannot be validated. But it remains well formed.

> **NOTE:** Remember that if you use `loc:id` with an ID type, each value must be unique in the entire document, even when applied to different elements.

Using `<loc:note>`

Some notes might be simple remarks, whereas others might be important information that the translators must see in order to understand the source text correctly. These notes can be mixed with additional localization properties:

```
<panel name="main" loc:maxwidth='23' loc:minwidth='23'>
 <loc:note from='developer' type='normal'>The text must be right-aligned
➥and fit in 23 characters.</loc:note>
```

```
<label id="main_user">           Utilisateur :</label>
<label id="main_connection">          Machine hôte :</label>
<label id="main_used">  Temps d'utilisation :</label>
</panel>
```

Using Attributes and `<loc:span>`

The localization properties attributes are passed from parent elements to children. In Listing 8.3 for example, the `loc:maxwidth` attribute specified in the `<list>` element is applied to each `<item>` element.

The `<loc:span>` element enables you to target more precisely the content to which the properties should apply. For instance, the first occurrence in the sample file sets a portion of a `<label>` content to remain not translated, while the second occurrence sets the same property for two `<label>` elements.

LISTING 8.3

`LocPropUsage1.xml`—Example of Attributes and `<loc:span>` Elements

```
<?xml version='1.0' encoding='utf-8' ?>
<screen name='login' xml:lang='en'
 xmlns:loc='urn:Localization-Properties'>
 <group pos='1:1'>
  <label id='login1' loc:term='yes'>Login name:</label>
  <text maxinput='12'/>
 </group>
 <group pos='2:1'>
  <label id='login5'>Password:</label>
  <text maxinput='8' hidden='yes'/>
 </group>
 <group pos='1:3'>
  <label id='login2'>Language:</label>
  <list sorted='yes' loc:maxwidth='30'>
   <item id='login2lang_en' map='1'>English</item>
   <item id='login2lang_ja' map='2'>Japanese</item>
   <item id='login2lang_ru' map='3'>Russian</item>
   <item id='login2lang_iu' map='4'>Inuktitut</item>
  </list>
 </group>
<label pos='3:2' id='login6'>Welcome to the <loc:span localize='no'>
➥Redwall 3.2 Application Server</loc:span> Network. Please, select the
➥language you want to use, enter your login name and password, and press
➥Enter.</label>
 <loc:span localize='no'>
```

LISTING 8.3   CONTINUED

```
<label pos='3:3' id='login3'>Copyright © 2001 - Redwall Inc.</label>
<label pos='3:4' id='login4'>All rights reserved.</label>
</loc:span>
</screen>
```

Markup of Properties Within Non-XML Files

Because XML documents can contain or be affected by non-XML data, it is important to provide a mechanism to insert localization properties in non-XML data.

The same instruction set could be used with only a change in the method of encapsulating the statement. It should be adapted to a non-XML environment. Specialized comments can be used for such a purpose.

For example, the equivalent of the element

```
<loc:span localize='no'>...</loc:span>
```

inside a JavaScript could be coded as follows:

```
/*loc:span localize='no'*/.../*/loc:span*/
```

There is also the need for an extra construct because non-XML data do not have the automatic range elements offered in XML. An additional marker to apply properties to the next translatable item in the file could be handy:

```
/*loc:next localize='no'*/
```

The following two listings provide some examples of how the markers can be used in different situations. Listing 8.4 shows a file with external entities and Listing 8.5 displays an example of the properties in a PO (Portable Object) file.

LISTING 8.4

LocPropUsage2.ent—Localization Markup in an Entities File

```
<!--loc:span localize='yes' -->

<!ENTITY str_OptionsTab "Options">
<!--loc:note This is the verb to file not the noun! -->
<!ENTITY str_FileTab    "File">

<!--loc:next localize='no' -->
<!ENTITY str_Start      "Scanner">
```

LISTING 8.4   CONTINUED

```
<!ENTITY str_NotesTab    "Comments">

<!--loc:next localize='no' -->
<!ENTITY connection      "http://www.theSite.com/Main.xsql?page=home">

<!--/loc:span -->
```

LISTING 8.5

`LocPropUsage3.po`—Localization Markup in a PO File

```
#@@v1.0 gettext v2.3

#msgid "str_outputnum"
#msgstr "Stampa il numero della riga con le righe di output."

#loc:next datatype='html'
#msgid "err_dupdigits"
#msgstr "compaiono cifre in due diversi <emph>elementi di argv</emph>."

#loc:note The -W refers to the Wrap option.
#msgid "err_noarg"
#msgstr "L'opzione '-W' non accetta argomenti."

#msgid "err_recursiveloop"
#msgstr "loop ricorsivo di directory."
```

Summary

A document type correctly designed for internationalization does not automatically lead to the creation of documents that are easy to localize. The way each document is authored is also important. A good practice to follow is to always keep things distinct: Separate content from presentation and XML data from non-XML data. In addition, the use of localization markup within the file can go a long way in helping the localizers to understand the content better and to apply tools for verifying that the translation adheres to any possible requirement needed.

As the authoring tools for XML mature, one can envision editors capable of dealing with namespaces, linking, and other XML technologies. Any application that also includes support for localization properties gives its users an advantage in allowing the creation of documents that can be integrated seamlessly in the localization process.

# CHAPTER 9

Automated References

In This Chapter:

Working with XML documents in multiple languages provides a strong case for content developers to look at how data can be reused within the overall system. For example, in a project that includes user interface, documentation, and online help components, it is inevitable for parts of the user interface to be referenced in the documentation and the online help. Taking the common text from the UI source and porting it automatically to the two other components is not a new idea, but with XML, it is a much more feasible one.

In this chapter we will see what advantages and inconveniences automated references bring to the localization process. We will then discuss several methods to implement such mechanisms.

Advantages and Drawbacks

Automated references already offer a number of incentives when working with a single language. These advantages are compounded when the data need to be localized into several languages.

Three main parameters drive almost any localization project: cost, time, and quality. Automated references help in all these areas, although not necessarily in this order.

Better Quality

Better quality is obtained first by offering better consistency. Using the same instance of a term in different outputs prevents a mismatch. This is especially useful during localization because a different translator might work on each component and synchronizing the translated terms might not always be easy.

Although there is the disadvantage that when a mistake is made in the original source it will be automatically propagated in the various components, you must also to keep in mind that, once found, the problem has to be fixed only once. This is true as well when a change needs to be made for other reasons; for example, when the terminology is updated in one of the languages.

As a general rule, the more manual dependencies you have across different components, the more dangers you have that the quality will suffer, for the source and the target languages.

Reduced Time

Time is also affected by automated references; for example, less extensive verification needs to be done and less translation needs to be entered.

Overall, having a unique source makes updates (for bug fix or normal changes) much faster. If the documents that have the references are rendered, the update happens when the output is generated. In other cases, when the data are to be updated in place, and then the files compiled or otherwise converted, tools or scripts can offer efficient solutions to do this. The amount of time needed to update references is usually very small.

Lower Cost

The benefits gained in the cost side are directly linked to time and quality.

First, there is obviously less material to localize. Because a large part of localization cost is directly associated with the number of words to translate and verify, reusing text reduces the word count of translatable material and ultimately the final cost. This might not be too significant for UI elements, but using a single source of data for larger chunks of text such as legal notices, repetitive boilerplate paragraphs, or error messages can be noteworthy when compounded by the number of languages into which the documents are translated.

The more important cost savings provided by automated references is in the late stages of the localization process when modifications are to be done, for example when a menu item is changed or when a dialog box is modified. Such updates are usually very costly because they have dependencies on the documentation, help, screen shots, and so forth. With automated references, getting the new text in the documentation is a matter of running a few tools. You are also able to eliminate reporting of bugs and their resolution, and cut down on the cost of re-releases, support, and so forth.

Also keep in mind that automated references do not always pertain to text data. XML documents can contain graphics or style references as well.

Dangers

The main weakness of using automated references is that in some circumstances the changing context around the reference can pose problems for the translator. This especially increases when multiple languages are involved. Reusing an identical text in different contexts is bound to cause some trouble when translating. In many regards you find here the same issues as you do when dynamically building a message from different variables. Most of the time translation is done within a single context (if any), and the data, once localized, might not fit the other contexts any more.

To avoid this issue, make sure the referenced text is self-contained and is used only after careful consideration. In some cases the use of references is natural, and in others you need to exercise good judgment. As a general rule, the smaller the reference will be (for example, a word versus a paragraph) the more likely you will run into problems. However, in many situations, even short references are safe to use. Referencing UI elements such as menu items, button labels, and captions makes sense because they will be clearly out of context in the destination documents and will already be treated as such (for example, put between quotes, or in a different font or style).

Reusing text should be done with strict guidelines on the authoring side and should be verified through testing procedures as part of the development cycle, before localization starts. Such tests could, for example, include pseudotranslation.

Before you start implementing automated references, you must assess whether the benefit you would gain is worth changing your source documents. There is no formula that works for all cases. It depends on many factors not necessarily linked to XML: the overall architecture of your product, the file formats involved, the tools developers and authors use, and so forth.

Automating the generation of documents means extra dependencies on the mechanism that offers the automation: scripts, tools, or even someone's knowledge. It also means some documentation to maintain, maybe more training, and so forth.

Entities

One mechanism by which to implement references is a built-in feature of XML (and SGML): the entities. They enable you to declare shorthands not only for a given character (for example `&aacute;` for 'á'), but also for a word, a term, a sentence, and even an arbitrary chunk of XML data. In many respects it is comparable to a `#define` statement in C++.

Entities can be declared in a separate file and changed independently of the document in which they are invoked. They also can be invoked from different documents, offering a way to declare a text only once and use it several times.

Entities are resolved when the document is open, before the rest of the document is parsed. Make sure the file where the entities declarations are stored is in the same encoding as the documents that use it.

Entities can be used efficiently for short strings, such as for a user interface coded in XML, or for constant text, such as product names, captions, and table headings.

One example of the use of external references is XUL (pronounced "zool"). XUL is the XML vocabulary utilized to define the user interface of the various components of Mozilla, the open source browser of Netscape.

In this instance, entities do not aim at reusing the same text in different places, but at simply separating the localizable text from the other common UI elements (scripts, options, layout, and so forth). A XUL file contains no translatable text, but only references to external entities. The definition of all the entities is listed in a separate DTD file.

Figure 9.1 shows the relationships between the DTD file (the file where the entities are located), the XUL document, and the resulting running application. Although it is not done in this case, you could easily have a single DTD for the labels that are common to all dialog boxes, such as the **Cancel** button.

Entities have several drawbacks that you must weigh carefully before making use of them extensively.

The first aspect to look at is the performance degradation: The more entities you have, the longer it will take to load a file. Obviously if the source files are compiled or converted to a runtime format, this problem goes away.

Offering the text for translation outside its normal location might not be always the best solution. Today's localization tools should have no problem dealing with XML files. The vocabularies can have clear indications of what is localizable and what is not, as we have seen in Chapter 7, "Creating Internationalized Document Types," and Chapter 8, "Writing Internationalized Documents."

Another use for entities is style. You may find it very handy to define only once a set of CSS statements that you can simply reference from different places. SVG (Scalable Vector Graphic) files often have part of their styles written that way. This helps when a manual adjustment needs to be made during localization, for example to change the font, the font size, or even the writing direction of the text. Listing 9.1 shows such a document and Figure 9.2 displays it in a browser.

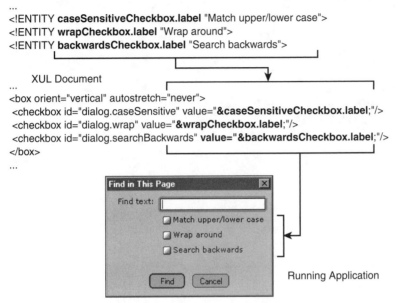

DTD File

```
...
<!ENTITY caseSensitiveCheckbox.label "Match upper/lower case">
<!ENTITY wrapCheckbox.label "Wrap around">
<!ENTITY backwardsCheckbox.label "Search backwards">
```

XUL Document

```
...
<box orient="vertical" autostretch="never">
 <checkbox id="dialog.caseSensitive" value="&caseSensitiveCheckbox.label;"/>
 <checkbox id="dialog.wrap" value="&wrapCheckbox.label;"/>
 <checkbox id="dialog.searchBackwards" value="&backwardsCheckbox.label;"/>
</box>
...
```

Running Application

FIGURE 9.1

Creation of the user interface for the Find dialog box in Netscape Navigator.

LISTING 9.1

`Style_Entities.svg`—Example of Entities in SVG

```
<?xml version="1.0" ?>
<!DOCTYPE svg PUBLIC "-//W3C//DTD SVG 20000303 Stylable//EN"
 "http://www.w3.org/TR/2000/03/WD-SVG-20000303/DTD/
➥svg-20000303-stylable.dtd"
 [
  <!ENTITY common "font-size:18;font-family:Arial;">
  <!ENTITY commonZH "font-size:18;font-family:SimSun;">
 ]>
<svg  id="svg-root" width="400" height="200">
 <title id="1">Style Entities</title>
 <g id="content">
  <text x="18" y="60" style="&common;font-style:italic;">Italic</text>
  <text x="142" y="60" style="&common;font-weight:bold;">Bold</text>
  <text x="278" y="60" style="&common;">Plain</text>
```

LISTING 9.1   CONTINUED

```
<text x="60" y="120" style="&common;font-weight:bold;">Odnośik</text>
<text x="220" y="120" style="&commonZH;">格式化</text>
</g>
</svg>
```

FIGURE 9.2

Rendering of the SVG file: The style, defined once, is applied to different parts of the text.

Overall, entities are probably the most useful for UI-type text where each unit is a rather short self-contained item, or for constants such as product names and versions.

XML Linking

Another way to implement automated references is to use the XML Linking features. The XML community has rapidly seen the need to standardize a single mechanism to link different parts of XML documents. The effort, initially led by the XML Core Working Group, is now the mandate of a separate Working Group (XML Linking) that oversees different standards: XLink, XBase, and XPointer.

XInclude, another related mechanism, is still owned by the XML Core Working Group.

> **NOTE:**   These related technologies are at different stages of definition. As always, check the latest versions on the W3C Web site.
>
> XLink is a proposed recommendation and its specifications can be found at `http://www.w3.org/TR/xlink`.
>
> XPointer is a working draft (last call stage) and its specifications are available at `http://www.w3.org/TR/xptr`.

> XBase is a proposed recommendation and its specifications can be seen at
> `http://www.w3.org/TR/xmlbase`.
>
> XInclude is a working draft and its specifications are available at
> `http://www.w3.org/TR/xinclude`.

XLink and XInclude address how to link or include data, whereas XPointer defines the way of describing the part of the referred resource that needs to be linked or included. Finally, XBase offers a generic attribute to solve URIs with relative paths.

XLink

XLink is a set of standard attributes grouped in a single namespace. It provides a generic method of describing relationships between documents or parts of documents. You can use XLink attributes in any vocabulary.

There are two categories of links: the *extended* links and the *simple* links. All links are actually extended links, but the simple links are the shorter versions in which default values are assumed for most of the parameters.

A simple link offers basically the same functionality as the `<A HREF="url" ALT="Title">` tags in HTML. Listing 9.2 shows a simple document where the word "here" is bracketed by an element `<ref>` that uses XLink attributes. The referenced page is offered in English or Polish.

LISTING 9.2

`Simple_Links.xml`—Simple Link Example

```
<?xml version="1.0" ?>
<?xml-stylesheet type="text/css" href="Classic.css"?>
<doc xmlns="urn:SampleLink"
     xmlns:xlink="http://www.w3.org/1999/xlink"
     xml:lang="en">
 <para>An error has occurred.</para>
 <para>To see more information about the problem, please click
  <ref xlink:type="simple" xlink:href="RefFile_en.xml">here</ref>.
 </para>
 <para xml:lang="pl">Aby zobaczyć więcej informacji na temat tego
  problemu, kliknij <ref xlink:type="simple"
  xlink:href="RefFile_pl.xml">tutaj</ref>.
 </para>
</doc>
```

The display of that file in Netscape 6 is shown in Figure 9.3. Notice that the underlining decoration is a built-in default.

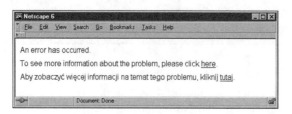

FIGURE 9.3

Simple Link implementation under Netscape 6.

If you click one of the links, the application behaves as if `xlink:actute=`
`"onRequest"` and `xlink:show="replace"` were set: Here it opens the referenced
file as shown in Figure 9.4.

FIGURE 9.4

Result of clicking on the link: The referenced file replaces the document from which the call originated.

XLink attributes, like any other attributes, need to be defined when using a DTD. In
our preceding example, the `<ref>` element could be defined as shown in Listing 9.3.

LISTING 9.3

`Simple_Links.dtd`—DTD for Simple Links

```
<!ELEMENT doc (para)* >
<!ATTLIST doc
   xmlns:xlink    CDATA        #FIXED "http://www.w3.org/1999/xlink"
   xml:lang       CDATA        #IMPLIED

<!ELEMENT ref ANY >
<!ATTLIST ref
   xmlns:xlink    CDATA        #FIXED "http://www.w3.org/1999/xlink"
   xlink:type     (simple)     #FIXED "simple"
```

LISTING 9.3   CONTINUED

```
xlink:href    CDATA         #IMPLIED
xlink:title   CDATA         #IMPLIED
xlink:arcrole CDATA         #IMPLIED
xlink:role    CDATA         #FIXED "http://www.company.com/reflink.xml"
xlink:actuate (replace)     #FIXED "replace"
xlink:show    (onRequest)   #FIXED "onRequest" >

<!ELEMENT para #PCDATA | ref >
<!ATTLIST para
   xml:lang    CDATA         #IMPLIED >
```

From an internationalization perspective you may want to convert the URI specified for the `xlink:ref` attribute in its correctly escaped form if it contains any disallowed characters. The rules to code internationalized URIs are given in Chapter 2, "Character Representation."

Beyond simple links, extended links offer many more options and enable a very wide range of relationships between documents.

An extended link is an element that has the attribute `xlink:type="extended"` and contains several child elements. Each child element can also have an `xlink:type` attribute that specifies its class: Locator-type, Arc-type, Resource-type, or Title-type. The other XLink attributes have various roles depending on which type of element they are.

A Title-type element can use the `xml:lang` attribute to specify to which locale the title information corresponds.

XLink is too rich and complex to be explained efficiently in the limited scope of this book, but it is a promising technology for localization because it will enable the development of composite documents regardless of the language of their content. In other words, it will enable sharing the same data across different structures, an aspect closely related to single sourcing.

The main drawback for the moment is the lack of implementations. As we have seen, Netscape supports simple links, but not yet extended ones. There are a few other applications and some libraries available that provide some level of support. It is too early to find many stable implementations of XLink, but they will come soon.

XPointer

XPointer is the language used in XLink to locate specific data within the resource described in a link. It is built on top of XPath, the notation also used in XSL and other XML-related standards.

Note that XPointer only works with resources of type `text/xml` and `application/xml`.

There are three main forms of identification: Full, Bare Names, and Child Sequences. For example, consider the following XML document (named `errors.xml` and located at `http://www.somewhere.com`):

```
...
<messages>
 <errors>
  <prompt id="opfail">Process failed.</prompt>
  <prompt id="norights">No read rights on this file.</prompt>
  ...
 </errors>
 <warnings>
  <prompt id="missingend">Query not closed.</prompt>
  <prompt id="toomanyblocks">More than 255 blocks.</prompt>
  ...
 <warnings>
<messages>
```

You can point to the prompt "Query not closed." in three different ways.

```
xlink:href="http://www.somewhere.com/errors.xml
↪#xpointer(id('missingend'))"
```

Full: The expression, enclosed in `xpointer()` (the schema name), uses the `id()` function. All the XPath functions and syntax are available also.

```
xlink:href="http://www.somewhere.com/errors.xml#missingend"
```

Bare Name: If `id` is declared as an ID data type in the document schema, you can simply call the identifier of the targeted element. This works regardless of the name of the identifier attribute.

```
xlink:href="http://www.somewhere.com/errors.xml#1/2/1"
```

Child Sequences: This is like walking through the nodes of the document. Our prompt is accessible by going to the first node of the document (`<message>`), then to the second node of `<messages>` (`<warnings>`), and finally to the first node of `<warnings>` (`<prompt id="missingend">`).

Overall, the use of IDs is encouraged with XLink. This goes well with a good preparation for localization. Text with unique identifiers can be manipulated and reused much more efficiently than raw data. It is especially effective to tie together the different translations of the same item. If you use IDS, they will pay off.

Another internationalization-related aspect of XPointer is the coding of the URIs. Here again the URI that XPointer uses should respect the encoding rules for internationalized URIs, as described in Chapter 2.

XPointer is very rich and offers extensions to XPath for specifying ranges, or more precise locations within a document fragment down to the character level. The principal problem is that implementing such a powerful set of functions will not come quickly. But once in place, XLink and XPointer will play an important role in constructing documents from different fragments.

XBase

This standard defines a new attribute, `xml:base`, which can be used as a base reference for resolving relative URIs. The mechanism is similar to the `BASE` attribute of HTML.

The attribute can be used several times in a document. When it is used in a child element, the part defined in the parent element is used as the prefix of the value defined in the child element. In other words, `xml:base` values are concatenated up as you go deeper in the document hierarchy.

Listing 9.4 shows an example of how `xml:base` is used in conjunction with XLink.

LISTING 9.4

`Base_Attribute.xml`—Using `xml:base` with XLink

```
<?xml version="1.0" ?>
<?xml-stylesheet type="text/css" href="Classic.css"?>
<doc xmlns="urn:SampleLink"
     xmlns:xlink="http://www.w3.org/1999/xlink"
     xml:lang="en"
     xml:base="http://www.opentag.com" >
 <para>Read about how
  <ref xlink:type="simple" xlink:href="otfandxlt.htm">XSL
   can be used with OpenTag</ref>.</para>
 <para xml:base="samples">And see an
  <ref xlink:type="simple" xlink:href="framedata1.htm">
   example</ref>.</para>
</doc>
```

The second occurrence of `xml:base` defines an addition to the first one because `<para>` is a child of `<doc>`, where the first `xml:base` was specified. Therefore, the complete URI for the last `xlink:href` is `http://www.opentag.com/samples/framedata1.htm`, not just `samples/framedata1.htm`.

As usual, it is recommended that you escape the value of `xml:base` when it contains any disallowed characters. The syntax for internationalized URIs is described in Chapter 2.

XInclude

The last XML mechanism related to references is XInclude. As its name indicates, this standard provides a way to insert external XML blocks inside a document.

XInclude defines a single empty element, `<include/>`, with the attributes listed in Table 9.1.

TABLE 9.1

Attributes for XInclude

Name	Presence	Description
href	Required	URI reference for the resource to include
parse	Optional	Indicator specifying whether to include the resource as XML (`parse="xml"`) or text (`parse="text"`)—the default is `parse="xml"`
id	Optional	Identifier of the `include` element

XInclude can prove handy to integrate common boilerplate text into several other documents. Because it uses XPointer, an extension of XPath, it also offers ways to select resources in specific languages. The reference URI can use XPointer to specify the exact location and range of the fragment to include.

For example, Listing 9.5 shows an XML repository that contains a legal note in several languages. That note is to be inserted at the end of different documents using XInclude. One of them is displayed in Listing 9.6. For this example we will assume that the note must appear in two languages for some legal reasons.

After the document is processed, the relevant included resources are now part of the output file, as shown in Listing 9.7.

`Inc_Repository.xml`—Common Text Repository

```xml
<?xml version="1.0" ?>
<repository>
 <block id="Legal1">
  <data xml:lang="en">
   <para><small>Note:</small></para>
   <para><small>This document is in accordance to the regulations
    outlined by the international treaty of electronic communications
    regarding documentation for medical equipment
    (ITECDME-13022000-AK47).</small>
   </para>
  </data>
  <data xml:lang="ru">
   <para><small>Примечание:</small></para>
   <para><small>Настоящий документ соответствует правилам, приведенным в
    международном соглашении об электронных коммуникациях в отношении
    документации по медицинскому оборудованию
    (ITECDME-13022000-AK47).</small>
   </para>
  </data>
  <data xml:lang="fr">
   <para><small>Remarques :</small></para>
   <para><small>Ce document est en accord avec les règlements promulgués
    par le traité international des communications électroniques
    concernant la documentation de matériel médical
    (ITECDME-13022000-AK47).</small>
   </para>
  </data>
 </block>
</repository>
```

`Inc_Document.xml`—Referencing Document

```xml
<?xml version="1.0" ?>
<document xmlns:xinclude="http://www.w3.org/1999/XML/xinclude">
 <title>Table of Contents</title>
 <para>This manual includes the following sections</para>
 <list>
  <item><para>Overview</para></item>
  <item><para>Blood Test CR-564 Protocol</para></item>
```

LISTING 9.6   CONTINUED

```
<item><para>Blood Test PT-2290 Protocol</para></item>
<item><para>HLA Group B Tests</para></item>
</list>
<xinclude:include
 href="Inc_Repository.xml#xpointer(id('legal1')/data[@xml:lang='en'])"
 parse="xml"/>
<xinclude:include
 href="Inc_Repository.xml#xpointer(id('legal1')/data[@xml:lang='fr'])"
 parse="xml"/>
</document>
```

LISTING 9.7

`Inc_Result.xml`—Referencing Document After Inclusion

```
<?xml version="1.0" ?>
<document xmlns:xinclude="http://www.w3.org/1999/XML/xinclude">
 <title>Table of Contents</title>
 <para>This manual includes the following sections</para>
 <list>
  <item><para>Overview</para></item>
  <item><para>Blood Test CR-564 Protocol</para></item>
  <item><para>Blood Test PT-2290 Protocol</para></item>
  <item><para>HLA Group B Tests</para></item>
 </list>
 <data xml"lang="en">
  <para><small>Note:</small></para>
  <para><small>This document is in accordance to the regulations outlined
   by the international treaty of electronic communications regarding
   documentation for medical equipment (ITECDME-13022000-AK47).</small>
  </para>
 </data>
 <data xml:lang="fr">
  <para><small>Remarques :</small></para>
  <para><small>Ce document est en accord avec les règlements promulgués
   par le traité international des communications électroniques
   concernant la documentation de matériel médical
   (ITECDME-13022000-AK47).</small>
  </para>
 </data>
</document>
```

The repository file used in this example could contain several blocks of common text, each in several languages. XInclude provides the way to pick the parts you need. A similar behavior can be obtained with XLink using the `show="embed"` options.

You must be careful with included resources. Because they become part of the referencing document they must result in a well-formed fragment in the new document instance. Some XML constructs might refer to declarations made in parent elements, such as namespaces and base URIs. The processing tool needs to carry over that information in the inclusion.

Customized Implementations

As you have already seen, one current problem of XML Linking mechanisms is the lack of implementations available. Mozilla offers basic support for simple links, but nothing for extended links. Only a few XML libraries have support for these technologies as of now. The implementation of XPointer is not trivial and it will take time for new releases of various products and libraries to provide better support. An alternate solution is to partially use XLink and have your own implementation.

As for using automated references to streamline localization, you can probably adapt a system with minimal effort compared to the interesting features you will get in return.

One important aspect of external references that is not completely addressed by the XML Linking methods is the modification of the referenced data.

For example, if you link an error message stored in a UI component to a section of an online help document, the original message might have characteristics that need to be altered to be used properly in the referring context. For instance, the message can have variables that need to be converted into human-readable text, as illustrated in Figure 9.5.

XPointer offers the `translate()` function that permits some very basic conversions of the referenced string, but only at the character level (and only one-to-one). This is not sufficient for our needs.

Beyond simple characters in some cases you might have to deal with inline elements that need to be removed or transformed appropriately. For instance, in VoiceXML (one of the XML vocabularies for voice-oriented data) a `<prompt>` element can contain one or more `<variable/>` elements, which are the equivalents of the `{0}` placeholder in the example shown in Figure 9.5.

Another issue not directly addressed by XML Linking is the resources in a non-XML format. Although XPointer offers powerful mechanisms to fetch data at the character level if needed, the implementation is still left up to the tool vendors. One way to bypass the problem is to use an XML document or a database as the intermediary between the referring files and the resource.

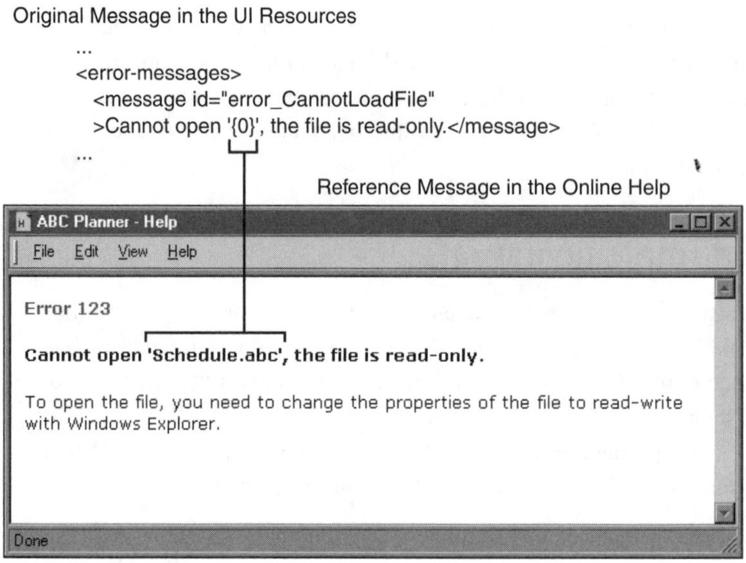

Original Message in the UI Resources

```
...
<error-messages>
  <message id="error_CannotLoadFile"
  >Cannot open '{0}', the file is read-only.</message>
...
```

Reference Message in the Online Help

ABC Planner - Help

File   Edit   View   Help

Error 123

Cannot open 'Schedule.abc', the file is read-only.

To open the file, you need to change the properties of the file to read-write with Windows Explorer.

Done

FIGURE 9.5

The message variables might need to be modified to be usable in other components.

Let's examine if and how it is possible to truly use different files in different formats (some XML, some not) for automated reference with the aim of reducing the manual dependencies between different components of a product.

The Scenario

We are part of a successful company that specializes in communications. Our main product (let's call it HandyPal-345) is a solution composed of different components, both software and hardware.

- **First, we have a handheld device of some sort**—It includes several embedded applications, written in Java and with the text of the user interface stored in property files. In addition, our little product sports a voice interface to drive its basic functions. The source text of the audio interface is stored in VoiceXML documents.
- **Second, we have a desktop application that provides some functions for the users to exchange data between a desktop computer and the handheld device**—The application is written in C++ and compiles on various platforms.

The localizable strings are coded like Windows resources, but are stored in PO (Portable Object) file for more efficient cross-platform development.

- **Finally, our solution comes with a complete user manual**—It is available both online (as XHTML files), and as a printed booklet. Both outputs are generated from a single source: a set of documents written in a proprietary XML vocabulary.

The user manual has many references to the three interfaces: the device UI, the desktop UI, and the audio interface. Our product is very popular and we must now localize it into 15 languages. The goal is to make sure the references to the various interfaces are reused automatically in the user manual.

The Solutions

The first idea that comes to mind is to have a single source file for the text that is used both in the interfaces and the documentation, as shown in Figure 9.6.

From an abstract viewpoint it make sense: The common file can be an XML document and the various necessary transformations can be applied during the process of updating the destination files.

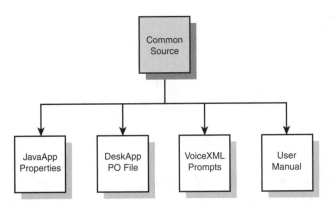

FIGURE 9.6

First possibility: one single source for all reusable messages.

But, after careful analysis, it appears to be too complicated for the user interface part.

Developing the dialogs and messages outside the normal development environment will be very cumbersome and time-consuming. For example, having an external reference instead of the real text for a label in a dialog box can cause problems: Changing the text in the common file and applying the update will not change the coordinates. From a development viewpoint it seems more efficient to have each resource in its original format.

So, the second solution aims at having less impact on the non-XML file formats and still allowing the same type of reuse across components.

This time we envision a common file that acts as an intermediary between the UI components and the documentation. The model, shown in Figure 9.7, still allows for referencing between UI files as well, if it becomes a need at some point. Each file can be either a referenced file (that is, containing the original text of a reference) or a referencing file (that is, containing a reference).

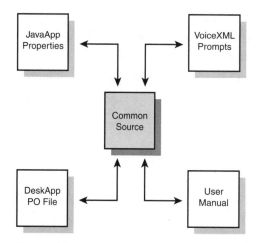

FIGURE 9.7

Second possibility: All files can be the source or destination of the references, and go through a single common middle file.

This model has two main drawbacks. The first is that an update must be done in two steps instead of one:

1. Update the common file from the original files.
2. Update the destination files from the common file.

However, this should not be a big inconvenience because the process is meant to be automated.

The second disadvantage is that we need to come up with tools to both extract from the source files and update the destination files. In the first solution no extraction was needed.

But it is probably a reasonable price to pay for having the luxury to still work within the normal development environment and still create and maintain the user interface components efficiently. In some other scenarios, it might be too costly to develop a sophisticated system for automated updates. This is a call that must be made in each situation. But keep in mind that even with a small number of references to the UI, let's say 250, when it might not be worth the effort with only one language, the stakes are different with 15 languages (3,750 references).

The Implementation

When the time comes to implement our solution we have to keep internationalization in mind. For example, when creating the Perl or AWK scripts, or the Java or C++ programs that will extract the text from PO files and properties files, we must take into account the fact that, if the text is now in ASCII, later on we will need to go from various encodings to UTF-16 or UTF-8 in the common reference file.

A possible fallback solution to deal with encodings is to add a step by converting each source file into a temporary file encoded in UTF-8, and then apply the extraction tools that update the reference file. As always, check first to see that someone else has not already come up with freeware utilities to execute some of these steps.

For the type of tasks our example requires, we can use Rainbow (http://www. opentag.com). This Windows application is a toolbox of various utilities pertaining to localization tasks. As we have already seen in Chapter 2, it provides, for example, a function to transcode text-based and XML documents from one encoding to another.

Here we want to use a utility that updates external references. It offers both update modes: from the referenced files to a reference database, and from the database to the referencing files.

The middle reference file could be implemented in various ways: As an XML document, we could use DOM to update and query it. Or, as with Rainbow, a mixture of database and XML document can be used.

The references are stored in a database, but an XML document is used to allow the creation and editing of substitution rules. This document has the same name as the database, but carries a .subst extension. It is generated at the end of each update of the database. When processing the referencing files, if the document has been modified since the last time it was created from the database, the application reads it first to update the database with the changed substitutions, and only then processes the destination files to update the external references.

When necessary, the operator can simply open the substitution document between the two processes and make any appropriate changes.

Because some of the replacement text might need to be localized, having an XML document for the substitutions offers another advantage: By using an XML file, the text is easily accessible.

The substitution mechanism itself is simple.

You can define generic substitutions first at the file level and then at the level of each extracted reference.

In addition, because the replacement text can vary from one output to the other, you might need to define several replacement texts for one given original token. The `class` attribute allows you to differentiate the various new text items.

There are a few rules to take into account when specifying substitutions:

- **The changes are applied in the order in which they are listed in the substitution document**—Be sure to avoid side effects of accidentally converting the replacement of a first token when processing the next one. Check that the new text of each substitution is not accidentally a pattern of the original text of the subsequent substitutions.
- **Make sure replacing a character is limited in its scope**—For example, in Windows resources & precedes the hotkey for the given string. You might need to replace it with an empty string in the documentation, but be careful with the escaped &. It is coded && and would be removed as well.

  To solve the problem:
  Replace && with $@$ (or any nonexistent pattern)
  Replace & with '' (empty string)
  Replace $@$ wih &&

To demonstrate how the whole process would work, we can run it on a few sample files. Listing 9.8 shows one of the properties files used with the Java embedded applications. Listing 9.9 displays one of the PO files for the desktop-side program, and Listing 9.10 shows one of the Prompts documents used by the voice system.

LISTING 9.8

JavaApp.properties—Java Properties File

```
# HandyPal error messages for connection module

err_cantopenfile = Cannot open {0}.
err_lostconnect = The connection with {0} has been lost.
err_readonly = The file is in read-only mode.
err_badprotocol = Invalid protocol declaration.
```

LISTING 9.9

DeskApp.po—Portable Object File

```
# DeskApp strings
# Connection DLL
# uses lib Orange, getstring() version 4.82

msgid  "menu_file"
msgstr "&File"
msgid  "menu_file_open"
msgstr "&Open Connection..."
msgid  "menu_file_reconnect"
msgstr "&Re-Connect"
msgid  "menu_help"
msgstr "&Help"
msgid  "menu_help_about"
msgstr "&About HandyPal-345..."

msgid  "dlg_about_caption"
msgstr "About HandyPal-345"
msgid  "dlg_about_copy"
msgstr "Copyright (c) 1937-2001 - Gandlaf Corp.\n"
       "Parachute - Colorado - USA"

msgid  "str_ok"
msgstr "OK"
msgid  "str_cancel"
msgstr "Cancel"
msgid  "str_close"
msgstr "&Close"
```

LISTING 9.10

Prompts.vxml—VoiceXML Document

```
<?xml version="1.0"?>
<vxml version="1.0">
 <form id="welcome">
  <field name="confirm" type="boolean">
   <prompt id="StartConnect">
    You have just connected to a PC.
    Would you like to start your pre-defined upload?
   </prompt>
   <filled>
```

LISTING 9.10   CONTINUED

```
  <if cond="confirm">
   <submit next="start_upload"/>
  </if>
 </filled>
 </field>
 </form>
</vxml>
```

Along with these three source files for the different types of user interfaces we also
have a file coming from the documentation side; Listing 9.11 displays it.

It includes several references to various items in the three interface source files
(marked in bold). The references are obtained using the `xref:ref` attribute. The initial
text inside the elements that will be updated does not matter much; in the original file
they are simply placeholders, and will be replaced by real text as soon as you execute
an update.

The documentation also uses external references for some of the common text that is
not coming from the interfaces: captions for the buttons on the panel of the handheld
device, product name, and so forth. Listing 9.12 shows the declaration for these entities.

LISTING 9.11

`Section6.xml`—Documentation File

```
<?xml version="1.0" ?>
<!DOCTYPE CaptionText SYSTEM "CommonText.ent" >
<section id="6" xmlns:xref="urn:Rainbow:XRef1">
 <header>
  <title>Interrupted Connection</title>
 </header>
 <body>
  <para id="234">Error:</para>
  <para xref:ref="JavaApp.properties#err_lostconnect">_errormsg_</para>
  <para>This error can be caused by a mis-connection. To reconnect the
➥&Handy; with the PC, execute the following steps:</para>
  <list>
   <item><para>In the Desktop application: select the
    <ui xref:ref="DeskApp.po#menu_file">_menuname_</ui> menu.
   </para></item>
```

LISTING 9.11   CONTINUED

```
<item><para>Select the
 <ui xref:ref="DeskApp.po#menu_file_reconnect">_menuopt_</ui> option.
 </para></item>
<item><para>Once reconnected, your &Handy; emits a short beep and,
 if your voice option is activated, it also says:
 <voice xref:ref="Prompts.vxml#StartConnect">_prompt_</voice>
 Ignore the question and press the &PanelBtn_Resume; button on the
 panel. You are now back at the point where the connection was
 interrupted.</para></item>
 </list>
 </body>
</section>
```

LISTING 9.12

`CommonText.ent`—External Entities Declarations

```
<!ENTITY Handy           "HandyPal-345" >
<!ENTITY VersionNum      "5.33" >

<!ENTITY PanelBtn_OK     "OK" >
<!ENTITY PanelBtn_Back   "Back" >
<!ENTITY PanelBtn_Resume "Resume" >
<!ENTITY PanelBtn_Cancel "Cancel" >
<!ENTITY PanelBtn_Up     "Up" >
<!ENTITY PanelBtn_Down   "Down" >
```

The first step is to build the initial reference database. Rainbow uses a Microsoft Access database through the ADO (ActiveX Data Object) engine. To create the initial reference database, we will execute the following steps:

1. Start Rainbow.
2. Enumerate the files we want to extract references from, in the list of the main window. To add the files in the list you can drag and drop the files or use the **Add** button. Here our input files are `DeskApp.po`, `JavaApp.properties`, and `Prompts.vxml`. The three sample files are located in the `Samples` subfolder under the folder where Rainbow is installed (`C:\Program Files\RWS Tools\Rainbow` by default).
3. Select the **Tools** menu.
4. Select the **XML Utilities** submenu.
5. Select the **Update External References** option. At this point a dialog box opens.

6. Enter the pathname for the reference database to create. For example,
   `C:\Program Files\RWS Tools\Rainbow\Samples\References.mdb`.
7. Select **Original Files** for the type of input file. This specifies that we want to extract the references, not to update referencing documents.
8. The option **Create a New Reference File** is set by default. Leave it as it. This would be used if we already had a database of the same name and wanted to re-create it. If the option is not set and the database does not exist it will be created.
9. Set the **Locale** to `English`.
10. Set the **Default Encoding** to `Windows, Western European (cp1252)`. Even if the files are only in `iso-8859-1`, this will not hurt since `window-1252` is a superset of `iso-8859-1`.
11. Set the root for the file identifiers to `C:\Program Files\RWS Tools\Rainbow\Samples`. This allows Rainbow to use relative paths for the filenames, while keeping the possibility to have same filenames in different sub-folders. The root is the longest path common to all files in the database. Now you should have the dialog box shown in Figure 9.8.

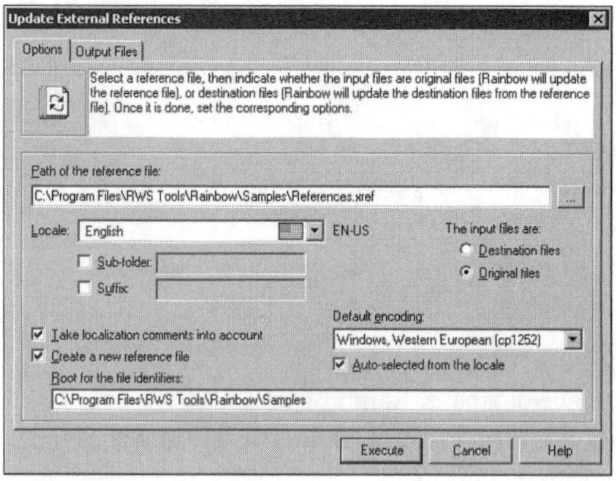

FIGURE 9.8

Options for extracting references to a database with Rainbow.

12. You have now finished setting the extraction options. The **Output Files** tab is not used in this mode, because the only file modified is the reference database.
13. Click **Execute**.

The input files are processed and the new database is created. At the end of the extraction the substitutions definition document is generated. It is shown in Listing 9.13.

References1.subst—Initial Substitutions File

```xml
<?xml version="1.0" ?>
<xrefsubst version="1.0">

 <!-- To add a substitution, add this element after the
      appropriate <text> element and set the attributes
      with the relevant values.

  <subst id="1" original="text to replace">
   <var id="1" class="class name" new="new text"/>
  </subst>

 -->

 <ref id="DeskApp.po#*" xml:lang="EN-US" status="new">
 </ref>

 <ref id="DeskApp.po#menu_file" xml:lang="EN-US" status="new">
  <text>&amp;File</text>
 </ref>

 <ref id="DeskApp.po#menu_file_open" xml:lang="EN-US" status="new">
  <text>&amp;Open Connection...</text>
 </ref>

 <ref id="DeskApp.po#menu_file_reconnect" xml:lang="EN-US" status="new">
  <text>&amp;Re-Connect</text>
 </ref>

 <ref id="DeskApp.po#menu_help" xml:lang="EN-US" status="new">
  <text>&amp;Help</text>
 </ref>

 <ref id="DeskApp.po#menu_help_about" xml:lang="EN-US" status="new">
  <text>&amp;About HandyPal-345</text>
 </ref>

 <ref id="DeskApp.po#dlg_about_caption" xml:lang="EN-US" status="new">
  <text>About HandyPal-345</text>
 </ref>
```

LISTING 9.13   CONTINUED

```
<ref id="DeskApp.po#dlg_about_copy" xml:lang="EN-US" status="new">
 <text>Copyright (c) 1937-2001 - Gandlaf Corp.\
➥nParachute - Colorado - USA</text>
</ref>

<ref id="DeskApp.po#str_ok" xml:lang="EN-US" status="new">
 <text>OK</text>
</ref>

<ref id="DeskApp.po#str_cancel" xml:lang="EN-US" status="new">
 <text>Cancel</text>
</ref>

<ref id="DeskApp.po#str_close" xml:lang="EN-US" status="new">
 <text>&amp;Close</text>
</ref>

<ref id="JavaApp.properties#*" xml:lang="EN-US" status="new">
</ref>

<ref id="JavaApp.properties#err_cantopenfile" xml:lang="EN-US"
➥status="new">
 <text>Cannot open {0}.</text>
</ref>

<ref id="JavaApp.properties#err_lostconnect" xml:lang="EN-US"
➥status="new">
 <text>The connection with {0} has been lost.</text>
</ref>

<ref id="JavaApp.properties#err_readonly" xml:lang="EN-US" status="new">
 <text>The file is in read-only mode.</text>
</ref>

<ref id="JavaApp.properties#err_badprotocol" xml:lang="EN-US"
➥status="new">
 <text>Invalid protocol declaration.</text>
</ref>

<ref id="PromptsApp.vxml#*" xml:lang="EN-US" status="new">
</ref>
```

LISTING 9.13   CONTINUED

```
<ref id="Prompts.vxml#StartConnect" xml:lang="EN-US" status="new">
 <text>You have just connected to a PC. Would you like to start your
➥pre-defined upload?</text>
 </ref>

</xrefsubst>
```

To edit the substitutions, open the document in a UTF-8–enabled application, such as Word 2000. Notepad and WordPad will also do fine if you are running under Windows 2000. Because we have only English text for now, it does not matter too much, but when non-ASCII characters are present you should be careful with encoding. Rainbow always uses UTF-8 to generate the substitution file.

Each extracted reference has a corresponding <ref> element where you can add new substitution rules.

In addition, each input file has a corresponding entry. This entry is to specify any substitution that is done for any reference from the given file. The IDs for these entries are the path of the file (without the root part), the # character, and the * character. For example: id="DeskApp.po#*".

The substitutions we need to define are simple:

For DeskApp.po we need to remove the & characters that prefix hotkeys and the ... sequences that have no meaning in the documentation. This should be done at the file level because it will apply to any entry in the PO document.

For JavaApp.properties we need to replace every variable placeholder such as {0} with a meaningful name. This obviously must be done at the reference level.

Listing 9.14 shows the parts of the document that have changed after the editing is done.

LISTING 9.14

References2.subst—Added Substitutions

```
<?xml version="1.0" ?>
<xrefsubst version="1.0">

  ...

  <ref id="DeskApp.po#*" xml:lang="EN-US" status="new">
   <subst id="1" original="&amp;&amp;">
```

LISTING 9.14   CONTINUED

```
  <var class="" new="$#$"/>
 </subst>
 <subst id="2" original="&amp;">
  <var class="" new=""/>
 </subst>
 <subst id="3" original="$#$">
  <var class="" new="&amp;"/>
 </subst>
 <subst id="4" original="...">
  <var class="" new=""/>
 </subst>
</ref>

<ref id="DeskApp.po#menu_file" xml:lang="EN-US" status="new">
 <text>&amp;File</text>
</ref>

...

<ref id="JavaApp.properties#*" xml:lang="EN-US" status="new">
</ref>

<ref id="JavaApp.properties#err_cantopenfile" xml:lang="EN-US"
↪status="new">
 <text>Cannot open {0}.</text>
 <subst id="4" original="{0}">
  <var class="" new="[File Name]"/>
 </subst>
</ref>

<ref id="JavaApp.properties#err_lostconnect" xml:lang="EN-US"
↪status="new">
 <text>The connection with {0} has been lost.</text>
 <subst id="4" original="{0}">
  <var class="" new="[Host Name]"/>
 </subst>
</ref>

...

<ref id="Prompts.vxml#StartConnect" xml:lang="EN-US" status="new">
```

LISTING 9.14 CONTINUED

```
<text>You have just connected to a PC. Would you like to start your
↪pre-defined upload?</text>
</ref>

</xrefsubst>
```

Note the workaround to avoid removing the literal & character for the strings from the PO file.

After the file is saved, we can move to the next step: updating the documentation from the reference database.

1. Go to Rainbow.
2. Enumerate the referencing files you want to update. Here we have only one input file: `Section6.xml`.
3. Select the **Tools** menu.
4. Select the **XML Utilities** submenu.
5. Select the **Update External References** option. At this point a dialog box opens.
6. Enter the pathname of the reference database to use, in our case `C:\Program Files\RWS Tools\Rainbow\Samples\References.xref`.
7. Select **Destination Files** for the type of input file. This specifies that we want to update referencing documents, not extract text to the database.
8. Set the **Locale** to `English`. The dialog box should look like the one shown in Figure 9.9.

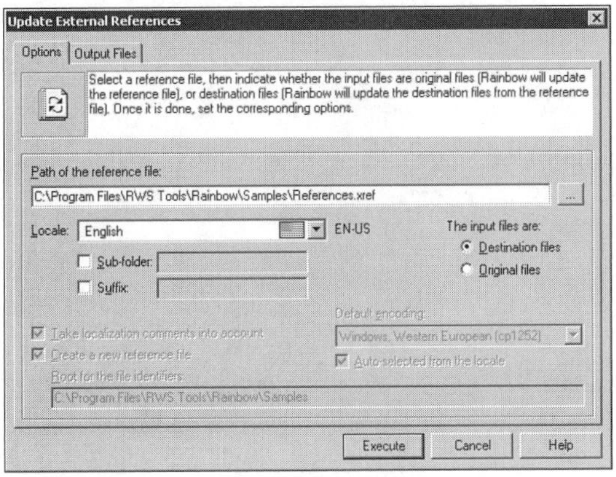

FIGURE 9.9

Options for updating the referencing files with Rainbow.

9. Move to the **Output Files** tab.

10. Set the option **Use the Following Extension Instead of the Original** and enter
    .out for the new extension. Most of the time you would simply overwrite the
    input files, but here we want to compare both documents after the update. The tab
    should now look like Figure 9.10.

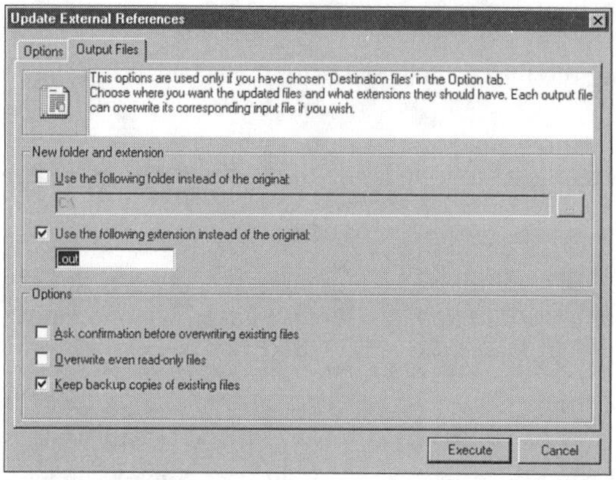

FIGURE 9.10

Output options: The new file will be named Section6.out.

11. Click **Execute**.

Rainbow creates the new XML document as shown in Listing 9.15. As you can see, the
text between the various elements with xref:ref attributes has been updated.

LISTING 9.15

Section6.out—Updated Documentation

```xml
<?xml version="1.0" ?>
<!DOCTYPE CaptionText SYSTEM "CommonText.ent" >
<section id="6" xmlns:xref="urn:Rainbow:XRef1">
 <header>
  <title>Interrupted Connection</title>
 </header>
 <body>
  <para id="234">Error:</para>
  <para xref:ref="JavaApp.properties#err_lostconnect">The connection with
➥[Host Name] has been lost.</para>
  <para>This error can be caused by a mis-connection. To reconnect the
➥&Handy; with the PC, execute the following steps:</para>
```

LISTING 9.15   **CONTINUED**

```
<list>
 <item><para>In the Desktop application: select the
  <ui xref:ref="DeskApp.po#menu_file">File</ui> menu.
 </para></item>
 <item><para>Select the
  <ui xref:ref="DeskApp.po#menu_file_reconnect">Re-Connect</ui> option.
 </para></item>
 <item><para>Once reconnected, your &Handy; emits a short beep and,
  if your voice option is activated, it also says:
  <voice xref:ref="Prompts.vxml#StartConnect">You have just connected
➥to a PC. Would you like to start your pre-defined upload?</voice>
  Ignore the question and press the &PanelBtn_Resume; button on the
➥panel.
  You are now back at the point where the connection was interrupted.
 </para></item>
 </list>
 </body>
</section>
```

The second time you run the first step (references extraction), the substitution file will have the `status` attributes set appropriately: `new` for the references that have been added, `same` for the references that are the same as the last time the extraction was run, or `changed` for the references that existed already in the database but have been modified in the source files. This allows a more efficient edit of the document.

Working with localized files will be no different. For example, the same source files in Polish can go through the same process. The translated files have the same names as the English, with a `_pl` suffix. Simply make sure to set the option **Suffix** and enter `_pl` in the corresponding box, choose the proper locale when setting Rainbow's options, and specify the correct default encoding for the source files (for Polish, use `windows-1250`). Listing 9.16 shows the Polish document after it has been updated with the corresponding Polish reference dababase.

LISTING 9.16

`Section6_pl.out`—Updated Documentation in Polish

```
<?xml version="1.0" ?>
<!DOCTYPE CaptionText SYSTEM "CommonText.ent" >
<section id="6" xmlns:xref="urn:Rainbow:XRef1">
 <header>
  <title>Przerwane Połączenia</title>
```

LISTING 9.16   CONTINUED

```
</header>
<body>
 <para id="234">Błąd:</para>
 <para xref:ref="JavaApp.properties#err_lostconnect">Połączenie z
➥nazwa hosta zostało przerwane.</para>
  <para>Ten błąd może być spowodowany wadliwym połączeniem. Aby ponownie
połączyć &Handy; z komputerm PC, wykonaj następujące kroki:</para>
  <list>
   <item><para>Wybierz <ui xref:ref="DeskApp.po#menu_file">Plik</ui> menu
➥w aplikacji Pulpitu.</para></item>
   <item><para>Wybierz opcję <ui xref:ref=
➥"DeskApp.po#menu_file_reconnect">Połącz ponownie</ui>.</para></item>
   <item><para>Po ponownym uzyskaniu połączenia &Handy; wyda krótki
➥sygnał dźwiękowy i jeśli opcja głosu jest również aktywna usłyszysz
➥zdanie: <voice xref:ref="Prompts.vxml#StartConnect">Właśnie połączyłeś
➥się z komputerem PC. Czy chcesz rozpocząć uprzednio zdefiniowane
➥nagranie?</voice> Pomiń pytanie i naciśnij na panelu przycisk
➥&PanelBtn_Resume;. Jesteś z powrotem w punkcie, gdzie połączenie
➥zostało przerwane.</para></item>
  </list>
 </body>
</section>
```

This example is far from a perfect solution and many improvements could be added. One is to offer a mechanism to specify the substitutions from the source files themselves instead of relying on an intermediate document.

Summary

In this chapter we have seen how important automated references can be for improving localization quality and cost.

Several methods are available: Entities work best with short strings, for example in a user interface. The W3C is also working on defining a complete and powerful system of links and inclusions through XLink, XPointer, Xbase, and XInclude. XML Linking promotes the use of unique IDs in your documents. This goes in the same direction as making your data more localization-friendly. You should use IDs.

Whatever strategy you choose, always keep in mind that you can highly customize XML files to fit your specific needs. The method of using an intermediary database demonstrated here is a good example of the flexibility of XML.

References

Some online reference documents are listed in the following text. The documents are identified as either working drafts or proposed recommendations and are still works in progress at the time of this book's publication. Make sure you get the latest information.

(working draft) XPointer Specifications: `http://www.w3.org/TR/WD-xptr`

(proposed recommendation) XLink Specifications: `http://www.w3.org/TR/xlink`

(working draft) XInclude Specifications: `http://www.w3.org/TR/xinclude`

(proposed recommendation) XBase Specifications: `http://www.w3.org/TR/xmlbase`

CHAPTER 10

Segmentation

In This Chapter:

- Principles of Segmentation   207
- Issues   208
- Possible Solutions   214

Translation tools, regardless of whether they are machine translation engines, computer-assisted translation workbenches, or leveraging utilities, all must process the text by units, usually called *segments*. The mechanism used to break the text into separate segments is called *segmentation*.

In this chapter you will see how tools can have different approaches to segmentation and what effect this has on the leveraging as well as on the exchange of translation memories.

The problems related to segmentation are obviously not specific to localizing XML documents but, as you will see, in some cases XML can be more conducive than other formats to solutions that reduce the volume of data that needs to be segmented.

Principles of Segmentation

The two main types of translatable text in XML documents are paragraph type and string type.

Paragraph-type text is the most common kind. It corresponds to text that flows from one sentence to another, with some formatting and embedded elements such as graphics. In this type of data, meaningful paragraph boundaries are usually clear, and dealing with text expansion is not too difficult. Web pages, documentation, online help, and any other narrative-oriented formats are some examples of paragraph-type content.

String-type text corresponds to some of the strings found in databases, resource files, prompts, dialog boxes, property files, and so forth. String-type text corresponds to user interface elements. In many cases this translatable text is rather short and often does not need to be broken down into segments.

When the text is translated with the help of a tool, the first thing that must be done is to break down the content of the elements into separate text units that are more manageable. For example, as shown in Figure 10.1, a <p> element of an XHTML document can be divided into two segments rather than translated as a single unit.

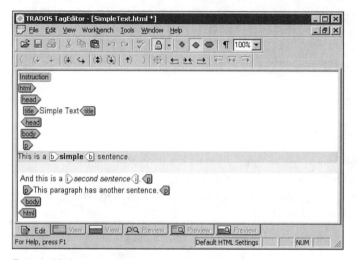

FIGURE 10.1

Translation segment by segment with TRADOS TagEditor.

Breaking sentences for Latin-based languages is usually not too difficult. But the rules can vary from one language to another. For example, the list of abbreviations you would consider to avoid creating "false breaks" is different, and the conventions for the number of spaces after a closing punctuation sign can differ (such as two spaces after a period in English, but only one in French).

These differences and other factors make segmentation as a task rather difficult to achieve, and also affect the use of the segments later on.

Issues

Segmentation problems can be sorted into two main categories: the problems of achieving the correct sentence breaks, and the problems appearing later in the process created by the fact that the text is now segmented.

Segmentation Challenges

Because languages use different scripts, the principles that drive how a sentence is constructed and delimited are different. One area where this aspect is quite visible is alignment.

Alignment, in the context of localization, is the task of taking two documents in different languages and creating a single list of paired entries where original and translation text are kept together.

Segmenting the entries in both languages means that the tool must apply different rules for each text. Because many tools are biased toward using English as the source language, some will have difficulty offering a very efficient segmentation in other languages. For example, Thai does not have spaces between words and loosely uses punctuation between sentences. Segmenting a text in Thai requires a very different algorithm than breaking sentences in any Latin-based language.

Another issue is the question of where to place the boundary of the segment. For example, do the white spaces between sentences go at the end of the first segment or at the beginning of the next? Should the tool even consider these white spaces as part of a segment or not? What rules should be used when the terminal part of a segment is not white space but, for instance, a closing parenthesis or bracket: should it be kept with the segment even if the opening character is not in that same segment? And then, what about the start of segments with characters that have a paired closing mark that might not be in the first segment?

Most of these questions are handled without too much difficulty, but sometimes the choices made for one tool are very different from the ones made for another.

An additional problem with segmentation is that on occasion, from one version to another, tools change the segmentation algorithm they use, creating loss of matches the next time you run your TM (translation memory) on the same document.

In the same line, because segmentation is not always reliable, tools usually offer a way for the translator to fix the segment manually so it makes sense. In many cases you can even change the segmentation rules altogether. This flexibility is necessary, but it has the side effect of losing matches again the next time the tool is used to leverage the same document. Its segmentation is not the same as the one used by the translator the first time.

Segmented Text Shortcomings

Regardless of whether the segmentation was done correctly, the use of segmented text brings problems during leveraging.

One main issue is the lack of context. Translation memory segments are stored in a database separated from the source and translated documents. As soon as a segment leaves its original location, a translator should verify any subsequent use of its translation. This is where reusing becomes recycling.

You cannot ensure that a segment taken from the TM is indeed the exact same instance as the one taken from the document. The text itself can be exactly the same, but the context in which you are recycling it can be very different from the original and can require a different translation. Worse, you can rarely verify with absolute certainty that in any given location you are using the segment that was taken from there originally. In short, there are no more links between the TM database and the documents, except the text itself.

For example, Listing 10.1 shows an excerpt of an XHTML document that contains two segments with the term "Help": once as a menu item, the second time as a button label.

LISTING 10.1

`Context.html`—Identical Segments in Different Context

```
<?xml version="1.0" ?>
<html xmlns:html="http://www.w3.org/TR/xhtml1">
 <head>
  <title>Overview</title>
 </head>
 <body>
  <p>Menu option: Help</p>
  <p>Select this option to open the online help.</p>
  <p>...</p>
  <p>Button: Help</p>
  <p>Click this button to open the online help.</p>
 </body>
</html>
```

The file translated into French is shown in Figure 10.2. As you can see, the two occurences of `Help` are translated differently. This is a simple case of terminology difference, but there are many other cases where a different translation is needed despite the fact that two source segments are identical. Grammar rules, especially with nouns, pronouns, and adjectives, can yield very different constructions in different contexts.

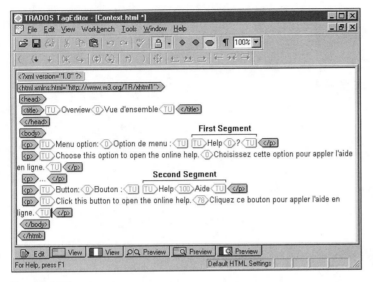

Figure 10.2

Two identical source segments here need two different translations.

Here the translator was able to correct the second segment as the translation for the first one was proposed. That is what you would expect from the TM: It offers choices and the translator can validate or correct them.

The problem comes the next time you use the translation memory. Imagine you have an updated version of the same set of files and run a pretranslation with the tool. The document has not changed at all. Figure 10.3 shows the document after a pretranslation. All segments have been leveraged, but the first Help segment now has an incorrect translation. If no verification is made for this file (and remember that there is no reason to do one because the file has only 100% matches) the leveraged document will go to production with a mistake.

The tool is not entirely to blame here: TagEditor behaves like many other tools. A quick look at the exported TM for this file shows that there are 6 translation units for 7 segments in the file, despite the fact that the duplicated segment has two different translations. It could be argued that a better approach would be to store an additional translation unit for the second Help segment rather than update the translation unit for the first segment. This could yield a fuzzy match for each Help segment and force a validation phase.

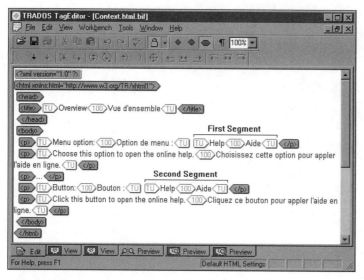

FIGURE 10.3

After pretranslation of the same file with the TM created in the first pass, the two identical source segments are translated the same way.

The bottom line is that the process would most likely not include a verification of the pretranslated file despite the fact that leverage done out of context can generate incorrect translation.

This is probably one of the main drawbacks of using translation memories with segmented text. TMs were developed originally to work along with the translators to provide suggestions they could quickly validate or correct. But the pressure for a shorter and cheaper localization cycle has pushed many to use this extremely useful tool in a way it was not designed to be used originally: batch pretranslation with little or no verification of the exact matches.

Aside from context-related problems, the segmentation of a document with the purpose of recycling text also brings a conflict of interest: You want to keep the segment as similar as possible to the original to make sure to get an exact match, but at the same time you try to make it as generic as possible to offer it as a possible fuzzy match for other segments. Finding the right balance is not easy, and here again, different tools make different choices.

XML documents also offer another interesting challenge with regard to segmentation. In XML, the translatable content flows normally from element to element, but on occasion, some translatable text also occurs as an attribute value, at the middle of the text flow.

For example, in the following excerpt of an XHTML file, the value of the `title` attribute is translatable, but it occurs at the middle of the main sentence.

```
<p>Click <a title="Start the service now" href="go.xml">here</a>
 to start the service.</p>
```

Using a translatable attribute is not usually recommended, but it does occur nevertheless and it generates segments embedded within other segments, or *subsegments*.

Two strategies are available to deal with a subsegment: Leave it within its parent segment or move it outside for the duration of the localization process.

With the first method, illustrated in Figure 10.4, both segments are seen as a single one by the translation tool, shown by the following code:

```
Click [code]Start the service now[code]here[code] to start the service.
```

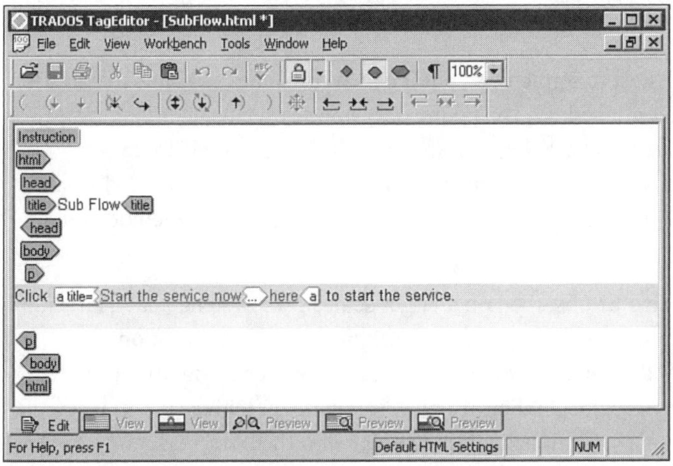

FIGURE 10.4

Subsegments in TagEditor: Both segments are merged into a single one.

With the second method, demonstrated in Figure 10.5, the subsegment is extracted from its parent segment and treated as a normal segment. The tool takes care of putting it back in the appropriate location when rebuilding the document, shown by the following code:

```
Click [code]here[code] to start the service.
Start the service now
```

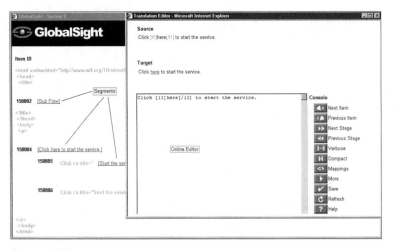

FIGURE 10.5

Subsegments in System 3: The attribute value is treated as a separate segment. SDLX and Déjà Vu also use this method.

The first option is the easiest to implement, but it generates some problems that can be avoided by using the second method. By having only one segment rather than two, some precision is lost during leveraging. For instance, if the `title` attribute is removed in a second version of the document, a tool that uses the first method would have to fix the translated segment, whereas a tool that uses the second method would have nothing to do.

The same problem can also be observed on a larger scale: Two systems that deal with subsegments in different ways will not be able to efficiently share translation memories. Not only will they end up with different segment breaks, but in this case, with a different number of segments. For instance, if you begin with a system using the first method, migrating to a system using the second method will decrease the number of exact matches (and fuzzy matches) you will be able to recycle. If the document type you are using has many translatable attributes this can be an issue to take into consideration.

Possible Solutions

Solving the various issues of creating reliable and consistent segments and using them for leveraging is not easy. We will explore first how to address the creation of segments. Then we will try to see possible workarounds when it comes to leveraging.

Standard Segmentation

Trying to come up with a method that all tools can use to segment text is very difficult. Each tool uses different techniques to find the break location. Some, like Transit, use regular expressions whereas others utilize a parser and a set of rules with parameters.

Common elements can be shared, such as the lists of exceptions ("etc.", "a.k.a.", "Mon.", and so forth), but this would not go very far.

If a set of common parameters could be defined, they could be attached to the translation memories files. But it seems unlikely such effort will take place.

In XML documents there might be a way to enforce a specific segmentation: Most translation tools offer the option to disable their default parameter, and all break segments at the structural element level by default.

This would create segments equivalent to the content of each structural element. If you want to further break the segment, you can use a specialized element to do so.

The main disadvantage of such a method is that it would decrease the number of reusable segments: the larger the segment, the fewer chances it has to be used several times.

Overall, it seems unlikely that the localization industry will ever manage to use a standard set of segmentation rules, or a way to transport tool-specific rules along with translation memories. But there might be ways to reduce the amount of text on which segmentation-based leveraging is done, making all these issues less important.

Reuse Versus Recycling

The various problems caused by segmentation would not exist if we did not use segments. But then how could we efficiently leverage previous translation? After all, the translation units are at the very heart of how a translation memory works.

Everything comes down to how we use translation memories. They are fine at translation time, when the linguists can validate or fix the suggestions of the machine. In short, they are fine when used for recycling purposes.

But the true reuse of text can be done before it comes to the translators, and without translation memories. In XML this can be done in such a way that exact matches are true exact matches: not because they happen to have matching content, but because they are two versions of the same instance of text.

Comparison of two XML documents represented in tree structures is much easier than dealing with other types of files where there is rarely a solid construction to rely on.

Furthermore, having unique IDs is not only easy to support in XML, but recommended. Identifiers would make the comparison a trivial programming exercise.

Assuming we have documents with unique IDs for each translatable element (let's call these identified elements *entries*), the leveraging/translation process can be executed using the two following steps:

1. Document comparison: Reuse at the entry level.

```
for each entry in the new source
    if ( same entry exists in the old source )
        then if ( both contents are the same )
            then if ( corresponding entry exists in old translation )
                then reuse it.
                else mark the entry for translation.
            else mark the entry for translation.
        else mark the entry for translation.
```

2. Translation: Recycling of the segments within each entry.

```
for each entry marked for translation
    for each segment within the entry
        search the TM for a segment with matching text.
        if ( exact match found )
            then recycle it as exact match
            else if ( fuzzy match found )
                    then recycle it as fuzzy match
                    else translate from scratch
```

The first step would be done prior to sending the document to translation and would generate an output where reused translation is already in place.

The second step would be done during translation with the understanding that, here, exact matches must be verified.

For example, with an XML document, if we used a specialized attribute (here `loc:id`) to identify each translatable structural element we would get a file such as the one shown in Listing 10.2.

LISTING 10.2

`Section_v1.xml`—XML Document with Unique IDs

```
<?xml version="1.0" ?>
<?xml-stylesheet type="text/css" href="StdOutput.css"?>
<doc xmlns="urn:myDocumentType"
    xmlns:loc="urn:Localization-Properties-Document:v1"
    xml:lang="en">
```

LISTING 10.2   CONTINUED

```
<section>
 <title loc:id="1">Saving a File in XML Format</title>
 <para loc:id="2">To save the current document into XML format execute
➥the following steps:</para>
 <steplist>
  <step>
   <para loc:id="3">Select the command <ui>Save As</ui> from the
➥<ui>File</ui> menu.</para>
  </step>
  <step>
   <para loc:id="4">Enter the name of the XML document. If a file with
➥the same name already exists you will be prompted to confirm the
➥replacement of the old file by the one you are saving now.</para>
  </step>
  <step>
   <para loc:id="5">Select the option <ui>XML Document</ui> in the
➥<ui>Format</ui> list box.</para>
  </step>
  <step>
   <para loc:id="6">Click the <ui>OK</ui> button.</para>
  </step>
 </steplist>
 </section>
</doc>
```

The identifier attribute could be part of the main namespace, as long as it could be used in any translatable element.

After the first version of our document is localized, the source text is modified and needs to be sent to localization again. Listing 10.3 shows the new version, with the modification in bold text.

LISTING **10.3**

`Section_v2.xml`—Second Version of the Document

```
<?xml version="1.0" ?>
<?xml-stylesheet type="text/css" href="StdOutput.css"?>
<doc xmlns="urn:myDocumentType"
     xmlns:loc="urn:Localization-Properties-Document:v1"
     xml:lang="en">
 <section>
  <title loc:id="1">Saving a Document in XML Format</title>
```

LISTING 10.3   CONTINUED

```
   <para loc:id="2">To save the current document into XML format execute
↪the following steps:</para>
   <steplist>
    <step>
     <para loc:id="3">Select the command <ui>Export</ui> from the
↪<ui>File</ui> menu.</para>
    </step>
    <step>
     <para loc:id="4">Enter the name of the XML document. If a file with
↪the same name already exists you will be prompted to confirm the
↪replacement of the old file by the one you are exporting now.</para>
    </step>
    <step>
     <para loc:id="7">Make sure the extension of your filename is
↪xml.</para>
    </step>
    <step>
     <para loc:id="5">Select the option <ui>XML Document</ui> in the
↪<ui>Format</ui> list box.</para>
    </step>
    <step>
     <para loc:id="6">Click the <ui>OK</ui> button.</para>
    </step>
   </steplist>
  </section>
</doc>
```

Applying our algorithm, we find that entries 1, 3, and 4 existed in the previous version, but have been modified, and that entry 7 is a new one.

Only these four entries need to be sent for translation. The translation previously done can be reused directly for the other entries, as shown in Listing 10.4.

LISTING 10.4

Section_v2_fr.xml—Pretranslated Second Version of the Document

```
<?xml version="1.0" ?>
<?xml-stylesheet type="text/css" href="StdOutput.css"?>
<doc xmlns="urn:myDocumentType"
     xmlns:loc="urn:Localization-Properties-Document:v1"
     xml:lang="fr">
 <section>
```

LISTING **10.4** CONTINUED

```
<title loc:id="1" xml:lang="en">Saving a Document in XML Format</title>
<para loc:id="2">Pour enregistrer le document courant au format XML,
executez les instructions suivantes :</para>
<steplist>
 <step>
  <para loc:id="3" xml:lang="en">Select the command <ui>Export</ui>
from the <ui>File</ui> menu.</para>
 </step>
 <step>
  <para loc:id="4" xml:lang="en">Enter the name of the XML document.
If a file with the same name already exists you will be prompted to
confirm the replacement of the old file by the one you are exporting
now.</para>
 </step>
 <step>
  <para loc:id="7" xml:lang="en">Make sure the extension of your
filename is xml.</para>
 </step>
 <step>
  <para loc:id="5">Sélectionnez l'option <ui>Document XML</ui> dans la
liste <ui>Format</ui>.</para>
 </step>
 <step>
  <para loc:id="6">Cliquez <ui>OK</ui>.</para>
 </step>
</steplist>
</section>
</doc>
```

At this point our process encounters a problem: The translation tools currently on the market are not designed to use input files already half-translated. This is unfortunate, especially for XML where the language of each element can be easily identified with xml:lang. However, because of the growing need for such features, some efforts have been done in that direction. For example, a new extraction format like XLIFF (XML Localisation Interchange File Format) is especially designed to provide pretranslated text along with the text to localize. See Chapter 17, "Extracted Text," for more details.

In the meantime, there are two workarounds.

First, we could extract the entries that need work and send them as isolated strings. But this is far from being the preferred way: The translator would lose the context around each entry to translate. Always remember that the less context you offer to the translators, the more difficult and less accurate their translation will be.

The second solution is to send our bilingual file, but in a format that translation tools can deal with, and where only the remaining English text is marked as translatable.

One of the formats that allows this is RTF, with specific styles for the nontranslatable parts.

In Figure 10.6, our bilingual document is prepared with an RTF layer that uses TRADOS conventions (except for the background colors, which have been changed to be more visible in the screen capture).

You will notice that the xml:lang attributes marking the English entries have been removed because they are not used in this environment. The file is then ready to be translated into French after it is saved as plain text in UTF-8 or UTF-16.

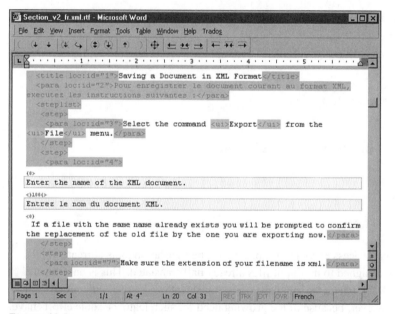

FIGURE **10.6**

A bilingual document with an RTF Layer where the nontranslatable text is in special styles (with a darker background).

The translation memory used during the localization of the first version is available, and we can utilize it for fuzzy matches and entries that have several segments, some untouched. For example, the first segment of entry 4 has not been modified and the exact match can be used as-is.

We obviously have the same segment-related issues as before, but this time the text that could be affected is only the entries that have changed. Like entry 2, any entry that was the same in the new and old source documents has been reused without going through the TM mechanism. On a complete set of documents, this makes a significant difference.

There are different ways to implement such a leveraging method:

It can be done through specialized programs that use the DOM (Document Object Model) interface to compare the two versions of the XML documents. A more robust approach is to use a database, either as an intermediate repository (like a "smarter" TM) or as the repository where the original text is stored and from where the XML documents are generated. At this point we are reaching the boundaries of document management solutions, which are the true solution for reuse.

An issue with this type of leveraging is the question of unique IDs. Most authoring tools will not generate and manage IDs. This is an area where they need to improve: Identifiers are often very useful with XML, not just for localization.

A fallback solution is to write a tool that would go through any XML document and add IDs to specified elements. This obviously does not prevent duplications you can introduce into a document with Copy/Paste changes.

As the providers of XML tools better understand the need for identifiers, these technical issues will be solved step by step.

Summary

This chapter showed how difficult it is to achieve a consistent and reliable segmentation. This causes problems when migrating translation memories from one system to another. Solutions that use standard methods for segmenting or exchanging segmentation information are problematical to implement.

To solve some of the issues brought by the segmentation-based mechanism used by the translation tools, you might want to look at alternative ways to pretranslate the XML documents and manage the reuse of translation upstream in the localization process.

However, at translation time, the TM-based tools remain important and efficient to use as a recycling engine on the parts that cannot be reused automatically.

# CHAPTER 11

Mixed Data

In This Chapter:

The number of technologies used to build a single application has risen dramatically in the past five years. More products are now based on N-tier architectures, and this is a factor in the increased complexity of the way translatable data are handled: Each component can use different programming languages and different resource mechanisms, reside on different platforms, and offer different levels of internationalization support.

Today you can have scenarios such as the following: An application with a Web interface (partially through standard UI, partially through Web pages) uses queries (coded in both stored procedures and application resources) to get data from a database, and displays the results using auxiliary files such as XSL templates and cascading style sheets (CSS).

You can have script source code in XML documents, and XML markup in software strings. More complex schemes are frequent too; for example, some XML markup in strings within a script source code, itself encapsulated inside an XML fragment that is stored in a database.

The combinations are infinite and the developers, being imaginative by nature, have an astonishing capacity to come up regularly with new, interesting variations. When it is time to do the localization, if all these creative efforts have not been thought out with internationalization in mind, they often shatter against a sudden concrete wall of realities with a resounding impact on cost and schedule.

Mixed data, even when it represents only a small fraction of the material to localize, can be expensive to deal with. You can separate mixed data into two main categories (although combinations of both are not rare):

- XML documents that contain non-XML data (for example, a script in an XHTML file).
- XML fragments encapsulated in non-XML containers (for instance, XSQL statements in a resource file string).

In this chapter we look at the different problems related to the localization of such data and discuss the possible workarounds.

Problems with Mixed Data

Regardless of the category involved, mixed data usually offer the same types of challenges.

One challenge is the difficulty of identifying the subset of embedded data. Where does it start in the stream of code and text, where does it end, and what is its type? For example, in Listing 11.1, there are no easy ways to distinguish which strings are XML codes only, which are text only, and which contain both. In addition there are no indications about the specific vocabulary used for the XML data.

LISTING 11.1

`Sample.js`—Example of Embedded XML

```
function PrintInfo ( p_sLogin, p_sPermissions )
{
   sOut = "<cell>User: " + "<emphasis>" + p_sLogin
        + "</emphasis></cell><cell>"
        + "Permissions: " + p_Permissions + "</cell>";
   document.write("<row class='info'>" + sOut + "</row>");
}
```

Another problem concerns escaped characters. Most of the time tools will be used to extract or mark up the text for translation. When several types of data are embedded, escaped characters cause various problems:

- The tools might not be able to switch to a different filter when they find a run of embedded data, and therefore the escape mechanism they expect might still be the one for the parent data.

- The tools have difficulty matching these entries with the ones that are coming from non-embedded source where the escaped characters are not the same or are not escaped in the same way.
- If the translation includes characters that must be escaped, multiple levels of escapes are more likely to be entered incorrectly.

Finally, in Client/Server architecture, the original source documents are often not the same as the ones presented on the client side. The source of an XML file served up over the Internet can be in a very different form than when it is displayed on the client. In many cases the final document does not exist as a single original instance, but rather as an assortment of separate parts in different formats, sometimes in different locations. These parts undergo various transformations (that can involve yet another set of ancillary files) to compose the final document. When localizing, you then must work with data in proprietary formats or in an incomplete form. This adds to the complexity of preparing for localization. Using good development practices, including testing and pseudo-translation, can reduce the impact of this type of architecture.

Non-XML Data in XML Containers

Two categories of non-XML data can be found in XML containers:

- Data that are expected by the XML vocabulary in which they are embedded. This could be, for example, a block of data in JGSF (Java Grammar Speech Format) in a VoiceXML document, or a script in an XHTML page.
- Data that occur because the XML document is not in its final form. Strictly speaking, the container is not an XML document, but in practice it will often be treated as XML. This is true, for instance, in the case of some forms of JSP (JavaServer Pages), ASP (Active Server Pages), and other server-side formats.

There are different ways to encapsulate these blocks in an XML stream. They include NOTATION declarations, legal comments, Processing instructions, and special markers. In addition, CDATA sections and DOCTYPE declarations can also present some aspects related to mixed data.

NOTATION Declarations

XML permits the use of NOTATION declarations. This construct enables you to declare a specific type of content (anything you want) and use it through unparsed entities. The notation type must be declared in your DTD. For example:

```
...
<!NOTATION DosShell    SYSTEM "dosshell">
<!NOTATION CShell      SYSTEM "cshell">
```

```
...
<!ELEMENT Shell         (#PCDATA) >
<!ATTLIST Shell
    type   NOTATION     (DosShell | CShell) #REQUIRED
    file   ENTITY       #REQUIRED
>
...
```

Then, in the document, you use entities to invoke the data:

```
...
<!ENTITY cmdFormat SYSTEM "cmdFormat.bat" NDATA DosShell >
...
<Shell type="DosShell" file="cmdFormat">
 This command format file1.tmp after sorting.
</Shell>
...
```

This could be used, for instance, to insert image or multimedia data in your documents. While most translation tools do not process the content of an element or an attribute based on the DTDs, this mechanism at least isolates the non-XML data from the XML content.

Comments

Comments are often seen as an easy way to hide non-XML data from the XML processors, enabling only tools that specialize in parsing a given type of document to recognize the special comments and treat them accordingly.

For example, Sybase PowerDynamo uses comments to embed instructions in XML templates. An example is shown in Listing 11.2.

LISTING 11.2

`Sales.xml`—PowerDynamo Instructions in Comments

```
<?xml version="1.0" ?>
<?xml-stylesheet type="text/css" href="Sales.css" ?>
<results>
 <para class='title'>Sales per Associate</para>
 <list>
 <!--SCRIPT
     connection = site.GetConnection("theConnection");
     query = connection.CreateQuery("SELECT nameid totalamount FROM
➥Sales");
     while ( query.MoveNext() )
```

LISTING **11.2** CONTINUED

```
    {
        xOut = "<item>";
        xOut += "<name>" + query.GetValue(1) + "</name>;
        if ( query.GetValue(2) >= 10000 )
        {
            xOut += "<score>High</score>;
            xOut += <amount class='high'>";
        }
        else
        {
            xOut += "<score>Low</score>";
            xOut += "<amount>";
        }
        xOut += query.GetValue(2) + "</amount>";
        xOut += "</item>";
        document.writeln(xOut);
    }
  -->
 </list>
 <para>The item in red indicate the sales greater or equal to
➥$10,000.</para>
</results>
```

The special instructions will be completely ignored by a normal XML parser because they are comments. Beware that some tools or editors can even remove comments.

For this type of non-XML data, translation utilities must be written to understand the specific instructions and be able to find translatable text in them.

In HTML, scripts and style definition were often enclosed inside comments as well. Note that in XHTML these elements should be enclosed in CDATA sections, not in comments.

The following is incorrect:

```
<script language="JavaScript">
<!-- // Hide the code from XML processors
   function myFunction ()
   {
   ...
   }
//-->
</script>
```

However, use of the CDATA section in the following is correct:

```
<script language="JavaScript">
<![CDATA[
   function myFunction ()
   {
   ...
   }
]]>
</script>
```

Processing Instructions

Usually, processing instructions do not contain translatable text, but sometimes they can have parameters that need to be changed: encoding declarations, URLs, and so forth. As an example, look at the standard `xml-stylesheet` statement:

```
<?xml-stylesheet type="text/css" href="classic_en-us.css" ?>
```

If the authoring tools used to create and deploy the XML documents use processing instructions, you must make sure this is communicated to the localizer, along with the parts that might have to be changed to adapt the file for a different language.

Some server-side formats, such as PHP (Personal Home Page), use the processing instructions to encapsulate their directives. As for other server-side languages, a specialized filter needs to be used by the translation tools to isolate any possible localizable parts.

In the case of PHP, you can use a function such as `gettext()` that enables you to externalize the translatable text in separate files, leaving only code-related data in the PHP blocks.

Special Markers

Some other server-side formats have chosen to use their own delimiters; for example, JSP and ASP use `<% ... %>`.

In some cases these special markers have opted for XML-like syntax but are not following the XML namespace usage, making parsing difficult. For example, ColdFusion tags can be embedded in XML documents and contain text parts.

Alternatives to special markers are also sometimes available. For example, in XML documents JSP is now enabled to use namespaces, a better solution than special markers.

For localization, all these languages require processing by filters that understand their specific syntax and are able to make the difference between translatable text and codes.

Avoiding the presence of translatable text in the embedded instruction, when possible, is helpful. For example, with JSP, you can define a Tag Library that can use Java's rich API to deal with resource bundles, formatted messages, and other aspects related to localization.

CDATA Sections

CDATA sections are blocks of data where characters are not escaped and XML tags cannot be used. Given that, by definition, non-XML data has no tags, CDATA can be an efficient encapsulation method.

As we have already seen, XHTML promotes the use of CDATA sections for script and style definitions, but this can be extended to any special content. For instance, the following is a block of JSGF code (Java Speech Grammar Format) inside the `<grammar>` element with VoiceXML:

```
...
<grammar type="application/x-jsgf">
 <![CDATA[
  public <toppings> = (mushrooms | pepperoni | pineapples | anchovies)
    {topping};
  [I (want | would like)] ({topping} [and])*;
 ]]>
</grammar>
...
```

DOCTYPE Declarations

Because DOCTYPE declarations are part of the XML specifications, translation tools should be able to handle them efficiently.

They might need to be parsed and examined for localizable content as well: Entity definitions might have to be translated or adapted as shown in Listing 11.3.

LISTING 11.3

EntSample.svg—DOCTYPE Declaration with Localizable Parts

```
<?xml version="1.0" ?>
<!DOCTYPE svg PUBLIC "-//W3C//DTD SVG 20000303 Stylable//EN"
 "http://www.w3.org/TR/2000/03/WD-SVG-20000303/DTD/
➥svg-20000303-stylable.dtd"
```

LISTING 11.3   CONTINUED

```
[
 <!ENTITY common "font-size:18;font-family:Arial;">
 <!ENTITY SampleText "The Quick Brown Fox" >
]>
<svg  id="svg-root" width="400" height="200">
 <title id="1">Using Entities</title>
 <g id="content">
  <text x="18" y="30" style="&common;
➥font-style:italic;">&SampleText;</text>
  <text x="18" y="60" style="&common;
➥font-weight:bold;">&SampleText;</text>
  <text x="18" y="90" style="&common;">&SampleText;</text>
 </g>
</svg>
```

Workarounds

The first option to consider for avoiding non-XML data inside an XML container is to use external files. The inclusion can happen when the document is parsed rather than in the physical source material. Use, for example, XInclude or an external entity so the original source for the non-XML data can be dealt with separately. Most server-side scripts also offer an `include` function that can be used.

In some cases, there are no ways to externalize the text, or the performance cost would be too high to do so. In these circumstances, and only if no better solution is available, you might want to consider marking up the embedded translatable text so tools can easily distinguish it from the rest of the data. Although this solution is far from perfect it might help during the localization process. Despite not being XML, the data could use, for example, the same properties that are described in Chapter 8, "Writing Internationalized Documents," but this time encapsulated in special comments markers.

XML Data in Non-XML Containers

When an XML document is generated, you will often find its parts stored in various places such as hard-coded source code, database entries, resource files, stored procedures, and even quite often non-XML data inside an XML container.

Source Code and Resources

The same general requirements that apply when writing source code apply here: avoid hard-coded strings that have localizable parts.

For example, the command

```
fprintf(pFile, "<?xml version='1.0' encoding='iso-8859-1' ?>\n");
```

might be sufficient in English, but you will have to change it to make sure the encoding can be safely specified for many other languages:

```
fprintf(pFile, "<?xml version='1.0' encoding='%s' ?>\n", p_szEncoding);
```

In some cases, the text is correctly externalized in a resource or properties file, but it must include XML tags as shown in Listing 11.4.

LISTING 11.4

`XMLResource1.str`—Resource File with Mixed Data

```
#include "strres.h"
STRINGTABLE
BEGIN
 S_CURUSR "User name: <emph>%1</emph> (Last logged on %2)."
 S_GTLNK "Go to <a href=""%s"" title=""Click to go to this
➥location"">%s</a>"
 S_PAKNGO "<a href=""%s"" title=""Pack &amp; Go"">Click here to package
➥the file and send it</a>"
 S_START1 "<p style='tr bgcolor='%s'><td><a title='Start Now!' href='"
 L_SELLABEL "&Selected package:"
 L_RDLABEL "R&&D Options:"
END
```

Most of the time the XML fragment will have no translatable data, only codes, but on some occasions you might have some text included. Another problem is that fragmentation could occur to such an extent that some strings have only partial tags (in other words, invalid XML). There is rarely an excuse for such a bad practice because it can usually be avoided.

Separate locale-specific data from the rest of the codes so they can be changed. Keep in mind that such data include not only text, but also encoding specification, style and presentation settings, coordinates and other placement information, and so forth. In short, it includes anything that has to do with displaying, parsing, or transforming text.

If the codes and text must stay together, use markers to indicate the ones to localize, the ones that are XML-specific, and the strings targeted to a different environment. It is important that the tools know the proper context in order to deal with format-specific aspects such as escaped characters.

Listing 11.5 shows a possible way of marking up and fixing our previous example. As
we have already seen, the same localization properties used for an XML document can
be used in a non-XML source, using comments for encapsulation instead of a
namespace.

LISTING 11.5

XMLResource2.str—Better Resource File

```
#include "strres.h"
STRINGTABLE
BEGIN
 //loc:bspan datatype="xml"
 S_CURUSR "User name: <emph>%1</emph> (Last logged on %2)."
 S_GTLNK "Go to <a href=""%s"" title=""Click to go to this
➥location"">%s</a>"
 S_PAKNGO "<a href=""%s"" title=""Pack &amp; Go"">Click here to package
➥the file and send it</a>"
 // S_START1 "<p style='tr bgcolor='%s'><td><a title='Start Now!' href='"
 // Codes have been hard-coded and the string is called
➥as a parameter now
 S_START1 "Start Now!"
 //loc:espan
 L_SELLABEL "&Selected package:"
 L_RDLABEL "R&&D Options:"
END
```

Database Access

Data can also be mixed in the places where an application performs queries or formats
the results of queries. Chapter 12, "XML and Databases," explores this topic in more
detail, but regardless of the technology used you should avoid mixing XML codes and
text when possible.

For example, Listing 11.6 shows a simple stored procedure where some text is coded
within the Oracle PL/SQL script that creates the result file.

LISTING 11.6

ListEvents1.sql—Stored Procedure with Text

```
CREATE OR REPLACE PROCEDURE ListEvents ( p_theVenue VARCHAR2 ) IS
BEGIN
   htp.p('<?xml version="1.0" encoding="utf-8" ?>');
   htp.p('<results>');
```

LISTING 11.6   CONTINUED

```
    htp.p(' <title>Events at '|| p_theVenue ||' this year.</title>');
    htp.p(' <list>');
    FOR r IN ( SELECT *
                  FROM Events
                  WHERE venue = "'"|| p_theVenue ||"'" )
    LOOP
       htp.p('  <event>');
       htp.p('    <id>'|| r.eventid ||'</id>');
       htp.p('    <location>'|| r.location ||'</location>');
       htp.p('    <name>'|| r.name ||'</name>');
       htp.p('    <dates>'|| r.dates ||'</dates>');
       htp.p('  </event>');
    END LOOP;
    htp.p(' </list>');
    htp.p('</results>');
END;
```

The string parameter of each `htp.p()` call is potentially translatable text. But in this procedure most of the text is XML code and only the third occurrence has four words to translate. This will require several steps, which are not always easy to execute.

1. Get the code of the stored procedure from the database.
2. Isolate the strings within the source code.
3. Identify which string or which part of a string is translatable.
4. Translate.
5. Put everything back together.

One possible alternate approach is to use specialized comments in the code to indicate what to localize. The type of markers discussed in Chapter 8 could be used, as shown in Listing 11.7.

LISTING 11.7

`ListEvents2.sql`—Stored Procedure with Text and Localization Markers

```
CREATE OR REPLACE PROCEDURE ListEvents ( p_theVenue VARCHAR2 ) IS
BEGIN
    --loc:bspan localize='no'
    htp.p('<?xml version="1.0" encoding="utf-8" ?>');
    htp.p('<?xml-stylesheet type="text/css" href="ListEvent.css" ?>');
    htp.p('<results>');
    --loc:item localize='data' datatype='xml'
```

LISTING 11.7   CONTINUED

```
htp.p(' <title>Events at '|| p_theVenue ||' this year.</title>');
htp.p(' <list>');
FOR r IN ( SELECT *
              FROM Events
              WHERE venue = "'"|| p_theVenue ||"'" )
LOOP
   htp.p('  <event>');
   htp.p('    <id>'|| r.eventid ||'</id>');
   htp.p('    <location>'|| r.location ||'</location>');
   htp.p('    <name>'|| r.name ||'</name>');
   htp.p('    <dates>'|| r.dates ||'</dates>');
   htp.p('  </event>');
END LOOP;
htp.p(' </list>');
htp.p('</results>');
--loc:espan
END;
```

But such a system would require the translation tools to understand the specialized comments, and this is currently not in place.

Instead, when possible, you want to truly separate the creation of the resultset from its presentation and move any localizable parts into the definition of the presentation. For our example, as shown in Listing 11.8, the title would be replaced by a simple element that would contain the parameter and could then be used by the XSL template to build the correct text.

LISTING 11.8

`ListEvents3.sql`—Alternate Stored Procedure

```
CREATE OR REPLACE PROCEDURE ListEvents ( p_theVenue VARCHAR2 ) IS
BEGIN
   htp.p('<?xml version="1.0" encoding="utf-8" ?>');
   htp.p('<?xml-stylesheet type="text/xsl" href="ListEvents1.xsl" ?>');
   htp.p('<results>');
   htp.p(' <venue>'|| p_theVenue ||'</venue>');
   htp.p(' <list>');
   FOR r IN ( SELECT *
                 FROM Events
                 WHERE venue = "'"|| p_theVenue ||"'" )
   LOOP
```

LISTING 11.8 **CONTINUED**

```
        htp.p('   <event>');
        htp.p('     <id>'|| r.eventid ||'</id>');
        htp.p('     <location>'|| r.location ||'</location>');
        htp.p('     <name>'|| r.name ||'</name>');
        htp.p('     <dates>'|| r.dates ||'</dates>');
        htp.p('   </event>');
    END LOOP;
    htp.p('  </list>');
    htp.p('</results>');
END;
```

Applying a template such as the one shown in Listing 11.9, you see a result similar to the one displayed in Figure 11.1.

LISTING 11.9

`ListEvents1.xsl`—XSL Template to Display the Resultset

```
<?xml version="1.0" ?>
<xsl:stylesheet xmlns:xsl="http://www.w3.org/1999/XSL/Transform"
➥version="1.0">

 <xsl:template match="/results">
  <HTML>
   <BODY>
    <p>Events at
     <B><xsl:value-of select="venue"/></B>
     this year.
    </p>
    <TABLE BORDER="1" WIDTH="100%" CELLPADDING="5"
     CELLSPACING="0" BGCOLOR="lightblue">
     <TR>
      <TD ALIGN="top"><B>ID</B></TD>
      <TD ALIGN="top"><B>Location</B></TD>
      <TD ALIGN="top"><B>Event</B></TD>
      <TD ALIGN="top"><B>Dates</B></TD>
     </TR>
     <xsl:for-each select="list/event">
      <TR>
       <TD><xsl:value-of select="id"/></TD>
       <TD><xsl:value-of select="location"/></TD>
       <TD><xsl:value-of select="name"/></TD>
```

LISTING 11.9   CONTINUED

```
        <TD><xsl:value-of select="dates"/></TD>
      </TR>
    </xsl:for-each>
   </TABLE>
  </BODY>
 </HTML>
</xsl:template>

</xsl:stylesheet>
```

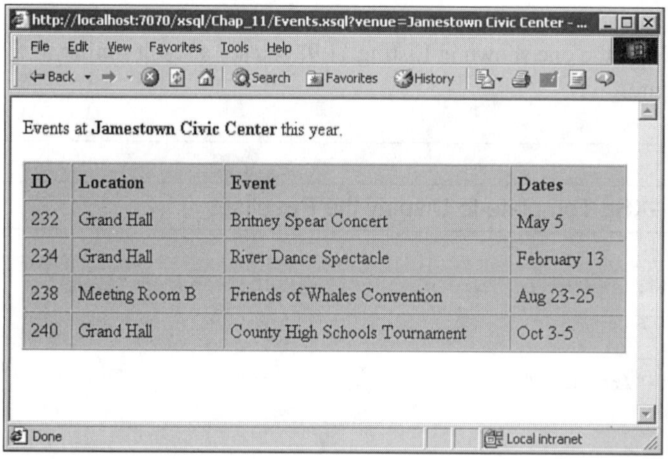

FIGURE 11.1

Rendering of the XML resultset, using XSLT.

You could go one step farther and use the various new techniques offered by most database systems such as Oracle, SQL Server, or Sybase. These now offer ways to directly generate XML results from simple queries or even from external server-side XML documents. The result of the queries is free of translatable text and can be converted into the relevant output using, for example, an XSL template as we have done already.

For example, Oracle 8i can be used with the XSQL servlet to generate such results. Listing 11.10 shows the XSQL page that can create the output shown in Figure 11.1. You need to slightly modify the XSL template. The differences are shown in bold, in Listing 11.11.

LISTING 11.10

`Events.xsql`—Same Query with XSQL

```xml
<?xml version="1.0"?>
<?xml-stylesheet type="text/xsl" href="ListEvents2.xsl" ?>
<page connection="xmli18n" xmlns:xsql="urn:oracle-xsql">
 <xsql:include-request-params/>
 <xsql:query rowset-element="list" row-element="event"
  tag-case="lower" >
  SELECT * FROM Events
  WHERE venue = ('{@venue}')
 </xsql:query>
</page></sql:query>
```

LISTING 11.11

`ListEvents2.xsl`

```xml
<?xml version="1.0" ?>
<xsl:stylesheet xmlns:xsl="http://www.w3.org/1999/XSL/Transform"
➥version="1.0">

 <xsl:template match="/page">
  <HTML>
   <BODY>
    <p>Events at
     <B><xsl:value-of select="request/parameters/venue"/></B>
     this year.
    </p>
    <TABLE BORDER="1" WIDTH="100%" CELLPADDING="5"
    CELLSPACING="0" BGCOLOR="lightblue">
    <TR>
     <TD ALIGN="top"><B>ID</B></TD>
     <TD ALIGN="top"><B>Location</B></TD>
     <TD ALIGN="top"><B>Event</B></TD>
     <TD ALIGN="top"><B>Dates</B></TD>
    </TR>
    <xsl:for-each select="list/event">
     <TR>
      <TD><xsl:value-of select="eventid"/></TD>
      <TD><xsl:value-of select="location"/></TD>
      <TD><xsl:value-of select="name"/></TD>
      <TD><xsl:value-of select="dates"/></TD>
     </TR>
```

LISTING 11.11   CONTINUED

```
        </xsl:for-each>
      </TABLE>
    </BODY>
  </HTML>
 </xsl:template>

</xsl:stylesheet>
```

Escaped Characters

When creating XML output from various sources, you can run into the problem of dealing with different ways of escaping the same character, or escaped characters that would not usually be escaped if the text fragment were in its natural container.

For instance, referring to Listing 11.4, the Windows RC file has three character ampersands and they should all be treated differently: & when used as hot-key marker, && when used as literal in Windows, and & when used as literal in XML.

Server-side scripts often offer utilities to automatically escape a string. For instance, you can use the function xmlEscape() with PowerDynamo to automatically create CDATA sections or escape any relevant characters.

For example

```
 <!--SCRIPT document.writeln(xmlEscape("Research & Development"));-->
```

produces

```
Research &amp; Development
```

while the statement

```
<!--SCRIPT document.writeln(xmlEscape("Research & Development",
➥true)); -->
```

generates the following:

```
<![CDATA[Research & Development]]>
```

In ColdFusion the XMLFormat() function can be used

```
<CFOUTPUT>
   <title>#XMLFormat("Research & Development")#</title>
</CFOUTPUT>
```

to get this output:

```
   <title>Research &amp; Development</title>
```

It is important to be consistent in using or not using such functions because you want to make sure that segments can be matched whenever possible when leveraging. Using different escape notations would prevent this.

Summary

In this chapter we have seen the different ways XML data and non-XML data can be combined and the problems such occurrences bring to the localization process.

To minimize these challenges, when creating content with mixed data, consider the following points:

- When possible, avoid embedding a block of data of a different type than the rest of the XML container. Instead use external files so that each data type can be dealt with separately.
- If you must mix different types of data in the same document, use any mechanism possible to clearly identify where the types change and what types are involved.
- Often, encapsulating the embedded format in CDATA sections will help with resolving escaped character mismatches.
- Ensure that the translation tools used on mixed data have the capability to switch filters to isolate the correct translatable parts.
- Provide documentation to the localizer about any specific data type included in your material, such as proprietary processing instructions or special comments.

# CHAPTER 12

XML and Databases

In This Chapter:

XML data are by nature very structured and lend themselves well to communicating with databases. Many database-related applications involve XML and localized content.

A number of the internationalization aspects in this area are more related to database architecture than to XML, but a few facets concern both. The best way to review them is to go through an example and see some of the various stages of interaction that a multilingual database and XML documents have.

Imagine we are working for a sophisticated travel agency that uses a database containing information about a set of vacation special packages. These offers should be published to our customers through two different interfaces: A classic Web site and a Web site for wireless devices. The first case requires a simple HTML page and the second requires a WML (Wireless Markup Language) document. We receive the original data in English, but because we have a strong presence in Central Europe we also need to localize the special package information into Polish.

Our database is hosted on Microsoft SQL Server 2000. The two tables related to the special deals are `Packages`, which contains any generic and nontranslatable data such as price, operator contact, and so forth, and `Descriptions`, which contains the different translatable fields. This last table is the one of interest for localization. It has the following columns:

Field	*Description*
`PackageID`	The unique identifier for the package
`Lang`	The locale code in the same format as for the XML `xml:lang` attribute: English is `EN` and Polish `PL`

Field	Description
Status	A flag set to `new` when the entry is new, `updated` when the entry has been changed since the last time a translation was done, and `ok` when the string has been translated and nothing has changed
Title	A short title for the package
Summary	A longer description of what is included in the package

The first internationalization aspect to take care of is not linked to XML, but to the database system itself: It must support languages using different alphabets, in our case, Latin-1 for English and Latin-2 for Polish. Most databases now offer support for Unicode through at least a few types of data. In SQL Server, for example, the `Title` and `Summary` fields should be of type `nchar` and `ntext` rather than `char` and `text`. This enables us to store any language supported by Unicode in these two columns. In Oracle, you can be even more specific and select the character set used for the `NCHAR` type in your database. Sybase has similar alternatives.

> **NOTE:** Always verify the type of your text fields: Some databases use encoding conversion mechanisms that try to use the closest ASCII character when they are not able to use a given extended character: In many Latin-based languages the result string does not appear corrupted to a person who does not speak the given language. For example, the phrase "Spędź tydzień na zacisznej plaży na Mikonos" would be converted to "Spedz tydzien na zacisznej plazy na Mikonos." Character corruption is more easily detected in languages using non-Latin–based alphabets such as Russian, or those using ideographs such as Chinese.

In this example, we go through two main processes: first, how to translate the data of the `Descriptions` table and second, how to generate the HTML and WML documents for each locale.

Translating Database Content

Localizing the content of a database can usually be done in three steps (excluding any testing):

1. The extraction of the translatable fields
2. The translation tasks
3. The merging of the new or modified data back into their respective tables

There are many ways to execute these steps, but using XML as the container for the translatable text during the process has a number of advantages. For example, any encoding conversion will be taken care of by the database utilities interfacing with XML documents. Also, the XML documents can be translated directly without additional conversion steps.

In this example, we will use XLIFF as the translation format. We also want to use only readily available tools, and not to develop any special utility. Finally, we want the process to be flexible enough that it can be easily ported to a different database if necessary.

Extraction

First, let's look more closely at the output format we want to generate. XLIFF (XML Localization Interchange File Format) is an XML format designed to store extracted text. It is the result of a recent collaboration by Oracle, Novell, IBM/Lotus, Sun, and a few other partners. In our case we only need to use a subset of its functionality. The two fields we are translating do not have inline codes, and can be merged back into the database without using the skeleton file that XLIFF filters normally would use. XLIFF is discussed in detail in Chapter 17, "Text Extraction."

All databases offer some XML capability from their query system. We could write an XLIFF document from a query directly, but because we want to stay flexible it is better to decompose the extractions in two parts: creating a simple XML document and then converting that document into XLIFF. This way, if we need to migrate the data to a different database system or stop using a database, the simple XML output will be very easy to port, and we can reuse the same method to create the XLIFF document, where the bulk of the conversion is.

Our output document requires all the information we have in the `Descriptions` table, but organized in such a way that it can be accessed easily. One possible type of layout is the following:

```
<Row PackageID="10" Lang="EN" Status="new">
 <Title>Cancun Paradise</Title>
 <Summary>5 days all-inclusive in Tulum most luxurious hotel.</Summary>
</Row>
```

Each `<Row>` element contains all the fields, and the translatable text is easily accessible. Note also that, following good internationalization practices, we do not use attributes to store localizable text.

The document will contain all the rows of the table, mixing any translation already available with the source data. The following step, the conversion to XLIFF, will group and filter these entries as needed.

SQL Server 2000 provides various methods to create XML files. The easiest one, the XML view, does not involve any query. You can create a schema to map the fields of a table to an XML structure and by invoking that schema, get the XML output.

The schema is written using XDR (XML Data Reduced). XDR is a simplified version of XML Data, a more complex schema language. The role of a schema is similar to the role of a DTD: to describe the structure and relationships of an XML vocabulary. For XDR this structure also has a default mapping mechanism that associates elements and attributes of the vocabulary to tables or columns in the database. Listing 12.1 shows the XDR schema for structuring our table into the type of output we want.

LISTING 12.1

`Descriptions.xdr`—XDR **Schema for the** `Descriptions` **Table**

```
<?xml version='1.0'?>

<Schema xmlns='urn:schemas-microsoft-com:xml-data'
        xmlns:sql='urn:schemas-microsoft-com:xml-sql'>

 <ElementType name='Title' content="textOnly"/>
 <ElementType name='Summary' content="textOnly"/>

 <ElementType name='Descriptions'>

  <AttributeType name='PackageID' />
  <AttributeType name='Lang'/>
  <AttributeType name='Status'/>

  <attribute type='PackageID' />
  <attribute type='Lang'/>
  <attribute type='Status' />
  <element type='Title'/>
  <element type='Summary'/>

 </ElementType>

</Schema>
```

The only difference between this and our initial idea is that the `<Row>` element will be named `<Descriptions>`, using the default mapping. We could use the XDR annotation features and force the element to be renamed `<Row>`, but there is no real reason to do so. If nothing else, using `<Descriptions>` is a good reminder of the name of the table we are working with.

Also note that we use `Lang` and not `xml:lang` for the attribute specifying the locale of the entry. We are not doing this mapping because, in addition to the same reason behind `<Descriptions>` and `<Row>`, XDR also does not let you easily map an element or attribute name to different namespaces at the field level.

You can see the view of the `Descriptions` table at any time by calling the schema from a browser. Listing 12.2 shows the output of the sample table before conversion to XLIFF. As you can see, two entries are in Polish already, one corresponding to a source entry with a `Status` attribute set to `ok`, the other one to an updated entry. This means that entry 41 has already been localized and has not changed since, while entry 22 has some old translation that can be reused for the updated source text. All the other entries are new and need translation.

LISTING 12.2

`RawOutput.xml`—XML Output Using the `Descriptions.xdr` **Schema**

```
<?xml version="1.0" ?>
<Translations>
 <Descriptions PackageID="10" Lang="EN" Status="new">
  <Title>Cancun Paradise</Title>
  <Summary>5 days all-inclusive in Tulum most luxurious hotel.</Summary>
 </Descriptions>
 <Descriptions PackageID="20" Lang="EN" Status="new">
  <Title>The Migration</Title>
  <Summary>See the herds migration in the Serengeti plains. 2 weeks
➥all-inclusive plan.</Summary>
 </Descriptions>
 <Descriptions PackageID="22" Lang="EN" Status="updated">
  <Title>Blue Greece</Title>
  <Summary>The Island where the shade is a dream: Spend a week on the
➥quiet beach of Mikonos. Includes a day trip to Delos.</Summary>
 </Descriptions>
 <Descriptions PackageID="25" Lang="EN" Status="new">
  <Title>The Reef</Title>
  <Summary>5 days all-inclusive sojourn to the incredible Great Barrier
➥Reef of Australia. Daily dive from Cairns included.</Summary>
 </Descriptions>
```

LISTING 12.2   CONTINUED

```
<Descriptions PackageID="41" Lang="EN" Status="ok">
 <Title>Peaceful Silence</Title>
 <Summary>Regenerate your body and soul spending a week in the Frigolet
➥monastery. No talking allowed, no warm water, bread and cheese at all
➥meals: you will love it!</Summary>
 </Descriptions>
 <Descriptions PackageID="22" Lang="PL">
 <Title>Błękitna Grecja</Title>
 <Summary>Spędź tydzień na zacisznej plaży na Mikonos. Oferta zawiera
➥jedno-dniową wycieczkę na Delos.</Summary>
 </Descriptions>
 <Descriptions PackageID="41" Lang="PL">
 <Title>Kojąca Cisza</Title>
 <Summary>Zregeneruj ciało i duszę spędzając tydzień w klasztorze
➥Frigolet. Zakaz rozmów, brak ciepłej wody, tylko chleb i ser do
➥posiłków: bedziesz wniebowzięty!</Summary>
 </Descriptions>
</Translations>
```

This type of output can be generated very easily from other databases (for example, by using XSQL with Oracle or through PowerDynamo templates for Sybase). You can see an example of the use of XSQL in Chapter 11, "Mixed Data."

Now that we have the raw XML output of the table, we can convert it to XLIFF using a simple XSLT template. For our purpose, XLIFF can be used with the following structure:

```
<xliff>
<file>
 <header>...</header>
 <body>
  <trans-unit>...</trans-unit>
  <trans-unit>...</trans-unit>
  ...
 </body>
</file>
```

Each <trans-unit> element corresponds to one of our translatable elements, <Title> and <Summary>, and is organized as follows:

```
<trans-unit>
 <source>...</source>
 <target>...</target>
```

```
[<alt-trans>
  <target>...</target>
 </alt-trans>]
</trans-unit>
```

The English text goes into the `<source>` element and the translation into the
`<target>` element. If any translation is available, we can also put it into an
`<alt-trans>` group so the translator can have suggestions, and later keep track of
the various phases the translation went through.

Listing 12.3 shows the template used to transform the raw XML output into the XLIFF
document. We do not want to send any entry for translation that has a `Status` attribute
set to `ok` for the source: These package descriptions have already been translated and
have not changed. In our case, for example, entry 41 will not go to translation.

LISTING 12.3

`ToTrans.xsl`—XSLT Template to Convert to XLIFF

```
<?xml version="1.0" ?>
<xsl:stylesheet xmlns:xsl="http://www.w3.org/1999/XSL/Transform"
 version="1.0">

 <xsl:output encoding='utf-8' indent='yes' doctype-system='xliff.dtd'/>
 <xsl:param name='Target'>PL</xsl:param>

 <xsl:template match="/Translations">

  <xliff version='1.0' xml:lang="en">
   <xsl:element name='file'>
    <xsl:attribute name='original'>db-output</xsl:attribute>
    <xsl:attribute name='datatype'>database</xsl:attribute>
    <xsl:attribute name='source-language'>EN</xsl:attribute>
    <xsl:attribute name='target-language'>
➥<xsl:value-of select="$Target"/></xsl:attribute>

    <header>
     <phase-group>
      <phase phase-name='prep1' process-name='preparation'></phase>
     </phase-group>
    </header>

    <body>
     <xsl:for-each select="Descriptions[@Lang='EN' and @Status!='ok']">
```

LISTING 12.3   CONTINUED

```xsl
      <xsl:variable name='UnitID'>
       <xsl:value-of select="@PackageID"/>
      </xsl:variable>

      <!-- translation unit for Title  -->
      <xsl:element name='trans-unit'>
       <xsl:variable name='SugTitle'>
        <xsl:value-of select="/Translations/Descriptions
➥[@PackageID=$UnitID and @Lang=$Target]/Title"/>
       </xsl:variable>

       <xsl:attribute name='id'><xsl:value-of select="$UnitID"/>
➥-t</xsl:attribute>
       <xsl:attribute name='restype'>title</xsl:attribute>
       <xsl:element name='source'>
        <xsl:attribute name='xml:lang'>
➥<xsl:value-of select="@Lang"/></xsl:attribute>
        <xsl:value-of select="Title"/>
       </xsl:element>
       <xsl:element name='target'>
        <xsl:attribute name='xml:lang'>
➥<xsl:value-of select="$Target"/></xsl:attribute>
        <xsl:attribute name='state'>
➥<xsl:value-of select="@Status"/></xsl:attribute>
        <xsl:if test="$SugTitle!=''">
         <xsl:value-of select="$SugTitle"/>
        </xsl:if>
        <xsl:if test="$SugTitle=''">
         <xsl:value-of select="Title"/>
        </xsl:if>
       </xsl:element>
       <xsl:if test="$SugTitle!=''">
        <alt-trans>
         <xsl:element name='target'>
          <xsl:attribute name='xml:lang'>
➥<xsl:value-of select="$Target"/></xsl:attribute>
          <xsl:attribute name='phase-name'>prep1</xsl:attribute>
          <xsl:value-of select="$SugTitle"/>
         </xsl:element>
        </alt-trans>
       </xsl:if>
```

LISTING 12.3   CONTINUED

```
    </xsl:element>

    <!-- translation unit for Summary   -->
    <xsl:element name='trans-unit'>
     <xsl:variable name='SugSummary'>
      <xsl:value-of select="/Translations/Descriptions
➥[@PackageID=$UnitID and @Lang=$Target]/Summary"/>
     </xsl:variable>

     <xsl:attribute name='id'><xsl:value-of select="$UnitID"/>
➥-s</xsl:attribute>
     <xsl:attribute name='restype'>summary</xsl:attribute>
     <xsl:element name='source'>
      <xsl:attribute name='xml:lang'>
➥<xsl:value-of select="@Lang"/></xsl:attribute>
       <xsl:value-of select="Summary"/>
     </xsl:element>
     <xsl:element name='target'>
      <xsl:attribute name='xml:lang'>
➥<xsl:value-of select="$Target"/></xsl:attribute>
      <xsl:attribute name='state'>
➥<xsl:value-of select="@Status"/></xsl:attribute>
      <xsl:if test="$SugSummary!=''">
       <xsl:value-of select="$SugSummary"/>
      </xsl:if>
      <xsl:if test="$SugSummary=''">
       <xsl:value-of select="Summary"/>
      </xsl:if>
     </xsl:element>
     <xsl:if test="$SugSummary!=''">
      <alt-trans>
       <xsl:element name='target'>
        <xsl:attribute name='xml:lang'>
➥<xsl:value-of select="$Target"/></xsl:attribute>
        <xsl:attribute name='phase-name'>prep1</xsl:attribute>
        <xsl:value-of select="$SugSummary"/>
       </xsl:element>
      </alt-trans>
     </xsl:if>
    </xsl:element>

   </xsl:for-each>
```

LISTING 12.3   CONTINUED

```
    </body>

   </xsl:element>
  </xliff>

 </xsl:template>

</xsl:stylesheet>
```

All the original information is carried into the document. Unlike most XLIFF documents, we do not need to use an auxiliary file (called a skeleton file in XLIFF) to merge the data back.

The template is designed to use a `Target` parameter if we need to prepare the file for a language other than Polish. By default its value is set to `PL`. Variables are also used to store different values and to simplify the template. They are used, for example, to optionally create the `<alt-trans>` element if we have translation candidates.

The `id` attribute is required in a `<trans-unit>` element. In our case, because we have two `<trans-unit>` elements for each original entry, we add a short suffix to the original identifier: `-s` for the summaries, and `-t` for the titles. Each `<trans-unit>` for the same entry is also distinguished by its `restype` attribute: `title` or `summary`.

When creating the attribute values, be careful not to accidentally add any unwanted white spaces by formatting the XSL source code itself. Usually the content of `<xsl:attribute>` should be on a single line, with only significant white spaces.

To create the XLIFF document, apply the template to the `RawOutput.xml` document. This can be done with the Microsoft XSL command-line processor, MSXSL:

```
msxsl RawOutput.xml ToTrans.xsl > to_translation.xlf
```

Listing 12.4 shows the result of the command.

LISTING 12.4

`to_translation.xlf`—XLIFF Output

```
<?xml version="1.0" encoding="utf-8"?>
<!DOCTYPE xliff SYSTEM "xliff.dtd">
<xliff version="1.0" xml:lang="en">
<file original="db-output" datatype="database" source-language="EN"
↪target-language="PL">
<header>
```

LISTING **12.4** CONTINUED

```
<phase-group>
<phase phase-name="prep1" process-name="preparation"></phase>
</phase-group>
</header>
<body>
<trans-unit id="10-t" restype="title">
<source xml:lang="EN">Cancun Paradise</source>
<target xml:lang="PL" state="new">Cancun Paradise</target>
</trans-unit>
<trans-unit id="10-s" restype="summary">
<source xml:lang="EN">5 days all-inclusive in Tulum most luxurious hotel.
↪</source>
<target xml:lang="PL" state="new">5 days all-inclusive in Tulum most
↪luxurious hotel.</target>
</trans-unit>
<trans-unit id="20-t" restype="title">
<source xml:lang="EN">The Migration</source>
<target xml:lang="PL" state="new">The Migration</target>
</trans-unit>
<trans-unit id="20-s" restype="summary">
<source xml:lang="EN">See the herds migration in the Serengeti plains. 2
↪weeks all-inclusive plan.</source>
<target xml:lang="PL" state="new">See the herds migration in the
↪Serengeti plains. 2 weeks all-inclusive plan.</target>
</trans-unit>
<trans-unit id="22-t" restype="title">
<source xml:lang="EN">Blue Greece</source>
<target xml:lang="PL" state="updated">Błękitna Grecja</target>
<alt-trans>
<target xml:lang="PL" phase-name="prep1">Błękitna Grecja</target>
</alt-trans>
</trans-unit>
<trans-unit id="22-s" restype="summary">
<source xml:lang="EN">The Island where the shade is a dream: Spend a week
↪on the quiet beach of Mikonos. Includes a day trip to Delos.</source>
<target xml:lang="PL" state="updated">Spędź tydzień na zacisznej plaży na
↪Mikonos. Oferta zawiera jedno-dniową wycieczkę na Delos.</target>
<alt-trans>
<target xml:lang="PL" phase-name="prep1">Spędź tydzień na zacisznej plaży
↪na Mikonos. Oferta zawiera jedno-dniową wycieczkę na Delos.</target>
</alt-trans>
</trans-unit>
```

LISTING 12.4   CONTINUED

```
<trans-unit id="25-t" restype="title">
<source xml:lang="EN">The Reef</source>
<target xml:lang="PL" state="new">The Reef</target>
</trans-unit>
<trans-unit id="25-s" restype="summary">
<source xml:lang="EN">5 days all-inclusive sojourn to the incredible
➥Great Barrier Reef of Australia. Daily dive from Cairns
➥included.</source>
<target xml:lang="PL" state="new">5 days all-inclusive sojourn to the
➥incredible Great Barrier Reef of Australia. Daily dive from Cairns
➥included.</target>
</trans-unit>
</body>
</file>
</xliff>
```

The file is now ready for translation.

One problem relates to the way our translatable text is stored in the `Descriptions` table: The two text fields are associated with the same `Status` field. Therefore, we cannot know whether it is the `Title` or the `Summary` column that has been changed and we must send both for verification. This is a relatively minor issue in our specific setup. In different circumstances where you have several fields with larger content, you probably want to have a status for each localizable field. In some cases, you might want to use separate tables. Another way to organize your translatable data would be to use a table with only one text field and an additional field to indicate the type of text.

These choices are often driven by the overall application and the design of the database itself. But it is wise, when creating the structure of the database, to look at how easily you can generate XML documents from it.

Translation

The translation step is no different for our file than for other XML documents. Because we put the source text in both the `<source>` and the `<target>` elements, we can use any XML-enabled translation tool to translate the content of the `<target>` element and protect everything else.

Any tool designed specifically to work with XLIFF documents can use the various features of the format to be more efficient in terms of keeping track of the different translation versions: translation, edit, proof, and review.

Regardless of how you do the work, the final document will look like the one shown in Listing 12.5. Note that, to illustrate a feature of XLIFF, we have also added the `approved` attribute to each `<trans-unit>`. Our merging process will verify that this flag is set to `yes` before integrating the data into the table.

LISTING 12.5

`from_translation.xlf`—Translated Document

```
<?xml version="1.0" encoding="utf-8"?>
<!DOCTYPE xliff SYSTEM "xliff.dtd">
<xliff version="1.0" xml:lang="en">
<file original="db-output" datatype="database" source-language="EN"
➥target-language="PL">
<header>
<phase-group>
<phase phase-name="prep1" process-name="preparation"></phase>
<phase phase-name="trans" process-name="translation"></phase>
</phase-group>
</header>
<body>
<trans-unit id="10-t" restype="title" approved='yes'>
<source xml:lang="EN">Cancun Paradise</source>
<target xml:lang="PL" state="new">Raj Cancun</target>
</trans-unit>
<trans-unit id="10-s" restype="summary" approved='yes'>
<source xml:lang="EN">5 days all-inclusive in Tulum most luxurious hotel.
➥</source>
<target xml:lang="PL" state="new">5 dni z pełną ofertą usług w
➥najbardziej luksusowym hotelu w Tulum.</target>
</trans-unit>
<trans-unit id="20-t" restype="title" approved='yes'>
<source xml:lang="EN">The Migration</source>
<target xml:lang="PL" state="new">Migrujące stada</target>
</trans-unit>
<trans-unit id="20-s" restype="summary" approved='yes'>
<source xml:lang="EN">See the herds migration in the Serengeti plains. 2
➥weeks all-inclusive plan.</source>
<target xml:lang="PL" state="new">Zobacz migrujące stada na równinach
➥Serengeti. Oferta 2 tygodniowa zawierająca wszystkie usługi.</target>
</trans-unit>
<trans-unit id="22-t" restype="title" approved='yes'>
<source xml:lang="EN">Blue Greece</source>
<target xml:lang="PL" state="updated">Błękitna Grecja</target>
```

LISTING 12.5 CONTINUED

```
<alt-trans>
<target xml:lang="PL" phase-name="prep1">Błękitna Grecja</target>
</alt-trans>
</trans-unit>
<trans-unit id="22-s" restype="summary" approved='yes'>
<source xml:lang="EN">The Island where the shade is a dream: Spend a week
➥on the quiet beach of Mikonos. Includes a day trip to Delos.</source>
<target xml:lang="PL" state="updated">Wyspa, na której cień jest
➥marzeniem: Spędź tydzień na zacisznej plaży na Mikonos. Oferta zawiera
➥jedno-dniową wycieczkę na Delos.</target>
<alt-trans>
<target xml:lang="PL" phase-name="prep1">Spędź tydzień na zacisznej plaży
➥na Mikonos. Oferta zawiera jedno-dniową wycieczkę na Delos.</target>
</alt-trans>
</trans-unit>
<trans-unit id="25-t" restype="title" approved='yes'>
<source xml:lang="EN">The Reef</source>
<target xml:lang="PL" state="new">Rafa</target>
</trans-unit>
<trans-unit id="25-s" restype="summary" approved='yes'>
<source xml:lang="EN">5 days all-inclusive sojourn to the incredible
➥Great Barrier Reef of Australia. Daily dive from Cairns
➥included.</source>
<target xml:lang="PL" state="new">5 dniowa wyprawa na niesamowitą Wielką
➥Rafę Koralową u wybrzeży Australii, z pełną ofertą usług. Pobyt
➥obejmuje także dzienne wyprawy nurkownia z Cairns.</target>
</trans-unit>
</body>
</file>
</xliff>
```

With the translated file back, we have only one more step to execute: the merging.

Merging

Merging data back to an original format is usually the most difficult part of a translation process that uses extraction. However, when dealing with databases, things are often not difficult because the database systems provide various efficient means to put the data back in their correct location.

SQL Server offers several methods: You could use a stored procedure with the OPENXML function, the SQLXMLBulkLoad object, updategrams, and different variations of other XML utilities. The simplest way is probably to use updategrams.

An *updategram* is a fragment of XML data processed through a template; it provides the XML data for a before and an after stage, letting SQL Server perform the necessary SQL INSERT, UPDATE, or DELETE commands to make the database match the after description. This is very powerful because almost the only thing you have to do is provide an XML document with the correct updategrams.

For example, the following updategram changes the text of the field mapped to the <population> element from 3.56 to 4.4 in the row with the id set to pg.

```
<u:sync mapping-schema="Countries.xdr"
        xmlns:u="urn:schemas-microsoft-com:xml-updategram">
 <u:before>
  <country id="pg">
   <population>3.56</population>
  </country>
 </u:before>
 <u:after>
  <country id="pg">
   <population>4.4</population>
  </country>
 </u:after>
</u:sync>
```

As you can see, this mechanism also uses an XDR schema to map the XML input to the database fields. In our case we can simply reuse the one we have already defined for the Descriptions table (refer to Listing 12.1).

The only work to do is to create another XSLT template to go from the XLIFF translated document to the XML file with the updategrams. Listing 12.6 shows the template source code.

LISTING 12.6

FromTrans.xsl—XSLT Template to Convert XLIFF to Updategrams

```
<?xml version="1.0" ?>
<xsl:stylesheet xmlns:xsl="http://www.w3.org/1999/XSL/Transform"
 version="1.0">

 <xsl:output encoding='utf-8' indent='yes' />
 <xsl:param name='Target'>PL</xsl:param>
```

LISTING 12.6   CONTINUED

```xsl
<xsl:template match="/xliff/file/body">

 <Translations>
  <u:sync xmlns:u="urn:schemas-microsoft-com:xml-updategram"
          mapping-schema="Descriptions.xdr">

   <xsl:for-each select="trans-unit[@restype='title' and
➥@approved='yes']">

   <xsl:variable name='PackageID'><xsl:value-of
➥select="substring-before(@id, '-')"/></xsl:variable>
    <xsl:variable name='SummaryID'><xsl:value-of select="$PackageID"/>
➥-s</xsl:variable>
    <xsl:variable name='Title'><xsl:value-of select='target'/>
➥</xsl:variable>

    <xsl:variable name='Summary'><xsl:value-of
     select="/xliff/file/body/trans-unit[@restype='summary' and
➥@approved='yes' and @id=$SummaryID]/target"/></xsl:variable>

    <xsl:if test="$Title=''">
     <xsl:message terminate='yes'>Empty value found for title id=
➥<xsl:value-of select='$PackageID'/></xsl:message>
    </xsl:if>
    <xsl:if test="$Summary=''">
     <xsl:message terminate='yes'>Empty value found for summary id=
➥<xsl:value-of select='$SummaryID'/></xsl:message>
    </xsl:if>

    <u:before>
     <xsl:element name='Descriptions'>
      <xsl:attribute name='PackageID'>
➥<xsl:value-of select="$PackageID"/></xsl:attribute>
      <xsl:attribute name='Lang'>EN</xsl:attribute>
      <xsl:attribute name='Status'>
➥<xsl:value-of select="target/@state"/></xsl:attribute>
     </xsl:element>
    </u:before>
    <u:after>
     <xsl:element name='Descriptions'>
      <xsl:attribute name='PackageID'>
➥<xsl:value-of select="$PackageID"/></xsl:attribute>
```

LISTING **12.6**   CONTINUED

```
        <xsl:attribute name='Lang'>EN</xsl:attribute>
        <xsl:attribute name='Status'>ok</xsl:attribute>
      </xsl:element>
    </u:after>

    <u:before/>
    <u:after>
     <xsl:element name='Descriptions'>
      <xsl:attribute name='PackageID'>
➥<xsl:value-of select="$PackageID"/></xsl:attribute>
      <xsl:attribute name='Lang'>
➥<xsl:value-of select="$Target"/></xsl:attribute>
      <Title><xsl:value-of select="$Title"/></Title>
      <Summary><xsl:value-of select="$Summary"/></Summary>
     </xsl:element>
    </u:after>

   </xsl:for-each>

  </u:sync>
 </Translations>

</xsl:template>

</xsl:stylesheet>
```

There are two tasks to perform: updating or inserting the row for the translation and updating the Status field of the corresponding English entry to ok.

We also want to build a few checks: An entry is updated only if both the title and the summary text are not empty. We also take from the XLIFF input only the <trans-unit> elements with an accepted attribute set to yes.

We need to make sure we use the correct identifier. Remember that we added a suffix to it so that we could tell the difference between title and summary. The XPath function substring-before(@id, '-') fixes that problem easily: It returns, for example, the value 10 from the id="10-s".

Figure 12.1 shows the result of our conversion from the translated XLIFF document to the file with the updategrams.

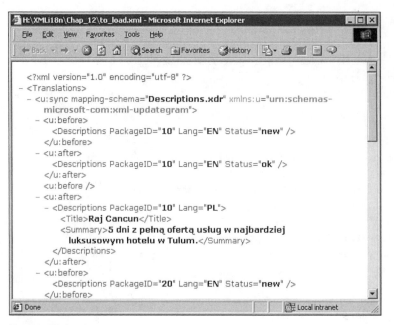

FIGURE 12.1

A list of the updategrams to use for the merge.

After the updategrams file is ready, we can call it from a browser as a template and the synchronization takes place.

Publishing XML from a Database

When our data have been localized, we need to generate the two types of presentation required: HTML and WML.

Here again the process can be broken down into different queries and templates to enable easier portability. The tasks are displaying the entries in a given language and then rendering the output either as an HTML page or as a WML document. The WML file can be compiled into a WMLC page ready to be served up to any device enabled for WAP (Wireless Application Protocol): for example, cell phones and other handheld devices.

Getting the Records

Our list of special deals can be queried from the database by various means. As we have already seen, all database systems have an arsenal of XML utilities and functions to generate XML documents.

This time we can use a SQL Server XML Query template. Listing 12.7 shows the file for performing the task. It uses a parameter to specify which language to query. It is set to EN by default, but you should specify the value of the Lang column for the locale you want to display.

LISTING 12.7

GetSpecials.xml—**XML Query**

```
<?xml version='1.0' ?>
<Output xmlns:sql='urn:schemas-microsoft-com:xml-sql'>

 <sql:header>
  <sql:param name="lang">EN</sql:param>
 </sql:header>

 <sql:query>
   SELECT      1                         as Tag,
               NULL                      as Parent,
               Descriptions.PackageID    as [Entry!1!ID],
               Title                     as [Entry!1!Title!element],
               Summary                   as [Entry!1!Summary!element],
               Price                     as [Entry!1!Price!element]
   FROM        Descriptions, Packages
   WHERE       ((Descriptions.PackageID = Packages.PackageID) AND (Lang =
➥@lang))
   ORDER BY    Descriptions.PackageID
   FOR         XML EXPLICIT
 </sql:query>
</Output>
```

In SQL server, XML SQL files are documents that include special elements containing SQL queries. These queries are evaluated and replaced with their resulting output. The FOR XML option enables you to indicate that the query result must be formatted as an XML fragment.

As mentioned already, if you are using a database other than SQL Server, you can use a similar mechanism. For example, as we have seen in the preceding chapter, Oracle can use a stored procedure, making use of the HTP object.

You could also develop XSQL or JSP pages using the JDeveloper package. Oracle's XML development Kit (XDK) offers a rich set of components to create solutions that tightly integrate XML and databases.

In SQL Server, the FOR XML option is especially powerful when used with its EXPLICIT mode. It enables you to structure the output in different levels, to assign the various database fields to attributes or elements, and to map names (with or without namespace prefixes). The query we are using is rather simple because the output required is very basic and involves only one column from the Packages table and three from the Descriptions table. The result is shown in Listing 12.8.

LISTING 12.8

QueryResults_en.xml—Raw Packages Descriptions List in English

```
<?xml  version="1.0"?>
<Output xmlns:sql="urn:schemas-microsoft-com:xml-sql">
 <Entry ID="10">
  <Title>Cancun Paradise</Title>
  <Summary>5 days all-inclusive in Tulum most luxurious hotel.</Summary>
  <Price>599</Price>
 </Entry>
 <Entry ID="20">
  <Title>The Migration</Title>
  <Summary>See the herds migration in the Serengeti plains. 2 weeks
➥all-inclusive plan.</Summary>
  <Price>2399</Price>
 </Entry>
 <Entry ID="22">
  <Title>Blue Greece</Title>
  <Summary>The Island where the shade is a dream: Spend a week on the
➥quiet beach of Mikonos. Includes a day trip to Delos.</Summary>
  <Price>699</Price>
 </Entry>
 <Entry ID="25">
  <Title>The Reef</Title>
  <Summary>5 days all-inclusive sojourn to the incredible Great Barrier
➥Reef of Australia. Daily dive from Cairns included.</Summary>
  <Price>899</Price>
 </Entry>
 <Entry ID="41">
  <Title>Peaceful Silence</Title>
  <Summary> Regenerate your body and soul spending a week in the
➥Frigolet monastery. No talking allowed, no warm water, bread and cheese
➥at all meals: you will love it!</Summary>
  <Price>1999</Price>
 </Entry>
</Output>
```

The next step is to transform this document into HTML or WML. We will do that by using an XSLT template. The template can be associated with the XML query itself if needed, making the two steps a single action.

Locale-Specific Output

The language of the final output is already set at the query level. For the transformation we have only one locale-specific issue to solve: the price. We want to show it in U.S. dollars or in złoty (the currency of Poland), depending on the language. The original price is always stored in U.S. dollars.

In addition, we want to make sure the price is formatted nicely according the locale: In this case, `$1,000` for a price in dollars, and `1 000 zł` for one in złoty.

XSL offers a function called `format-number()` that provides exactly what we need. You can use any formatting pattern necessary, including one to define the text of the currency symbol and its position. For example, `$#,###` can be used for dollars. When our output is WML, because that format uses the `$` sign as a special marker, we need to escape it (`$$#,###`).

Converting to złoty requires more work: The decimal and grouping separators are not the same as for the U.S. A non-breaking space and a comma respectively should replace them. The `<xsl:decimal-format>` element of XSL enables us to specify these changes and to use `# ### zł` as a parameter for the `format-number()` function.

Set all these options in the source template so all is ready when it needs to be modified. For example, all calls to the `format-number()` use the optional format pattern, which is not done by default.

We must localize the XSLT template as well as the database: Using `<xsl:variable>` to define the different locale-specific options does not work because they are not really variables. You cannot define them several times in the same XSLT template, even enclosed inside `<xsl:if>` elements.

The localized settings for the currency formatting looks like this for Polish:

```
<xsl:decimal-format name='pl'
 decimal-separator='.' grouping-separator=' '/>
<xsl:variable name="fmt">pl</xsl:variable>
<xsl:variable name="currency"># ### zł</xsl:variable>
```

As for the conversion rate, we can use a parameter with a default value. Ideally the rate would come from another table or some repository kept up-to-date.

The remaining part of the template is separated into the section for HTML and the section for WML. Which one is used is determined by the `output` parameter.

Conversion to HTML

The conversion to HTML is very simple. The special deals descriptions are displayed as a table. Each entry is set into three `<TD>` elements:

```
<xsl:when test="$output='html'">
 <HTML>
  <BODY BGCOLOR="ivory">
   <H3>Special Deals Available Now!</H3>
   <TABLE BORDER="1" WIDTH="100%" CELLPADDING="7" CELLSPACING="3">
    <xsl:for-each select="Entry">
     <TR>
      <TD VALIGN="TOP"><B><xsl:value-of select="Title"/></B></TD>
      <TD VALIGN="TOP"><xsl:value-of select="Summary"/></TD>
      <TD VALIGN="TOP"><xsl:value-of select="format-number((Price*$rate),
➥$currency, $fmt)"/></TD>
     </TR>
    </xsl:for-each>
   </TABLE>
  </BODY>
 </HTML>
</xsl:when>
```

An example of the result is displayed in Figure 12.2.

Conversion to WML

The WML file is more complex to create because WAP devices have more constraints as far as layout goes. A WML file uses the concept of a deck of cards rather than a page. A card is usually limited to the small amount of text that can be displayed on a small LCD screen. In our example, we want to have each package on a separate card, so the user can move back and forth using the intrinsic navigation functions provided by WAP devices.

The code for that navigation is enclosed in the `<do>` statements and generated depending on where the item is in the deck: The first one will have only a `Next` function and the last one will have only a `Prev` function, while any other will have both. This can be achieved using the `count()` and `position()` XPath functions offered by XSLT.

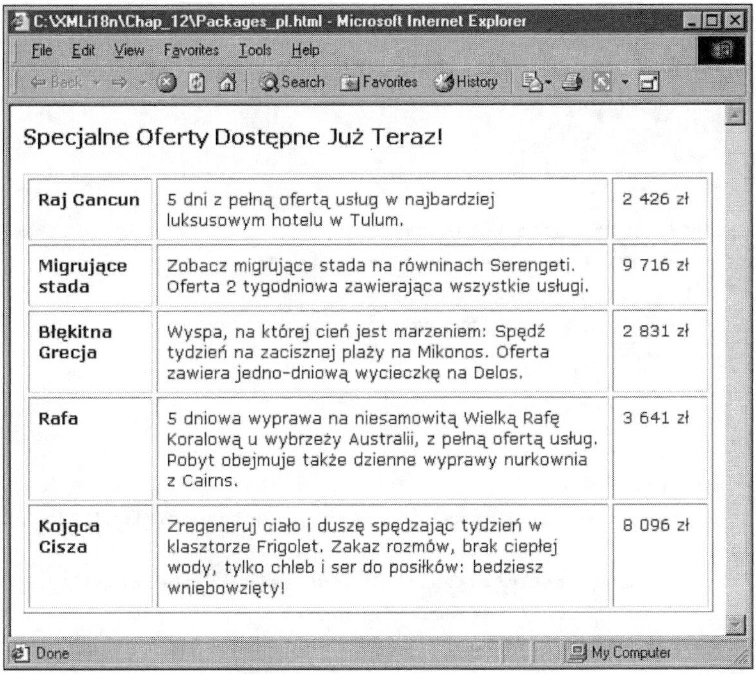

FIGURE 12.2

Special deals queried from the database, in Polish.

Listing 12.9 shows the complete XSL template, with the WML-specific section highlighted.

LISTING 12.9

Rendering_pl.xsl—Localized Template for Both HTML and WML Output

```
<?xml version="1.0" encoding="utf-8"?>
<xsl:stylesheet xmlns:xsl="http://www.w3.org/1999/XSL/Transform"
↪version="1.0">

 <xsl:param name="output">wml</xsl:param>
 <xsl:param name='rate'>4.05</xsl:param>

 <xsl:decimal-format name='pl'
  decimal-separator='.'
  grouping-separator=' '/>
 <xsl:variable name="fmt">pl</xsl:variable>
 <xsl:variable name="currency"># ### zł</xsl:variable>
```

LISTING 12.9   CONTINUED

```xml
<xsl:output encoding="us-ascii" indent="yes"/>

<xsl:template match="/Output">
 <xsl:choose>

  <xsl:when test="$output=&apos;wml&apos;">
   <xsl:variable name="Total" select="count(Entry)"/>
   <xsl:text disable-output-escaping="yes">
    &lt;!DOCTYPE wml PUBLIC "-//WAPFORUM//DTD WML 1.1//EN"
      "http://www.wapforum.org/DTD/wml_1.1.xml">
   </xsl:text>
   <wml>
    <xsl:for-each select="Entry">
     <xsl:element name="card">
      <xsl:attribute name="id">ID_<xsl:value-of select="position()"/>
</xsl:attribute>
      <xsl:attribute name="title">(<xsl:value-of select="position()"/> z
<xsl:value-of select="$Total"/>)</xsl:attribute>
      <xsl:if test="position()!=1">
       <do type="accept" label="Wstecz"><prev/></do>
      </xsl:if>
      <xsl:if test="$Total!=position()">
       <do type="prev" label="Dalej">
        <xsl:element name="go">
         <xsl:attribute name="href">#ID_
<xsl:value-of select="position()+1"/></xsl:attribute>
        </xsl:element>
       </do>
      </xsl:if>
      <p><small><b><xsl:value-of select="Title"/></b>-
       (<xsl:value-of select="format-number((Price*$rate), $currency,
$fmt)"/>)
       <xsl:value-of select="Summary"/></small>
      </p>
     </xsl:element>
    </xsl:for-each>
   </wml>
  </xsl:when>

  <xsl:when test="$output=&apos;html&apos;">
   <HTML><HEAD><META HTTP-EQUIV="Content-Type" CONTENT="text/html;
charset=utf-8"></META></HEAD>
```

LISTING **12.9** CONTINUED

```
    <BODY BGCOLOR="ivory">
     <H3>Specjalne Oferty Dostępne Już Teraz!</H3>
     <TABLE BORDER="1" WIDTH="100%" CELLPADDING="7" CELLSPACING="3">
      <xsl:for-each select="Entry">
       <TR>
        <TD VALIGN="TOP"><B><xsl:value-of select="Title"/></B></TD>
        <TD VALIGN="TOP"><xsl:value-of select="Summary"/></TD>
        <TD VALIGN="TOP" WIDTH="60"><xsl:value-of
➥select="format-number((Price*$rate), $currency, $fmt)"/></TD>
       </TR>
      </xsl:for-each>
     </TABLE>
    </BODY>
   </HTML>
  </xsl:when>

  <xsl:otherwise>
   <xsl:message terminate="yes">
    Error: invalid output parameter:
    The output parameter must be 'wml' or 'html'.
   </xsl:message>
  </xsl:otherwise>

  </xsl:choose>
 </xsl:template>

</xsl:stylesheet>
```

To be used by a WAP device, the WML page must be compiled into a binary format (WMLC), so we need a physical output from our template. We can use MSXSL again. For example, you can execute the following command line that uses the default parameters for the Polish data (WML and 4.05 conversion rate):

```
msxsl QueryResults_pl.xml Rendering_pl.xsl -o Packages_pl.wml
```

At this point the WML file can be compiled to WMLC and posted for WAP device access.

During localization, the verification of the WMLC file can be accomplished using one of the WAP emulators that several communication companies offer: for example, Nokia's WAP Toolkit or Ericsson's WapIDE. You can also emulate the various devices on a few Web sites. Figure 12.3 shows one of the cards generated by the template

served on a generic emulator. The corresponding WML document is shown in Listing
12.10.

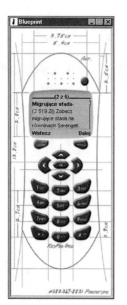

FIGURE 12.3

Display of the package deals on the generic emulator provided with Nokia's WAP Toolkit.

LISTING 12.10

`Packages_pl.wml`—WML Output from the Rendering Template

```
<?xml version="1.0" ?>
    <!DOCTYPE wml PUBLIC "-//WAPFORUM//DTD WML 1.1//EN"
     "http://www.wapforum.org/DTD/wml_1.1.xml">
    <wml>
<card id="ID_1" title="(1 z 5)">
<do type="prev" label="Dalej">
<go href="#ID_2"/>
</do>
<p><small><b>Raj Cancun</b>-
        (2 426 z&#x142;)
        5 dni z pe&#x142;n&#x105; ofert&#x105; us&#x142;ug w najbardziej
➥luksusowym hotelu w Tulum.</small>
</p>
</card>
<card id="ID_2" title="(2 z 5)">
<do type="accept" label="Wstecz"><prev/></do>
```

LISTING 12.10 CONTINUED

```
<do type="prev" label="Dalej">
<go href="#ID_3"/>
</do>
<p><small><b>Migruj&#x105;ce stada</b>-
        (9 716 z&#x142;)
        Zobacz migruj&#x105;ce stada na r&#xf3;wninach Serengeti. Oferta
➥2 tygodniowa zawieraj&#x105;ca wszystkie us&#x142;ugi.</small>
</p>
</card>
<card id="ID_3" title="(3 z 5)">
<do type="accept" label="Wstecz"><prev/></do>
<do type="prev" label="Dalej">
<go href="#ID_4"/>
</do>
<p><small><b>B&#x142;&#x119;kitna Grecja</b>-
        (2 831 z&#x142;)
        Wyspa, na kt&#xf3;rej cie&#x144; jest marzeniem:
➥Sp&#x119;d&#x17a; tydzie&#x144; na zacisznej pla&#x17c;y na Mikonos.
➥Oferta zawiera jedno-dniow&#x105; wycieczk&#x119; na Delos.</small>
</p>
</card>
<card id="ID_4" title="(4 z 5)">
<do type="accept" label="Wstecz"><prev/></do>
<do type="prev" label="Dalej">
<go href="#ID_5"/>
</do>
<p><small><b>Rafa</b>-
        (3 641 z&#x142;)
        5 dniowa wyprawa na niesamowit&#x105; Wielk&#x105; Raf&#x119;
➥Koralow&#x105; u wybrze&#x17c;y Australii, z pe&#x142;n&#x105;
➥ofert&#x105; us&#x142;ug. Pobyt obejmuje tak&#x17c;e dzienne wyprawy
➥nurkownia z Cairns.</small>
</p>
</card>
<card id="ID_5" title="(5 z 5)">
<do type="accept" label="Wstecz"><prev/></do>
<p><small><b>Koj&#x105;ca Cisza</b>-
        (8 096 z&#x142;)
        Zregeneruj cia&#x142;o i dusz&#x119; sp&#x119;dzaj&#x105;c
➥tydzie&#x144; w klasztorze Frigolet. Zakaz rozm&#xf3;w, brak
➥ciep&#x142;ej wody, tylko chleb i ser do posi&#x142;k&#xf3;w: bedziesz
➥wniebowzi&#x119;ty!</small>
```

LISTING 12.10   CONTINUED

```
</p>
</card>
</wml>
```

Testing is very important because not all devices support WML equally: Many have restrictions in the navigation features they offer, or very different ways to implement them.

Another possible problem is the character sets supported by the WML compilers. In some occurrences these limitations even include UTF-8 and UTF-16. To work around the problem you can specify US-ASCII as the output encoding of the XSL template. This will force any extended character to be written as a numeric character entity, which is usually correctly supported. Note that not all Windows systems have US-ASCII encoding support installed by default: In those cases you will get an error when using MSXSL.

Database fields often have restricted size. To reduce the number of errors, make sure these limitations are integrated in the translation file. XLIFF provides various attributes specialized for this. For example, if a translatable field can only contain 29 bytes, the XLIFF entry can be written:

```
<trans-unit id="123" maxwidth="20" size-unit="byte">
<source>Text to translate</source>
</trans-unit>
```

Summary

XML and databases complement each other very well. From an internationalization viewpoint, XML brings a great deal of reliability to data extraction and presentation because of its built-in internationalization support.

All database systems now have a wide range of utilities and features that make interfacing with XML documents easy. There are no standards for the different functions that link XML and databases, but some are currently being developed, such as XML Query.

XML and databases go well beyond the few glimpses you saw in this chapter. Object-oriented database storage, for example, makes interfacing with XML even more natural. From a localization viewpoint, as more and more applications use database back ends to store some of their messages and interface components, XML can be used to easily import and export the data to localize. This makes the process not only easier but also safer. It also adds new opportunities; for example, creating pseudotranslated data to test the application that uses the database is easy, and it enables better preparation for localization.

References

The following books and Web sites are some places to look for additional information about XML and databases. The document identified as a draft is still a work in progress at the time of this book's publication. Make sure you get the latest information.

Kevin William et al., *Professional XML Databases*. Wrox Press, 2000, ISBN 1-86100-358-7.

Steve Muench, *Building Oracle XML applications*. O'Reilly, 2000, ISBN 1-56592-691-9.

(draft) XML Query Specifications: `http://www.w3.org/TR/xquery`

XQL: `http://www.w3.org/TandS/QL/QL98/pp/xql.html`

Microsoft XML SDK: `http://msdn.microsoft.com/library/psdk/xmlsdk/xmls6g53.htm`

Oracle XDK: `http://technet.oracle.com/tech/xml`

Localizing XML Material

In This Part:

Localization Kits

In This Chapter:

If you are a customer of localization services, one area in which you can make a positive impact on a project is with the type of material you provide to your vendors. This set of files and information is often called a *Localization Kit*.

Obviously this topic goes far beyond dealing with only the localization of XML documents, and most of the advice for documentation and software applications that have no XML components can be applied in this case as well.

When starting a localization project, vendors are usually selected after providing a proposal. The content of a Request For Quotes/Proposal (RFQ/RFP) is usually a subset of the Localization Kit.

The Localization Kit can be viewed as a framework not only for handing off files and tasks to a localization vendor, but also for defining and laying out the whole localization effort, including how localized deliverables will be integrated into your development and release efforts. There are as many varieties of Localization Kits as there are different types of projects. However, some components are always present, or should be.

General Information

The general information about the project usually consists of the following elements:

Contacts

Contacts include the main project manager and possibly the contact responsible for the financial side of the project.

In addition, for each component of the product, you may want to provide the localizer with contacts who have a good technical understanding of the component. Examples are an author who participated in developing the document type of the XML files and an engineer who knows how the XML files are put together with the XSL templates and the scripts source code.

Ideally you have someone who oversees the internationalization aspect of your product. This person should also be one of the contacts provided.

At some point, you will want to involve in-country reviewers: people in your organization who have a direct interest with regard to the localized version of the product and who are in touch with the targeted market. These people should be involved in approving the terminology, for example.

Product Description

A clear description of what the product is, what it does, and how the different components interact is important. It will help the localizer to gain a good comprehension of the overall architecture and perhaps to discover some potential problems related to localization that might have been missed during the original design.

Naming each component clearly and consistently and associating the components with sets of files will make the picture clearer for the localizer.

Make use of the old wisdom that Descartes described in his famous *Discours de la méthode* four centuries ago. Describing a product is just like trying to solve a problem. When you have a complex problem to solve, the best way to approach it is to break it down into smaller problems. Each small problem is then much easier to resolve. Apply the same principle to your description and it will become easier to understand quickly.

Requirements

It is important to convey specific requirements for the project to the localizer. The following are a few questions to consider:

- Are there any length limitations for the elements to be localized?
- Is there any preformatted text that should be kept in a certain layout?

- Does the translation of some of the content need to be limited to a subset of characters?
- Are there any parts of the documents that should stay in the source language?
- Do you need translation for the file or directory names?

If possible and when appropriate, mark up all these specific requirements within the XML documents using the localization properties as described in Chapter 8, "Writing Internationalized Documents."

Provide information about what hardware or software is needed to work with the source files and the final product: for example, platform, operating system version, service pack upgrades, Web server application, database back end, browser and its version, compilers, specialized editors, development environments, and XML tools.

Also give any information needed to set up the development environment and the running product: system variables to set, command-line paths, virtual directories to use, and any other related information.

Delivery

Clearly specify what you expect back from the localization provider. This will help you avoid any last minute confusion and misunderstandings.

What are the target languages? In some cases you want to be very specific. If Spanish is one of the target languages, which market are you targeting: Europe, Mexico, or some of the Latin American countries? The localizer can help you with these questions if necessary.

What type of files should be delivered? Normally you always want the source documents, but in some cases you might also want some output form of the documents. For example, if the XML files are used to generate printed manuals, do you want the localized versions of the files after they have been converted to the required output format (PDF, PostScript, RTF, and so forth)?

Specify any preferences for the translated documents: In what encoding should it be? For example, a Japanese document could be in UTF-8, Shift_JIS, EUC-JP, or a number of other encodings. Indicate the encoding that makes sense for you. The same is true for the type of line breaks to use: Windows/DOS, Unix, or Macintosh?

In general, the localization provider will try to deliver files as similar as possible to the source data, and matching the usual expectations for the platform you are working in, but it never hurts to clearly specify these details in writing.

File and Folder Names

Related to the delivery specification are the instructions about how to handle file and directory names. XML projects often involve many documents in directory structures that can be complex. You can also have auxiliary files that are part of the structure (DTDs, entity declaration files, CSS style sheets, XSL templates, scripts, include files, and so forth). The way all these files need to be organized in the localized versions must be spelled out so you can seamlessly integrate the set of localized files in your environment.

A well-internationalized product will have a directory structure in place that provides rules to indicate where the translated files should go, how the various language directories should be named, what convention is to be used (for example, ISO language codes), and so forth.

In addition, specify whether the filenames and directory names should be translated. They usually are not, but you can make exceptions when appropriate.

Directory structure and possible translation of path are important because they can impact any link or query information you have in the files: URL, XPath or XPointer expressions, XSQL settings, and other related data.

Also, avoid using full paths in your project; use relative paths whenever possible. This will make the work of the localizer much easier when moving documents from one place to another.

Another possible source of problems is the way source files are named. For example, if the only difference in the name of two translatable files is their extensions, some tools, which replace the extensions when processing the files, will overwrite the first file with the second. Some other tools might not be very good at dealing with two different files with the same name located in two different directories. If these files are taken out of their original location at some point in the process, they will conflict.

Most of the tools have solved those issues nowadays, but a few still do not handle them well. Knowing whether you have files like this can help the localizer to take some steps to work around the problem early on rather than discovering it during the project.

Internationalization Assumptions

An outline of the possible internationalization issues for the product is helpful. It is made up of the list of the parts that have not been internationalized properly, as well as any other assumptions made in the development about how the localization will be done.

This will help the localizer to identify possible areas where more attention is needed. In addition, it will provide a way to indicate what internationalization means for you.

Process Definition

An outline of the expected localization process is a good document to provide to the vendor. If you prefer, the localizer can do this. In all cases the vendor should be able to point out some potential problems, based on experience with previous similar projects. Working out a final process that is clearly understood by all parties will pay off during the project.

Such process definition would include, for example, the different steps of the localization and when you expect them to occur as well as any contingency plans you might want to prepare. This process should also include the mechanism for inserting updated source material during the project, the procedure for reporting bugs and issues to your development team, and so forth.

Schedule and Time Frame

Indicate when you would like to receive the deliverable files for each component and each target language. Work out a schedule with the project manager on the vendor side.

It is wise to have milestones for completions as well as predefined points in the schedule to give updates to the vendor. This latter aspect should be discussed and planned along with your general strategy for updates.

The time frame in which the project needs to be done is important because it will drive much of the decision on how the documents will be processed. For example, more translators might have to be used in order to translate the same volume in a shorter period of time. This can impact the consistency and quality of the project.

Source Material

The source material to localize is obviously the most important part of the Localization Kit. It encompasses the source documents to localize as well as any collateral and reference material that can be critical to correct translation.

Along with the source material, an indication of the stability of the source should be provided: Are updates expected, and if yes, for which part of the material?

Source Documents

The localizer needs the original source files, not the final output files. There is often a difference between the files used by the endusers and the files that are the source for creating these final documents.

For example, in a Web site project, you want to give the source data (server-side files) to your localizer, not the served-up pages you can see by browsing the site. Auxiliary files such as XSL templates, DSSSL, CSS, XSL-FO style sheets, script source code, and any other documents or resources that participate in the creation of the final output are needed as well. Even files that have no translatable text might need to be modified: For instance, styles and presentation settings might need to be adapted.

If you are using you own XML vocabularies, provide at least the corresponding DTDs or schema files. They will be needed to create filters or set up translation tools to parse your documents. If possible, provide a document that supplies more precise localization-related information about the vocabularies and which elements and attributes are translatable, for example. See Chapter 7, "Creating Internationalized Document Types," for a detailed description of such a document.

User interfaces or documentation usually include graphics. The localizer needs the source files for those as well. If necessary, the additional resources used to create the final graphic might be needed. For instance, for GIF or JPEG files, you want to give the Photoshop source files, or any other layer-based original format you used to generate the final graphics, and also the palettes information, preferred fonts, and any design specifications that you have used to create the original graphics.

Another component most products have is an installer. If it needs to be localized as well, make sure to include the corresponding source material.

Ideally, the source files should come with a manifest that lists all of them, along with their respective format and information such as the ones that do not have translatable text, graphics that include text, and so forth.

Obviously the localizer will be able to make such list, but it makes sense for the developer to have it ready for the source documents.

Reference Material

The source material also includes any reference material that is useful to understand the translatable text better and to see it in context.

For example, if the XML documents are the repository of the user interface for an application, it is essential to provide the running application as well, or to offer a way to access it though the Web. Translation done out of context is more costly because the linguists must guess about what some of the words really are (verb, noun, adjective, and so forth) and the way they are used. The time spent asking questions and fixing inappropriate translation will have an impact on the project.

Supplying a way to see the content within its final context (or contexts if you are using the document as single-source material) reduces the difficulties caused by these issues.

The well-known principle of separating text and code cannot be applied blindly in XML because the border between what is code and what is text is very blurry and depends on each XML application. In many cases the code is really the structure of the document and is better left with the content. In other cases, the text is minimal and most of the document is non-translatable data. In these circumstances, externalizing the text can sometimes be appropriate. However, always be careful to keep the translatable text with its context as much as possible.

Word Counts

Translators are usually paid by the word, and therefore a large part of the localization project cost depends on the number of words to translate. Because this sometimes leads to disagreements between the different parties, getting accurate word counts is important.

The problem you will immediately face is the discrepancy between word counts done by different tools. The reason for this is that each utility tends to use different rules to define what a "word" is. For example: Is the character ' a separator? (Is "can't" one or two words?) If a word starts or is made only of digits and/or non-alphabetic characters, is it a word or not?

A quick test with the simple document shown in Listing 13.1 can be run through various tools to confirm this problem.

LISTING 13.1

`WordCount.htm`—Simple Document for Word Count Test

```
<?xml version='1.0' ?>
<html>
 <head>
  <title>text</title>
 </head>
 <body>
  <p>text;text-text/text,text.text_text text'text(text) 123456 +++++
↪text<b>text</b>text</p>
 </body>
</html>
```

The file, processed with some of the commercial or free tools available that support XML, is shown in Table 13.1.

TABLE 13.1	
Word Count Differences	
Application	*Word Count*
Déjà Vu	14
SDLX	11
System3	11
Translator's Workbench	10
Transit	5
Unix wc (with xmln/grep/awk)	8
WebBudget (default settings)	8
Word 2000	5

As you can see, the total word count varies from 5 to 14. Granted, the document has been made to emphasize the discrepancies, but it is easy to see how on large volumes you can get significant differences in proposals when your vendors use different tools.

> **NOTE:**   Everyone can claim to be correct because there are no standard rules for word breaking.
>
> At some point it would be positive for the translation industry to come up with a set of rules on how to count words. The various proprietary and commercial applications could then conform to this set of rules and generate responses to requests for quotes that could be compared with more realism.

One solution while waiting for a standard is to provide an estimated word count and ask rates per language. That way you can do better comparisons. Also compare your own tally to the word count provided by the vendor. In all cases, make sure to agree on final word count before the translation starts.

In addition to the discrepancy issue, there are possible problems with the source language. If it uses an ideograph-based script (such as Chinese or Japanese) the word count is usually based on a character count, where each Han character is counted as a word. Not all tools will have support for this, so you want to keep an eye on these numbers.

Also, in some languages like Thai, where there is no space between words but complex linguistic rules, most of the tools will not be able to come up with a meaningful count.

Terminology

The glossary is one of the most important resources used throughout the project. Terminology management enables you to ensure consistency across product lines and different releases of the same product. For the localizer, it is a key reference used to ensure consistency between components (such as the UI and the documentation). It is used at all points of the localization process and must be carefully maintained.

Creation

Some glossaries are simple bilingual lists of the software messages. Although this type of reference is important, you want to make the creation of your terminology a more comprehensive part of your development cycle.

XML offers some flexibility not always available in other formats: You can use inline specialized markers to indicate terms within the documents, making the creation of the terminology lists easier and the identification of these same terms much more efficient when translating.

Automated terminology extraction tools can also take advantage of the markup by inserting the special tags rather than extracting the terms, allowing for an easier review in context.

Your terminology is an asset, an investment you want to carry from one project to the next and reuse across products. Spending some time and money to do it right will pay back tenfold during localization.

Revision and Maintenance

When translating the glossary, usually at the very beginning of the project, the localization provider will want to validate the results with someone from your in-country staff who is involved with the customers if possible.

These reviews should be integrated in the schedule. Make sure that a format is agreed on for the glossary: Many terminology tools are available, and you can decide to use a specific one, but always be prepared to provide the data in a generic format that can be easily exchanged. The upcoming TBX/DXTL standard, described in Chapter 19, "Terminology Exchange," might be a solution in the future. Most of the time, if the fields you are using are simple enough, a simple tab-delimited format can also be used.

Any modification of the glossary will have repercussions on any translation memories you have. When providing the Localization Kit, make sure to note whether any change has been made in the existing terminology that was not propagated in the translation memories.

Existing Translation

Dealing with existing translation is often frustrating because the high expectations most software publishers have are often difficult to fulfill.

Using an existing translation for a new or modified document is called *leveraging*. During a localization project, leveraging applies in two situations:

- At the start of the project, when you want to utilize existing translation of an older product or version for the new project
- During the course of the project, when new or modified material is integrated into the XML documents that have already been through part of the localization process

Have a plan for both situations before you start the work. Here again, the localizer should be able to draw on past experiences and help you define the best approaches for your specific needs.

Reusing Previous Projects

If you use a document management system, or have implemented a reuse mechanism similar to the one discussed in Chapter 9, "Automated References," you might be able to provide the localizer with a set of preleveraged documents instead of simple source files.

Make sure the vendor can deal with such types of file: Very few tools currently let you translate preleveraged files if the files have not been leveraged using their own proprietary mechanisms.

Many of these tools will require the creation of a translation memory from the old source and target files and will leverage the new documents based on that database. Besides the additional alignment work (which could be costly), a number of potential pitfalls exist in batch pretranslation with TMs, as we have seen in Chapter 10, "Segmentation." Therefore, try to work out with the vendor the best way to use any preleveraged files you can provide.

The first draft of the new XML Localisation Interchange File Format (XLIFF) was released in May and should help solve that problem. However, it is mostly oriented toward extracted text and might not always be suitable for your purpose.

Ideally the vendor should be able to deal with pretranslated files in their original XML format, where any entry that has not been leveraged is marked as source language with the xml:lang attribute, while the rest of the document is in the target language. This could apply, for instance, to an XHTML file, as shown in Listing 13.2.

LISTING 13.2

PreLeverage.html—Preleveraged XML Document

```
<?xml version='1.0' encoding='iso-8859-1' ?>
<html xmlns="http://www.w3.org/1999/xhtml"
 xmlns:loc="urn:Localization-Properties"
 xml:lang='fr'>
<head>
 <title loc:id='1'>Convertir des URIs en URIs avec codes
↪d'échappement</title>
</head>
<body>
 <h1 id='2'>Convertir des URIs en URIs avec codes d'échappement</h1>
 <p id='3' xml:lang='en'>This function allows you to convert URIs
↪ (Universal Resource Identifiers) to escaped URIs. URIs are
↪ASCII-based and cannot have extended characters in raw format: they
↪need to be escaped.</p>
 <p id='4'>Cette fonction change les URIs de la façon suivante :
↪Convertit le contenu du Presse-Papier en UTF-8, puis convertit chaque
↪octet superieur á 128 au format d'échappement %HH oú HH est la valeur
↪héxadecimale de l'octet.</p>
 <p id='5'>Par exemple : <code>"http://www.ábç.org"</code> est
↪convertit en <code>http://www.%C3%A1b%C3%A7.org"</code>.</p>
 <p id='9' xml:lang='en'>To use the function:</p>
 <ol>
  <li id='6'>Dans l'application dans laquelle vous travaillez,
↪sélectionner l'URI á convertir.</li>
  <li id='7' xml:lang='en'>Copy it to the Clipboard (or double copy
↪it).</li>
  <li id='8'>Copier le contenu du Presse-Papier par-dessus la
↪sélection.</li>
 </ol>
 <p id='10'>Pour plus d'informations á propos des URIs internationaux
↪reportez-vous au site Web suivant : <a href="http://www.w3.org/
↪International/O-URL-and-ident.html">www.w3.org/International/
↪O-URL-and-ident.html</a>.</p>
 </body>
</html>
```

If you use pretranslated files, also provide the original documents in the source language as reference material.

If you do not have the capability to provide pretranslated documents, the solution is to use translation memories. Sending the TMs of a previous project with the Localization Kit will be helpful, but always keep in mind the various possible drawbacks of using TMs. One is that the translation in the TMs might not be the latest version of the translated files of the old project: Review changes or glossary modifications might have been made in the documents and never propagated in the TMs.

Often a realignment of the old source and target document is necessary so that an up-to-date TM can be used for the new project.

One of the details to work out with the vendor is the precise meaning of exact matches, fuzzy matches, and repetitions in their estimate of the leveraging. Not all tools work the same way and the analysis results are not always exactly comparable. Agreement on word count and on which tools are used is important.

At the end of the project, make sure you get back TMs with the translated documents. The TMs should be listed as one of the deliverables. In addition, agree with the vendor on how exactly these TMs will be updated. If they do not include edit and review changes, they are not worth as much as if they actually reflect the final translation that is in the localized files that are delivered.

Ensure that the TMs are delivered in a format you can reuse. TMX (Translation Memory eXchange) is a good bet for exchanging TM data across tools, but not in all cases: some tools do not support TMX well. For example, Translator's Workbench Edition 3 still supports only level 1 of TMX: Any inline element will be lost. Also keep in mind the problems related to segmentation that can affect TM exchange. See Chapter 10 for more details on that subject.

Update Strategy

During the project itself, you might have to integrate last-minute changes that have been made to the source documents. The Localization Kit should outline the expected process for these updates. Drawing on past experiences, the vendor should also be able to help out here.

One important aspect is to define points in the schedule where these changes can be integrated, and not keep sending changes bit by bit every day.

A version control system can go a long way toward helping you maintain a good handle on what files have changed during the project. A better alternative is to use a document management system able to generate the delta between the different versions.

It is essential to keep track of the changes you make in the files that are currently undergoing localization. Obviously, if possible, try to avoid any updates at all.

Ownership

Localization providers (and the freelance translators they might use) need to have a clear understanding of your position with regard to ownership of translation memories created during the project.

Do not rely on some implicit rules: There are none. Make sure all parties agree on who is the owner of the TMs and how they can (or cannot) be used outside of the project.

There are currently heated debates on this topic and the best way to prevent any misunderstandings is to clearly put in writing what is agreed on.

Test Material

Translation tools are usually designed to preserve any nontextual information embedded in the body of the document such as links, image references, and so forth. However, after translation, you might want to, at least, spot-check these elements, or run automatic functions that verify the translated document against its source.

Regardless of the level of testing that you decide the localizer will do, the Localization Kit should also include any material related to testing procedures or context verification: This will help in understanding how the product works.

Scripts and Roadmaps

When developing the original material, you also most likely must develop some sort of testing mechanism: automated scripts or at least roadmaps for manual testing.

Providing this material to the localizer will eliminate the duplication of efforts. Naturally, for automated scripts, this implies that the scripts have been designed with internationalization in mind. For example, they do not rely on hot keys to navigate through the interface.

The minimum test you should expect from the localizer is to return to you translated documents that are well formed and valid (if the relevant schemas and DTDs are available).

Test Sites

Systems that use N-tier architecture might require more logistics than other projects.

Whether the XML files are the source for a user interface, an online help system, or any other type of output, they need to be verified, and possibly tested, in context.

Make sure you have a test site in place for this purpose. It is usually much more efficient to provide the localizer with the relevant access rights to a test server you have already set up than to try to replicate one on the vendor side. By being able to upload or modify files in the server without your direct involvement, the localizer can carry on the testing tasks without wasting time in back-and-forth exchanges of data.

The same setup can be used early on by the translators to see the running product in its normal context. Make sure the Localization Kit contains all the necessary information to log on or otherwise access the relevant parts of your test server.

Summary

Beyond a simple way of providing files, the Localization Kit is a way of setting up the framework for the whole project.

Providing all the source files is the most important part. But the Localization Kit should also include other essential information such as a clear explanation of the product architecture, a strategy for updates, terminology data, means to access running product in context, and a detailed list of the deliverables expected.

Starting with a complete and well-organized Localization Kit can make a significant positive impact on the way the whole project will be handled and save costly misunderstandings.

References

Although they do not specifically address XML, the following books provide valuable information that is also valid for XML-based projects.

Bert Esslink, 2000, *A Practical Guide to Localization.* John Benjamins B.V., ISBN 1-58811-006-0.

Fergus O'Connell, 1996, *How to Run Successful Projects II: The Silver Bullet.* Prentice Hall, ISBN 0-132-39856-7.

Sue Ellen Wright and Gerhard Budin, 2000, *Handbook of Terminology Management.* John Benjamins, ISBN 1-556-19502-8.

# CHAPTER 14

XML-Enabled Translation Tools

In This Chapter:

As XML is used more frequently, translation tool vendors are adapting what they offer to the market and upgrading their products to support XML material.

In this chapter we will take a close look at various commercial tools from the XML viewpoint. The goal is to assess whether a given tool can handle XML documents.

We are looking here only at the XML aspect of each product. This is not a comparison between tools or an evaluation of their overall capabilities. How they manage translation memories, terminology, and other features is not taken in account. Neither is the learning curve, the intuitiveness of the interface, or other usability-related aspects. In other words, a poor result with XML does not preclude the tool from being very good in other areas, and conversely.

Although the results of the evaluation presented will change as new versions of the tools are released, the test documents listed here can be reused easily for your own test on any translation tool that offers XML support.

Getting Started

The tools evaluated here are Déjà Vu from Atril, SDLX from SDL International, TagEditor from TRADOS, and Transit from STAR. They are among the most-used commercial translation tools and all claim support for XML. They are all Windows applications (commercial translation tools are rare on other platforms). The evaluation has been done on a machine running Windows 98, U.S. version, with support for all languages available installed. Tests that failed were run again under Windows 2000 with all language support installed.

To see how each tool fares with a basic document, we can use the one displayed in Listing 14.1. It contains all the elements of the first sample DTD, shown in Listing 14.2.

LISTING 14.1

`Test_Simple.xml`—A Simple XML Document

```
<?xml version="1.0" encoding="iso-8859-1"?>
<doc>
 <para title="Title">Text to translate including <block>special
➥text</block>.</para>
 <BLOCK>Data not to translate</BLOCK>
</doc>
```

LISTING 14.2

`Test.dtd`—Document Type Definition for the Test Files

```
<!ELEMENT doc (para | BLOCK)* >
<!ATTLIST doc
   xml:lang     CDATA     #IMPLIED
   xml:space    CDATA     #IMPLIED >

<!ELEMENT para (#PCDATA | block)* >
<!ATTLIST para
   title        CDATA     #IMPLIED
   xml:lang     CDATA     #IMPLIED
   xml:space    CDATA     #IMPLIED >

<!ELEMENT BLOCK (#PCDATA) >

<!ELEMENT block (#PCDATA) >
```

The DTD is very simple. The root element <doc> can contain <para> or <BLOCK> elements. The <para> element can have an attribute title and contain an inline element called <block>. The content of all elements except <BLOCK> is translatable. In addition, the two XML attributes xml:lang and xml:space can be used in <doc> and <para>.

Déjà Vu

Atril Software, based in Madrid, is the developer of Déjà Vu. The product tested here is version 3.0.16, available on Atril's Web site (`http://www.atril.com`).

SGML/XML is one of the various input formats offered. The first step is to create a new file that defines which elements and attributes are translatable and which are not. This is a new *filter* in Déjà Vu's terminology, and it is done through the SGML Filter Maintenance tool.

There are two ways to create the new filter: manually or by importing a sample file. The **Read from SGML File** command gives the result shown in Figure 14.1.

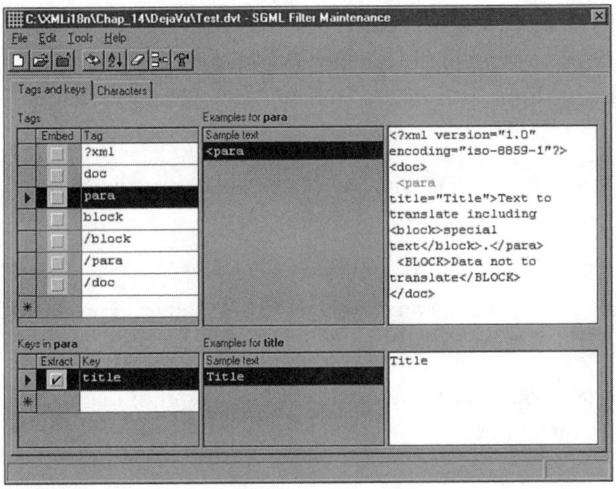

FIGURE 14.1

Déjà Vu SGML Filter Maintenance tool after reading the `Test_Simple.xml` *file.*

Note that the elements listed include opening and closing tags and the XML declaration is listed as one of the tags. This is somewhat puzzling: A standard parser would only need the name of each element and would not treat the XML declaration as an element.

The attributes (called *keys* in Déjà Vu's terminology) are set as translatable by default. Make sure to go through all attributes and set the flags appropriately.

The `<block>` element is not set as an embedded (inline) element. Make sure to go through each element and set the flags properly.

A more alarming problem is the absence of the `<BLOCK>` element. It has been visibly confused with the `<block>` element. XML is case sensitive and apparently the parser is not. Although using case difference to distinguish element or attribute names is not common (and probably not recommended), it is part of the XML specifications and should be supported.

Another issue is the impossibility of specifying when an element is not translatable. This is rather problematic because in the translation environment the tag names are not visible and the linguist has no way to guess the non-translatable extracted segments.

SDLX

SDL International, headquartered near London, is the developer of SDLX. The product tested here is version 3.5.0, available on SDL's Web site (`http://sdlx.sdlintl.com`).

When creating a new project, the **Project Import** dialog box offers SGML/XML as one of the file types supported. When you select it, the **Options** button enables you to access the **SGML/XML Extract Options** dialog box. Here you can specify the localization properties for your XML vocabulary.

SDL uses a definition file, Analysis file (`.anl`), where each element and attribute can be associated with various properties: translatable or not, inline or not, and so forth.

The Analysis file can be created from sample files or from an existing DTD. You can also create the Analysis file in a text editor from an existing one; it is, after all, an XML file itself.

Because we have a DTD for our test vocabulary, we can use it. The result of the Analysis command is shown in Figure 14.2.

FIGURE 14.2

SDLX analysis result for the `Test.dtd` *file.*

No surprise so far: All elements and attributes have been identified correctly. The
<block> element has been detected as an inline element, and <BLOCK> is seen as a
separate element, not inline. By default, elements are translatable and attributes are not.
We need to correct that for the <BLOCK> (not translatable for us) and the title attribute of the <para> element (translatable in our case).

The final Analysis file is displayed in Listing 14.3.

LISTING 14.3

Test.anl—SDLX Analysis File

```
<?xml version="1.0" encoding="ISO-8859-1"?>
<ANAL FILE="C:\XMLi18n\Chap_14\SDLX\Test.dtd">
 <ELM ID="doc" CONTENT="(para | BLOCK)*" INLINE="NO" XLATE="YES">
  <ATTRIB ID="xml:lang" ELEMENT="doc" VALUE="CDATA" XLATE="NO"/>
  <ATTRIB ID="xml:space" ELEMENT="doc" VALUE="CDATA" XLATE="NO"/>
 </ELM>
 <ELM ID="para" CONTENT="(#PCDATA | block)*" INLINE="NO" XLATE="YES">
  <ATTRIB ID="title" ELEMENT="para" VALUE="CDATA" XLATE="YES"/>
  <ATTRIB ID="xml:lang" ELEMENT="para" VALUE="CDATA" XLATE="NO"/>
  <ATTRIB ID="xml:space" ELEMENT="para" VALUE="CDATA" XLATE="NO"/>
 </ELM>
 <ELM ID="BLOCK" CONTENT="(#PCDATA)*" INLINE="NO" XLATE="NO">
 </ELM>
 <ELM ID="block" CONTENT="(#PCDATA)*" INLINE="YES" XLATE="YES">
 </ELM>
</ANAL>
```

After the Test_Simple.xml file is imported, only the relevant text is offered to the
translators, as shown in Figure 14.3.

TagEditor

TRADOS GmbH, based in Stuttgart, Germany, develops TagEditor. The product
evaluated here is version 3 build 139, available on TRADOS' Web site
(http://www.trados.com).

TagEditor is the SGML/XML specialized editor included in the TRADOS Translation
Workbench suite. The definition of the localization properties of a vocabulary is done
through the **DTD Settings Wizard**.

You can create the new settings file from an existing DTD or from an existing settings
file. The result of the import with our DTD is shown in Figure 14.4.

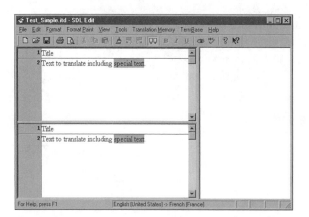

FIGURE 14.3

`Test_Simple.xml` *after extraction in SDLX.*

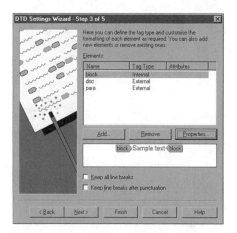

FIGURE 14.4

DTD settings imported from the `Test.dtd` *file.*

The `<block>` element has been recognized as an inline (internal) element. However, no attributes have been imported; we must add them manually.

Another problem is that the `<BLOCK>` element is not recognized as different from `<block>`. Trying to add it manually will simply result in replacing `<block>` with the new definition for `<BLOCK>` the next time the settings file is loaded.

The best solution in this specific case is to use `<block>`; otherwise we would get segmentation problems because `<block>` is an inline element, and more importantly is translatable, whereas `<BLOCK>` is neither.

Non-translatable elements can be specified by using the **Group** property. The **Non-Xlatable** type also prevents the translation of a given element, but seems much more cumbersome to use.

Transit

Transit is developed by STAR GmbH. The product evaluated here is version 3.0 build 182. You cannot download a demonstration version from STAR's Web site, but you can obtain one on a CD.

Transit offers various filters and among them is one for SGML/XML. As shown in Figure 14.5, the tool uses regular expressions to map the tags of the source documents to the internal XML format it uses during the translation. The default settings might be enough for some document types.

In our case we can try to create new parameters for our specific DTDs. The task is not easy: Very little documentation is available and the paradigm used is quite different from the one utilized in other tools. This makes guessing how to set up the properties for a new filter rather challenging. As a matter of fact, it was not possible to achieve in this evaluation. Transit technical support was helpful and responsive but time constraints made it impossible to get the settings correct for this evaluation. The tests were done using the default parameters, which obviously puts the tool at a disadvantage and prevents us from determining whether Transit supports some of the capabilities tested here.

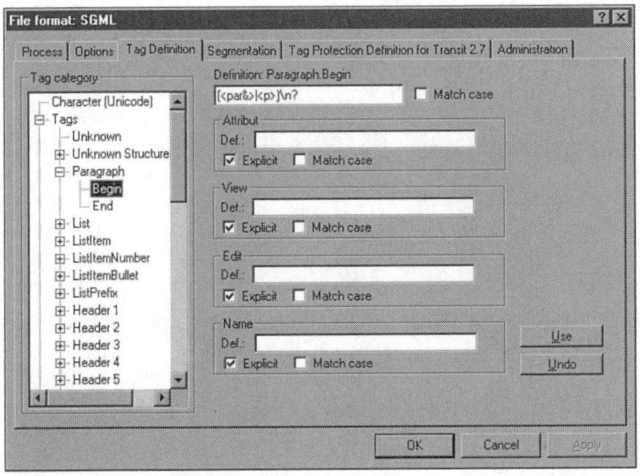

FIGURE 14.5

The Transit dialog box to set the property of a filter, here with the default settings for XML.

Conditional Properties

One aspect of translatable XML that could not be tested here is conditional translatable text. For example, Listing 14.4 displays an XML document in which only one word is translatable.

LISTING 14.4

`Test_Conditions.xml`—An XML Document with Conditional Translatable Text

```xml
<?xml version="1.0" ?>
<page>
 <entry class="topic" level="1">
  <param type="descr">Overview</param>
  <param type="source">overview.xml</param>
 </entry>
 <entry class="button">
  <param type="action">open(windows1)</param>
  <param type="descr">bold; pushlike;</param>
  <param type="source">openBtn.png</param>
 </entry>
</page>
```

The `<param>` element is translatable only if the `type` attribute is `descr`, but also only if the class attribute of the `<entry>` parent element is `topic`.

Currently none of the tools evaluated here makes provision for such occurrences. With the growing number of proprietary XML vocabularies that are used, cases similar to this are happening more often. Although it is obviously not a good idea to develop vocabularies that yield this type of problem, it would be an important step forward to have translation tools capable of handling conditional translatable text.

Input Encoding

One of the first expectations of an XML-enabled translation tool is that it supports UTF-8 and UTF-16. This is, after all, a requirement for any XML processor.

Listing 14.5 shows a simple document with a few extended characters. It has been encoded in three forms: UTF-8, UTF-16LE (little-endian), and UTF-16BE (big-endian).

LISTING 14.5

`Test_UTF16LE.xml`—Simple Text with a Few Extended Characters

```
<?xml version="1.0" ?>
<doc>
 <para>Ø = O-slash, þ = thorn</para>
 <para>Œ = OE-ligature, ı = dotless-i</para>
</doc>
```

The test is simple: trying to import the three files in each translation tool.

Déjà Vu

Atril's product does not score well in this test: None of the three encodings imports correctly. The two `UTF-16` files are simply truncated right at the first null byte: Déjà Vu does not support 16-bit documents. The `UTF-8` file is imported as a file encoded in `iso-8859-1`, as shown in Figure 14.6.

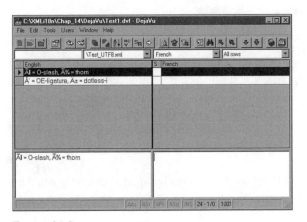

FIGURE 14.6

Invalid import of the file encoded in `UTF-8` *in Déjà Vu.*

In XML, no encoding declaration at the top of a document means that the document is in either `UTF-8` or `UTF-16`. To check whether the problem is simply a lack of support for the correct default encoding, we can add the relevant encoding declarations and try again. No luck: The results are the same.

SDLX

The SDLX Project Import Wizard offers a **Use UTF-8** check box to use for the `UTF-8` document. Aside from the fact that, once in the editor module, you must manually set the font of the source text to see the characters properly, all works as expected, as you can see in Figure 14.7.

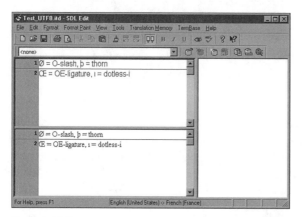

FIGURE 14.7

A `UTF-8` *document imported in SDLX.*

Results are not as good for the `UTF-16` test documents. Both produce an empty extracted file. Here as well, adding the encoding declaration does not change the outcome.

TagEditor

TagEditor acts as expected with the three files. They are all imported correctly into the editor. You can see as an example the `UTF-16` big-endian in Figure 14.8.

A quick additional test shows that the application correctly saves the translated files into the encoding used originally for each.

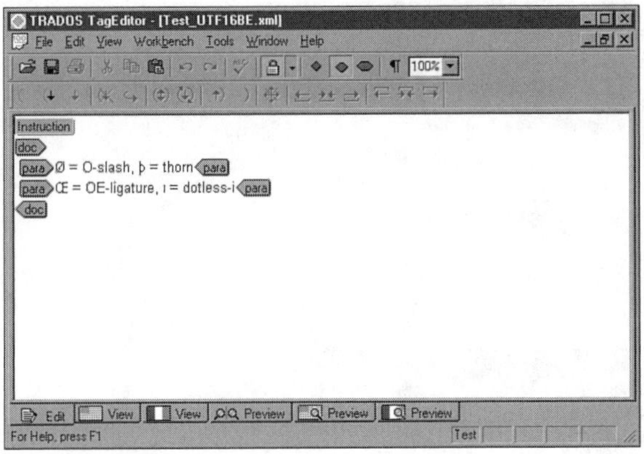

FIGURE 14.8

A `UTF-16BE` *document imported in TagEditor.*

Transit

Testing encoding is independent from the DTD used, so we can do this with the default DTD settings.

Importing the three documents in Transit does not generate any error. However, when the language pair files are opened, as shown in Figure 14.9, it appears that the editor does not support the encodings correctly. The extended characters for all files appear as if they were `UTF-8`, but they are interpreted as `windows-1252`. This means the `UTF-16` documents, and probably the `UTF-8` file as well, were parsed correctly, but somehow Transit editor failed to carry the conversion to the system code page properly.

An option in the **Options** tab of the **File Format** dialog box offers a list of conversion tables named **Utf-16**, **SGML**, **FINFO**, and so forth. The help does not give any information about its role. Repeating the test with that parameter set respective to **Utf-8** and **Utf-16** does not change the final outcome in the editor.

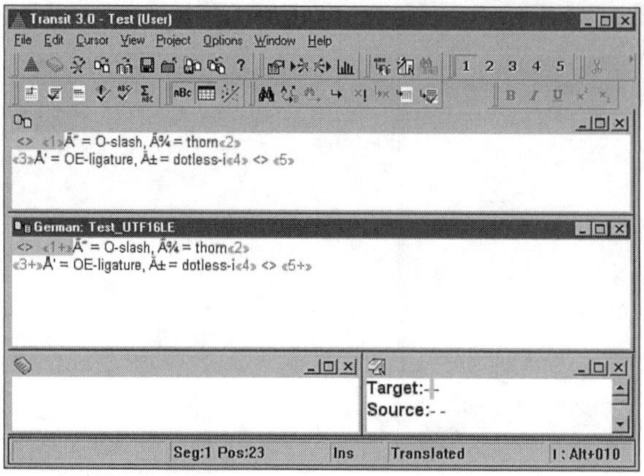

FIGURE 14.9

A `UTF-16LE` *document after import in Transit. The 16-bit characters have been converted, but the editor treats the file as if it were in* `windows-1252`.

CDATA Sections

The next test is to see how the different tools treat the CDATA sections.

A CDATA section is, simply put, a chunk of non-XML data within an XML document. Content inside such a section is not escaped, and cannot include elements. Listing 14.6 shows the example we are using.

LISTING 14.6

`Test_CDATA.xml`—Example of a CDATA Section

```
<?xml version="1.0" encoding="iso-8859-1"?>
<doc>
 <para><![CDATA[
line 2 of a pre-formatted and non-escaped
text. <=lt, &=amp, >=gt, "=quot, '=apos
&amp; &lt; &quot; &apos; (all literal)
last line with two spaces:  .]]></para>
</doc>
```

Déjà Vu

The test file imports without error in Déjà Vu, but the result is not good. As displayed in Figure 14.10, the text is treated as normal content, except for the terminal mark `]]>`. The start marker `<![CDATA[` is included in the translated text, and the literal text that looks like character entities is converted to raw characters.

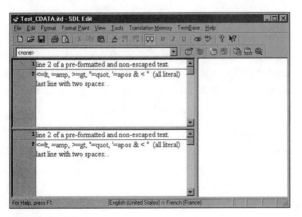

FIGURE 14.10

CDATA section incorrectly imported in Déjà Vu.

The export function is consistent with the import: Special characters are escaped, which means for example that `<![CDATA[` becomes `&lt;![CDATA[`. There is an option in the **Export** function to output the special characters as they are, but it applies to the whole file and would not fix all problems anyway. The CDATA sections must be fixed manually after translation, no matter what.

SDLX

The SDL tool goes halfway to support CDATA. The markers are excluded from the extracted text, but as you can see in Figure 14.11, entity-like text is treated as a real entity.

FIGURE 14.11

CDATA section in SDLX.

The output generated is consistent with this and also must be fixed manually.

TagEditor

In TagEditor, the CDATA section imports correctly. The result is shown in Figure 14.12.

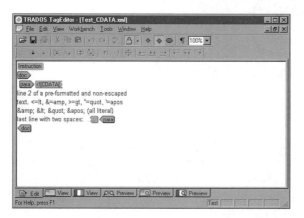

FIGURE 14.12

CDATA section in TagEditor.

However, the output is not quite perfect: All special characters ($\&$, $<$, and so forth) are escaped as if they were outside of a CDATA section. Here again the file must be fixed manually after translation.

Transit

Transit imports the document without error, but the CDATA content is marked as a code as shown in Figure 14.13. This can be caused by some of the default settings: The `<![CDATA[` marker matches the regular expression defined for the beginning of an unknown structure. The tool offers a way to include the content of the CDATA section as a translatable part, but by default it does not recognize the XML construct.

Creating the translated file results in a document where the CDATA content has been preserved, including its white spaces.

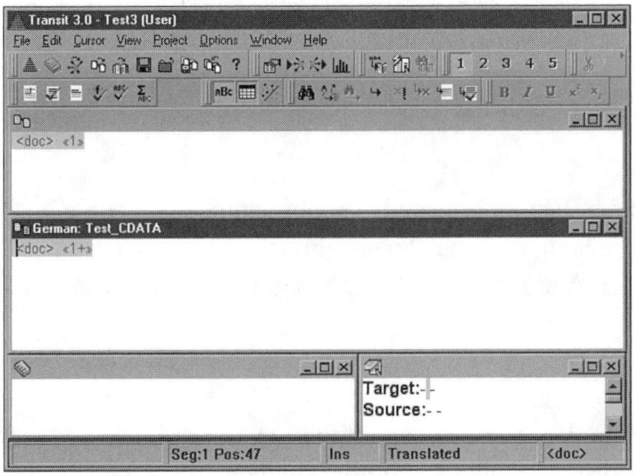

FIGURE 14.13

Result of the CDATA section imported in Transit with the default XML settings.

Special Statements and Output Encoding

XML documents can include a number of special statements in addition to CDATA, such as comments, processing instructions, and document type declarations. The translation tools should be able to mask these entries from the user but output them unchanged in the translated files. Obviously, if any extended character is included in these statements, it should be converted if necessary to reflect any encoding changes as well.

The test file for this is shown in Listing 14.7. It includes one `<para>` element and examples of the various special statements.

LISTING 14.7

`Test_Quotes.xml`—Special Statements Test Document

```
<?xml version='1.0' encoding='iso-8859-1'?>
<!DOCTYPE Test SYSTEM "Test.dtd" >
<doc>
 <!-- Comments
      that should remain untouched -->
 <para title='First text to translate'
 >Second text to translate.</para>
 <?xyz some processing instructions not to localize
  with extended characters: á=a-acute ?>
</doc>
```

LISTING 14.7   CONTINUED

```
<!-- A last comment with extended chars:
      á=a-acute, è=e-grave -->
```

It can also be useful to check whether the tools correctly support single and double quotes to enclose attributes, because both are legal. To test this, the file uses only attribute values between single quotes. (We have already seen that double quotes work.)

Déjà Vu

The file imports without error in Déjà Vu, but the value of the `title` attribute, although extracted, is also truncated and includes its starting single quote. A few additional tests show that the tool simply does not handle single-quoted attributes correctly.

To test how extended characters are handled in the output, we can translate the two entries into Russian and export the file. A first look at the file shows that the encoding declaration of the output file is still the original `iso-8859-1`, while the text is now in `windows-1251`. Figure 14.14 shows the document set with a Cyrillic font.

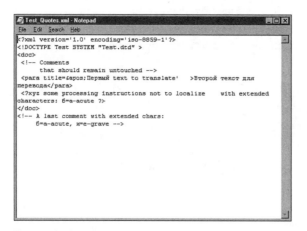

FIGURE 14.14

Déjà Vu output of `Test_Quotes.xml` *translated into Russian.*

Note the extended characters that were in the special statements have not been converted to make up for the fact that the document is now not in the same encoding, and they are now displayed incorrectly: 'à' as 'б', and 'é' as 'и'.

SDLX

In SDLX the test document imports without problem. The Russian output file is encoded in `windows-1251`, and the encoding declaration is correctly updated as shown in Figure 14.15.

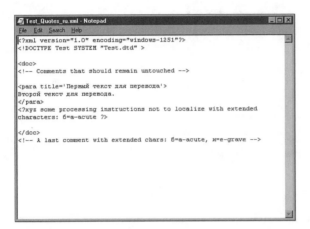

FIGURE 14.15

SDLX output of `Test_Quotes.xml` *translated into Russian.*

The special statements are preserved, except for the white spaces. The extended characters included in the non-translatable parts of the file are not converted and are now incorrect.

TagEditor

TagEditor imports the test file correctly. The special statements are accessible to the linguist but protected and, if needed, can be compressed in a short symbol.

The translated document is encoded in `windows-1251`, but the encoding declaration is not updated, as you can see in Figure 14.16.

The extended characters in the special statements have changed: the á is now a simple a, and the è a plain e. This transformation is rather appropriate because `windows-1251` does not support the two original characters, and numeric character references cannot be used there. The original Windows line breaks (carriage return + line feed) within the special statement have been curiously converted to Unix line breaks (line feed), but the other white spaces have been preserved.

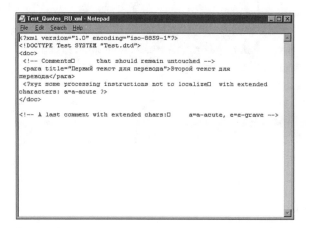

FIGURE 14.16

TagEditor output of `Test_Quotes.xml` *translated into Russian.*

Transit

The demonstration version of Transit comes with only one target language, German, so we cannot run our test from English into Russian. However, because the choice for the source is not limited and includes Russian, we can translate from Russian to German. This will provide the same conditions for the test as far as code sets, only reversed. The test file used is shown in Listing 14.8.

LISTING 14.8

`Test_QuotesRU.xml`—Russian Test File

```
<?xml version='1.0' encoding='windows-1251'?>
<!DOCTYPE Test SYSTEM "Test.dtd">
<doc>
 <!-- Comments
      that should remain untouched -->
 <para title='Первый текст для перевода'
 >Второй текст для перевода</para>
 <?xyz some processing instructions not to localize
  with extended characters: б=cyr-letter-be ?>
</doc>

<!-- A last comment with extended chars:
     б=cyr-letter-be, и=cyr-letter-i -->
```

The file imports correctly in Transit (see Figure 14.17). Note that because we use the default XML settings, the `title` attribute has not been extracted.

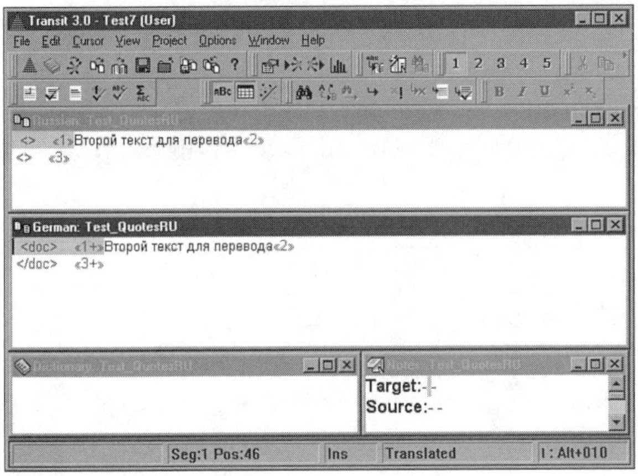

FIGURE 14.17

Russian source text imported in Transit.

The file exported after translation does not have its encoding declaration updated. Note also that extended characters are converted into character entities, a default not supported by XML. More interestingly, the two extended characters б and и in the last comments are converted into NCRs: `&#65505;` and `&#65512;` but the letter б in the processing instruction is changed into `&bcy;`. This inconsistency reveals a problem with converting extended characters in comments. You will notice that 65505 and 65512 are respectively 0xFFE1 and 0xFFE8 in hexadecimal. Those are the 16-bit negative values for 0xE1 and 0xE8, which are the original code points of the two extended characters in `windows-1251`. There is a bug involving an unsigned value converted to a signed value somewhere in the source code of Transit.

`xml:lang` and `xml:space` Attributes

As we have already seen, XML offers two predefined attributes: `xml:lang` and `xml:space`.

The `xml:lang` attribute identifies the language of a given element content. This is obviously a feature of XML that we could expect translation tools to support. Content marked up in a language different from the source language should not be treated as translatable. In the same way, any `xml:lang` attribute of the document that had the source locale for value should be updated to the target locale in the translated document.

The `xml:space` attribute, when set to `preserve`, indicates that the content should be treated like a preformatted text where all white spaces must be left intact. This is important information for the tools because they must offer the same mechanism in the translation environment.

Our test file for these two XML features is shown in Listing 14.9. It is a simple document with a set of `<para>` elements in different languages, clearly identified, but using different variations of the language code. One of the elements also has the `xml:lang` attribute set to `preserve`.

LISTING 14.9

`Test_Attributes.xml`—**Test File for** `xml:lang` **and** `xml:space`

```
<?xml version="1.0" encoding="windows-1252"?>
<doc xml:lang="en">
 <para>Text 1 in English</para>
 <para xml:lang="en">Text 2 in English.</para>
 <para xml:lang="fr">Texte 1 en français.</para>
 <para xml:lang="fr-fr">Texte 2 en français.</para>
 <para>Text 3 in English</para>
 <para xml:lang="en-us" xml:space="preserve">Text 4 in English: line 1
Line 2 with several spaces: [    ]
Line 3.</para>
</doc>
```

All tools evaluated enable us to specify a source language; we will use English and see how the text marked as French is handled.

Déjà Vu

The file imports without error in Déjà Vu, but the two paragraphs identified as French have been extracted as well, as shown in Figure 14.18. Also, the white spaces in the paragraph with the `xml:space` attribute have not been preserved.

The XML document created from the translation has all its `xml:lang` attributes untouched, just like the original. They will need to be updated manually after translation.

In output, any line breaks you have inserted during translation are lost; however, extra spaces are preserved so you can partially fix the lost formatting in the tool.

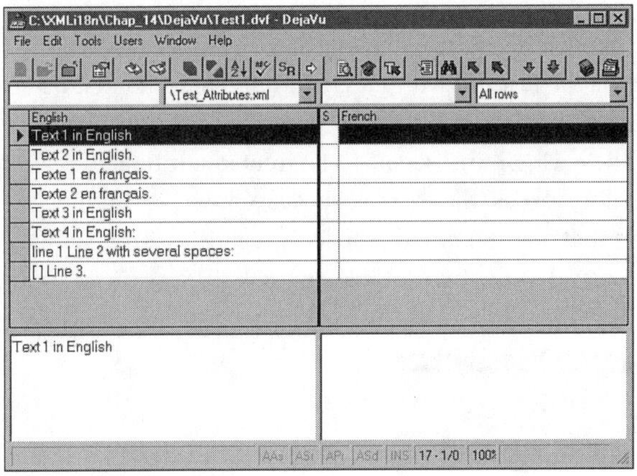

FIGURE 14.18

No language distinction is made when importing the text to Déjà Vu.

SDLX

In SDLX the test document imports without problem, but here also the text in both languages is set for translation, as illustrated in Figure 14.19. The preformatted paragraph is again not imported with its white spaces preserved.

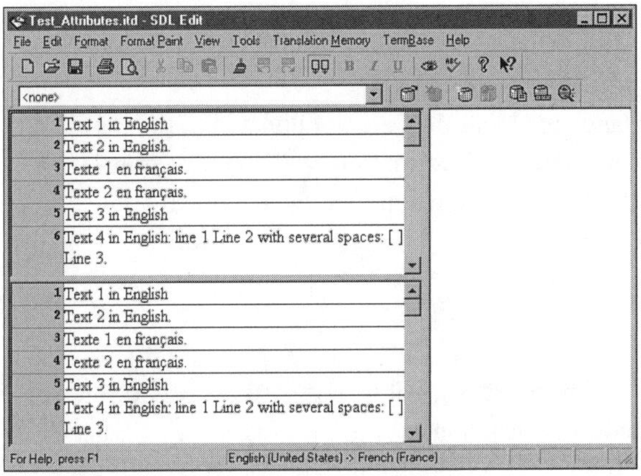

FIGURE 14.19

The text in both French and English is extracted to SDLX.

The `xml:lang` attributes are not updated in the exported file. They will need to be fixed manually. The formatting of the last paragraph is also lost and cannot be fixed in SDLX Edit itself.

TagEditor

Like the other tools, TagEditor opens the test file without error, but makes no distinctions between the paragraph marked as English and the one already in French. The result is displayed in Figure 14.20. The xml:space seems to be treated a little better: although the line breaks are reduced to spaces, the extra spaces are preserved in the imported text. A rapid check shows that any run of extra spaces, regardless of whether xml:space is defined, will be preserved in the translatable content.

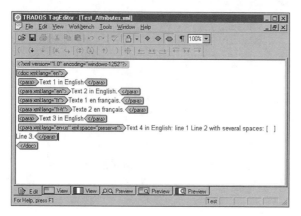

FIGURE 14.20

TagEditor does not take into account the xml:lang *attribute when importing the XML documents.*

Again, as with the other tools, the language identifiers are not updated in the translated document and need to be changed manually. Any formatting you do in the translated text is preserved in the output, so the last paragraph could be fixed manually in TagEditor and saved formatted.

Transit

The test document imports without error in Transit. All text, regardless of the value of the xml:lang attribute, is presented for translation as shown in Figure 14.21. The white spaces in the paragraph with the xml:space attribute are not preserved.

Here again, it is possible that some settings would enable the user to specify a given behavior for elements that have the xml:space present, but the help does not provide enough information to test this.

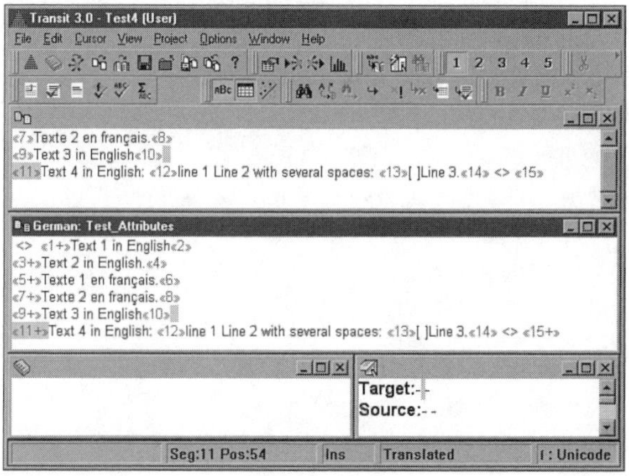

FIGURE 14.21

Transit does not take into account `xml:lang` *and* `xml:space`.

It is not possible to enter a line break manually in the editor, and the output file generated from the tool does not preserve extra white spaces. The preformatted paragraph must be fixed manually. As with the other tools, the `xml:lang` attributes are not updated automatically.

Entities

XML uses various types of entities that should be supported by the translation, in both import and export:

- The five predefined character entities (`&lt;`, `&amp;`, `&gt;`, `&apos;`, and `&quot;`)
- The numeric character references (NCRs), both decimal (`&#DDDD;`) and hexadecimal forms (`&#xHHHH;`)
- Any external entities

The last category can be handled in different ways. Ideally, the tool should be able to offer to translate the source in context, clearly marked. At worst, it should preserve the entity calls and offer alternative ways to translate their corresponding declarations.

To verify the way the tools behave with entities we can use the document in Listing 14.10. It includes all forms of entities in both attribute values and element content.

LISTING **14.10**

`Test_Entities.xml`—A Sample of All Forms of XML Entities

```
<?xml version="1.0" ?>
<!DOCTYPE doc [
<!ENTITY UserEntity "Text to localize (with &#225; and &#xe1;)">
]>
<doc>
<para title="&lt;=less-than">&lt;=less-than</para>
<para title="&amp;=ampersand">&amp;=ampersand</para>
<para title="&gt;=greater-than">&gt;=greater-than</para>
<para title="&apos;=apostrophe">&apos;=apostrophe</para>
<para title="&quot;=quote">&quot;=quote</para>
<para title="&#xe1;=a-acute">&#xe1;=a-acute</para>
<para title="&#225;=a-acute">&#225;=a-acute</para>
<para title="&UserEntity; = entity">&UserEntity; = entity</para>
</doc>
```

When parsed, the document should be represented as displayed in Figure 14.22.

FIGURE **14.22**

Parsed entities of the `Test_Entities.xml` *document shown in Internet Explorer.*

Déjà Vu

The document opens correctly in Déjà Vu. The definition of the external entity is extracted and available for translation. The references in the document are simply included as-is in the text.

One problem is that the tool also sees the semicolon in the entities as a segment break. This issue can possibly be fixed by changing the rules for breaking sentences. A **Join Sentences** function can put the split text back together, but it would be cumbersome to use it every time an entity is in the text.

All predefined character entities are converted appropriately. Note that they must be declared in the SGML filter you create with the SGML Filter Maintenance utility.

The decimal numeric character reference is converted to a raw character, but the hexadecimal form is interpreted as `xe1;`, as shown in Figure 14.23.

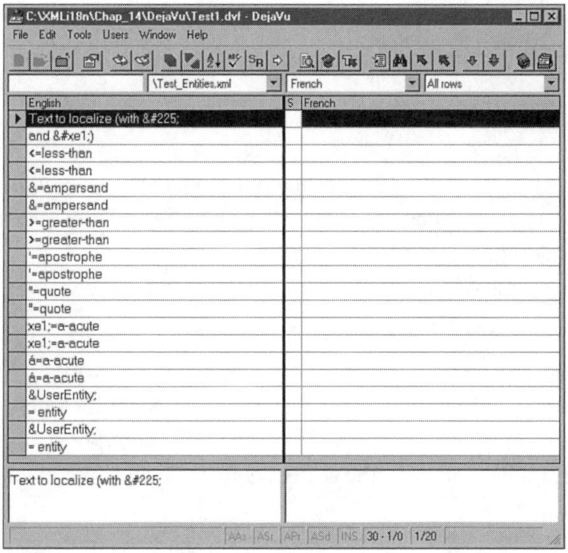

FIGURE 14.23

Entities and numeric character references imported in Déjà Vu.

The conversion, when it works, works for both attribute values and element content.

When exporting the translation, all entities are conserved, except the hexadecimal NCR that was lost when importing the file. The decimal form is output as a raw character with a `windows-1252` code point. This is fine because `a-acute` exists in that encoding. The problem is that the document was really a `UTF-8` file, so you must fix the encoding declaration as we have already seen.

SDLX

The test file imports without error in SDLX. But the text offered for translation as shown in Figure 14.24 includes several problems.

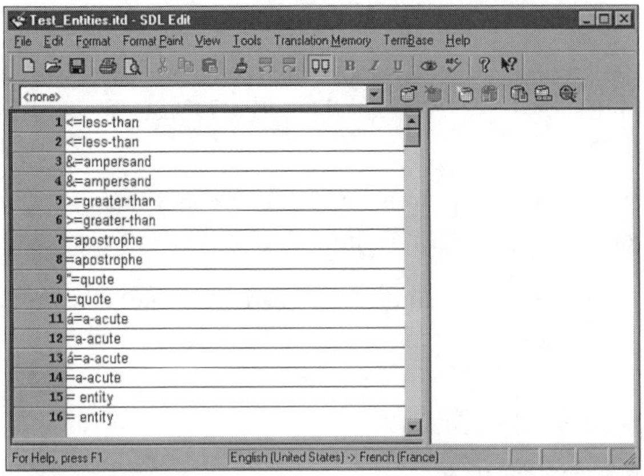

FIGURE 14.24

`Test_Entities.xml` *after import in SDLX.*

The `&apos;` character reference is apparently not supported at all: both entries 7 and 8 should have one. A second surprise is the presence of an apostrophe at line 10 where you should have a double quote. Also, the numeric character references, both hexadecimal and decimal, are not supported inside elements, while they are in attribute values.

The definition for the `&UserEntity;` external references is not extracted and will need to be localized separately. Its reference in the last `<para>` element is not included in the text presented to the translator (only `= entity` is displayed). This could be a problem if, for grammatical reasons, the position of the entity needs to be changed in some target languages.

The output of the file is displayed in Listing 14.11. It also includes a few errors.

LISTING 14.11

`Test_Entities_SDLX.xml`—Output of the Test Document with SDLX

```
<?xml version="1.0" encoding="windows-1252"?> <!DOCTYPE doc
➥[ <!ENTITY UserEntity "Text to localize (with &#225; and &#xe1;)"> ]>
<doc>
<para title="&lt;=less-than">
&lt;=less-than
</para>
<para title="&amp;=ampersand">
&amp;=ampersand
</para>
<para title="&gt;=greater-than">
```

LISTING 14.11   CONTINUED

```
&gt;=greater-than
</para>
<para title="'=apostrophe">
&apos;=apostrophe
</para>
<para title="'=quote">
'=quote
</para>
<para title="á=a-acute">
&#xe1;=a-acute
</para>
<para title="á=a-acute">
=a-acute
</para>
<para title="= entity">
&UserEntity; = entity
</para>
</doc>
```

The apostrophe in the `title` attribute has disappeared, while it still exists in the element content despite the fact it was not shown to the translator.

The double quote in the `title` attribute is not escaped anymore, marking the file invalid.

The decimal form of the NCR does not exist in the element content anymore, while it has been preserved as a raw character in the attribute value.

Finally, the `&UserEntity;` has disappeared in the attribute value in the last `<para>` element.

TagEditor

The test document can be opened in TagEditor without error. All predefined character entities and NCRs are converted properly, as shown in Figure 14.25.

The only problem is the impossibility of accessing the definition of `&UserEntity;` in the `DOCTYPE` declaration. It must be translated outside of TagEditor.

A minor change in the output is that the numeric character references are converted into raw `UTF-8` characters, which are valid as well.

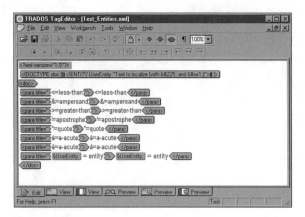

FIGURE 14.25

`Test_Entities.xml` *opened in TagEditor.*

Transit

The test document imports without error in Transit. Because we were not able to define a settings file, the editor presents only the content of the `<para>` element as translatable, even if the `title` attribute contains extractable text as well. The result is displayed in Figure 14.26.

FIGURE 14.26

`Test_Entities.xml` *opened in Transit.*

All character entities are converted correctly, except the apostrophe, which displays as a block. The numeric character references have also been correctly converted. One oddity is that all NCRs are recognized as text (black) whereas the character entities are marked as code (blue), except for the quote. This distinction can have an effect on translation memory export where the inline codes will be marked up differently from the simple text.

The &UserEntity; code is marked as a code, but there is no direct access to its definition and that part must be translated outside of Transit.

The file after it is exported from the tool is shown in Listing 14.12.

LISTING 14.12

Test_Entities_Transit.xml—Output from Transit

```
<?xml version="1.0" ?>
 <!DOCTYPE doc [
 <!ENTITY UserEntity "Text to localize (with &#225; and &#xe1;)">
 ]>
<doc>
 <para title="&lt;=less-than">&lt;=less-than</para>
 <para title="&amp;=ampersand">&amp;=ampersand</para>
 <para title="&gt;=greater-than">&gt;=greater-than</para>
 <para title="&apos;=apostrophe">&apos;=apostrophe</para>
 <para title=""=quote">"=quote</para>
 <para title="&aacute;=a-acute">&aacute;=a-acute</para>
 <para title="&aacute;=a-acute">&aacute;=a-acute</para>
 <para title="&UserEntity; = entity">&UserEntity; = entity</para>
</doc>
```

Almost all characters are correctly escaped, but the literal quote in the attribute value is not escaped, making the file invalid. The character à is coded as á as for an HTML file. In XML, character entities other than the five predefined ones must be defined in a DTD. The tool should use numeric character references instead.

Latin-1 Tag Names

Most of the XML formats use only ASCII characters in the names of their elements and attributes, but XML is not limited to such a small character set: Almost any UCS character can be used. A few DTDs using non-ASCII tag names are already appearing among localization customers.

To test this feature with the tools, first we will try the tools with a vocabulary that uses ASCII and Latin-1 (iso-8859-1) characters, as displayed in Listing 14.13. Only the content of <texte> is localizable.

LISTING 14.13

`Test_TagLatin1.xml`—Document with Tag Names in Latin-1

```xml
<?xml version="1.0" encoding="iso-8859-1" ?>
<début>
 <requête numéro="1">
  <priorité>Urgente</priorité>
  <texte>Premier text à traduire.</texte>
 </requête>
 <requête numéro="2">
  <priorité>Normale</priorité>
  <texte>Deuxième text à traduire.</texte>
 </requête>
</début>
```

To make sure the extended characters are handled correctly we will translate the French entries into Russian and see the resulting files. Note that the output encoding must support both Russian (the content) and French (the tag names). In other words, it must be `UTF-8` or `UTF-16`.

Déjà Vu

The creation of a new filter with the SGML Filter Maintenance tool goes well: All tags are entered correctly in the filter definition, as shown in Figure 14.27.

FIGURE 14.27

Latin-1 elements and attributes in the SGML Filter Maintenance tool.

The file imports correctly in Déjà Vu. Note that, as we have already seen, because there are no ways to specify that an element should not be translated, the two entries for `<priorité>` should be left in French.

The problems start when creating the output after translation (see Figure 14.28). The encoding is not switched to one that could support both Latin-1 and Cyrillic. Consequently the extended characters in the tag names are now Cyrillic.

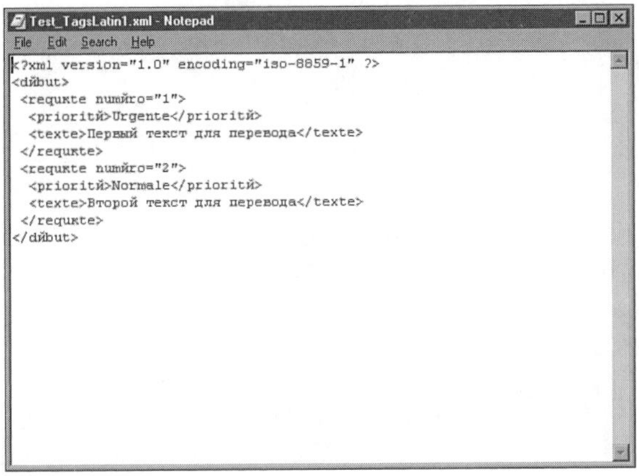

FIGURE 14.28

Déjà Vu output of the `Test_TagLatin1.xml` *file.*

Note also that the encoding declaration must be updated to reflect the use of `windows-1251`. Fixing such a file is a matter of converting it from `windows-1251` to `UTF-8` (or `UTF-16`), and then doing search and replace to substitute the now incorrect tag names with the original ones (in the UTF variant used).

SDLX

The creation of the Analysis file goes well, as shown in Figure 14.29. All tags are added correctly to the list. We can change the default settings to set only the `<texte>` element as translatable.

When creating the new project to translate from French to Russian, make sure to specify the use of `UTF-8` for the translated file so it can include both Latin-1 and Cyrillic characters. The input document imports without problems into SDLX. Only the translatable text is presented to the linguist and can be translated into Russian, as shown in Figure 14.30.

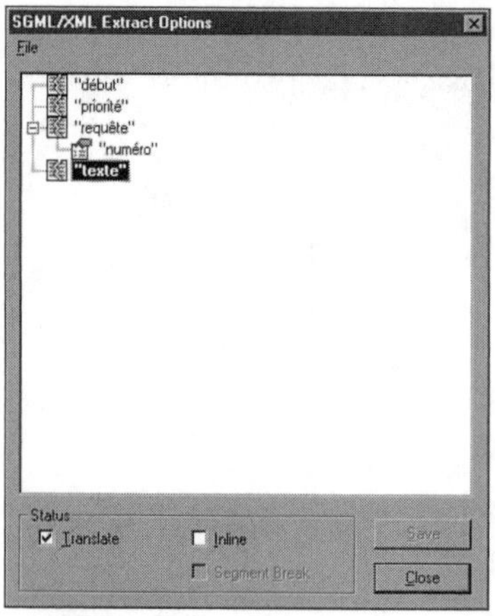

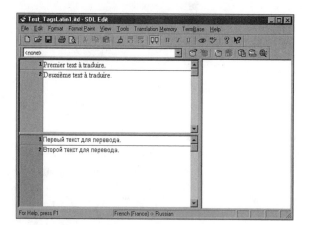

FIGURE 14.29

Analysis file for the `Test_TagLatin1.xml` *document.*

FIGURE 14.30

File with Latin-1 tag names imported with SDLX Edit.

When creating the translated document, SDLX uses `UTF-8` as we specified in the project settings. Unfortunately, only the translated parts are converted: The tag names remain in `iso-8859-1`. Such a file is invalid and, when opened in a `UTF-8`–capable application like Word, as displayed in Figure 14.31, it shows problems.

Not only are the extended characters in the tag names lost, but also some of the Russian text (for example, the letters П and В at the beginning of each `<texte>` element) are misinterpreted and not displayed properly. The actual encoding sequences for these specific characters in the XML document are correct, but the presence of the invalid Latin-1 characters creates confusion for Word.

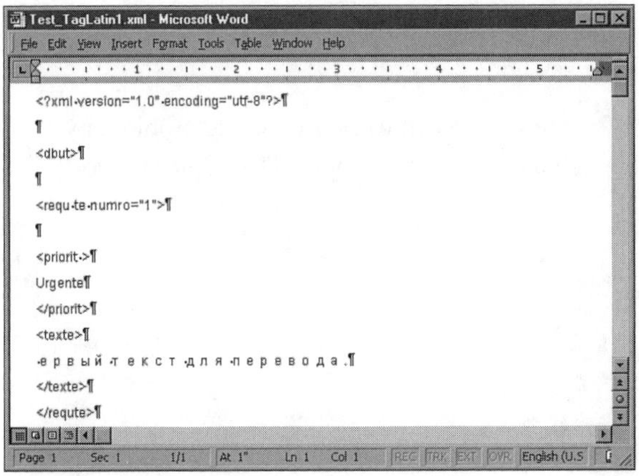

FIGURE 14.31

Translated document in UTF-8, *with tag names still in* iso-8859-1.

To cover all options we can try to go through the same process, but this time with the input file encoded in UTF-8 rather than iso-8859-1. It does not work: When importing the document, SDLX gives errors for each tag with non-ASCII characters.

TagEditor

To create a new DTD Settings file for TagEditor we can use the DTD corresponding to the French document type. The file is shown in Listing 14.14.

LISTING 14.14

Test_TagsLatin1.dtd—**DTD for** Test_TagsLatin1.xml

```
<!ELEMENT début (requête)* >


<!ELEMENT requête (priorité | texte)* >
<!ATTLIST requête
  numéro      CDATA      #IMPLIED >


<!ELEMENT texte (#PCDATA)* >


<!ELEMENT priorité (#PCDATA)* >
```

TagEditor does not read the file correctly. Only two elements are created: priorit and texte. A few additional tests show that any tag name with a non-ASCII character is either discarded or has its extended characters removed. The DTD file is in iso-8859-1, which is for this purpose the same as windows-1252, the default code set of the system where the test is done. A try with the DTD encoded as UTF-8 and another with UTF-16 gives exactly the same result.

We cannot rely on the DTD import feature but we can work around the problem by manually entering the properties for each element and attribute. That seems to work, and the result is shown in Figure 14.32.

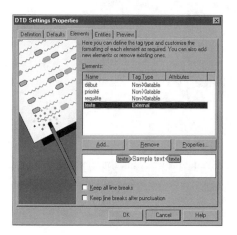

FIGURE 14.32

TagEditor DTD Settings after manually fixing the missing or incorrectly imported tags.

Because only the <texte> element is translatable, the other tags are set to **Non-Xlatable** (we could have also used the **Group** property to specify this).

With the DTD Settings finished, we can open the test document. The result is shown in Figure 14.33.

Although the <texte> element behaves as expected, the others are interpreted as inline (marked with a white background in our example) instead of non-translatable. Changing the properties and using **Group** has the same result. In fact, any property defined for an element that has a tag name with extended characters is not applied. You can try, for example, to associate a format such as bold and red to the tag. TagEditor acts as if it does not recognize the tag and applies the default properties to it.

Incorrect inline tags do not prevent the translation. They will cause important problems for leveraging, fuzzy matching, and other functionalities, but we still can enter the Russian text and save the translated file. The output is shown in Figure 14.34.

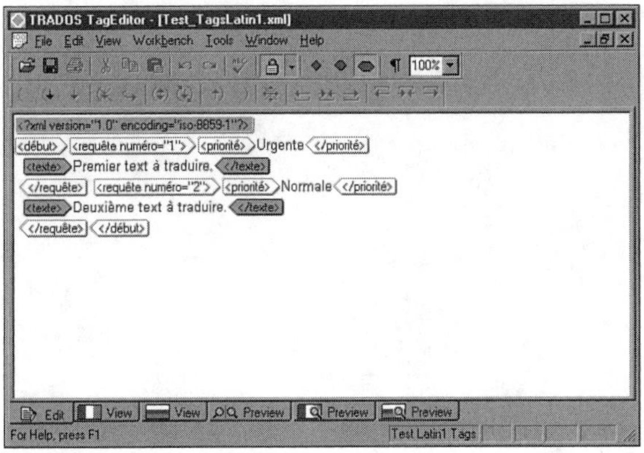

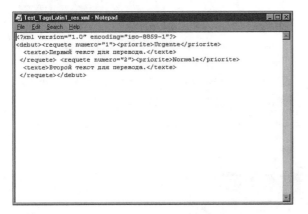

FIGURE 14.33

Test file imported in TagEditor. Non-translatable elements are incorrectly marked as inline tags.

```
Test_TagsLatin1_res.xml - Notepad
File  Edit  Search  Help
<?xml version="1.0" encoding="iso-8859-1"?>
<debut><requete numero="1"><priorite>Urgente</priorite>
 <texte>Первый текст для перевода.</texte>
 </requete>  <requete numero="2"><priorite>Normale</priorite>
 <texte>Второй текст для перевода.</texte>
 </requete></debut>
```

FIGURE 14.34

Output of TagEditor with the translation in `windows-1251` *when the input file is in* `iso-8859-1`*.*

The resulting file is consistent with the behavior we have already observed when testing the special statements and the output encoding: The file encoding is in `windows-1251` (although the encoding declaration is not updated) and any extended character not available in this encoding is converted to its closest ASCII equivalent if one exists. This means all tag names are stripped of accents and the resulting file is invalid.

There is a solution for this. If the input document is in `UTF-8`, TagEditor creates output also in `UTF-8` where all extended characters are preserved. Figure 14.35 displays the resulting file when the input is in `UTF-8`.

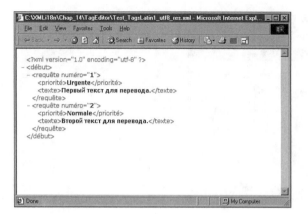

FIGURE 14.35

Output of TagEditor when the input file is in UTF-8.

Transit

Because of the limitation of the demonstration version that only allows German, a Latin-1 language, as the target language, it is not easy to run the same test with Transit as with the other tools. However, we can at least see whether tag names using Latin-1 characters can be used.

The test file imports without error and seems to work properly when loaded in Transit, as shown in Figure 14.36.

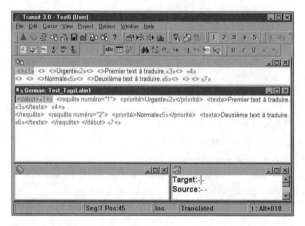

FIGURE 14.36

Document with tag names in Latin-1 loaded in Transit.

The exported file is shown in Listing 14.15 and is consistent with the behavior noted previously. All extended characters are escaped as character entities.

`Test_TagsLatin1_Transit.xml`—Output of Latin-1 Tag Names from Transit

```
<?xml version="1.0" encoding="iso-8859-1" ?>
<d&eacute;but>
 <requ&ecirc;te num&eacute;ro="1">
 <priorit&eacute;>Urgente</priorit&eacute;>
 <texte>Premier text &agrave; traduire.</texte>
 </requ&ecirc;te>
 <requ&ecirc;te num&eacute;ro="2">
 <priorit&eacute;>Normale</priorit&eacute;>
 <texte>Deuxi&egrave;me text &agrave; traduire.</texte>
 </requ&ecirc;te>
</d&eacute;but>
```

Character entities must be defined in XML, and element and attribute names cannot use any type of escaped characters.

UCS Tag Names

Element and attribute names are not limited to Latin-1 characters. They could use almost any character of the UCS repertoire. Because we have already established that some of the tools do not support Latin-1 tags, there is no point in testing them for support of UCS tag names. TagEditor and, to a lesser extent, Transit were the only tools that were able to go through the process (with quite a few fixes needed). Let's see how they behave with UCS characters.

Our test file shown in Listing 14.16 and its associated DTD shown in Listing 14.17 are encoded in `UTF-16`.

`Test_TagsHan.xml`—Test Document with Tag Names in Chinese

```
<?xml version="1.0" ?>
<测试>
 <标题>Title</标题>
 <输入>Entry with <黑体>bolded text</黑体>.</输入>
```

LISTING 14.16   CONTINUED

```
<输入>Entry with <斜体>italicized text</斜体>.</输入>
<格式化 xml:space="preserve">Pre-formatted text:
- Line 1
- Line 2</格式化>
</测试>
```

LISTING 14.17

`Test_tagsHan.dtd`—DTD for `Test_TagsHan.xml`

```
<!ELEMENT 测试 (标题 | 输入 | 格式化)* >

<!ELEMENT 输入 (#PCDATA | 黑体 | 斜体)* >

<!ELEMENT 黑体 (#PCDATA | 斜体)* >

<!ELEMENT 斜体 (#PCDATA | 黑体)* >

<!ELEMENT 格式化 (#PCDATA)* >
<!ATTLIST 格式化
  xml:space   CDATA     #IMPLIED >
```

TagEditor

From the previous test we can determine that the TagEditor DTD Settings function does not correctly read `UTF-16` DTD files, so we must enter the parameters manually. What was working with Latin-1 characters does not work with Chinese ones. You must either work on a localized version of Windows or switch the default system code page to the Chinese one to be able to enter the correct characters. This is possible under Windows 2000, in the **Regional Settings** dialog box of the **Control Panel**.

When the default code page is Chinese, the settings file can be created from the DTD file and the file opened, as shown in Figure 14.37.

While opening and closing the segments, however, some tag names become corrupted; for example, the second translated segment is a fuzzy match obtained from the first segment. Somehow during the internal leveraging process the element <黑体> was misinterpreted into <Ð±Ìå>. The translated output and the translation memory also contain the corrupted tags.

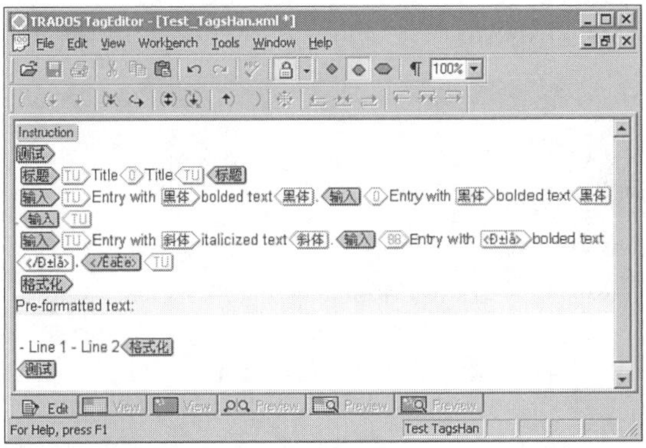

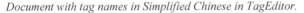

FIGURE 14.37

Document with tag names in Simplified Chinese in TagEditor.

Transit

For Transit we already know we will not be able to define specific rules for the test DTD, but we can try the document with the default settings to see whether tags are at least recognized correctly.

Again the test is done on a Windows 2000 machine with Chinese system installed and set as the default. The result of the import is shown in Figure 14.38.

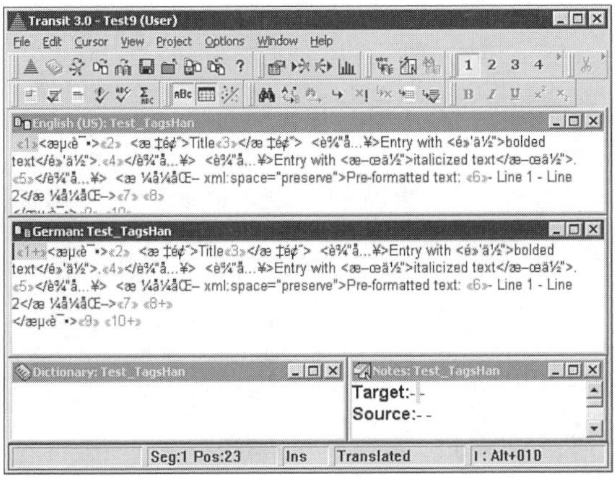

FIGURE 14.38

`Test_TagsHan.xml` *imported in Transit with default settings.*

As before, the Unicode characters seem to be read correctly by the parser, but at some point Transit does a `UTF-8` conversion and does not convert back to the code page of the font used.

The output of the file results in invalid character entities in the text and in the element and attribute names.

Namespaces

A part of XML that is used more and more is the capability to mix different vocabularies within the same document. As we have already seen, this is achieved through the concept of namespaces. Translation tools must be able to process such files correctly. For example, `abc:text` and `xyz:text` should be seen as two distinct attributes belonging to their respective vocabularies.

Looking at the way the tools are mapping elements and attribute names, it is clear that they do not offer a simple way to support namespaces directly. They do allow the definition of element and attribute names that have a namespace prefix, as demonstrated with the XSL default support in TagEditor, but the supports stops there. There are no built-in mechanisms to handle `xmlns` and its different default rules.

However, at this time few documents use complex namespace setup and current support is, for the most part, enough to deal with documents such as XSL templates where you have XSLT elements mixed with another vocabulary such as XHTML.

Summary

The results of this series of tests are consolidated in Table 14.1. Note that some capabilities were not determined for Transit because it was impossible to create DTD-specific settings due to of the lack of documentation.

Overall, the tests show that there is room for improvement. None of the tools reviewed was able to measure up to all expectations. In some cases the XML support is clearly insufficient to deal with real XML formats. With the large number of good XML parsers freely available, the tools should be able to offer a much better handling of XML documents.

TABLE 14.1

Summary of XML Support with the Translation Tools Evaluated

Functionality	Déjà Vu	SDLX	TagEditor	Transit
Supports `UTF-8`	No	Yes	Yes	No
Supports `UTF-16LE`	No	No	Yes	No
Supports `UTF-16BE`	No	No	Yes	No

TABLE 14.1 CONTINUED				
Functionality	*Déjà Vu*	*SDLX*	*TagEditor*	*Transit*
Allows defining of structural versus inline elements	Yes	Yes	Yes	TBD
Allows locking of specific elements from translation	No	Yes	Yes	TBD
Allows locking of specific attributes from translation	Yes	Yes	Yes	TBD
Is case sensitive	No	Yes	No	TBD
Imports CDATA	No	No	Yes	No
Exports CDATA	No	No	No	No
Recognizes xml:lang in input	No	No	No	No
Updates xml:lang in output	No	No	No	No
Updates encoding declaration in output	No	Yes	No	No
Preserves comments	Yes	Yes	Yes	Yes
Preserves processing instructions	Yes	Yes	Yes	Yes
Supports xml:space in input	No	No	No	No
Supports xml:space in output	No	No	Yes[1]	No
Supports tags in Latin-1 characters	No	No	Yes[2]	Yes[3]
Supports tags in Unicode characters	No	No	No[4]	No
Supports single quotes	No	Yes	Yes	Yes
Supports predefined character entities in attributes	Yes	Not well	Yes	Yes
Supports predefined character entities in elements	Yes	Not well	Yes	Yes
Supports decimal numeric character references in attributes	Yes	Yes	Yes	Yes
Supports decimal numeric character references in elements	Yes	No	Yes	Yes
Supports hexadecimal numeric character references in attributes	No	Yes	Yes	Yes
Supports hexadecimal numeric character references in elements	No	No	Yes	Yes
Allows direct translation of external entity definitions	Yes	No	No	No

TABLE 14.1 CONTINUED				
Functionality	*Déjà Vu*	*SDLX*	*TagEditor*	*Transit*
Handles external entities in attributes	Yes	No	Yes	TBD
Handles external entities in elements	Yes	No	Yes	Yes
Supports namespaces	Yes[5]	Yes[5]	Yes[5]	Yes[5]

[1] *In output, all elements, regardless of whether they have an* xml:space *attribute, are treated as if* xml:space=preserve *were set.*

[2] *Only if the input file is in* UTF-8 *or* UTF-16, *and the properties associated with each element and attribute are not handled correctly in all cases.*

[3] *The extended characters in the output are escaped, which makes any tag name with extended characters invalid.*

[4] *It almost works, but some tags become corrupted during translation.*

[5] *Support limited to element and attribute names with predefined prefix. No support for* xmlns *mechanism.*

Some shortcomings, such the lack of support for xml:space, or non-ASCII element names, can be forgiven because some XML processors or browsers do not support this either. But the lack of support for basic features such as single-quoted attributes, hexadecimal NCRs, UTF-8 and UTF-16 encodings and so forth, is not acceptable.

As XML becomes more important, we can expect some progress in its support by the commercial translation tools. Additionally, XML is often handled in the broader context of content management systems, and specific localization processes also exist in that area.

# CHAPTER 15

Online Translation

In This Chapter:

- Principles 329
- Advantages 330
- Disadvantages 331
- Features 333

With the rapid development of the Internet, new ways of providing online translation have appeared in the past few years. They are mostly integrated systems that offer a simple translation portal, a globalization workflow solution for managing Web sites, or a more elaborate Content Management System (CMS).

XML is included in these developments because it is both a choice medium for Internet data and a medium used for the localization process regardless of the type of data to translate.

Principles

An online translation system is a client/server application designed to manage the translation of various localizable material through a Web-based interface. Figure 15.1 shows the general organization of the different parts.

The server side hosts the filters, rendering engines, workflow mechanisms, business logic, and other core components, as well as the translation memories, glossaries, and other reference mechanisms, enabling them to be shared as they are updated.

The client side is a Web interface usually hosted in browser-based forms or Java applets. It provides the editing components as well as all the necessary code to communicate with the shared resources on the server.

Online translation systems often take advantage of a number of Internet-related as well as server-side–specific technologies. Although the client side is usually cross-platform (even though in practice the products are typically tested on only a few main platforms), the server side is frequently limited to one or two platforms (usually Windows and Solaris).

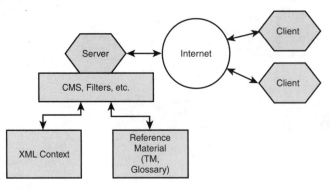

FIGURE 15.1

Components of an online translation system.

In addition to its Internet-oriented architecture, the system often includes various mechanisms to track changes, offers leveraging mechanisms, and provides some type of automated workflow.

Such systems have pros and cons. We will look here only at the considerations related to working online.

Advantages

The various advantages of online translation systems are usually associated with the benefits of collaborative work.

Resource Sharing

One obvious advantage is the capability to share resources: translation memories, lexicons, terminology databases, rendering engines, and so forth can be shared across many different users.

As each translator makes progress with its set of documents, new translations become available and can be recycled by the other translators. In XML documents where there are numerous repetitions, this could prove time saving and also very efficient for keeping consistency across documents.

Turnaround Time

One of the main advantages of an online translation system is that it often provides a very fast turnaround time for the translation.

Most online systems are coupled with some comparison mechanisms and workflow procedures that enable the user to expedite the file-handling process and automatically go from one stage to the next. The automation can include continual monitoring of the changes done to the source documents and dispatching process working around-the-clock.

Add this to the capability of rendering the final output from the translation environment (therefore testing it immediately), and you have a reduced turnaround time because all tasks are optimized and the time between tasks is also reduced.

This could be especially useful for XML documents served on Web sites where updates must be short and efficient.

Lighter Maintenance

Because the core of the application resides on the server, the client side is a lightweight interface that is downloaded whenever needed, and therefore is always up-to-date.

This reduces the risk of problems due to version discrepancies. However, keep in mind that some components on the client side must be set up and periodically updated, for example the Java virtual machine if the application uses Java components.

Owner Control

Another attractive aspect for the owners of the source material, if they are also the administrators of the system, is that they have a much tighter control over how the translation is done. Word counts and leveragability are known parameters, progress can be monitored, and shared resources are centrally maintained.

Ultimately, this gives owners of the source material more control over the costs, the progress, and to some level, the quality of the localization.

Disadvantages

As with any other solution, online translation comes with its share of drawbacks. Some problems are linked to infrastructure and technology, whereas some others are related to user preferences.

Bandwidth

Not all countries have the infrastructure available in the United States, and connectivity is not always completely reliable in any country. Working online means staying connected for a sustained period of time: This is simply not always possible in many locations.

Efficiency issues are linked to the infrastructure that is available to the users. In many cases, for financial or technical reasons, the linguists might not have T1 or DSL connections. Working online using a slow modem is then much more difficult.

The situation should improve over time, but meanwhile online systems should provide some mechanisms to alleviate the consequences of connection instability and smaller bandwidth. Such mechanisms include file recovery systems, smaller transmission packets, and offline alternatives. One additional issue is the problem of dealing with linguists who use free Internet Service Providers (ISPs). Many of those free ISPs include advertisement data in the flow of packets. This can cause some problems with online systems that are not prepared for unexpected data interspersed with the normal transmission flow.

Costs

Connection costs are related to these bandwidth issues. Billing policies vary from one country to another and some translators may not have access to local deals for unlimited connection time. Many providers bill according to the duration of the connection, and this is a strong deterrent for any type of online work.

In addition, if you are buying the system to integrate it into your Web infrastructure or document management system, the costs can be high. Some level of customization will be needed, so you are more likely to need consulting services, which add a significant associated cost. Make a careful evaluation of the possible return on investment when selecting your system.

Such evaluation can be a drawback by itself because the lack of information, benchmarking, and the need to map out the implications of using the new system in your existing framework can be long and costly.

Format Support

Because of the cost involved, make sure the solution you select offers support for the source format you are using. If such a system can be used for only part of the data you have to localize, many advantages disappear.

The online systems usually work well with small tag-based documents, but do not often provide efficient mechanisms for graphics, desktop-publishing formats, or software resources. Depending on your overall needs, this may diminish the efficiency you are expecting.

A completely localized output is not ready for release until the last component is done. Like any other solution, your online system will be only as strong as its weakest link.

Usability

An area where problems are often difficult to solve is the editing environment provided to the linguists. For example

- Spelling and grammar checkers might not be available, or when they are, they might not be as efficient as those offered in traditional word processing packages.
- Although a rendering mechanism is often provided, the translation itself is often done out of context, or with only a small context such as the previous and the next sentences.
- Online systems are usually recent and may not always have the refined leveraging features older systems have slowly developed. For example, fuzzy matching may be only partially, if at all, implemented.
- The powerful editing tools you would find in a word processor application are often scaled down in the online editor: no user macros, fewer options for search and replace, and so forth.

Some of these shortcomings also exist, to a lesser degree, in some of the offline translation tools using their own editor, but such environments can usually offer more functionality because they are desktop applications. Applets or light client front ends are usually more restricted because they must balance feature set with code size and performance carefully.

Features

Testing classic translation environments such as those discussed in Chapter 14 is one thing, but evaluating online systems is another. It proves to be more complicated for several reasons:

- Because all these systems are often quite expensive and require more complex client/server setup (compared to the classic translation tools), they usually do not come with trial versions.
- Some companies are also a little more reticent to offer full access to their product for evaluation purposes.
- Many of these systems have yet to move to full support for XML. They have been designed mostly for HTML, and are only now reaching a point where they can be efficiently used with any XML document types.

Because of these different issues, rather than go through the same motions as we did earlier and test several products, the following section discusses the main aspects of online translation tools from the viewpoint of using them for XML documents. A few examples are included for illustration.

Administration

Most online translation tools offer different components: These usually include an administrator module and a translator module.

Like the rest of the interface, the administrative features handle the various file manipulation tasks from a Web-based UI. Using FTP, documents can be uploaded to the server site, assigned to a specific project, and run through the process. Keep in mind that many of these systems are meant to be integrated within the owner's architecture, so a great deal of customization is usually allowed.

Administration also includes the settings to establish working folders, user lists, access rights, and so forth. An important aspect of this is how the different XML document types and their localization properties are identified.

For example, System3 from GlobalSight provides an interface to define profiles, as shown in Figure 15.2.

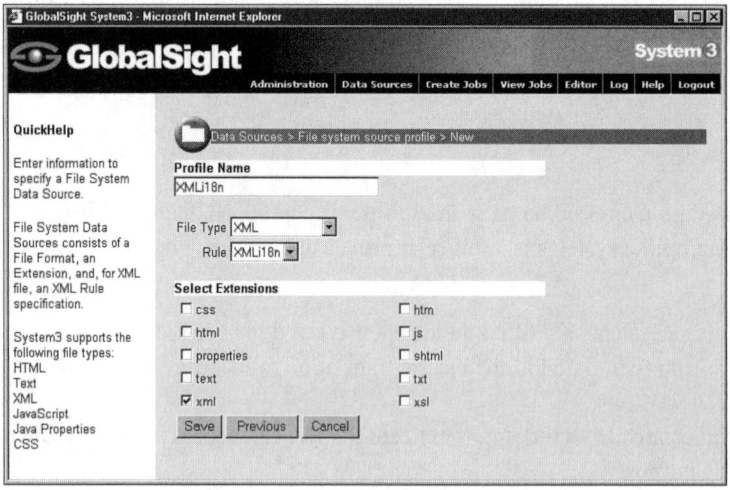

FIGURE 15.2

Creating profiles for XML projects in System3.

Each XML profile is associated with a Rule file. This Rule file is the equivalent of the localization property document discussed in Chapter 7, "Creating Internationalized

Document Types." The approaches are very similar. For example, Listing 15.1 shows the complete Rule file we could use if we had to process the different test documents we used in Chapter 14, "XML-Enabled Translation Tools."

LISTING 15.1

`XMLi18n.xml`—Rule File

```
<?xml version='1.0' encoding='iso-8859-1' ?>
<schemarules>
 <ruleset schema='doc'>
  <translate path='//@title' />
  <translate path='//block' inline='yes' />
  <dont-translate path='//BLOCK' />
 </ruleset>
 <ruleset schema='page'>
  <dont-translate path='//entry[@class="topic"]/param[@type!="descr"]' />
  <dont-translate path='//entry[@class!="topic"]/param' />
 </ruleset>
 <ruleset schema='début'>
  <translate path='//texte' />
  <dont-translate path='//priorité' />
 </ruleset>
 <ruleset schema='&#x6D4B;&#x8BD5;'>
  <translate path='//&#x9ED1;&#x4F53;' inline='yes' />
  <translate path='//&#x659C;&#x4F53;' inline='yes' />
 </ruleset>
</schemarules>
```

The salient feature of the Rule file is the use of an XPath expression in the `path` attribute to specify the scope of each rule. This allows for more flexibility. For instance, the conditional translations that none of the desktop tools that we evaluated were able to handle can be simply defined here (`<ruleset>` for `page`).

With the increase of databases using XML to provide translatable files, this type of conditional translation is growing. Although workarounds involving, for instance, XSLT templates can be found, it is always better to control these parameters directly from the translation system itself.

The only minor shortcoming of System 3 in this area is that it does not offer the possibility of defining a default behavior for elements and attributes. The default is built in and set to translate the elements and not the attributes.

Setting the localization properties for the various XML Document types is usually not as sophisticated in other systems, but most of them include some degree of flexibility there. This is definitely an area you must explore when evaluating a content globalization product.

Workflow

Many online translation systems offer some kind of workflow functionality. The idea is to automate the flow of the data through the process as much as possible using triggers, schedulers, and e-mail notifications.

A popular function is to regularly scan a list of source documents to see whether any have changed, prepare the changed or new text for translation, and route the package to a predetermined translator and to an editor. When the linguists have finished their work, the new translation is integrated into the final target documents. At any point in this process you might have checkpoints where a manager can monitor costs, progress, and other variables and make changes in the workflow if necessary.

Such automation is especially efficient for the maintenance of multilingual Web sites or databases. Working with more complex document structures, or a more important volume of translation, will probably have to involve more people and some manual work.

Although it is unlikely that you will be able to completely remove all human management elements from the localization process, these workflow features show that you can probably simplify it.

Change Tracking

Tracking changes is not directly related to online translation, but this is a feature that is offered more often in these systems than in the more classic translation tools. One reason for this is that integrated systems are working directly from the original source material and content management is easier to set up at that level.

Tracking changes can be done in many different ways on XML documents. Time stamps and size are a first factor, and then more detailed analysis of the documents is needed. Because a document can be parsed into a tree structure you can use tree-comparison algorithms. Another method is to use unique IDs and check whether content has changed or new elements have been added or removed.

Obviously any changes that affect only the structure or the codes but not any translatable data should be resolved automatically using the localized documents of the previous version of the document.

In addition to version changes, the systems are now using some new methods with regard to selecting the type of change that should occur for the translatable material. The classic model where each paragraph or component of the original document is simply translated has been extended to a more flexible model. You can often apply rules to each item that you want to localize: set it to be simply translated, adapted, or even omitted. The adaptation aspect enables the change of the content or the creation of brand new material for a given locale. In these cases, tracking changes becomes more complex because you do not have a one-to-one match between the source document and its localized versions.

Translation

The translation environment is an important piece of the system and implementations vary widely. Although all applications offer translation memory matches, access to a glossary is not often supported.

As for the translatable text, some packages such as SDLWebFlow from SDL International provide linguists with a list of entries, as shown in Figure 15.3.

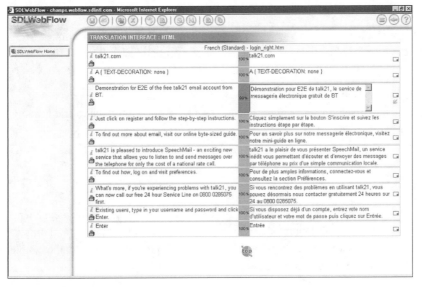

FIGURE 15.3

XHTML document edited with SDLWebFlow.

Other applications have opted for a paragraph-by-paragraph approach, for example JCAT from RWS, as shown in Figure 15.4.

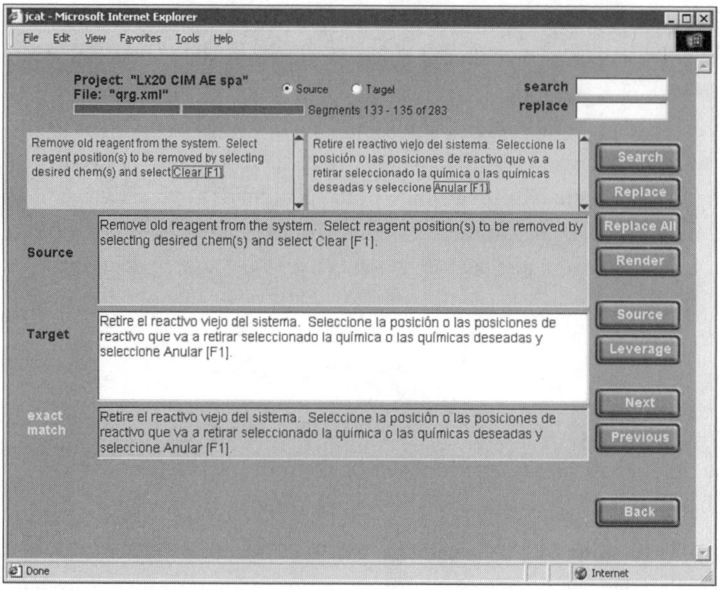

FIGURE 15.4

JCAT online editor.

These two approaches and their variations have advantages and drawbacks linked to performance and ease of use. Favoring one interface over another, as long as they work correctly, often boils down to personal preference of the users.

Overall the functions are often the same: access to fuzzy matches from a server-side translation memory, search and replace features, sometimes an interface to add inline codes for formatting, some terminology support, concordance searches, and spell-checking capability.

Rendering

Most online systems also include some type of rendering facility that enables the client application to see the XML document after it has been transformed into its final output (or outputs, in the case of single-sourcing). For instance, Figure 15.5 shows an example of XHTML documents rendered from the online interface of SDLWebFlow.

With XML, in many cases having the server provide the rendering is very useful because a simple merging of the original document would not be enough and you would need to have some conversion process, sometimes heavily involved, to create the final output. These conversion tools might not be available on each translator desktop because they might require the setup of one or more tools such as Perl, AWK, or OmniMark, or they might more simply include parts in JSP, XSQL, PHP, or other server-side scripting mechanisms. It is more efficient to set up the translation server for this task.

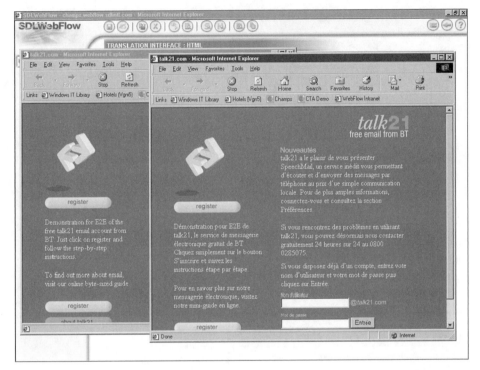

FIGURE 15.5

Rendering of documents with SDLWebFlow.

Offline Alternatives

Because of the problems linguists sometimes encounter when working online, many systems offer an offline alternative whereby you download a set of documents to localize and work with it outside of the system, as shown in Figure 15.6.

The formats of files provided for offline translation vary widely. These files could be RTF documents, special formats dedicated to an offline application also provided, or simple text files such as the example shown in Figure 15.7.

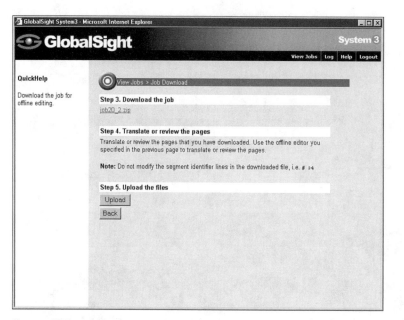

FIGURE 15.6

Downloading offline packages with System 3.

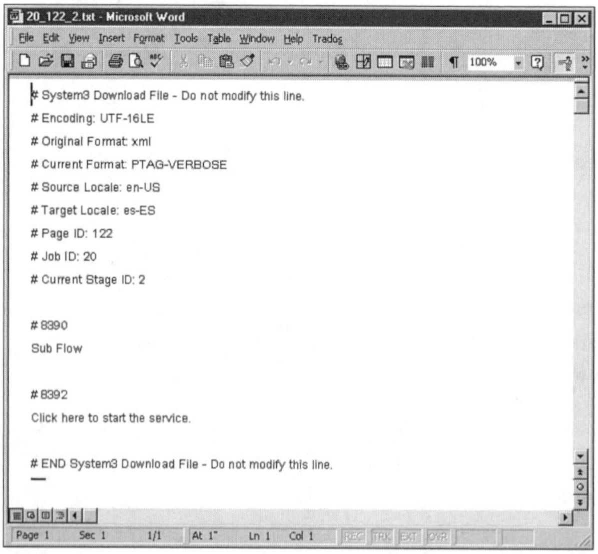

FIGURE 15.7

An option of System 3: a UTF-16 *text file the linguists can open and translate in any editor. Here two segments are to be translated.*

Some systems also provide matches along with the translatable text, either as translation memory in TMX or another tool-specific format, or directly in the documents. For
example, GLOBELIX from Alpnet provides an editor, the Java Translation Editor
(JTE), along with documents that are pretranslated as shown in Figure 15.8.

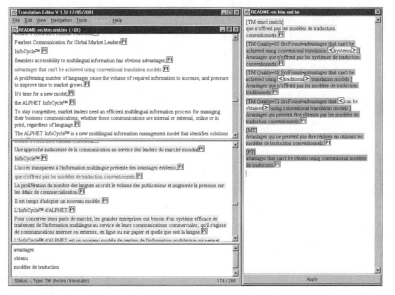

FIGURE 15.8

Alpnet Java Translation Editor.

The recent availability of XLIFF, which includes a mechanism for storing preleveraged
text, will probably make this more common.

Summary

Online translation is definitely an aspect you want to consider for XML localization.
Depending on your needs and the architecture of your data repository it can be a very
attractive solution, especially for Web sites. There are, however, several things you
must keep in mind:

- Many features offered by online translation systems are not necessarily related to
  working online. For instance, project management and change tracking are two
  important aspects that are now also offered in the more classic translation tools.
- Many online translation systems currently promoted have to do with efforts to
  cash in on the dot-com burst of the past few years. There is a lot of marketing
  hype in this domain: Make sure you evaluate carefully any system you might

want to adopt. If you have or plan to have XML data, it is recommended that you run a series of tests identical to the one presented in Chapter 14 with each system you are evaluating. A thorough analysis of the true cost of implementation and a pilot project are also in order.

Online translation systems have the ability to do what classic translation tools have not been able to achieve or promote efficiently so far: to move the starting point of the localization process upstream where it belongs, right along with content development. This approach is especially efficient with XML documents.

Overall, using Internet-related technologies for building localization solutions is obviously a good idea. However, the actual task of translating a document using an online editor still has many drawbacks. Most of these drawbacks are related to bandwidth and infrastructure problems that are beyond the control of tools developers.

Finally, note that successfully implementing an online system always requires a certain amount of customization and important changes in your processes and possibly in the structure of your organization. A successful implementation of an online system also depends on the correct internationalization of your content.

Using XML to Localize

In This Chapter:

There are different approaches to using XML for localization. One approach is to use XML as a storage format for text extracted from other formats. A second approach is to use XML directly as the original container of the text with converters or filters generating the final format needed for the targeted application.

Regardless of whether the XML documents to localize are the original source files or temporary repositories, they all can be processed the same way and benefit from the many XML-enabled utilities offering various text-manipulation functions.

Taking Advantage of XML

Extracting text from a given format to an XML document is discussed in detail in the next chapter. The main trait of this scenario is that you can use XML as a temporary format for most of the duration of the localization.

XML is used more and more often as the original storage format with filters or converter tools to transform the XML documents into the targeted format. This is logical when you consider the overall architecture of an internationalized product: XML is not only very well suited to deal with many languages, but it is also an ideal format to be converted to any output you need, to interact with databases, and to be reused in different components.

There are different variations of this methodology and the following are some possible applications of it.

Firmware

In some domains the localizable data must be partially compiled or processed to be placed in its final destination, regardless of the format it is stored in: for example, burned in a PROM (Programmable Read-Only Memory) or uploaded in a device. This is the case with printers, copiers, fax machines, PDAs, barcode scanners, and medical apparatus. The generic term used for this special category of software is *firmware*.

Linked to the particularities of their final destination, firmware-related data often have many more constraints than data for other types of user interface. For example, the available memory can be limited and the display screens might be small LCD panels. Information about these restrictions must be available during localization so you can make sure the translation fits the requirements.

Traditionally, firmware text is either hard-coded in source code files or stored in some proprietary file formats that are more or less appropriate for localization.

The use of XML instead of these various formats could bring much flexibility to the process not only from a localization viewpoint but also in the general organization of the firmware components.

To illustrate this, we can see how an imaginary XML document type could be used for handling the messages of a product such as a copier, a printer, or a scanner.

The Challenges

Our firmware has two main restrictions:

- The text is displayed on an LCD panel that can show 2 lines of 22 characters at most.
- The memory space reserved for the bitmapped fonts and the text is very limited.

This leads to several interesting challenges.

Because of the memory limitation, only fonts of 255 characters can be used. One of the target languages is Japanese and the character set available is restricted to Halfwidth Katakana. However, a few strings are not displayed on the panel, but on the printed test pages, and can use any `Shift-JIS` characters. In other words, some messages must be in Katakana, whereas others can be in any Japanese characters.

Because of the memory limitation, the amount of storable text is smaller than the amount of text needed for the messages. The solution has been to use dynamic messages where duplicated parts of messages are shared across different messages and referenced by placeholders. For example, these messages

```
"Open the side panel"   (19 bytes)
"Close the side panel"  (20 bytes)
```

```
"Change the cartridge"    (20 bytes)
"Open the top cover"      (18 bytes)
```

are handled as dynamic strings

```
"%1%2"                    (4 bytes)
"Close %2"                (8 bytes)
"Change the cartridge"    (20 bytes)
"%1the top cover"         (15 bytes)
```

along a shared table where

```
1 = "Open "               (5 bytes)
2 = "the side panel"      (14 bytes)
```

With that method, our four messages are stored in 66 bytes instead of the 77 bytes needed if each message were in its complete form. The difference is even more significant when you take in account all messages.

A concern with this method is that each message is limited to 2 lines of 22 characters (or less) each, so the various dynamic string combinations must fit within that limit.

In addition, messages can have parameters. The values of the parameters are treated like the duplicate strings and can also have variable lengths that must fit the different messages where they appear. This line of code

```
"Orientation: $1"
```

has this associated value:

```
1 = "Landscape|Portrait"
```

This generates the following combinations on the LCD panel:

```
Orientation: Landscape
Orientation: Portrait
```

The Solutions

The first issue to solve is the problem of the dynamic strings. Splitting a message in several pieces is never good for localization. However, in this firmware environment we must find a way to do so because it is the only way to overcome the memory restrictions.

A possible solution is to move the cause of the problem to a different point in the process. Relying on the breaking of the English text will not work for other languages, but if the breaking apart of the messages occurs after localization, it cannot affect the translation anymore.

The source material would be stored in the XML document and would be made of complete messages:

```
<msg>Open the side panel</msg>
<msg>Close the side panel</msg>
<msg>Change the cartridge</msg>
<msg>Open the top cover</msg>
```

A utility would take these messages and break them down to minimize the storage space. The output is the original firmware code

```
"%1%2%3"                 (6 bytes)
"Close%2%3"              (9 bytes)
"Change%2cartridge"      (17 bytes)
"%1%2top cover"          (13 bytes)
```

along with the table where

```
1 = "Open"               (4 bytes)
2 = " the "              (5 bytes)
3 = "side panel"         (10 bytes)
```

The automated utility that creates the dynamic messages can be more efficient than the human programmer because sentence construction does not matter at this point: The generated file will not be used for translation. The algorithm can be optimized to take advantage of every duplicate part of text, even if the parts are not within word boundaries. For example, by storing " the " as a shared variable you save 2 more bytes (64 versus 66). When taking into account the full list of messages, such improvement will be even greater. In addition, working with complete messages is a huge improvement for the localization.

The investment required to create the utility that reads the XML source document and creates the output files with broken messages and reference tables is probably not much compared to the savings in time and efficiency to be gained from using it.

The second problem to solve is making sure the different values for a parameter fit into the various messages where they are used.

A specialized tool that can exercise all combinations and warn when one of them exceeds the length limit is probably the best way to approach this problem.

The parameters tables in XML format enable you to use any scripting or programming language that has an XML parser, such as Perl, Java, Python, or C++.

Listing 16.1 shows an example of an XML document that could be used to store our firmware message sample. We used the localization properties markup described in

Chapter 8, "Writing Internationalized Documents," whenever one of the requirements to specify could be indicated that way.

LISTING 16.1

`Firmware_en.xml`—XML Document for Firmware Messages

```
<?xml version='1.0' ?>
<?xml-stylesheet type='text/xsl' href='FirmwareCheck.xsl' ?>
<fwdata xml:space="preserve"
 xmlns:loc="urn:Localization-Properties">
 <parameters>
  <param id='orient'>
   <value id='1'>Portrait</value>
   <value id='2'>Landscape</value>
  </param>
  <param id='OnOff'>
   <value id='1'>On</value>
   <value id='2'>Off</value>
  </param>
 </parameters>
 <messages>
  <msg id="panelOpenSide" loc:maxwidth="22"
  >Open the side panel</msg>
  <msg id="panelCloseSide" loc:maxwidth="22"
  >Close the side panel</msg>
  <msg id="panelChgCart" loc:maxwidth="22"
  >Change the cartridge</msg>
  <msg id="panelOpenCover" loc:maxwidth="22"
  >Open the top cover</msg>
  <msg id="panelReset" type="Panel" status="changed"
       loc:maxwidth="22" loc:nblines="2"
  >Reset the copier:
Press CTRL+SET</msg>
  <msg id="panelOrientation" loc:maxwidth="22"
  >Orientation: <var id='orient'/></msg>
  <msg id="panelOnOff" loc:maxwidth="18"
  >Ecomony Mode: <var id='OnOff'/></msg>
 </messages>
</fwdata>
```

Even without offering a high level of sophistication, such as checking the length of messages with variables, a simple XSL template like the one shown in Listing 16.2 can help the developer and the localizer to verify many of the messages.

LISTING 16.2

`FirmwareCheck.xsl`—XSL Template to Render the Messages

```xml
<?xml version="1.0" ?>
<xsl:stylesheet xmlns:xsl="http://www.w3.org/1999/XSL/Transform"
 xmlns:loc="urn:Localization-Properties"
 version="1.0">

 <xsl:template match="/fwdata">
  <HTML>
   <HEAD>
    <SCRIPT>
     function MakeTopRuler ( p_nWidth )
     {
        var strNum = "12345678901234567890123456789012345678 90";
        var strLine = "";

        for ( var i=1; i!=p_nWidth; i++ )
        {
           if ( i % 5 ) strLine += '-';
           else strLine += '+';
        }
        strLine += '|';
        document.writeln(strNum.substring(0, p_nWidth));
        document.write(strLine);
     }
     function MakeBottomRuler ( p_nWidth )
     {
        var strNum = "12345678901234567890123456789012345678 90";
        var strLine = "";

        for ( var i=1; i!=p_nWidth; i++ )
        {
           if ( i % 5 ) strLine += '-';
           else strLine += '+';
        }
        strLine += '|';
        document.writeln(strLine);
        document.write(strNum.substring(0, p_nWidth));
     }
    </SCRIPT>
   </HEAD>
   <BODY>
```

LISTING 16.2   **CONTINUED**

```
    <P>The text in <B>Bold</B> should be translated except the text in
<B><FONT COLOR="Red">Red</FONT></B>. Variables are represented by
markers in the form of [var], where var is the name of the variable.
Messages with variables are not in the correct length.</P>
    <xsl:apply-templates/>
  </BODY>
 </HTML>
 </xsl:template>

 <xsl:template match="//value">
 </xsl:template>

 <xsl:template match="//msg">
  <PRE>--- ID: <xsl:value-of select='@id'/>
    maximum width: <xsl:value-of select='@loc:maxwidth'/>
<BR/><SCRIPT>MakeTopRuler(<xsl:value-of
➥select='@loc:maxwidth'/>);</SCRIPT>
<BR/><B><xsl:apply-templates/></B><BR/>
<SCRIPT>MakeBottomRuler(<xsl:value-of select='@loc:maxwidth'/>);</SCRIPT>
</PRE>
 </xsl:template>

 <xsl:template match="//var">
  <FONT COLOR="Red">[<xsl:value-of select='@id'/>]</FONT>
 </xsl:template>

</xsl:stylesheet>
```

Our document can be processed with any XML-enabled tool and rendered as shown in Figure 16.1. You can see in this French translation that some of the messages will have to be wrapped, shortened, or somehow reworked to comply with the length limitation.

In addition to length restriction, for the Japanese documents that need to be in Half-width Katakana because of the limited font capability, we could also use the loc:charclass attribute to indicate the limitation and enable validation tools to check the text when it has been translated.

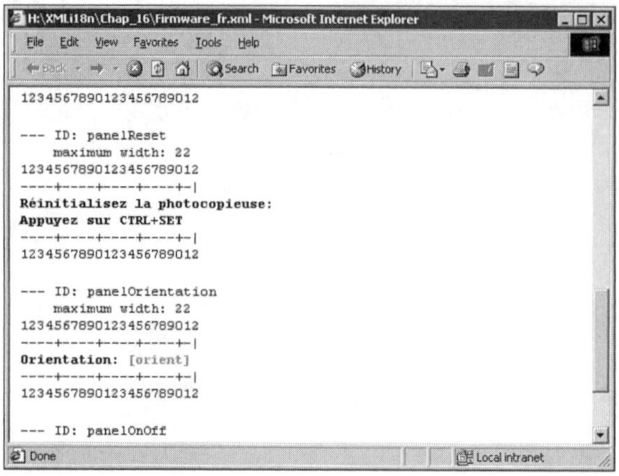

FIGURE 16.1

Rendering of a translated firmware document, offering some basic length verification.

Database Text

Many products have a substantial part of their translatable text stored in database tables. The localization of such text is not always easy because it involves extraction of the relevant fields to some format that can be easily handed to the linguists. Then the file must be merged back into the database.

The latest versions of any of the main commercial database systems such as Oracle, SQL Server, and Sybase now have built-in XML capability. Two simple SQL procedures can take care of extracting and merging the translatable text and can also handle any encoding conversion problems.

If XML is used as the transport format, you must make sure the names of the element and attributes to translate are provided to the localizer. Then the files can be dealt with as any other XML document.

For example, imagine that the strings to localize are stored in an Oracle database in a table called MESSAGES where the field LNG indicates the language code for the entry, and the field MSG contains the actual text of the message. The following query uses the Oracle DBXML package to generate an XML document directly as displayed in Listing 16.3:

```
CREATE PROCEDURE ExtractLanguage ( p_lng VARCHAR2 )
BEGIN
Dbxml.query('SELECT MsgId, Msg
            FROM Messages
            WHERE Lng = ''' || p_lng || '''');
END
```

LISTING 16.3

`DbResults.xml`—Simple Query Results

```
<?xml version="1.0" ?>
<!--Oracle DBXML Version 1.1.10 Query Results at 19-MAR-2001 16:10:34 -->
<!--
SELECT MSG
FROM Messages
WHERE Lng = 'en-US'
-->
<MESSAGESLIST>
 <MSGID>100</MSGID>
 <MSG>Checked</MSG>
 <MSGID>101</MSGID>
 <MSG>Updating all files...</MSG>
 <MSGID>102</MSGID>
 <MSG>Do you want to cancel the task currently in progress?</MSG>
 <MSGID>102</MSGID>
 <MSG>Updating all files...</MSG>
</MESSAGESLIST>
```

Such output can obviously be tuned to be even more localization-friendly. For more details, see some of the XML features that the different database systems offer in Chapter 12, "XML and Databases."

Flash Files

Flash, the popular application from Macromedia, is often used to provide animations on Web sites. Flash movies have always been time-consuming to localize because there is no easy way to access the translatable text, and the last resort of copying and pasting can offer some challenges when dealing with text in a code page different from the system code page of the machine where the work is done.

One way to externalize text in Flash is to use the dynamic text property of the symbols and assign variables. These variables can be set with values taken from a remote file using the `loadVariables()` or `loadVariablesNum()` methods.

This technique works but requires the external file to be in a format that, to say the least, does not lend itself very well to localization. For example, to set the following three variables

```
varIntro = "Introduction text";
btnHome  = "Home";
btnRD    = "R&D";
```

the text file must contain a single line formatted as follows:

```
varIntro=Introduction+text&btnHome=Home&btnRD=R%26D
```

The text must be in one line, each variable=value pair must be separated by a character
&, the spaces must be replaced by the character +, and all extended characters (and
some ASCII characters, such as +, /, ?, %, *, and &) must be escaped into the %HH form
where HH is the hexadecimal value for the given character.

Starting in version 5, Flash offers support for XML, which from a localization viewpoint could be a much better alternative to loadVariables().

You can create and manipulate XML DOM objects in the movie scripts. Again, using
the dynamic text property for each symbol, the text can be mapped to variables. However, this time the goal is to populate the variables in the frame actions script by loading an external XML document where each variable has a corresponding entry. As an
example, see the document shown in Listing 16.4.

LISTING 16.4

`FlashText_en.xml`—Storing Flash Text in XML

```
<?xml version='1.0' encoding='windows-1252' ?>
<data>
 <var id='varIntro'>Introduction text</var>
 <var id='btnHome'>Home</var>
 <var id='btnRD'>R&amp;D</var>
</data>
```

All the translatable data are outside of the movie and are easily translatable. In addition, the localization properties described in Chapter 8 could be used as well, making
the mechanism even more localization-friendly. Listing 16.5 shows the script code that
uses the XML object to read the entries and map them to the variables in the movie.
Note that a direct selection by ID would be much more efficient, but Flash does not
currently provide one.

LISTING 16.5

`FlashXML.fla`—Flash Script Loading XML File

```
var xmlDoc = new XML();

xmlDoc.onLoad = myOnLoad;
xmlDoc.load("FlashText_en.xml");
```

LISTING 16.5 **CONTINUED**

```
function myOnLoad ( p_bSuccess )
{
    if ( p_bSuccess )
    {
        tmp = xmlDoc.lastChild.previousSibling;
        tmp = tmp.lastChild.previousSibling;
        for ( i=0; i<3; i++ )
        {
            if ( tmp.attributes.id == "varIntro" )
            {
                varIntro = tmp.lastChild.nodeValue;
            }
            else if ( tmp.attributes.id == "btnRD" )
            {
                btnRD = tmp.lastChild.nodeValue;
            }
            else if ( tmp.attributes.id == "btnHome" )
            {
                btnHome = tmp.lastChild.nodeValue;
            }
            tmp = tmp.previousSibling.previousSibling;
        }
    }
    else
    {
        varIntro = "Problem loading the XML document";
    }
}
```

When the movie is published you can open the generated HTML file and see the result as shown in Figure 16.2.

There is a problem with encoding support. Flash documentation states that ActionScript (the Flash scripting language) supports only `iso-8859-1` and `Shift-JIS`. In most cases this means ActionScript supports only the default code set of the machine on which the player is running. For example, loading Japanese text from an English or Russian machine (with Japanese support) will not result in a correct Japanese output. This problem is not specific to the XML object; it also affects the `loadVariables()` function. Although this lack of code set support can be forgiven for the latter function, failure to support `UTF-8` and `UTF-16` with the XML object is unacceptable if you need to do any serious localization.

FIGURE 16.2

Flash movie with text loaded directly from the XML document.

Currently, to display extended characters properly the text must be broken apart into vector graphics on a machine set with the proper code page (and there are problems even then for some languages such as Chinese).

Until Macromedia fixes these basic problems, dealing with non-ANSI languages will always be tricky in Flash. However, on the positive side, despite the inability to access nodes by using IDs, the addition of the XML DOM object is encouraging. It opens the door for a much more efficient approach to localization with Flash.

PYX

If you are familiar with SGML and the SGML parsers such as `nsgmls` from James Clark, you may know about ESIS. *ESIS (Element, Structure, Information, Set)* is the structured-controlled output of the SGML document: how the document is composed in terms of elements, attributes, characters, and so on. The ESIS output is a line-based list of parsed data with a very simple notation that can be used by non–SGML-aware tools.

PYX is the same thing for XML. Because XML constructs are simplified versions of the SGML ones, the PYX output is also simpler. This alternative to other XML parsing methods such as in-memory storage with DOM (Document Object Model) or event-driven storage such as with SAX (Simple API for XML) offers some advantages when you need to execute operations with command-line utilities such as `awk`, `grep`, `wc`, and `sort`.

Several tools offer a PYX output, among them the original `xmln` and `xmlv` by Sean McGrath. The document is checked for validity if you use `xmlv`, whereas it is only checked for being well formed with `xmln`. These two utilities are available at `http://www.digitome.com/pyxie_download.html`.

Various PYX-related modules are available in Perl (see `http://search.cpan.org/search?mode=module&query=PYX` for details). For example, `pyxw` by Matt Sergeant is a tool enabling the conversion of PYX files back into XML format.

PYXToSAX and SAXToPYX from Shawn Silverman are two Java classes that can be used to enable a PYX input with a SAX parser and to generate PYX output from an XML document. You can download these classes at `http://members.home.net/sfs/xml`.

The PYX notation, derived from the original ESIS, is quite simple: Each parsed component is output in a single line with a character prefix that indicates what type of data it is. The notation is outlined in Table 16.1.

TABLE 16.1

PYX Notation

Code	Description
?	Processing instructions
(	Start tag
)	End tag
A	Attribute
–	Text

Empty elements are output as a start tag immediately followed by an end tag. Comments are ignored. Line breaks are represented by the code \n in a text line.

Both xmln and xmlv support only a few encodings: UTF-8, UTF-16, us-ascii, and iso-8859-1. To process any documents in other encodings you must first convert them to UTF-8 or UTF-16.

Note that the output is always in UTF-8. Any non-ASCII character in a subsequent command that you run after the PYX transformation, such as a grep command, must be written in UTF-8.

By piping different utilities you can achieve many functions. Listing 16.6 shows a sample XML document that we can use to illustrate various commands.

LISTING 16.6

SampleFile.xml—**Sample XML Document**

```
<?xml version='1.0' encoding='iso-8859-1' ?>
<document title='Sample XML File'>
 <!-- <emph> is used to make emphasized terms -->
 <para id='1'>Text in the <emph>first</emph> paragraph.</para>
 <para id='2'><emph>A</emph>nother paragraph.</para>
```

LISTING 16.6   CONTINUED

```
<para id='3'>Link to <link href='link1.xml'>Link1.xml</link>.</para>
<para id='4'>Link to <link href='link2.xml'>Link2.xml</link>.</para>
<para id='5'><image href='image.svg'/></para>
</document>
```

For example, we can try to get a word count of the file.

The default output of xmln for the sample document file is obtained by using the following command:

```
xmln SampleFile.xml
```

It generates the following output:

```
(document
Atitle Sample XML File
-\n
-
-\n
-
(para
Aid 1
-Text in the
(emph
-first
)emph
- paragraph.
)para
-\n
-
(para
Aid 2
(emph
-A
)emph
-nother paragraph.
)para
-\n
-
(para
Aid 3
-Link to
(link
```

```
Ahref link1.xml
-Link1.xml
)link
-.
)para
-\n
-
(para
Aid 4
-Link to
(link
Ahref link2.xml
-Link2.xml
)link
-.
)para
-\n
-
(para
Aid 5
(image
Ahref image.svg
)image
)para
-\n
)document
```

To take into account only the text, we can add a `grep` command as follows:

```
xmln SampleFile.xml | grep '^-'
```

This gives the list of the text lines only:

```
-\n
-
-\n
-
-Text in the
-first
- paragraph.
-\n
-
-A
-nother paragraph.
-\n
-
```

```
-Link to
-Link1.xml
-.
-\n
-
-Link to
-Link2.xml
-.
-\n
-
-\n
```

Because line breaks are getting in the way, we want to fine-tune the `grep` expression to get only the text lines that are not line breaks (all line breaks are output on separate text lines). Do not forget the `?` to allow lines that have only one character.

```
xmln SampleFile.xml | grep '^-[^\\][^n]?'
```

The output is now

```
-
-
-Text in the
-first
- paragraph.
-
-A
-nother paragraph.
-
-Link to
-Link1.xml
-.
-
-Link to
-Link2.xml
-.
-
```

To eliminate the text marker (the leading -), we can use `gawk` (the GNU version of `awk`) as follows:

```
xmln SampleFile.xml | grep '^-[^\\][^n]?' | gawk "{print substr($0,2)}"
```

This gives us the text content without the tags, comments, attribute values, or other XML-specific constructs.

```
Text in the
first
 paragraph.

A
nother paragraph.

Link to
Link1.xml

.

Link to
Link2.xml

.
```

The addition of the `wc` command finally provides the word count:

```
xmln SampleFile.xml | grep '^-[^\\][^n]?' | gawk "{print substr($0,2)}" |
↳wc -w
```

There are 16 words in this case. However, this is not perfect because the `<emph>` element was used to mark the first letter of the second paragraph and make the word "Another" into two text entries: A and `nother`. The other problem is that the `title` attribute is translatable text and was not included in the output either.

Despite these limitations (which you can work around most of the time) you can see that very useful functions are possible using a PYX output. The following are a few other examples.

To generate a list of the values of any `href` attributes in the file:

```
xmln SampleFile.xml | grep '^Ahref' | gawk "{print substr($0,7)}"
```

Output:

```
link1.xml
link2.xml
image.svg
```

You could use this for quickly verifying that a translated document has the same links as the original document (with the provision that some may be in a different order). The same principle could be used to check IDs, and so forth.

To count the number of `<link>` elements the document contains:

```
xmln SampleFile.xml | grep '\(link' | wc -l
```

Output:

2

To create a sorted list with no textual data in the document:

```
xmln SampleFile.xml | grep "^[^-]" | sort
```

Output:

```
(document
(emph
(emph
(image
(link
(link
(para
(para
(para
(para
(para
)document
)emph
)emph
)image
)link
)link
)para
)para
)para
)para
)para
Ahref image.svg
Ahref link1.xml
Ahref link2.xml
Aid 1
Aid 2
Aid 3
Aid 4
Aid 5
Atitle Sample XML File
```

This output could be used to compare the corresponding translated documents and detect any modification of the code part of the file. If, as in this example, localizable values are in some attributes, you can use a second grep command to remove them:

```
xmln SampleFile.xml | grep "^[^-]" | sort > tempfile
grep -v "^Atitle" tempfile > finalfile
```

The bottom line is that the PYX output is not XML anymore, but is now in a text file with a simple, predictable structure that you can use. The fact that any extended character would be in UTF-8 eliminates most parsing problems: You will never have trailing bytes that can be confused with ASCII characters in UTF-8.

Obviously not all XML documents will generate PYX output that will always be usable for complex functions. But for many documents, tools such as grep, awk, sed, perl, diff, and sort provide the means to execute almost any type of text manipulation, limited only by your imagination.

Validation

One of the first tasks of localizing XML documents is usually to make sure the files are well formed, and if a DTD is available, that they are valid.

Opening the documents in a validating XML tool such as the latest Internet Explorer would do, but it is not efficient if there are more than a few files to process.

Various validation tools are freely available. Among them are nsgmls from James Clark (available at http://www.jclark.com/sp/nsgmls.htm) or xmlv, already mentioned in the discussion of PYX. Many online validation utilities are also available. A rich list of XML validators and checkers is available at the OASIS (Organization for the Advancement of Structured Information Standards) at http://www. oasis-open.org/cover/check-xml.html.

If you are working on Windows, Microsoft XML SDK offers a command-line utility for this: xmlint. It allows specifying several documents at once. Any error is explained and clearly indicated, as shown in Figure 16.3.

FIGURE 16.3

Output of xmlint, *the Microsoft validation utility.*

The same functionality has been incorporated in Rainbow (`http://www.opentag.com`). The tool uses the same XML engine, but the interface, which enables you to quickly list various files scattered in different folders and subfolders, can be more convenient in some cases. After listing the documents to process in the main window, select the **XML Utilities** option from the **Tools** menu and choose the **Validate Documents** command. As displayed in Figure 16.4, the output is the same as for `xmlint`.

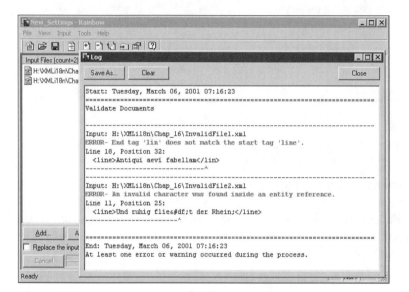

FIGURE 16.4

*Output of the **Validate Documents** function in Rainbow.*

One of the most negative aspects of HTML is the permissiveness of many HTML browsers, which do not enforce constructed documents correctly. This will not happen with XML and should enable a much easier handling of the files.

The Translation Process

Regardless of whether your XML document is native or an extraction of another format, it can go through the same translation process.

The steps of that process are obviously different according the set of tools you use, but they are generally divided into three main phases: The preprocessing, the translation, and the postprocessing.

Preprocessing

The preprocessing phase can be very involved or minimal depending on different factors. Figure 16.5 outlines the general workflow of the preprocessing.

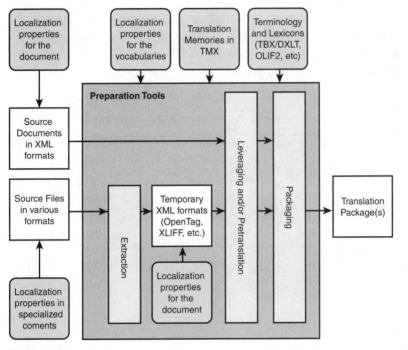

FIGURE 16.5

Preprocessing XML documents for translation.

The blocks with round corners indicate some of the types of technologies that can be involved in the different steps.

Source files may already be XML; if not, they go through an extraction or filtering step. Localization properties for document types can be used here to inform the filters of the elements and attributes to localize. The localization properties at the document level will help in adding context information: parts not to translate, glossary terms, length limitation, and other requirements.

Then, the XML documents can be preleveraged, possibly from other XML documents or from TMX translation memories. Terms can be searched for and matched against a glossary. The steps can be as easy as a drag-and-drop of the XML documents (such as for TagEditor), or can involve a batch process through a wizard (such as for SDLX), or anything in between. Each has advantages and drawbacks: drag-and-drop is easy, but not well suited for multiple documents and possible preleveraging. The batch process is more involved, but also more scalable.

At the end you have a translation package consisting of files ready to be opened in the translation environment.

To illustrate the process we can look at one XML document throughout the different steps. Our test file displayed in Listing 16.7 is a VoiceXML document. This document, along with other files used in this chapter, can be found in the `Samples` folder of the Rainbow application.

LISTING 16.7

`VoiceForm.xml`—VoiceXML Document to Localize

```xml
<?xml version="1.0"?>
<?xml-stylesheet type='text/xsl' href='VoiceXMLSimple.xsl' ?>
<vxml version="1.0">
 <form id="get_card_info">
  <block> We now need your credit card type, number, and expiration date.
➥</block>
  <field name="card_type">
   <prompt count="1">What kind of credit card do you have?</prompt>
   <prompt count="2">Type of card?</prompt>
   <!-- This is an in line grammar. -->
   <grammar><![CDATA[
    visa {visa}
    | master [card] {mastercard}
    | amex {amex}
    | american [express] {amex}
   ]]></grammar>
   <help> Please say Visa, Mastercard, or American Express. </help>
  </field>
  <!-- The grammar for type="digits" is built in. -->
  <field name="card_num" type="digits">
   <prompt count="1">What is your card number?</prompt>
   <prompt count="2">Card number?</prompt>
   <catch event="help">
    <if cond="card_type == 'amex'">
     Please say or key in your 15 digit card number.
    <else/>
     Please say or key in your 16 digit card number.
    </if>
   </catch>
```

LISTING 16.7   CONTINUED

```
  <filled>
   <if cond="card_type == 'amex' &amp; card_num.length != 15">
    American Express card numbers must have 15 digits.
    <clear namelist="card_num"/>
    <throw event="nomatch"/>
   <elseif cond="card_type != 'amex' &amp; card_num.length != 16"/>
    Mastercard and Visa card numbers have 16 digits.
    <clear namelist="card_num"/>
    <throw event="nomatch"/>
   </if>
  </filled>
 </field>
 <field name="expiry_date" type="digits">
  <prompt count="1">What is your card's expiration date?</prompt>
  <prompt count="2">Expiration date?</prompt>
  <help>
   Say or key in the expiration date, for example one two oh one.
  </help>
  <filled>
   <!-- validate the mmyy -->
   <var name="mm"/>
   <var name="i" expr="expiry_date.length"/>
   <if cond="i == 3">
    <assign name="mm" expr="expiry_date.substring(0,1)"/>
   <elseif cond="i == 4"/>
    <assign name="mm" expr="expiry_date.substring(0,2)"/>
   </if>
   <if cond="mm == '' || mm &lt; 1 || mm > 12">
    <clear namelist="expiry_date"/>
    <throw event="nomatch"/>
   </if>
  </filled>
 </field>
 <field name="confirm" type="boolean">
  <prompt>I have <value expr="card_type"/> number <value
⮡expr="card_num"/>,
   expiring on <value expr="expiry_date"/>. Is this correct?
  </prompt>
  <filled>
   <if cond="confirm">
    <submit next="place_order.asp" namelist="card_type card_num
⮡expiry_date"/>
```

LISTING 16.7   CONTINUED

```
  </if>
  <clear namelist="card_type card_num expiry_date acknowledge"/>
  </filled>
 </field>
</form>
</vxml>
```

The VoiceXML document type is designed for programming voice systems. During the translation phases, the linguist will have only the XML document for context. In this specific case, we can make the task of the translator a little bit easier by providing an XSL template to render the file in a table format where the text to translate is clearly visible. That is why the document contains the processing instruction to use an XSL template:

```
<?xml-stylesheet type='text/xsl' href='VoiceXMLSimple.xsl' ?>
```

This template will not be useful after translation, when the document is used in its final context by voice systems.

The principle of creating temporary views of documents to help the translation can be applied to any XML document, especially those that contain extracted text such as OpenTag, XLIFF, or any output from database queries.

Our example does not include existing translation memories, but, although most tools offer a preleveraging function, that function is no different from using the TMs interactively while translating.

To preprocess the document with SDLX, you must obtain an Analysis file that describes the VoiceXML vocabulary. It can be created from the DTD or the source file itself. To create the Analysis file and prepare our sample document, follow these steps:

1. Start SDLX, click the **Project Wizard** button, and select the option **Import Files into a New Project**.
2. In the **SDLX Project Import** window, check the **SGML/XML** filter, and click **Options**.
3. Select the **Analyse** command from the **File** menu.
4. We will use the source document to create the Analysis file. In the **Input File** edit box enter the name of the document: C:\Program Files\RWS Tools\ Rainbow\Samples\VoiceForm.xml. In the **Output** edit box enter a name for the Analysis file: for example, C:\Program Files\RWS Tools\Rainbow\ Samples\VoiceXML.anl, and then click **OK**. You will then see a warning

message telling you the file is not a DTD. Click **OK**. A second message tells you the Analysis file will be done from the source document. Click **OK**.

5. The list of the different elements appears. Go through the list of tags and change any default property that is not correct for VoiceXML. For our purposes, make sure the <grammar> element is set to be not translatable. Click **Save**, and then click **Close**.

6. In the **SDLX Project Import** window, click **Next**.

7. Make sure English (United States) is the **Source Language**, and add French (France) to the **Target Languages** list. Click **Next**.

8. Enter the location of the source document (C:\Program Files\RWS Tools\Rainbow\Samples) and click **Next**.

9. From the **Project Files** list, remove all files except VoiceForm.xml and click **OK**.

10. Leave the default **Target File Folder** location (same as the source). Click **Next**.

11. Leave the options as they are. Click **Next**.

12. Click **Next** again. The file is processed. You can save the project if you want. To quit, click **Close**.

A French folder has been created under the target file directory you have specified. It contains VoiceForm.itd, the file SDLX uses for the translation. To ensure any preview of the translated file can be done properly, copy the VoiceXMLSimple.xsl file into the French folder. The package is ready.

For TagEditor, you need a DTD Settings file for VoiceXML to process our sample document. You can create it from the VoiceXML DTD. To do so, follow these steps:

1. Start TagEditor and select the **DTD Settings** command from the **Tools** menu.

2. In the **DTD Settings** dialog box, click **Add**.

3. Select the first option: **Create a New DTD Settings File Using the DTD Settings Wizard** and click **OK**.

4. The **Wizard** dialog box opens. Click **Next**.

5. In the filename of the DTD box, browse to select the VoiceXML DTD: C:\Program Files\RWS Tools\Rainbow\Samples\voicexml1-0.dtd.

6. In the **File Name of the DTD Settings** box, select a name for the new DTD Settings file: C:\Program Files\RWS Tools\Rainbow\Samples\VoiceXML.ini.

7. Enter VoiceXML for the description and click **Next**.

8. Click **Next** again.

9. In the **Step 3** window, select the <grammar> element in the list and click **Properties**. Set the **Group** option in the **Markup** list. This will prevent the translation of the element content. Click **OK**, and then click **Next**.

10. In the **Step 4** window, check the **XML Default** options in the **Sets** list and make sure the **Convert Entities** option is also set. Click **Finish**.
11. In the **DTD Settings** dialog box click **OK**.

TagEditor is now ready to open VoiceXML documents.

In some circumstances, the traditional commercial tools will not work; bugs, unsupported XML features, or unsupported source languages are some of the reasons this could occur. One way to work around these issues is to provide an RTF file where the XML tags and the translatable text have been set to different styles. This method is widely used by many tools. One of the most popular RTF formats is the one used by TRADOS Translator's Workbench, with the `tw4winInternal` and `tw4winExternal` styles for inline and structural codes respectively, while the translatable text is in `Normal` style.

Sometimes you may have to come up with your own preparation process. Ideally this phase should be independent of the choice of the translation environments that will be used by the linguists. As an example of an alternative process, we can use the functions offered in Rainbow.

As with the other tools, you first need a file that specifies the localization properties for VoiceXML. It is already included with Rainbow. You can edit it if needed using the following commands:

1. Select the submenu **Localization Properties Definitions** from the **Tools** menu. Then select the **XML Document Types** command.
2. Select the **Open** command from the **File** menu and select the `VoiceXML` file listed in the default directory. Click **OK**. At this point the list of rules can be edited.
3. To quit, select the **Exit** command from the **File** menu.

In Rainbow, the XML document type to use is chosen from different criteria when each XML document is processed (root element, namespace, and so forth). In this way, documents of different types can be processed in the same batch of input files.

To proceed to the preparation itself, execute the following steps:

1. List the `VoiceForm.xml` file in the main window of the application by using the **Add** button or by dragging and dropping the document in the main window.
2. Select the **Prepare For Translation** command from the **Tools** menu.
3. In the **Work Environment** tab, select the option **Original File with Translator's Workbench RTF Layer**.

4. In the **Source Options** tab make sure English is selected. The default encoding does not matter because it is an XML document and its encoding will be detected by the filter. The file does not have any special localization markers.
5. In the **Target Options** tab select French as the **Locale** and select `UTF-8` as the **Encoding**.
6. In the **Package** tab enter a location for the package, for example `C:\Localization Projects`. Choose a name for the package, for instance `Pack1`. All output files will be under that subfolder in the folder destination you have selected. Choose whether you want to zip the package (you need WinZip 8.0 and its command-line plug-in for this option to work).
7. Click **Execute** to start the preparation. If you go to the `C:\Localization projects\Pack1` directory (you can quickly do this by selecting the **Open Last Package Folder** command from the **Tools** menu), you will find two subfolders: `Original` and `Work`. The first one contains the original XML document, whereas the second has the prepared RTF file. If several source files were in a hierarchy of folders, that structure would be replicated under the `Original` and `Work` folders as well.

To make sure the translator will be able to see the file in its simplified presentation, copy the `VoiceXMLSimple.xsl` file into both the `Original` and `Work` folders. Also make sure to refresh the ZIP file with these additions if you send the package.

Translation

When the files are ready for translation, the package can be sent to the linguists. Most tools share the same general characteristics shown in Figure 16.6: Source text is translated in an editor while a translation memory engine, fed through TMs, provides exact and fuzzy matches. In addition, a terminology engine locates terms in the source text and offers glossary terms. The tools also often provide a way to preview the translated documents.

After the translation is completed, the files can be packaged again to be sent for postprocessing.

With SDLX, the translation occurs in a specialized database-driven application, SDL Edit, shown in Figure 16.7.

This enables you to tightly control the modification of the text. In some cases, it has the drawback of hiding the codes, which on occasion could be helpful to understand the context.

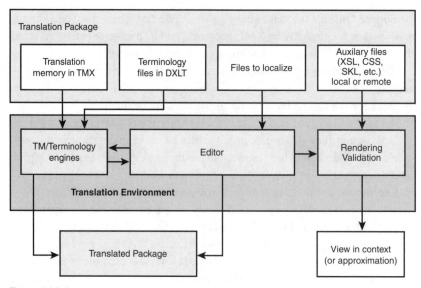

FIGURE 16.6

Translation environment with XML documents.

FIGURE 16.7

The VoiceXML document loaded in the SDLX translation environment.

With the **Preview Translation** command in the **File** menu, you can merge back the extracted text and display it in your browser, as shown in Figure 16.8.

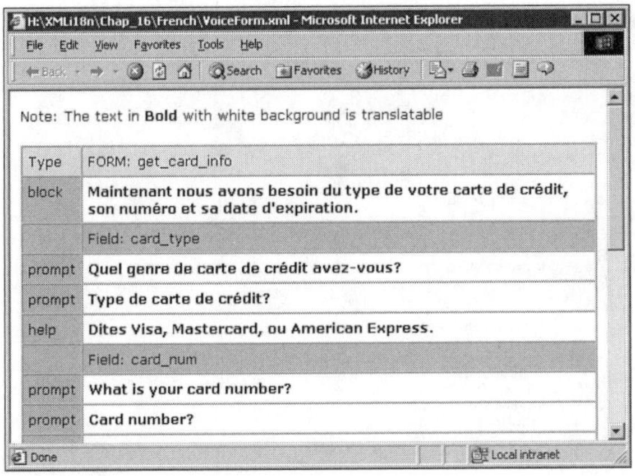

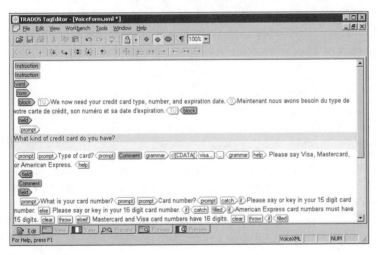

FIGURE 16.8

During translation, the localized merged file can be seen in the browser.

With TagEditor, our file can be opened directly in the application. As you see in Figure 16.9, the user has a little more context while translating because the codes, although they are protected, are visible.

FIGURE 16.9

The VoiceXML document loaded in TagEditor.

TagEditor also has a preview mode where you can see the source language, the target language, or both at the same time, as shown in Figure 16.10.

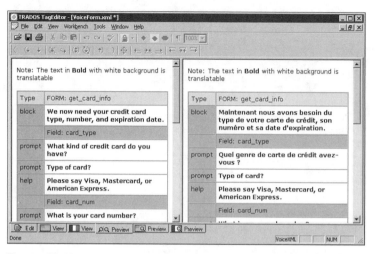

FIGURE 16.10

During translation, source and target documents can be rendered.

There are several drawbacks in using dedicated editors for translation, including

- There is little or no built-in support for preleveraged files (not using a TM and the tool, but inputting source files where any reusable text already exists).
- Specialized editors are usually not as powerful as editing environments such as Word, which offer macros, powerful spell checkers, grammar checkers, and so on.

Rainbow offers a few utilities that can help in localizing XML documents converted to RTF. The package created earlier has a file named `C:\Localization projects\ Pack1\Pack1.hrz`. This small file is the Settings file for the package and can be opened with Horizon, another tool that ships with Rainbow.

Essentially, Horizon serves as a rendering engine for files edited in Word. When opening the `Pack1.hrz` file, the first document of the package is displayed. Select the **Edit File** command from the **Tools** menu (or press Ctrl+E) to open the current document in Word.

At this point you can translate directly into the file, as shown in Figure 16.11, or use one of the tools that supports RTF to help while working in Word.

Any time you want to see the translation, save the RTF file in Word (no need to close the file), go to Horizon, and select the **Refresh** command from the **View** menu (or press F5). The text is converted from RTF to plain text with the encoding that was selected at preparation time (`UTF-8` in our example), and the file is displayed in Horizon as shown in Figure 16.12.

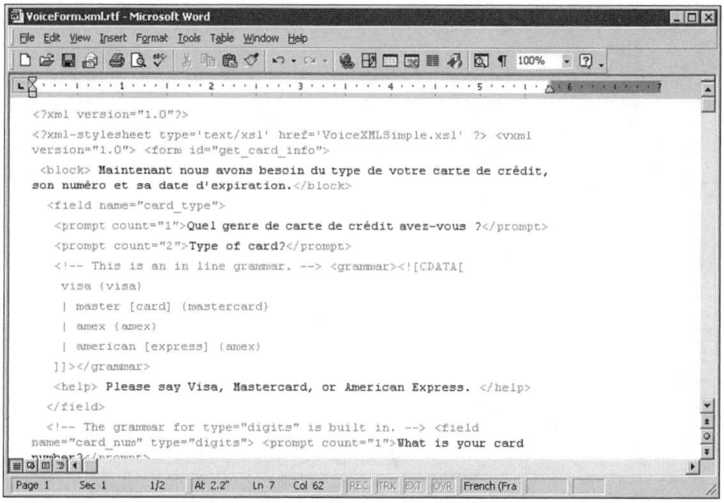

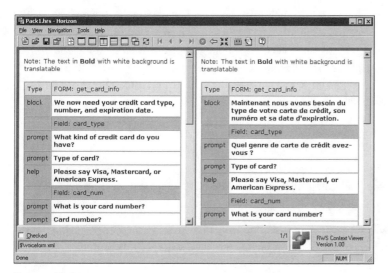

FIGURE 16.11

Translation of the text with color-coded styles.

FIGURE 16.12

Preview of the translation in Horizon.

As for the previews with SDLX or TagEditor, if any tag is deleted or some other XML
syntax error is introduced, the viewer displays an error message and points out the
problem, such as the example shown in Figure 16.13 where a `</prompt>` tag was accidentally modified.

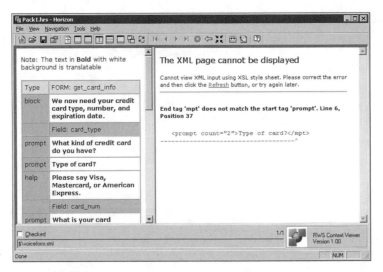

FIGURE 16.13

A verification of the XML syntax is done at the same time the translated document is viewed.

A tool such as Horizon can be also helpful when you deal with many documents organized in a complex directory structure. The Settings file keeps a list of the documents and makes navigating among them very easy. For example, browsing through all documents of a project is simply a matter of going from one to the other with the **Next** command from the **Navigation** menu (or pressing Ctrl+Right). Small details like this can sometimes make a big difference in saving time and increasing overall quality.

Postprocessing

The postprocessing phase consists of several tasks, displayed in Figure 16.14. These include creating the final output for each translated document and creating the final translation memories, if necessary.

In addition, if the XML document is a temporary repository created by extracting text from another file format, the file must be merged back into its native format.

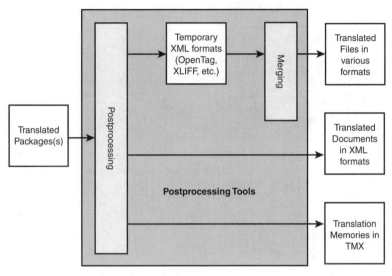

FIGURE 16.14

Postprocessing XML documents.

In most of these cases the tasks are easy to execute. For example, to create the final files you would

- In SDLX, load each ITD file and select the **Create Translation** command from the **File** menu.
- In TagEditor, load each BIF file and select the **Save Target As** command from the **File** menu.
- In Horizon, select the **Rebuild All Files** command from the **Tools** menu to re-create all documents of the project from their corresponding RTF files.

Summary

XML can be a tremendous ally in the localization process. It addresses any encoding problems efficiently, it has flexibility for adding specialized markup to help in the process, and it has a large number of tools (and libraries to build tools) available. These are some of the reasons for the appeal of XML.

In addition, XSL templates, CSS, and other technologies related to transformation and presentation provide an important benefit when it comes to offering better context for linguists during the localization process.

CHAPTER 17

Text Extraction

In This Chapter:

Most of the localizable data you find in today's projects are not stored in XML documents. They are kept in various file formats, a few of which are easy to localize, but many of which are difficult or impossible to use in a normal localization process.

In this chapter, we see how the data in formats that are not efficient for translation can be treated as XML data through text extraction. We discuss in detail two XML-extracted text formats, OpenTag and XLIFF, and see when it is appropriate to use them.

Text Extraction Principles

Separating the text to translate from its original format to facilitate localization is as old as localization itself. This process has been used most often with formats related to software. The mechanism is simple to implement and works as described in the following text and as illustrated in Figure 17.1.

1. **Extraction**—A tool, usually called a *filter,* takes the original format as input and separates the localizable parts from the nonlocalizable parts. The latter file is often called the reference file or *skeleton* file.
2. **Translation**—The localizable parts are sent for translation and related tasks.
3. **Merging**—After these tasks are done, the now localized parts are merged back together with the nonlocalizable parts to make a new file in the original format.

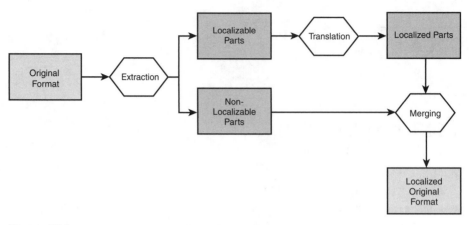

FIGURE 17.1

Principles of text extraction for localization.

Advantages

This system offers the advantage that, at the translation stage, you deal with only one type of file instead of the several different original formats.

Related to this, extracting the text provides you with an opportunity to abstract any inline codes through the use of a common notation. This makes for a much easier reuse of translation across different formats.

Another advantage is that most of the code part of the original file never goes to translation, lessening any risk of accidental modification. In some cases, when the file is merged back with the translated text, the nontranslatable data may need to be changed to accommodate the target language. This could be done automatically by the merging tool or by someone with a good understanding of the native file format.

Finally, extracting data to a common format provides some benefits when it comes to tool development and maintenance. After a new filter is created for a given original file format, you immediately have the opportunity to use any utilities that have been developed for the common format. For example, if you have a tool that generates pseudo-translation on your extracted text format, developing a filter for a new native format will give you pseudotranslation capability for that format right away. At the same time, when one of the native formats changes, you need to upgrade only its corresponding filter to support the new version, but none of the tools working on the extracted text need to be modified.

Drawbacks

Extracting text has a few negative aspects.

The most important drawback is that with extracted text you might not have much context information to offer to the linguists during translation. For example, a filter for the Windows RC file format may not extract control type information with the translatable text, making the work of the linguist more difficult. However, this type of issue is more an implementation problem than a drawback linked to the concept of extracted text. There is nothing that prevents good filters from providing any possible context information along with the translatable text.

The problem of rendering the extracted data is related to context. The translation environment used may not be able to generate the merged file on demand, and the linguist may not be able to see the WYSIWYG version of the translated document. This problem does not always exist, however. In many cases, extracted text is used on file formats for which you would not have rendering anyway. In these cases, using the extracted file with an XSL template can actually help the linguists to have a clearer view of the text than they would have with the original file.

To make the extraction and merging process truly efficient, you need to avoid making adjustments to the nonextracted part of the files. This means the file is internationalized correctly and if any code change is needed, it is done by the merging tool. These conditions might not always be true.

A final possible drawback is that using extracted text makes the overall localization process a bit more complicated because it adds two steps: extraction and merging. This can be significant if you have many files to localize.

When to Use Extracted Text

Extracted text is not meant to be used on every source file. It is merely a possible fallback solution when you cannot process the source file in a better way. The method is especially applicable when the original format of the file contains more codes than text and does not provide much context information.

A format like XLIFF provides the tools with an easy way to keep track of the modifications made to the translation. If your process requires this type of functionality, you might want to look at using extracted text.

This is also the case when the translatable text can be leveraged upstream in the authoring process and pretranslated files are sent to the linguists. The distinction between new text and text already translated is usually easier to handle in an extracted text format than in the original file where there is most likely no provision for this.

OpenTag

The first XML application for extracted text was OpenTag. The format was initially made public by International Language Engineering (ILE) in February 1997. The definition was refined with the help of various customers and partners.

Version 1.2 of OpenTag was released in September 1998 and a few adjustments have been made since to keep up with the various changes XML itself has undergone, such as namespaces or schema definitions. You can find more information on OpenTag in Appendix E, "OpenTag Quick Reference," and at http://www.opentag.com.

How It Works

OpenTag has a loose architecture: It offers only a few elements that can be combined in many different ways depending on your needs. The <grp> element enables you to group things together. This can be done at any depth because a <grp> element can contain one or more <grp> elements.

The basic unit of text is the <p> element, which corresponds to a text item (a label, a paragraph, the text of a cell in a table, and so forth). Inside a <p> element OpenTag substitutes the native inline codes with special elements: the <g> element for paired codes and the <x/> element for any other placeholders.

If necessary, you can presegment the content of a <p> element using the <s> elements (for example, when breaking down a paragraph into sentences).

In addition, the format offers various specialized elements to deal with features usually related to documentation-type data: index markers, references, conditional text, and so forth. Tools can also use the <prop> element and the ts attributes to code their specific metadata.

Example

If your original file is a Windows resource file such as the one shown in Listing 17.1, you can split it into two components: the OpenTag document (Listing 17.2) and its corresponding skeleton file (Listing 17.3).

LISTING 17.1

Sample1.rc—Original RC File

```
#include "resource.h"
IDD_DIALOG1 DIALOG DISCARDABLE  0, 0, 186, 57
STYLE DS_MODALFRAME | WS_POPUP | WS_CAPTION | WS_SYSMENU
```

LISTING 17.1 CONTINUED

```
CAPTION "Title"
FONT 8, "MS Sans Serif"
BEGIN
    LTEXT           "&Path:",IDC_STATIC,8,4,18,8
    EDITTEXT        IDC_EDIT1,8,16,100,14,ES_AUTOHSCROLL
    CONTROL         "&Validate",IDC_CHECK1,"Button",
                    BS_AUTOCHECKBOX | WS_GROUP |
                    WS_TABSTOP,8,40,41,10
    DEFPUSHBUTTON   "OK",IDOK,129,7,50,14,WS_GROUP
    PUSHBUTTON      "Cancel",IDCANCEL,129,24,50,14
END
```

There are no specifications for the format of the skeleton file, so it can be done in any way the filtering tool sees fit. Some filters will even avoid generating a skeleton file, and instead use the original document to reconstruct the translated copy.

LISTING 17.2

`Sample1.rc.otf`—OpenTag Document

```xml
<?xml version="1.0" encoding="windows-1252" ?>
<opentag version="1.2">
 <file lc="EN-US" ts="skl:964008261" datatype="winres"
  tool="WinRcFilter" original="Sample1.rc"
  reference="Sample1.rc.skl"
 >
  <grp id="1" type="dialog" rid="IDD_DIALOG1">
   <p type="caption">Title</p>
   <p id="2" type="label" rid="IDC_STATIC">&amp;Path:</p>
   <p id="3" type="check" rid="IDC_CHECK1">&amp;Validate</p>
   <p id="4" type="button" rid="IDOK">OK</p>
   <p id="5" type="button" rid="IDCANCEL">Cancel</p>
  </grp>
 </file>
</opentag>
```

LISTING 17.3

`Sample1.rc.skl`—Skeleton File

```
<OKFSKL100:RES:964008261>
#include "resource.h"
IDD_DIALOG1 DIALOG DISCARDABLE  0, 0, 186, 57
```

LISTING 17.3 CONTINUED

```
STYLE DS_MODALFRAME | WS_POPUP | WS_CAPTION | WS_SYSMENU
CAPTION "<xref$1>"
FONT 8, "MS Sans Serif"
BEGIN
    LTEXT           "<xref$2>",IDC_STATIC,8,4,18,8
    EDITTEXT        IDC_EDIT1,8,16,100,14,ES_AUTOHSCROLL
    CONTROL         "<xref$3>",IDC_CHECK1,"Button",
                    BS_AUTOCHECKBOX | WS_GROUP |
                    WS_TABSTOP,8,40,41,10
    DEFPUSHBUTTON   "<xref$4>",IDOK,129,7,50,14,WS_GROUP
    PUSHBUTTON      "<xref$5>",IDCANCEL,129,24,50,14
END
```

The principle used by OpenTag can be applied not only to RC files, string tables, properties files, and other similar resource-type data, but also to document-type data, where the text is not broken into strings, but flows into sentences and paragraphs.

Multilingual Documents

There are many ways to organize an OpenTag document, depending on what you want to do with it. You can use it as a repository for multiple translations of segments, for example. Figure 17.2 shows the extracted RC file with strings in several languages.

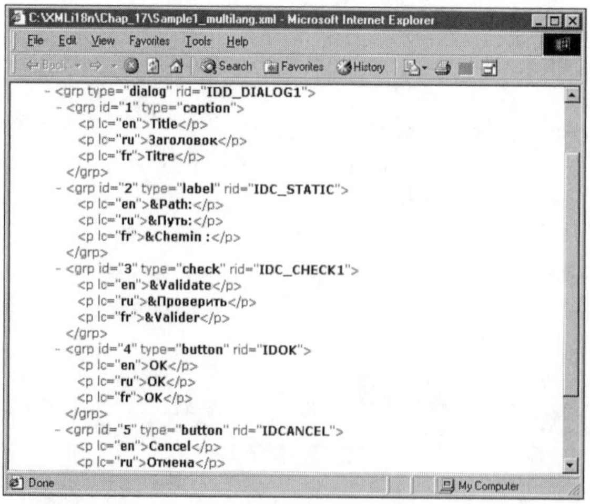

FIGURE 17.2

An OpenTag document with content in several languages.

The use of the `lc` attribute instead of the more standard `xml:lang` attribute is a remainder of the early design of OpenTag. The `lc` attribute has exactly the same values as `xml:lang` and will most likely be deprecated in favor of `xml:lang` the next time a version is released.

XML Localisation Interchange File Format

At the end of 2000, a group driven by companies including Oracle, Novell, Sun, and IBM/Lotus started to define an exchange format for translatable data: XLIFF (XML Localisation Interchange File Format).

The format is based on the principles defined by OpenTag and borrows some of its tags. It also adopts some of the ideas developed later in TMX and adds a few innovations of its own: project information, pretranslation and history, versioning, binary objects, and so forth.

The first draft of XLIFF was released in May 2001. The information provided here is subject to change as the draft is finalized. You can find the latest specifications and more information on XLIFF at `http://www.xliff.org`. There is also a discussion group at `http://groups.yahoo.com/group/DataDefinition`.

How It Works

XLIFF is close to OpenTag in many respects, but it is a more defined format, enabling fewer possibilities to express the same content in different ways, and therefore offering better interoperability.

The format also, for now, specializes in storing text extracted from software-type files and tagged documents. This more specialized aim eliminates the need for some compromises that OpenTag made to accommodate documentation-type data.

Listing 17.4 is an example of the XLIFF document generated from the sample Window RC file used earlier (refer to Listing 17.1). Obviously, as with OpenTag, additional localizable information such as coordinates or font information could also be extracted and stored in XLIFF if needed.

LISTING 17.4

`Sample1.xlf`—Example of an XLIFF Document

```
<?xml version="1.0" encoding="windows-1252" ?>
<xliff version="1.0" xml:lang='en'>
 <file source-language='en' target-language='fr' datatype="winres"
  original="Sample1.rc">
```

LISTING 17.4   CONTINUED

```
<header>
 <skl>
  <external-file href="Sample1.rc.skl"/>
 </skl>
</header>
<body>
 <group restype="dialog" resname="IDD_DIALOG1">
  <trans-unit id="1" restype="caption">
   <source>Title</source>
  </trans-unit>
  <trans-unit id="2" restype="label" resname="IDC_STATIC">
   <source>&amp;Path:</source>
  </trans-unit>
  <trans-unit id="3" restype="check" resname="IDC_CHECK1">
   <source>&amp;Validate</source>
  </trans-unit>
  <trans-unit id="4" restype="button" resname="IDOK">
   <source>OK</source>
  </trans-unit>
  <trans-unit id="5" restype="button" resname="IDCANCEL">
   <source>Cancel</source>
  </trans-unit>
 </group>
</body>
</file>
</xliff>
```

The base element of XLIFF is `<trans-unit>`. It corresponds to a unique item extracted from the original file (label, caption, paragraph, string, and so forth). The content of the item is stored in its `<source>` element for the source language, and, optionally, its `<target>` element for the target language.

Both `<source>` and `<target>` elements contain the text and any inline elements included with the text. Note that currently no mechanism is dedicated to break the item into smaller segments, for instance, sentences inside a paragraph.

Bilingual Files

As you can see from using `<source>` and `<target>`, a `<file>` element can contain only a source and one target language. However, an XLIFF document can contain several `<file>` elements, and the source and target locales of each `<file>` element can be different.

The `xml:lang` attribute can be used to indicate the language of the content at any level where there is text. The `source-language` and `target-language` attributes in the `<file>` element indicate the corresponding languages for `<source>` and `<target>`. To allow XML tools that are not XLIFF-aware to process XLIFF documents correctly, it is recommended that you still use `xml:lang` with `<source>` and `<target>`, even if some tools could guess the correct locales implicitly.

Skeleton Files

In XLIFF, the skeleton file can be stored either inside the XLIFF document or in a separate file.

When the skeleton file is stored inside the document, you can use a simple CDATA section to encapsulate its body, as shown in Listing 17.5:

LISTING 17.5

`Sample1_skl1.xlf`—An XLIFF Document with Embedded Skeleton

```
<?xml version="1.0" encoding="windows-1252" ?>
<xliff version="1.0" xml:lang='en'>
 <file source-language='en' target-language='fr' datatype="winres"
  original="Sample1.rc">
  <header>
   <skl>
    <internal-file>
<![CDATA[<OKFSKL100:RES:964008261>
#include "resource.h"
IDD_DIALOG1 DIALOG DISCARDABLE  0, 0, 186, 57
STYLE DS_MODALFRAME | WS_POPUP | WS_CAPTION | WS_SYSMENU
CAPTION "<xref$1>"
FONT 8, "MS Sans Serif"
BEGIN
    LTEXT           "<xref$2>",IDC_STATIC,8,4,18,8
    EDITTEXT        IDC_EDIT1,8,16,100,14,ES_AUTOHSCROLL
    CONTROL         "<xref$3>",IDC_CHECK1,"Button",
                    BS_AUTOCHECKBOX | WS_GROUP |
                    WS_TABSTOP,8,40,41,10
    DEFPUSHBUTTON   "<xref$4>",IDOK,129,7,50,14,WS_GROUP
    PUSHBUTTON      "<xref$5>",IDCANCEL,129,24,50,14
END]]>
```

LISTING 17.5   CONTINUED

```
    </internal-file>
   </skl>
  </header>
  <body>...
```

If the skeleton file is binary it can be coded in Base64 and inserted in the document. For example, Listing 17.6 shows how the previous example would look in Base64 form.

LISTING 17.6

`Sample1_skl2.xlf`—An XLIFF Document with Base64 Skeleton

```
<?xml version="1.0" encoding="windows-1252" ?>
<xliff version="1.0" xml:lang='en'>
 <file source-language='en' target-language='fr' datatype="winres"
  original="Sample1.rc">
  <header>
   <skl>
    <internal-file form="base64" crc="3a1e7daf">
```

PE9LRlNLTDEwMDpSRVM6OTY0MDA4MjYxPg0KI21uY21ZGUgInJlc291cmNlLmgiDQpJRERf
RElBTE9HMSBESUFMT0cgRElTQ0FSREFCTEUgIDAsIDAsIDE4NiwgNTcNClNUWUxFIERTX01P
REFMlJBTUUgfCBCXU19QT1BVUCB8IFdTX0NBUFRJT04gfCBCXU19TWVNNRU5VDQpDQVBUSU9O
ICI8eHJlZlQxPiINCkZPTlQgOCwgIk1TIFNhbnMgU2VyaWYiDQpCRUdJTg0KICAgIExxURVhU
ICAgICAgICAgICAiPHhyZWYkMj4iLElEQ19TVEFUSUMsOCw0LDE4LDgNCiAgICBCRFElUVEVY
VCAgICAgICAgSURDX0VVSVQxLDgsMTYsMTAwLDE0LEVTX0FVVE9IU0NST0xMDQogICAgQ09O
VFJPTCAgICAgICI8eHJlZiQzPiIsSURDX0NJRUNLMSwiQnV0dG9uIiwNCiAgICAgICAgICAg
ICAgICAgICAgQlNfQVVUT0NIRUNLQk9YIHwgV1NfR1JPVVAgfCANCiAgICAgICAgICAgICAg
ICAgICAgV1NfVEFCU1RPUCw4LDQwLDQxLDEwDQogICAgREVGUFVTSEJVVFRPTiAgICAgICI8
eHJlZiQ0PiIsSURPRSywxMjksNyw1MCwxNCxXU19HUk9VUA0KICAgIFBVU0hCVVVRUT04gICAg
ICAiPHhyZWYkNT4iLElEQ0FOQ0VMLDEyOSwyNCw1MCwxNA0KRU5EDQo=

```
    </internal-file>
   </skl>
  </header>
  <body>...
```

> **NOTE:** Base64 is a method used to compress and code any content, including binary data, into a subset of ASCII characters. Base64 is defined in section 5.2 of the RFC 1341. See `http://www.ietf.org/rfc/rfc1341.txt` for more details.

To allow the verification that the skeleton data have not been changed during the local-ization process, the tools can use a CRC (Cyclic Redundancy Check) signature through the `crc` attribute. This mechanism is available throughout the XLIFF document for most of the elements that contain data.

Binary Objects

An innovative aspect of XLIFF concerns binary objects. The format offers a way to transport any object and its associated localization metadata (project, phase, and so forth) as part of the document. The object itself, for example a bitmap from a resource file, is either embedded directly in the XLIFF document or referenced to an external file using the same methods as for the skeleton file.

The XLIFF tools can make the appropriate calls to choose the relevant applications needed to edit the object. The object is included in the `<bin-unit>` element that con-tains a `<bin-source>` and `<bin-target>` element. The type of the object is speci-fied in the `mime-type` attribute of the `<bin-unit>` (overridden in the `<bin-target>` element if the translated version of the object is in a different format).

Listing 17.7 shows how a bitmap and an audio file can be transported in the XLIFF document.

LISTING 17.7

`Sample2.xlf`—Binary Object Transport with XLIFF

```
<?xml version="1.0" ?>
<xliff version="1.0" xml:lang="en">
 <file source-language="en" target-language="fr-ca"
  datatype="winres" original="Object List">
  <header></header>
  <body>
   <bin-unit id="1" mime-type="image/bmp">
    <bin-source><external-file href="image1_en.bmp"/></bin-source>
    <trans-unit id="1">
     <source>Next</source>
    </trans-unit>
   </bin-unit>
    <bin-unit id="2" mime-type="audio/wav">
    <bin-source><external-file href="image2_en.jpg"/></bin-source>
   </bin-unit>
  </body>
 </file>
</xliff>
```

Each <bin-unit> element can also contain one or more <trans-unit> elements if you choose to offer some of the object's text in its extracted form as well.

Note that the file has no skeleton. This is allowed in XLIFF because, as in our example, you could have an XLIFF document that is only used to transport project and metadata information.

Project Information and Versioning

Other advantages of XLIFF compared to OpenTag include the predefined project information, pretranslation candidates, and version tracking data that can be stored along with the extracted text. This information can be coded in OpenTag as well by using tool-specific <prop> elements, not a standardized and dedicated structure.

The metadata works as follows:

The <header> element can contain a <phase-group> that lists the different steps the file went through. Each <phase> element is uniquely identified in its <file> by a phase-name attribute.

Each <trans-unit> can contain a set of <alt-trans> elements that act as suggestions, or can record a list of its previous versions of <source> and <target>. The <target> element (for both <alt-trans> and <trans-unit>) can have a phase-name attribute pointing to the <phase> element during which the change was made. The <phase> element has the information about tools, date, user, and so forth. A tool can make use of this mechanism to offer a very powerful pretranslation and versioning interface for the different users of the file during the process.

Listing 17.8 shows an example of the use of such tracking metadata. The three items to translate from French to Slovenian have been extracted (phase-name="p1"), and then leveraged (phase-name="p2"). At that time the <alt-trans> elements were inserted in the document. Then the file was sent for translation (phase-name= "trans").

LISTING 17.8

Sample3.xlf—Tracking Versions with XLIFF

```
<?xml version="1.0" ?>
<xliff version="1.0" xml:lang="en">
 <file source-language="fr" target-language="sl"
  datatype="pofile" original="Sample3.po" >
  <header>
   <phase-group>
```

LISTING 17.8 CONTINUED

```
    <phase phase-name="p1" process-name="preparation" tool="Rainbow
↪v2.00"
    date="2001-04-01T05:30:02" contact-name="Ernest Lafleur"></phase>
    <phase phase-name="p2" process-name="leverage" tool="Rainbow v2.00"
    date="2001-04-01T07:45:12" contact-name="Gertrude Kirkgard">
    <note>Used project-xyz version 3.2 TM.</note>
    </phase>
    <phase phase-name="trans" process-name="translation"
    date="2001-04-02T22:00:02" contact-name="Vlad Krasovsky"
    contact-email="vlad@krasovsky-inc.si"></phase>
   </phase-group>
  </header>
  <body>
   <trans-unit id="1">
    <source xml:lang="fr">Envoyer à...</source>
    <target xml:lang="sl" phase-name="trans">Pošlji v...</target>
    <alt-trans match-quality="95">
     <target xml:lang="sl" phase-name="p2">Naslovnik</target>
    </alt-trans>
   </trans-unit>
   <trans-unit id="2">
    <source xml:lang="fr">Italique</source>
    <target xml:lang="sl" phase-name="trans">Ležeče</target>
   </trans-unit>
   <trans-unit id="3">
    <source xml:lang="fr">Insérer un objet</source>
    <target xml:lang="sl" phase-name="trans">Vstavi predmet</target>
    <alt-trans match-quality="75">
     <source xml:lang="fr">Insérer</source>
     <target xml:lang="sl" phase-name="p2">Vstavljanje</target>
    </alt-trans>
   </trans-unit>
  </body>
 </file>
</xliff>
```

This aspect of XLIFF is important because it goes in the same direction as a trend that translation customers have shown recently: the need to have more control early in the process over the preparation of the localizable files. For example, this enables you to provide exact and fuzzy matches already associated with the source text, bypassing the use of translation memories for this first leverage. It permits the document authors to use other types of leveraging methods (database driven, or ID-based, for example).

Inline Codes

Inside the `<source>` and the `<target>` elements you can have inline codes. XLIFF offers support for the two main markup mechanisms:

- The substitution method consists of extracting each native code to the skeleton file and replacing it with a placeholder element. This also is how OpenTag deals with inline codes. The `<g>` replaces paired codes, while `<x/>` marks any stand-alone code. In addition, `<bx/>` and `<ex/>` offer a solution for paired codes that overlap and could not be marked up with a `<g>` element.

  For example, given the XHTML paragraph

  ```
  <p>The <b>big <i>black</i></b> dog runs fast.</p>
  ```

  an XLIFF entry using the substitution method generates the following:

  ```
  <source>The <g id='1' c-type='bold'>big <g id='2'
  ➥c-type='italic'>black</g></g> dog runs fast.</source>
  ```

- The encapsulation method consists of bracketing the native codes between XLIFF metatags. This is how TMX deals with inline codes. The `<bpt>` and `<ept>` elements are used to encapsulate paired codes; the `<it>` element is used for any isolated part of paired codes; and the `<ph>` element is used for any other standalone code. If any text occurs inside a sequence of encapsulated native code (for example, the text of an `alt` attribute in an `<img>` element in XHTML), you can use the `<sub>` element to delimit it. You might consider going a step further and creating a specific `<trans-unit>` for this type of text as well.

  For example, given the XHTML paragraph

  ```
  <p>The <b>big <i>black</i></b> dog runs fast.</p>
  ```

  an XLIFF entry using the encapsulation method generates the following:

  ```
  <p>The <bpt id='1' rid='1' c-type='bold'>&lt;b></bpt>big
  ➥<bpt id='2' rid='2' c-type='italic'>&lt;i></bpt>black
  ➥<ept id='3' rid='2'>&lt;/i></ept><ept id='4' rid='1'>&lt;/b>
  ➥</ept> dog runs fast.</p>
  ```

The attributes of all inline elements have been harmonized. The `id` attribute provides a reference to the skeleton file. The `c-type` attribute can be used to specify the type of inline code. The `rid` attribute is used to connect beginning and ending parts: `<bx/>` with `<ex/>`, and `<bpt>` with `<ept>`.

XLIFF offers many more powerful features to handle various aspects of the localization process: word count, context, coordinates, font and style information, and so forth. In addition, as with OpenTag, tools can add their own private metadata using the `<prop-group>` and `<prop>` elements as well as the `ts` attribute.

Translating Extracted Text

After the text has been extracted to OpenTag or XLIFF it can be translated using the same process as for any other XML documents. Some of these methods are described in Chapter 16, "Using XML to Localize."

Any XML-enabled tool will be capable of loading the extracted file. As long as you can specify which elements are translatable, the file can be dealt with like any other XML document. For example, as shown in Figure 17.3, you can load an OpenTag file in TagEditor.

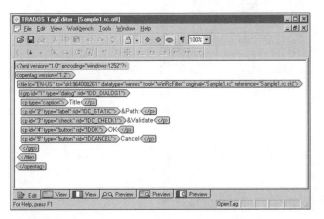

FIGURE 17.3

An OpenTag document in TagEditor.

Some tools even use extracted text formats as standard input. For instance, SDLX uses OpenTag as its default format. You can work directly with any OpenTag document you generate with your own filters. Figure 17.4 shows our sample document when it is loaded into SDL Edit.

If no XML-enabled translation environment is available, you can code the extracted text into a more generic format, such as RTF, that can be used in a word processor. Figure 17.5 displays an XLIFF document with an RTF layer opened in Word.

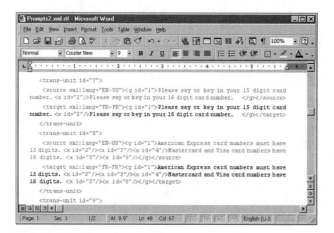

FIGURE 17.4

An OpenTag document in SDL Edit.

FIGURE 17.5

An XLIFF document in Word.

Different styles are used to indicate the text to translate from the rest of the document.

If the file cannot be merged during translation for a preview in context, you can at least provide a basic rendering of the extracted text that can help the linguist. For example, an XSL template such as the one shown in Listing 17.9 can be used to display any OpenTag document in a more user-friendly layout, as shown in Figure 17.6.

LISTING 17.9

`StdOTFDisplay.xsl`—Simple OpenTag Rendering

```
<?xml version="1.0" ?>
<xsl:stylesheet xmlns:xsl="http://www.w3.org/1999/XSL/Transform"
 version="1.0">

 <xsl:template match="/opentag/file">
  <HTML>
   <BODY>
    <P>Original File: <xsl:value-of select="@original"/></P>
    <TABLE BORDER="1" WIDTH="100%" CELLPADDING="5"
     CELLSPACING="0">
     <xsl:apply-templates/>
    </TABLE>
   </BODY>
  </HTML>
 </xsl:template>

 <xsl:template match="grp">
  <TR VALIGN="top">
   <TD BGCOLOR="LightBlue" WIDTH="100">
    <xsl:value-of select="@rid"/>
   </TD>
   <TD BGCOLOR="LightBlue">
    <xsl:if test="boolean(@type)">
     <B><xsl:value-of select="@type"/></B>
    </xsl:if>
    <xsl:if test="boolean(@type)=false">
     <B> </B>
    </xsl:if>
   </TD>
   <TD BGCOLOR="LightBlue">
    <B>Group</B>
   </TD>
  </TR>
  <xsl:apply-templates/>
 </xsl:template>

 <xsl:template match="p">
  <xsl:if test="text()!=''" >
```

LISTING 17.9   CONTINUED

```
  <TR VALIGN="top">
   <TD BGCOLOR="NavajoWhite">
    <xsl:value-of select="@id"/>
   </TD>
   <TD BGCOLOR="MediumTurquoise">
    <xsl:value-of select="@type"/>
   </TD>
   <TD BGCOLOR="White">
    <xsl:value-of select="text()"/>
   </TD>
  </TR>
 </xsl:if>
</xsl:template>

</xsl:stylesheet>
```

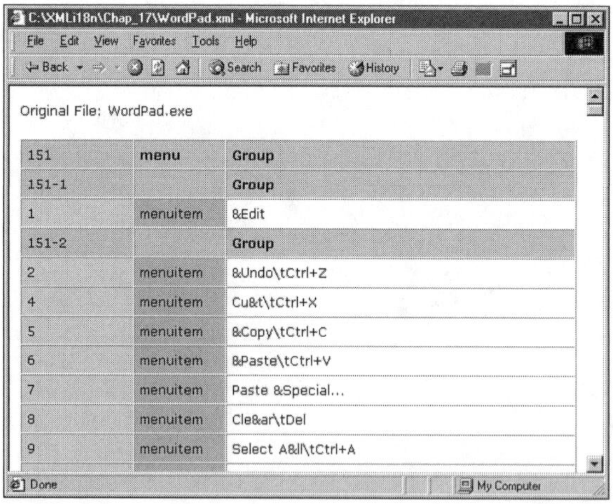

FIGURE 17.6

An OpenTag document viewed with an XSL template.

The same rendering system can be used for XLIFF documents as well. It is actually easier to come up with standard templates for XLIFF because the structure changes little compared to the OpenTag documents.

Summary

In this chapter we have seen that many non-XML formats can be extracted into a common XML format using a mechanism such as OpenTag or XLIFF. Although there are a few disadvantages in using extracted text, they are usually outweighed by the various advantages that the separation of text from source code and the internationalization features of XML bring.

You can find more information about the OpenTag format and some utilities at `http://www.opentag.com`. You can find a set of quick references for OpenTag in Appendix E. XLIFF is too new to have specifications set in stone yet, but you can find the latest draft at `http://www.xliff.org`.

# CHAPTER 18

TMX

In This Chapter:
- The Need   397
- How TMX Works   397
- Certification   402
- Implementation   403

TMX, the *Translation Memory eXchange* format, is an XML document type defined by the Localization industry to provide a common way to code translation memory exported files so they can be used with different translation tools.

The Need

As the number of translation tools increases and their use becomes more widespread, the need for a standard method of exchanging translation memories is evident.

After the OpenTag initiative made them realize the need for standardization, several localization customers, tool vendors, and translation providers met just before the *Localisation Industry Standards Association (LISA)* conference at Washington, D.C. in June 1997. The outcome of this meeting was the decision to start working on a standard way to exchange translation memory data between applications.

The effort was dubbed *Open Standard for Content And Container Reuse (OSCAR)* and its members went on to create the specifications for TMX within about a year. The latest version (1.2) was released in June 2000.

How TMX Works

TMX is a method of storing a collection of segments of arbitrary format in several languages. Each segment can contain native markup (inline codes).

Segments are grouped in translation units (`<tu>` elements). Each `<tu>` element contains one or more translation unit variants (`<tuv>` elements), which are the translations of the same text in different languages. Inside a `<tuv>`, the `<seg>` element contains the actual text of the segment.

Listing 18.1 shows a `<tu>` element as it appears inside a TMX document. There are three language variants: Greek, Croatian, and English. Each segment contains only text, no inline codes.

LISTING 18.1

`Sample1.tmx`—An Example of a TMX Document

```
<?xml version="1.0" ?>
<tmx version="1.2">
 <header creationtool="Rainbow" creationtoolversion="2.00"
  datatype="plaintext" segtype="sentence"
  adminlang="EN" srclang="EN" o-tmf="Cauldron">
 </header>
 <body>
  <tu tuid="1">
   <tuv lang="EL">
    <seg>Δοκιμάστε '-?' για περισσότερες πληροφορίες.</seg>
   </tuv>
   <tuv lang="HR">
    <seg>Za više informacija pokrenite '-?'.</seg>
   </tuv>
    <tuv lang="EN">
    <seg>Try '-?' for more information.</seg>
   </tuv>
  </tu>
 </body>
</tmx>
```

The example in Listing 18.2 is the same file, but this time the format of the text in HTML and the text -? have been replaced by a reference to a GIF file.

LISTING 18.2

`Sample2.tmx`—TMX File with Inline Markup

```
<?xml version="1.0" ?>
<tmx version="1.2">
 <header creationtool="Rainbow" creationtoolversion="2.00"
```

LISTING 18.2 CONTINUED

```
   datatype="html" segtype="sentence"
   adminlang="EN" srclang="EN" o-tmf="Cauldron">
 </header>
 <body>
  <tu tuid="1">
   <tuv lang="EL">
    <seg>Δοκιμάστε <ph x="1">&lt;img href="help.gif">&lt;/img></ph> για
➥περισσότερες πληροφορίες.</seg>
   </tuv>
   <tuv lang="HR">
    <seg>Za više informacija pokrenite
➥<ph x="1">&lt;img href="help.gif">&lt;/img></ph>.</seg>
   </tuv>
   <tuv lang="EN">
    <seg>Try <ph x="1">&lt;img href="help.gif">&lt;/img></ph> for more
➥information.</seg>
   </tuv>
  </tu>
 </body>
</tmx>
```

Levels

Tools can be categorized in three different levels depending on how they deal with content markup (inline codes). As an example, consider the following XHTML fragment:

```
<p>The <b>black</b> cat.</p>
```

This paragraph is a single segment in a translation memory, but it can be output in three different ways when it comes to the handling of the inline element <b>.

In the first level the segment is stripped of any inline markup codes and contains only text:

```
<tuv lang="en">
 <seg>The black cat.</seg>
</tuv>
```

This has the obvious drawback that it loses any formatting or other information coded within the text of the segment. But at least you will still get fuzzy matches.

For the second level the segment contains inline codes, but these codes are not in the original format of the file. Instead they are in whatever format the translation tool uses. For example, we can imagine a tool in which the original <b> and </b> inline codes are replaced by tool-specific markers such as [1#] and [#1].

```
<tuv lang="en">
 <seg>The <bpt i="1" type="bold">[1#]</bpt>black<ept i="1">[#1]</ept>
➥cat.</seg>
</tuv>
```

At this level, TMX preserves the information about the fact that inline codes are in the segment, where they are, and, if the tool is well written, what type of code it represents (for example, bold, font change, or link).

The third level is identical to the second, but the inline codes encapsulated inside the content elements are the native codes of the original file format.

```
<tuv lang="en">
 <seg>The <bpt i="1" type="bold">&lt;b></bpt>black<ept i="1">&lt;/b>
➥</ept> cat.</seg>
</tuv>
```

Note that inline codes are considered text data when coded in TMX. The characters < and & must be escaped. This third level is obviously the best for lossless exchange.

Note that for software messages, variable insertions such as %s, $1, or {1} are usually not considered inline markup but a part of the text. For this reason software localization tools such as Catalyst from Alchemy Software might support only Level 1 because there is no need to support more than that.

User-Defined Characters

In addition to segment content, TMX also makes provisions for user-defined characters. TMX, like any XML vocabulary, can use any character of the UCS repertoire. However, in some cases the text to exchange utilizes user-defined characters (in the Private Use area: U+E000 to U+F8FF). In some cases it might be useful to provide additional information on these characters in the TMX document itself.

The user-defined characters are grouped in <ude> elements. Each of them contains one or more <map/> elements. The <ude> element has a name attribute that identifies the set of user-defined characters and often a base attribute that specifies the encoding to which the code attributes are mapped. Each <map/> element provides a unicode attribute that is the user-defined character in the Private Use Area, and if necessary a code attribute that is the encoding (in hexadecimal) of the character in the base encoding.

Additionally, each `<map/>` element can have an `ent` attribute to describe a possible entity name, and a `subst` attribute to provide a possible alternative string or character if the original is not supported.

For example, the Macintosh encoding for Roman scripts includes one character that is not defined in UCS. Listing 18.3 shows how this character could be specified in a TMX document.

LISTING 18.3

`UserCharacters.tmx`—Using User-Defined Characters with TMX

```
<?xml version="1.0" ?>
<tmx version="1.2" xmlns="http://www.lisa.org/tmx">
 <header o-tmf="TWB-Horizon"
  creationtool="Rainbow" creationtoolversion="2.00"
  adminlang="EN" srclang="EN"
  datatype="MacRes" segtype="paragraph"
 >
  <ude name="Apple Additions" base="MacRoman">
   <map unicode="#xF8FF" code="#xF0" ent="apple" subst="(apple)"/>
  </ude>
 </header>
 <body>
  <tu tuid="STRING#1">
   <tuv lang="en">
    <seg>The character '&#xf8ff;' is specific to the Macintosh.</seg>
   </tuv>
   <tuv lang="fr">
    <seg>Le caractère '&#xf8ff;' est propre au Macintosh.</seg>
   </tuv>
  </tu>
 </body>
</tmx>
```

Segmentation

One of the most important aspects of exchanging translated segments is not covered by TMX: the segmentation. There is currently no provision in TMX to describe how the set of segments in a given TMX document has been broken down.

This type of information is very difficult to carry from one tool to another because each tool has different ways of handling sentence division.

This is not a problem limited to TMX: Any TM format will have the same issue when imported in a tool other than the original one.

Certification

To make sure the tools claiming TMX compliance are indeed implementing the standard correctly, the OSCAR Group provides a mechanism to certify the tools.

The certification is provided free by the *Language Technology Research Center (LTRC)* based in San Francisco, California, working with other organizations such as the *Localization Resource Center (LRC)* in Dublin, Ireland.

If you want to certify your implementation of TMX (for import and/or export) you might want to start by using the *TMX Development Kit (TDK)*. It is freely available and contains a set of test files that exercise most of the TMX constructs. This provides a good way to verify whether the import function of your application works correctly. The TDK also includes TMXCheck, a simple Windows application to validate TMX documents, helping you to test exported files. TMXCheck is illustrated in Figure 18.1.

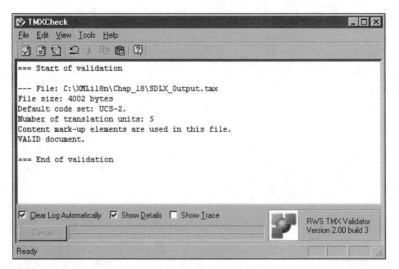

FIGURE 18.1

Validating TMX documents with TMXCheck.

The TDK as well as information about the TMX Certification are available online at http://www.lisa.org/tmx.

Implementation

Many tools now implement TMX at one level or another. First check carefully what level they claim to provide. A translation tool dealing with MIF, HTML, XML, or any document-type format that does not support at least Level 2 is very limited. It means you will lose all inline codes when saving to TMX. Ideally, tools should provide Level 3 support, or at least Level 2.

Listing 18.4 presents a simple XML document. It has been loaded in various translation tools, translated into German, and the resulting TM has been exported to TMX.

LISTING 18.4

`Test_Sample.xml`—Test XML Document to Generate TMX Files

```
<?xml version="1.0" ?>
<doc>
 <para>This is a simple text. With <emph>two</emph> sentences.</para>
 <para>Click <link ref="#help">'-h'</link> for more information.</para>
 <para>Click <image ref="help.gif" text="Help"/> for more
↪information.</para>
</doc>
```

The creation of the TMX files is easily done in all four tools. Listings 18.5–18.8 show the different outputs produced.

LISTING 18.5

`DejaVu_Output.tmx`—TMX File Generated by Déjà Vu

```
<?xml version="1.0" ?>
<!DOCTYPE tmx SYSTEM "tmx11.dtd">
<tmx version="1.1">
   <header
      creationtool="DejaVu2"
      creationtoolversion="2"
      datatype="PlainText"
      segtype="sentence"
      adminlang="EN-US"
      srclang="EN"
      o-tmf="DVMDB"
   >
   </header>
```

LISTING 18.5   CONTINUED

```
<body>
    <tu
        tuid="1"
        datatype="Text"
    >
        <tuv
            lang="en"
        >
            <seg>This is a simple text.</seg>
        </tuv>
        <tuv
            lang="fr"
        >
            <seg>Ceçi est un simple texte.</seg>
        </tuv>
    </tu>
    <tu
        tuid="2"
        datatype="Text"
    >
        <tuv
            lang="en"
        >
            <seg>With <ph x="1">{001}</ph>two<ph x="2">{002}</ph>
➥sentences.</seg>
        </tuv>
        <tuv
            lang="fr"
        >
            <seg>Avec <ph x="1">{001}</ph>deux<ph x="2">{002}</ph>
➥phrases.</seg>
        </tuv>
    </tu>
    <tu
        tuid="3"
        datatype="Text"
    >
        <tuv
            lang="en"
        >
            <seg>Click <ph x="1">{001}</ph>'-h'<ph x="2">{002}</ph> for
➥more information.</seg>
```

LISTING 18.5   CONTINUED

```
        </tuv>
        <tuv
            lang="fr"
        >
            <seg>Cliquez <ph x="1">{001}</ph>'-a'<ph x="2">{002}</ph>
➥pour plus d'information.</seg>
        </tuv>
    </tu>
    <tu
        tuid="4"
        datatype="Text"
    >
        <tuv
            lang="en"
        >
            <seg>Click <ph x="1">{001}</ph>Help<ph x="2">{002}</ph> for
➥more information.</seg>
        </tuv>
        <tuv
            lang="fr"
        >
            <seg>Cliquez <ph x="1">{001}</ph>Aide<ph x="2">{002}</ph>
➥pour plus d'information.</seg>
        </tuv>
    </tu>
  </body>
</tmx>
```

LISTING 18.6

`SDLX_Output.tmx`—TMX File Generated by SDLX

```
<?xml version="1.0" ?>
<!DOCTYPE tmx SYSTEM "tmx11.dtd">
<tmx version="1.1">
  <header
    creationtool="SDLX"
    creationtoolversion="1.0.0"
    datatype="unknown"
    segtype="sentence"
    adminlang="EN-US"
    srclang="EN-US"
```

LISTING 18.6   CONTINUED

```
  o-tmf="sdlxTM"
>
</header>
<body>
  <tu tuid="1">
    <tuv lang="EN-US">
      <prop type="SDLXCP">1252</prop>
      <seg>This is a simple text.</seg>
    </tuv>
    <tuv lang="FR">
      <prop type="SDLXCP">1252</prop>
      <seg>Ceçi est un simple text.</seg>
    </tuv>
  </tu>
  <tu tuid="2">
    <tuv lang="EN-US">
      <prop type="SDLXCP">1252</prop>
      <seg>With <bpt i="1" x="1">&lt;1&gt;</bpt>two<ept i="1">
➥&lt;/1&gt;</ept> sentences.</seg>
    </tuv>
    <tuv lang="FR">
      <prop type="SDLXCP">1252</prop>
      <seg>Avec <bpt i="1" x="1">&lt;1&gt;</bpt>deux<ept i="1">
➥&lt;/1&gt;</ept> phrases.</seg>
    </tuv>
  </tu>
  <tu tuid="3">
    <tuv lang="EN-US">
      <prop type="SDLXCP">1252</prop>
      <seg>Click <bpt i="1" x="1">&lt;1&gt;</bpt>&apos;-h&apos;
➥<ept i="1">&lt;/1&gt;</ept> for more information.</seg>
    </tuv>
    <tuv lang="FR">
      <prop type="SDLXCP">1252</prop>
      <seg>Cliquez <bpt i="1" x="1">&lt;1&gt;</bpt>&apos;-a&apos;
➥<ept i="1">&lt;/1&gt;</ept> pour plus d&apos;information.</seg>
    </tuv>
  </tu>
  <tu tuid="4">
    <tuv lang="EN-US">
      <prop type="SDLXCP">1252</prop>
```

LISTING 18.6   CONTINUED

```
      <seg>Click <ph x="1">&lt;1/&gt;</ph> for more information.</seg>
    </tuv>
    <tuv lang="FR">
      <prop type="SDLXCP">1252</prop>
      <seg>Cliquez <ph x="1">&lt;1/&gt;</ph> pour plus d&apos;
↪information.</seg>
    </tuv>
  </tu>
  <tu tuid="5">
    <tuv lang="EN-US">
      <prop type="SDLXCP">1252</prop>
      <seg>Help</seg>
    </tuv>
    <tuv lang="FR">
      <prop type="SDLXCP">1252</prop>
      <seg>Aide</seg>
    </tuv>
  </tu>
  </body>
</tmx>
```

LISTING 18.7

`TWB_Output.tmx`—TMX File Generated by Translator's Workbench

```
<?xml version="1.0" ?>
<!DOCTYPE tmx SYSTEM "tmx11.dtd">
<tmx version="version 1.1">
<header
    creationtool="TRADOS Translator's Workbench for Windows"
    creationtoolversion="Edition 3 Build 139"
    segtype="sentence"
    o-tmf="TW4Win 2.0 Format"
    adminlang="EN-US"
    srclang="EN-US"
    datatype="rtf"
    creationdate="20010122T034619Z"
    creationid="YVES"
>
<prop type="RTFFontTable">
{\fonttbl
{\f1 \fmodern\fprq1 \fcharset0 Courier New;}
```

LISTING 18.7 CONTINUED

```
{\f2 \fswiss\fprq2 \fcharset0 Arial;}}</prop>
<prop type="RTFStyleSheet">
{\stylesheet
{\St \s0 {\StN Normal}}
{\St \cs1 {\StB \v\f1\fs24\sub\cf12 }{\StN tw4winMark}}
{\St \cs2 {\StB \cf4\fs40\f1 }{\StN tw4winError}}
{\St \cs3 {\StB \f1\cf11\lang1024 }{\StN tw4winPopup}}
{\St \cs4 {\StB \f1\cf10\lang1024 }{\StN tw4winJump}}
{\St \cs5 {\StB \f1\cf15\lang1024 }{\StN tw4winExternal}}
{\St \cs6 {\StB \f1\cf6\lang1024 }{\StN tw4winInternal}}
{\St \cs7 {\StB \cf2 }{\StN tw4winTerm}}
{\St \cs8 {\StB \f1\cf13\lang1024 }{\StN DO_NOT_TRANSLATE}}}}</prop>
</header>

<body>
<tu creationdate="20010122T034944Z" creationid="YVES">
<tuv lang="EN-US">
<seg>This is a simple text.</seg>
</tuv>
<tuv lang="FR-FR">
<seg>Ceçi est un simple texte.</seg>
</tuv>
</tu>

<tu creationdate="20010122T035020Z" creationid="YVES">
<tuv lang="EN-US">
<seg>With two sentences.</seg>
</tuv>
<tuv lang="FR-FR">
<seg>Avec deux phrases.</seg>
</tuv>
</tu>

<tu creationdate="20010122T035048Z" creationid="YVES">
<tuv lang="EN-US">
<seg>Click &apos;-h&apos; for more information.</seg>
</tuv>
<tuv lang="FR-FR">
<seg>Cliquez &apos;-a&apos; pour plus d&apos;information.</seg>
</tuv>
</tu>
```

LISTING 18.7 CONTINUED

```
<tu creationdate="20010122T035105Z" creationid="YVES">
<tuv lang="EN-US">
<seg>Click Help for more information.</seg>
</tuv>
<tuv lang="FR-FR">
<seg>Cliquez Aide pour plus d&apos;information.</seg>
</tuv>
</tu>

</body>
</tmx>
```

LISTING 18.8

`Transit_Output.tmx`—TMX File Generated by Transit

```
<?xml version="1.0" ?>
<!-- Transit TMX document -->
<tmx version="1.1">
<header
    creationtool="Transit"
    creationtoolversion="3.0"
    datatype="Transit"
    segtype="block"
    adminlang="en"
    srclang="en-us"
    o-tmf="Transit"
    creationdate="20010128T005317Z"
    creationid="Yves"
    o-encoding="Unicode"
  >
<prop type="Project"></prop>
</header>
<body>
<tu>
<prop type="FileFormatGUID">{D2C9E572-4199-11D2-96CD-006008568A7A}</prop>
<prop type="Filename">Test_Sample</prop>
<tuv lang="en-us" changedate="20010128T004331Z" changeid="Transit">
<seg><ut>&lt;?xml version="1.0" ?&gt;
&lt;doc&gt;
 &lt;para&gt;</ut></seg>
</tuv>
```

LISTING 18.8   CONTINUED

```
<tuv lang="fr-fr" changedate="20010128T004342Z" changeid="Yves">
<seg><ut>&lt;?xml version="1.0" ?&gt;
&lt;doc&gt;
 &lt;para&gt;</ut></seg>
</tuv>
</tu>
<tu>
<prop type="FileFormatGUID">{D2C9E572-4199-11D2-96CD-006008568A7A}</prop>
<prop type="Filename">Test_Sample</prop>
<tuv lang="en-us" changedate="20010128T004331Z" changeid="Transit">
<seg>This is a simple text. </seg>
</tuv>
<tuv lang="fr-fr" changedate="20010128T004548Z" changeid="Yves">
<seg>Ceçi est un simple texte. </seg>
</tuv>
</tu>
<tu>
<prop type="FileFormatGUID">{D2C9E572-4199-11D2-96CD-006008568A7A}</prop>
<prop type="Filename">Test_Sample</prop>
<tuv lang="en-us" changedate="20010128T004331Z" changeid="Transit">
<seg>With <bpt i="1" type="inldel">&lt;emph&gt;</bpt>two<ept >
➥&lt;/emph&gt;</ept> sentences.</seg>
</tuv>
<tuv lang="fr-fr" changedate="20010128T004619Z" changeid="Yves">
<seg>Avec <bpt i="1" type="inldel">&lt;emph&gt;</bpt>deux<ept >
➥&lt;/emph&gt;</ept> phrases.</seg>
</tuv>
</tu>
<tu>
<prop type="FileFormatGUID">{D2C9E572-4199-11D2-96CD-006008568A7A}</prop>
<prop type="Filename">Test_Sample</prop>
<tuv lang="en-us" changedate="20010128T004331Z" changeid="Transit">
<seg><ut>&lt;/para&gt;
 &lt;para&gt;</ut></seg>
</tuv>
<tuv lang="fr-fr" changedate="20010128T004342Z" changeid="Yves">
<seg><ut>&lt;/para&gt;
 &lt;para&gt;</ut></seg>
</tuv>
</tuv>
</tu>
<tu>
```

LISTING **18.8**   CONTINUED

```
<prop type="FileFormatGUID">{D2C9E572-4199-11D2-96CD-006008568A7A}</prop>
<prop type="Filename">Test_Sample</prop>
<tuv lang="en-us" changedate="20010128T004331Z" changeid="Transit">
<seg>Click <bpt i="1" type="inldel">&lt;link ref="#help"&gt;</bpt>'-h'
➥<ept >&lt;/link&gt;</ept> for more information.</seg>
</tuv>
<tuv lang="fr-fr" changedate="20010128T004656Z" changeid="Yves">
<seg>Cliquez <bpt i="1" type="inldel">&lt;link ref="#help"&gt;</bpt>'-a'
➥<ept >&lt;/link&gt;</ept> pour plus d'information.</seg>
</tuv>
</tu>
<tu>
<prop type="FileFormatGUID">{D2C9E572-4199-11D2-96CD-006008568A7A}</prop>
<prop type="Filename">Test_Sample</prop>
<tuv lang="en-us" changedate="20010128T004331Z" changeid="Transit">
<seg><ut>&lt;/para&gt;
 &lt;para&gt;</ut></seg>
</tuv>
<tuv lang="fr-fr" changedate="20010128T004342Z" changeid="Yves">
<seg><ut>&lt;/para&gt;
 &lt;para&gt;</ut></seg>
</tuv>
</tu>
<tu>
<prop type="FileFormatGUID">{D2C9E572-4199-11D2-96CD-006008568A7A}</prop>
<prop type="Filename">Test_Sample</prop>
<tuv lang="en-us" changedate="20010128T004331Z" changeid="Transit">
<seg>Click <bpt i="1" type="inldel">&lt;image ref="help.gif"
➥text="Help"/&gt;</bpt> for more information.</seg>
</tuv>
<tuv lang="fr-fr" changedate="20010128T004719Z" changeid="Yves">
<seg>Cliquez <bpt i="1" type="inldel">&lt;image ref="help.gif"
➥text="Help"/&gt;</bpt> pour plus d'information.</seg>
</tuv>
</tu>
<tu>
<prop type="FileFormatGUID">{D2C9E572-4199-11D2-96CD-006008568A7A}</prop>
<prop type="Filename">Test_Sample</prop>
<tuv lang="en-us" changedate="20010128T004331Z" changeid="Transit">
<seg><ut>&lt;/para&gt;
&lt;/doc&gt;
 </ut></seg>
```

LISTING 18.8   CONTINUED

```
</tuv>
<tuv lang="fr-fr" changedate="20010128T004342Z" changeid="Yves">
<seg><ut>&lt;/para&gt;
&lt;/doc&gt;
 </ut></seg>
</tuv>
</tu>
</body>
</tmx>
```

First, except for the Transit output, all exported files pass the validation test of
TMXCheck. The document generated by Transit has one error: a missing mandatory
attribute i in all <ept> elements (this attribute enables you to match the <ept> element with its corresponding <bpt>).

The file generated by Déjà Vu is Level 2 and uses <ph> elements for all inline codes.
The encoding is UTF-16LE.

The document created from SDLX is also Level 2. It uses the <bpt> and <ept> elements to mark paired tags, and <ph> for isolated code. The encoding is UTF-16LE.

An interesting illustration of the segmentation problems discussed in Chapter 10,
"Segmentation," shows up in these samples: The value of the attribute title ("Help")
is translated in both tools, but Déjà Vu treats it as part of the segment where the <img>
element is located, whereas SDLX considers it a distinct segment and assigns a <tuv>
for it. The second approach is probably more efficient because it enables you to preserve an exact match when the only changes in a segment are update, addition, or deletion of attribute values.

Note that the Déjà Vu approach could use a small enhancement in TMX that would
make it more compatible with the SDLX approach. The <sub> element is designed to
indicate subflows of text within a main flow, which is exactly what "Help" is. A better
output for Déjà Vu that would require very little change would be to enclose the value
of any translatable attribute within a <sub> element.

Translation Workbench TMX is Level 1 only: All inline codes are stripped out. This
means you cannot even get exact matches if you are comparing it against the same
original document with the same tool. This limitation is rather puzzling because it is
difficult to see what type of technical difficulty would prevent support for inline codes.
In fact, BIF, the native format used to store bilingual files for TagEditor, is based on
TMX and utilizes the metatags to code inline elements. Note that this limitation is

supposed to be fixed in TRADOS 5. As is true for the two previous tools, the encoding of the TMX file is `UTF-16LE`.

Regarding the value of the attribute `title` that we discussed earlier, if Translator's Workbench had inline elements it would most likely be implemented as with Déjà Vu because like that tool, TagEditor offers "Help" as part of the main segment during translation.

The file generated by Transit is different from the ones generated by the three other tools. First note that, again because it was not possible to define a DTD-specific filter, the file was created using the default XML filter and the `title` attribute was not extracted.

Transit creates a Level 3 document. This means not only that the inline codes are present but also that their content is the original tag itself, whereas in Level 2 the content is whatever the tool uses to mark inline code in its translation environment (for example `{n}` for Déjà Vu and `<n>`, `</n>`, and `<n/>` for SDLX). As a matter of fact, the entire original document is present in the Transit TMX file. It is difficult to judge whether there is a merit to this; after all, TMX is meant to store fragments of text and the presence of structural codes such as `<doc>` in the inline codes can cause a mismatch when used with the other tools. On the other hand, such a property could be interesting. You could, for instance, reconstruct both the source and the target documents from the different `<tuv>` elements. The file is encoded in `UTF-8`, which means the version of the `<tmx>` element should probably be 1.2 and not 1.1.

As you can see, although TMX itself is now quite stable, its various implementations need to evolve to work out many potential exchange problems. All these issues exist regardless of what format you use, but TMX at least provides a common ground on which to build.

Summary

To help interoperability between translation tools, the LISA has defined an XML vocabulary to exchange translation memories: TMX. Most commercial tools and many in-house utilities now implement the format.

Keep in mind that the differences in the ways tools implement segmentation are an additional problem of exchanging TMs between different applications. The solution to this problem is quite difficult and is not currently addressed.

You can find a set of quick references for TMX in Appendix F. The complete TMX specifications are available online at `http://www.lisa.org/tmx`.

# CHAPTER 19

Terminology Exchange

In This Chapter:

Terminology is an important part of any translation work. As the localization process becomes more complex and involves more players and tools, problems related to interactions between different products with terminology databases have grown equally complicated.

This chapter discusses the need for terminology exchange and some of the solutions related to XML that have been developed.

The Need

Terminology data, simply put and in the context of localization, is a list of concept definitions in different languages. Such concept definitions can include various aspects such as descriptions, sources, examples of usage, grammatical information, synonyms, corresponding acronyms, and related terms. The following two main types of terminology databases can be used during localization:

- The terminology used directly by the translators as reference material during the translation, editing, and other steps of the product cycle.
- The terminology data used with NLP (Natural Language Processing) technologies, whether with human or machine interfaces: for example, the lexicons used by machine translation (MT) systems.

For simplicity's sake, in this chapter, we will refer to the first category as *termbase*, and the second as *lexbase*. These two types of terminology have many common properties, but they also include a wide range of different information.

> **NOTE:** Note that the term *glossary* often means different things depending on its use. In the localization industry, *glossary* frequently refers to a list of strings extracted from software or a documentation source that is used for reference when localizing the different components. This list is not always free of source code instructions, and does not always have information beyond the source and target text.
>
> In many respects such enumerations are very close to being translation memories, but they are used for terminology reference. This type of glossary can obviously be converted to one of the terminology exchange formats, but the scope of those formats is much broader.

As the list of tools used by linguists expands, it is important to ensure the sharing of the terms independently of the toolset used. In addition, some technologies that were rather uncommon yesterday now find their way to many projects. Examples include automated term extraction upstream and terminology validation downstream. An efficient exchange format in place ensures better interoperability and the integration of these mechanisms in the processes that are already in place.

As MT systems are implemented more and more often along with controlled language authoring, it is important to be able to leverage the traditional terminology work done by the translators into the lexicons used by machine translation. Conversely, the considerable work put into creating lexbases should be easily ported to the human-oriented termbases. In other words, developing and maintaining terminology should be done with both uses in mind.

The Solutions

Several projects are underway to standardize terminology representation. For various reasons, these endeavors have had mixed results until recently. An effort to consolidate these different activities into a coherent and collaborative framework has been made in the last few years.

The SALT project is probably the work that best illustrates this approach.

SALT, which stands for *Standards-based Access to multilingual Lexicons and Terminologies*, is an international project established in cooperation with the ISO Technical Committee 37, the OLIF2 Consortium, the OSCAR Group from LISA, the Text Encoding Initiative, and other related entities.

One objective of SALT is the development of XLT, the XML-based formats for lexicons and terminologies. XLT is a framework that harmonizes diverse aspects of various existing formats in different domains to give flexibility while maintaining interoperability both between the different termbase standards and between termbases and lexbases.

XLT

XLT is not a format in itself, but rather an architecture that provides components with which you can build an XLT-compliant markup language that can have a certain level of interaction with other XLT-compliant formats. More information on XLT can be found at http://www.ttt.org/oscar/xlt/dxlt.html.

XLT is designed to fit within the Terminology Markup Framework (TMF) currently developed by the ISO Technical Committee 37. This framework defines a set of criteria for Terminology Markup Languages (TMLs). In accordance with this, a given XLT format is defined by the logical combination of three components: the structure, the content, and the style.

The structure describes the core container of the documents. It is a constraint version of the core structure of ISO 12200, with some optional extensions that will be integrated as an amendment. ISO 12200, "Computer applications in terminology—*Machine-Readable Terminology Interchange Format*" is also called *MARTIF*.

The style is the form of markup used to represent the structure. In other words, to represent the same data, you could use a single element with a descriptive attribute or several specific elements. For example

```
<descript type="location">...</descript>
<descript type="definition">...</descript>
```

could also be represented as

```
<location>...</location>
<definition>...</definition>
```

However, this TMF distinction does not exist explicitly in XLT. All XLT formats use the same style (the first type).

Finally, the content consists of a subset of allowed data categories and values defined by ISO 12620, "Computer applications in terminology—*Data categories*." Each format differs from the others in terms of the data categories that it allows and the values they can take. This is represented by the DCS (Data Constraint Specification) document.

In other terms, an XLT format is composed of a core DTD/Schema (common to all XLT formats) and a specific content described by its DCS file, as illustrated in Figure 19.1.

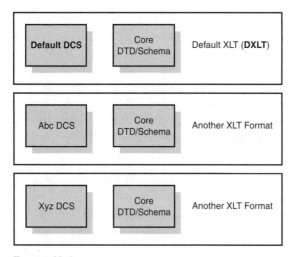

FIGURE 19.1

The components of XLT-based formats.

The framework also defines a default DCS and therefore a default application of XLT. This document type is called DXLT. (Some old documents may refer to it as DXF.)

The extensions slated for addition to MARTIF are composed of a few elements borrowed from the TMX content metatags (`<bpt>`, `<ept>`, and so forth). These inline elements offer more flexibility in the formatting of term entries.

OLIF2

The efforts of the SALT group that are related to lexicons are based on the work of the OLIF2 Consortium. OLIF2 is an XML document type developed as a continuation of the work done by the OTELO project. Detailed information can be found at `http://www.olif.net`.

OLIF2 is a reformulation in XML of the original OLIF (Open Lexicon Interchange Format) standard. The format is at the draft stage. Listing 19.1 shows an excerpt from an OLIF2 document: the contents of an `<entry>` element.

LISTING 19.1

`Olif2Sample.xml`—OLIF2 Sample Document

```
<entry EntryUserId="2312">
 <mono MonoUserId="2311">
  <keyDC>
   <canForm>Briefkurs</canForm>
```

LISTING 19.1 CONTINUED

```
   <language>de</language>
   <ptOfSpeech>noun</ptOfSpeech>
   <subjField>gac-fi</subjField>
   <semReading>b</semReading>
  </keyDC>
  <monoDC>
   <monoAdmin>
    <syllabification>brief-kurs</syllabification>
    <entryFormation>cmp</entryFormation>
    <originator>FISHERF</originator>
    <adminStatus>ver</adminStatus>
    <entrySource>sapterm</entrySource>
    <company>sap</company>
   </monoAdmin>
   <monoMorph>
    <morphStruct>brief:kurs</morphStruct>
    <inflection>like Tisch</inflection>
    <head>kurs</head>
    <gender>m</gender>
   </monoMorph>
   <monoSyn>
    <synType>cnt</synType>
   </monoSyn>
   <monoSem>
    <semType>meas</semType>
   </monoSem>
  </monoDC>
  <generalDC>
   <updater>HANSENPOU</updater>
   <modDate>1999-28-01</modDate>
   <usage>online</usage>
   <note>online-A</note>
  </generalDC>
 </mono>
 <transfer>
  <keyDC>
   <canForm>bank selling rate</canForm>
   <language>en</language>
   <ptOfSpeech>noun</ptOfSpeech>
   <subjField>gac-fi</subjField>
   <semReading>b</semReading>
  </keyDC>
```

LISTING **19.1**   CONTINUED

```
  <equival>full</equival>
 </transfer>
</entry>
```

TBX and DXLT

Following the development of TMX, LISA (Localisation Industry Standards Association) started to work on a format to exchange terminology: TBX (TermBase eXchange). As the work progressed it seemed clear that fitting into the new framework defined by the SALT project, the OLIF2 Consortium, and ISO TC 37 would be logical. The decision was finally made, at the end of 2000, to use the Default XLT format for TBX. Therefore, TBX and DXLT are now exactly the same format.

Most likely a small subset of the DXLT elements will be used in TBX documents, and TBX files will probably often look like minimal DXLT files, but this offers a great deal of flexibility.

XLT and DXLT are still under development and some descriptions that follow may be changed as the format is finalized. For example, the lang attribute in XLT probably will be replaced by the more standard xml:lang, allowing for better interoperability with other XML technologies such as XSL and XPath.

As shown in Figure 19.2, a TBX file is composed of a document header (the <martifHeader> element) and a main block (<text>) composed of an optional front matter (<front>), a <body> element, and an optional back matter (<back>). The <body> element contains a collection of <termEntry> elements.

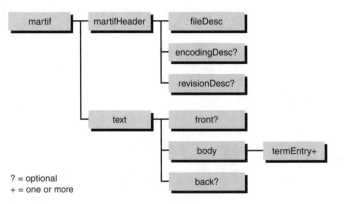

FIGURE 19.2

The Structure of a TBX/DXLT document.

Each <termEntry> element can store quite a complex structure if needed, but in many cases for localization projects, a smaller subset can be used. Listing 19.2 shows how a minimal TBX document looks.

LISTING 19.2

MinimalTBX.tbx—A Minimal TBX Document

```xml
<?xml version="1.0" ?>
<martif type="DXLT" lang="en">
 <martifHeader>
  <fileDesc>
   <sourceDesc>
    <p>Description of the source for "Hello World".</p>
   </sourceDesc>
  </fileDesc>
 </martifHeader>
 <text>
  <body>
   <termEntry>
    <langSet lang="en">
     <tig>
      <term>Hello World</term>
     </tig>
    </langSet>
   </termEntry>
  </body>
 </text>
</martif>
```

Obviously, a real-life TBX document will have one or more <langSet> elements for each <termEntry> element. In addition, a few pieces of auxiliary data will be also present. Listing 19.3 displays a TBX document that includes more useful information.

LISTING 19.3

Sample1.tbx—A More Elaborate Sample of TBX Data

```xml
<?xml version="1.0" ?>
<martif type="DXLT" lang="en">
 <martifHeader>
  <fileDesc>
   <sourceDesc>
    <p>Source: XYZ Translation Services.</p>
```

LISTING 19.3   CONTINUED

```
    </sourceDesc>
   </fileDesc>
 </martifHeader>
 <text>
  <body>
   <termEntry>
    <descrip type="definition">
     Part that goes on top of a book or some other published material.
    </descrip>
    <langSet lang="en">
     <tig>
      <term>Front cover<term>
     </tig>
    </langSet>
    <langSet lang="ja">
     <tig>
      <term>表紙<term>
      <termNote type="pronounciation">ひょうし</termNote>
     </tig>
    </langSet>
   </termEntry>
  </body>
 </text>
</martif>
```

As for each XLT-compliant format, the DCS for DXLT is defined in the form of a Microsoft XDR Schema. The XDR (XML-Data Reduced) language is based on the XML-Data specifications. The default DCS can be obtained from the XLT pages at `ftp://ftp.ttt.org./oscar/XLT`.

Summary

Although it is true that the landscape of terminology exchange formats can be a little bit confusing at times, the cooperative efforts started recently and the progress that has been made are encouraging.

The consolidation of the lexicon formats through OLIF2 and the XLT formats will enable a much more efficient cross-use of human-made glossaries and lexicons created for machine translation systems. However, keep in mind that this interoperability will be accomplished through tools that map content from one TML to another, not through the use of a single format.

For the glossaries used by traditional translation processes, consider TBX/DXLT as the solution for interchange between tools. Some translation environments such as Transit already offer support for MARTIF.

If your localization process also includes the use of a machine translation system, OLIF2 is the direction to go when you need to exchange lexicons between MT systems, as well as when you want to leverage data to and from human-oriented glossaries (with TBX/DXLT on the other side).

References

Here are some online reference materials. The documents identified as drafts are still works in progress at the time of this book's publication. Make sure you get the latest information.

SALT Web pages: `http://www.loria.fr/projects/SALT`

(draft) DXLT Specifications: `ftp://ftp.ttt.org./oscar/XLT`

OLIF2 Consortium Web pages: `http://www.olif.net`

(draft) OLIF2 Specifications: `http://www.olif.net/olif2/specification.htm`

| CHAPTER | 20 |

Conclusion

In This Chapter:

As you have seen throughout this book, the domains of application for XML are numerous and very different, but they usually match the areas where internationalization and localization are also needed. This alone is a good reason to invest time and resources to better understand how you can use XML to reach a more global market. Many processes, tools, and architectures you will come up with can apply and be ported to the various components of your products.

New Trends

With the emergence of XML as an important element of today's information technology, several trends are starting to take shape. The use of XML as the original storage medium for data that are not in formats easy to localize has been growing. Instead of having the data in the format native to the application for which they are used, the data are in XML and are converted or compiled into the native format at some point during production. The extra cost of developing the conversion process is quickly recovered by the various benefits XML offers for maintenance and localization.

Another growing use of XML is the role it plays in the localization of database content. The already efficient interaction mechanisms between databases and XML documents are bound to mature and become even better. This opens new avenues not only for localization but also for many new ways of using databases as repositories. With a minimal investment in time and work, you can develop efficient mechanisms to manage the multilingual content of your database.

User interfaces are also affected by XML. The browser-based interfaces that have been used for a while are now starting to change into more classic desktop interfaces with dialog boxes, tabs, windows, and so forth, to the point that they are not easily distinguished from classic interfaces. Many of them use a mixture of proprietary XML formats, XSLT, CSS, and JavaScript.

Finally, XML provides an excellent platform to store and manage multiple languages and to synchronize their translations. With the rise of more international development teams, content is now sometimes created in more that one source language. Databases and XML are helpful in creating systems taking this variable into account. In addition, the various aspects of workflow and content management are well served by XML.

All these tendencies bode well for localization because, through the flexibility and the internationalization capabilities of XML, localizable data are brought into the realm of more efficient reusability and reduced costs.

Some Drawbacks

However, a few issues with XML in certain situations can cause some limited problems. They are not alarming, but you will want to keep them in mind when assessing your use of XML.

The first issue is the growing complexity and interdependency that XML technologies are starting to show. This is an inevitable drawback of the powerful features XML brings. But, at times, it might affect your implementation decisions. For example, if you want to make use of XPath, you will almost be forced to use a DOM parser to process your documents.

It is inevitable that some technologies must work within a given set of constraints. You want to make sure these constraints do not force you to change the framework of your normal environment drastically without justification.

The second problem is one of scalability. XML technologies are mostly developed with the Web environment in mind and this does not always fit their use anymore. For example, using a DOM parser can, on occasion, lead to some performance problems with very large documents and documents with complex structures.

XML has outgrown its original domain and is utilized in many areas where the environment is not the Internet and where parameters and requirements can be quite different. Hopefully this is a reality that will be taken into account in the future of XML.

For now, the advantages that XML brings in terms of internationalization, flexibility, and ease of use outweigh by far any of these small drawbacks.

There is, however, one additional issue that, although not directly related to XML, can affect your migration to XML. A significant number of organizational and political aspects are linked to moving from a classic process to a process that involves XML and some form of content management. The traditional separations between software and documentation, as well as development and localization phases, are not so distinct with content-driven processes. New skills, procedures, and tools are needed, along with a new attitude and a different way of thinking. In addition, the notion of project may need to be redefined as the localization becomes an ongoing effort linked to the development of the content. The responsibilities and relationships between the different parties involved in the localization efforts must be adapted to this new model.

Adopting XML

In the last month of 333 BCE, Alexander the Great was setting camp on the coast of Lebanon, facing the island-city of Tyre. The Phoenician stronghold was reputed to be impregnable. It had never been captured, even after the 13 years of siege by the Babylonian armies of Nebuchadnezzar II. The main defense of the city was the eight hundred meter channel between the shore and the island. Instead of trying to solve that problem, Alexander decided to remove it, literally. He started to build a large causeway to reach the island and fight on the ground, where his troops were more efficient. Seven months later, Alexander's army broke through the high walls of Tyre and took the city. The causeway still exists today.

XML as a brand new solution for some of your localization problems is similar to Alexander's strategy. You bring the problem on a ground where it can be solved more efficiently. The very good internationalization support XML offers, along with its flexibility and adaptability, opens the way for new methodologies such as multilingual data management, single-sourcing, better interface between the different players of the process, and so forth.

However, keep in mind that using new approaches will often not be enough. In the summer of 332 BCE, when Alexander's causeway was about to reach the island of Tyre, the progress was stopped because of the depth of the channel and the proximity of the city defenders. The final assault leading to Alexander's success was carried out mostly from ships. The causeway was enormously helpful, but it alone could not bring victory.

In the same way, while embracing XML and its related new technologies, make sure you do not overlook the other areas where internationalization still needs to be done. For example, using XML to localize databases goes a long way toward making the process easier, safer, and more cost-effective, but it will not make your product capable of handling English, Russian, and Chinese together if your database itself has not been set up and designed to support multilingual data.

Internationalization and localization go well beyond selecting the most appropriate media to store your data. XML certainly adds a new dimension to the things you can do to improve your localization process and offers new avenues through a rich set of solutions. But the key to success is to seamlessly integrate these new and often fast-changing technologies into your existing framework without rebuilding everything or discarding proven mechanisms.

The Next Steps

The emergence of XML and its related implications create opportunities of which the industry should take advantage. Several important steps will make localization much easier and more cost-effective.

Many types of content are still far from being efficiently internationalized. Graphics are a good example of this. At a time when we have reuse of translation, version synchronization, translation memories, and so forth, we are still mostly reduced to basic copy and paste when it comes to translating text in graphics. An XML format such as SVG is definitely a step forward, but it is time to also see solutions for any other type of graphics. The addition of simple export and import functions in graphic applications would help immensely. Hopefully, companies such as Adobe or Macromedia will take some significant steps in that direction. Common formats such as XLIFF, OpenTag, or even proprietary XML formats would be good approaches to the problem.

The same is true for other categories of applications that produce localizable data: reporting tools, CAD and design applications, and so forth. In short, anything that creates documents with localizable text should include a mechanism to access it, and using XML for this is one of the best solutions.

As translation customers become more involved in the preprocessing stages of the localization process by integrating content management–related solutions and providing preleveraged documents, the need for two new standardization efforts increases.

The first of these standardization efforts is about word count. The current situation with regard to word count is about the same as Medieval Europe was with weights and measures. Everyone has his own standard. This cannot continue. With more cases where translatable data is provided in XML, it is inevitable that one piece of information carried along with the text will be its corresponding word count. It is the unit used to compare proposals, the unit used to pay translators, and the unit used in many types of estimations. It must be standardized, and should have been standardized long ago.

A second standardization effort, probably more of a long-term and progressive project, concerns translation tools API (Application Programming Interface). Here again, as the use of XML formats to carry localizable data increases, the need to provide context to the translators grows accordingly. A simple common API could be used to trigger the rendering of such documents through engines provided along with the file: Applets, DLLs, or server-side calls could provide any translation tools with a way of offering the linguists validation and rendering of proprietary formats. You can easily imagine new ways to provide localization packages. Some might include

- The XML documents in a given vocabulary (preleveraged when possible).
- A standard localization properties definition document that describes what is localizable in the given document type.
- Translation memories and glossaries in common formats.
- An engine for rendering (applets, DLL, and so forth) that can be easily triggered by a simple API call from the translation tools.

Vendors of translation tools could concentrate their developmental efforts in translation-related aspects of their products while localization customers would have the opportunity to interface their own viewing environment and therefore provide more efficient help to the translators. With XML as a common medium to carry localizable data, the development of common interfaces to describe and access these data is the next natural step.

The main advantages XML offers are openness, flexibility, and built-in internationalization features. XML is such a powerful and adaptable medium that its ability to meet your needs is for the most part limited not by technology but by your imagination.

Appendixes

In This Part:

APPENDIX A

Glossary

The following glossary entries provide definitions for the main terms found in this book. The terms in *italic* in a definition are terms that appear in the glossary.

Base character   A Unicode character that graphically combines with a succeeding *combining character* to form a *composite character*.

Base64   Format designed to represent arbitrary sequences of octets in a form that is not humanly readable, but is ASCII-compatible. Base64 is defined in the IETF RFC 1341.

Bicameral   Refers to a script that uses letters in two cases: uppercase and lowercase. For example, the Roman and Cyrillic scripts are bicameral, whereas Thai, Katakana, and Hebrew are not.

Big-endian   A computer architecture that stores multiple-byte numerical values with the most significant byte (MSB) values first. In a big-endian system the Unicode *Byte-Order-Mark* (U+FEFF) will be coded 0xFE followed by 0xFF. Motorola processors use a big-endian architecture. Big-endian is also known as *network byte order*.

BMP   (1) In the context of *character sets*: Basic Multilingual Plane, ISO/IEC 10646-1 that corresponds to the Unicode *code points* between U+000 and U+FFFF. (2) In the context of graphic formats: Bitmap. Extension for Windows bitmap files.

BOM   See *Byte-Order-Mark*.

Byte-Order-Mark   A special function of the Unicode character U+FEFF (ZERO WIDTH NO-BREAK SPACE). The Byte-Order-Mark placed at the beginning of Unicode files encoded in *UTF-16* distinguishes between *big-endian* and *little-endian* files. Byte-Order-Mark is often abbreviated *BOM*.

CAT tool   Computer-Assisted Translation tool.

Character set   Set of symbols used to represent text information.

Charset   (1) In IANA terminology a charset is the same as an *encoding*. (2) Otherwise, see *Character set*.

Chữ Hán   Vietnamese term for *Han character*.

CJKV   Chinese, Japanese, Korean, and Vietnamese. Common abbreviation used to refer to the languages that use *ideographic characters* (*Han characters*) in their writing systems. Note that Vietnamese uses ideographs more rarely nowadays.

Code point   Scalar value associated with a symbol of a *character set*. Character sets with associated code points are called *coded character sets*.

Code set   See *Coded character set*.

Coded character set   Set of symbols where each one is mapped to a specific value or *code point*. (same as *Code set*).

Combining character   A Unicode character that graphically combines with a *base character* to form a *composite character*.

Composite character   A Unicode character that is equivalent to a sequence consisting of a *base character* with one or more *combining characters*. Composite characters are also known as *precomposed characters*.

DLL   Dynamic Link Library. A shared, compiled component in Windows.

DOM   Document Object Model. Type of parser used to process *XML* documents. DOM parsers load the entire document in memory and represent it in a tree structure accessible through its nodes.

DSSSL   Document Style Semantics and Specifications Language. Style sheet language, precursor of XSL. DSSSL offers a rich feature set and can be used with *XML*.

DTD   Document Type Definition. File that contains the description of the structure of a given document (names of elements, attributes, their properties, and so forth).

Encoding   See *Encoding scheme*.

Encoding scheme   Function that maps the *code points* of a *coded character set* to a serialized representation in bytes. For example, Unicode is a coded character set and *UTF-8* and *UTF-16* are two of its encoding schemes.

Exact match   In the context of leveraging, a match that corresponds exactly to the source segment (as opposed to a *fuzzy match* or no match).

External code   See *Structural element*.

External tag   See *Structural element*.

Folding   Action of transforming a string or a character in a uniform case, with the intent of comparing it to another folded string or character.

FSS-UTF   File System Safe Unicode (or *UCS*) Transformation Format. Obsolete name for *UTF-8*.

FTP   File Transfer Protocol.

Fullwidth character   Type of East Asian character whose glyphs use the entire character display cell (as opposed to *halfwidth characters*). In legacy character sets, fullwidth characters are normally encoded in multiple bytes. The equivalent Japanese term for fullwidth characters is *zenkaku*.

Furigana   Japanese term equivalent to *Ruby text*.

Fuzzy match   In the context of leveraging, a source segment in the *translation memory* that closely corresponds to a source segment in the new document. By extension, the corresponding target segment. The degree of fuzziness is often expressed in percentage, 100% being an *exact match*.

Gisting   The translation of a document with a *machine translation* system to obtain an approximate translation that is sufficient to understand the general subject of the document.

Globalization   Globalization addresses the business issues associated with taking a product to the global market. Globalization usually involves *internationalization* and *localization*.

Halfwidth character   Type of East Asian character whose glyphs use half of the character display cell. In legacy character sets, halfwidth characters are normally encoded in a single byte. The equivalent Japanese term for halfwidth characters is *hankaku*.

Han character   Generic term to designate an ideographic character of Chinese origin. Han characters are called *Hanzi characters* in Mandarin Chinese, *Kanji characters* in Japanese, *Hanja characters* in Korean, and *Chữ Hán* in Vietnamese.

Hangul   Main script used to write the Korean language. Hangul is a *syllabary*.

Hanja character   Korean term for *Han character*.

Hankaku   Japanese term equivalent to *halfwidth character*.

Hanzi character   Mandarin Chinese term for *Han character*.

High-surrogate   The first part of a *surrogate pair*. A high-surrogate is a Unicode *code point* in the range between U+D800 and U+DBFF.

Hiragana   Japanese *syllabary* used for the representation of native Japanese words and grammatical elements.

HTTP   Hypertext Transfer Protocol.

I18N   Abbreviation often used for *internationalization* (because of the 18 letters between I and N).

IANA   Internet Assigned Numbers Authority. Organization that defines various Internet-related standards. One of them is the official list of values to use for text-encoding declarations.

Ideograph   (1) Any symbol that expresses an idea or a meaning, as opposed to a sound or pronunciation. (2) Common term used to refer to a *Han character*.

Ideographic character   See *Ideograph*.

IETF   Internet Engineering Task Force.

Inline code   See *Inline element*.

Inline element   In the context of localization, an element (often with a presentational function) which occurs inside the content of another element that can also have textual data (mixed content). For example, the element `<tspan>` in SVG is an inline element for the structural element `<text>`. Inline elements are also often called *inline codes*, *internal tags*, or *internal codes*.

Internal code   See *Inline element*.

Internal tag   See *Inline element*.

Internationalization   Addressing locale-specific aspects of a product so that it can handle multiple languages and cultural conventions without being modified.

Iroha   A Japanese collation method based on the order of a table of sounds.

ISO   International Organization for Standardization.

IURI   Internationalized URI. Form of *URI* in which all extended characters have been converted to canonical form and escaped.

Jamo   Basic element of the *Hangul* script.

Kanji character   Japanese term for *Han character*.

Kashida   Arabic elongation glyph used to connect characters in some rendering situations such as justification.

Katakana   Japanese *syllabary* used for the representation of borrowed vocabulary (other than vocabulary of Chinese origin), interjections, and so forth.

Kumimoji Japanese term for a special inline combination of characters. It consists of a group of up to five small characters combined to fit within the space of a single character.

L10N Abbreviation often used for *localization* (because of the 10 letters between L and N).

Linguist In the context of this book, *linguist* is used to designate a person executing one of the localization tasks for which knowledge of a given target language is required (for instance, translation, editing, proofing, or terminology work).

LISA Localisation Industry Standards Association.

Little-endian A computer architecture that stores multiple-byte numerical values with the most significant byte (MSB) values last. In a little-endian system the Unicode *Byte-Order-Mark* (U+FEFF) will be coded 0xFF followed by 0xFE. Intel processors use a little-endian architecture.

Locale (1) Combination of a language and a region or country. For example, French for France and French for Canada are two different locales. In the context of localization, the term "language" is often used for locale. Both terms need official definitions. (2) In the context of programming languages and operating systems, the concept of locale also applies to specific properties such as *encoding*, number formatting, currency, and so forth. For example, in Java, French for France using the Euro currency and French for France using the Franc currency are two different locales.

Localization Function of making a product linguistically and culturally appropriate for the target *locale*.

Low-surrogate The second part of a *surrogate pair*. A low-surrogate is a Unicode *code point* in the range between U+DC00 and U+DFFF.

Machine translation System to automatically translate a document from a given source language to a given target language.

MT Abbreviation for *machine translation*.

NCR See *Numeric character reference*.

Network byte order See *Big-endian*.

Numeric character reference An *SGML/XML* notation for characters. The syntax is &#xHHHH; or &#DDDD; where HHHH and DDDD are respectively the hexadecimal and decimal *UCS* values of the given character.

OpenTag An *XML* document type designed to store extracted text.

Precomposed character See *Composite character*.

Pseudotranslation   Replacing source text with automatically generated random text that contains extended characters and a different number of words and a different size for each word. The objective is to simulate a translation. This method enables you to test an application or a document for problems before the localization happens.

RFC   Request For Comments. Name given to the documents that describe the various standards defined by the *IETF*.

Ruby text   Short run of text associated with the base text, typically used in East Asian documents to indicate pronunciation or to provide a short annotation. An equivalent Japanese term for ruby is *furigana*.

SAX   Simple API for XML. Type of parser used to process *XML* documents. SAX parsers are event-driven and access the document sequentially.

SGML   Standard Generalized Markup Language. A standard framework for defining specific markup languages (formats). *XML* is a subset of SGML.

SOAP   Simple Object Access Protocol. *XML*-based standard used to exchange objects and data between applications.

Structural element   In the context of localization, an element that contains other structural elements, or textual data, with *inline elements*. Structural elements are also often called *external tags* or *external codes*.

Supplementary character   A Unicode encoded character that has a *supplementary code point*.

Supplementary code point   A Unicode *code point* between U+10000 and U+10FFFF.

Surrogate character   A misnomer for *supplementary character*. Do not use this term.

Surrogate pair   A coded character representation for a single abstract character that consists of a sequence of two parts: a *high-surrogate* and a *low-surrogate*.

SVG   Scalable Vector Graphic. An *XML* document type used to code vector-based images and text. From a localization viewpoint, SVG has the advantage of offering easy access to the text for translation.

Syllabary   An alphabet in which each symbol represents phonemes of a language. These phonemes are generally combinations of consonants and vowels. *Hiragana* and *Hangul* are syllabaries.

TM   Abbreviation for *translation memory*.

TMX Translation Memory eXchange. An *XML* document type designed to enable the exchange of translation memory data between translation tools.

Transcoder Term sometimes used to indicate a tool that offers a function to convert the encoding of a file, for example to convert a document from `Shift_JIS` to *UTF-8*.

Translation memory A collection of multilingual entries used by translation tools to leverage translated text. Translation memories are used to retrieve existing translated text by searching for matches at the source level. The term is often abbreviated *TM*.

UCS Universal Character Set. The repertoire of characters offered by Unicode/ISO 10646.

UCS-2 16-bit encoding method for Unicode/ISO 10646. `UCS-2` can be considered a subset of *UTF-16*.

UIML User Interface Markup Language. An *XML* document type designed to define user-interface components independently of the final device and application that will use them.

URI Uniform Resource Identifier.

URL Uniform Resource Locator.

URN Uniform Resource Name.

UTF-2 Obsolete name for *UTF-8*.

UTF-8 Unicode (or *UCS*) Transformation Format, 8-bit encoding form. `UTF-8` is the encoding method that serializes a Unicode/ISO 10646 scalar value (*code point*) as a sequence of one to four bytes.

UTF-16 Unicode (or *UCS*) Transformation Format, 16-bit encoding form. `UTF-16` is the encoding method that serializes a Unicode/ISO 10646 scalar value (*code point*) as a fixed sequence of two bytes, in either *big-endian* (`UTF-16BE`) or *little-endian* (`UTF-16LE`) format.

VoiceXML An *XML* document type designed to program audio interfaces for voice-driven devices.

Warichu Japanese term for an inline combination of characters used in some East Asian scripts. Warichu text is a run of small characters that appears as two lines of equal height and length whose combined height is equal to the height of the line in which they appear.

XLIFF XML Localisation Interchange File Format. An *XML* document type developed by a group of localization customers and suppliers for storing extracted text and localizable data.

XLink   XML Linking Language. Language that enables you to create and describe links between resources. It uses *XML* syntax to create structures that can describe the simple unidirectional hyperlinks of today's HTML as well as more sophisticated links.

XML   eXtensible Markup Language. Language to define formats. A format is also called a vocabulary, or a document type, or an XML application. XML is a subset of *SGML*.

XPath   Language used with various *XML* technologies to specify the address of a part of an *XML* document.

XPointer   XML Pointer Language. Used as the basis for a fragment identifier for any URI reference that locates a resource whose media type is `text/xml`, `application/xml`, `text/xml-external-parsed-entity`, or `application/xml-external-parsed-entity`. XPointer is used in *XLink* and is based on *XPath*.

XSL   eXtensible Stylesheet Language. An *XML*-based technology providing presentation and transformation mechanisms for *XML* documents. XSL encompasses *XSLT* and *XSL-FO*.

XSL-FO   XSL Formatting Objects. The part of *XSL* that deals with rendering data.

XSLT   XSL Transformations. The part of *XSL* that deals with transforming a document.

Zenkaku   Japanese term equivalent to *fullwidth character*.

APPENDIX B

Encoding Declarations

Various areas in XML-related resources require the declaration of the encoding of the text. Examples are the `encoding` attribute in the initial declaration of an XML document and the `@charset` rule in CSS.

The list of possible values used for these encoding declarations (called charsets) is defined by the *Internet Assigned Numbers Authority (IANA)*.

Table B.1 lists most of the commonly used values. The first column indicates the actual value of a charset, and the second column gives its corresponding description. The values are listed by alphabetical order. The charset values are not case sensitive.

The complete and official list of all charset values can be found at `http://www.iana.org/assignments/character-sets`.

TABLE B.1

Encoding Declarations

Charset	Description
big5	Traditional Chinese
cp437	IBM 437, U.S. Standard
cp850	IBM 850, Western European (for example, German)
cp852	IBM 852, Central European (for example, Polish)
cp857	IBM 857, Turkish
cp861	IBM 861, Icelandic
cp862	IBM 862, Hebrew
cp865	IBM 865, French Canadian
euc-jp	Japanese (Unix)
euc-kr	Korean (Unix)
gb2312	Simplified Chinese

TABLE B.1 CONTINUED

Charset	Description
hp-roman8	HP Roman-8, Western European (for example, German)
iso-8859-1	Latin-1, Western Europe (for example, German)
iso-8859-2	Latin-2, Central Europe (for example, Polish)
iso-8859-3	Latin-3, Southern Europe (for example, Maltese)
iso-8859-4	Latin-4, Northern Europe (for example, Estonian)
iso-8859-5	Cyrillic (for example, Russian)
iso-8859-6	Arabic
iso-8859-7	Greek
iso-8859-8	Hebrew
iso-8859-9	Latin-5, Turkish
iso-8859-10	Latin-6, Nordic (for example, Lappish)
iso-8859-13	Latin-7, Baltic (for example, Latvian)
iso-8859-14	Latin-8, Celtic (for example, Welsh)
iso-8859-15	Extended Latin-1, (also known as Latin-9 and Latin-0) Western European (with Euro sign)
koi8-r	Russian
koi8-u	Ukrainian
ks_c_5601-1989	Korean
shift_jis	Japanese (Windows)
tis-620	Thai
utf-8	UCS Transformation Format 8
utf-16	UCS Transformation Format 16
us-ascii	ANSI_X3.4-1968, Basic ASCII
windows-1250	Windows Central European (for example, Polish)
windows-1251	Windows Cyrillic (for example, Russian)
windows-1252	Windows Western European (for example, German)— counts more characters than Latin-1
windows-1253	Windows Greek
windows-1254	Windows Turkish
windows-1255	Windows Hebrew
windows-1256	Windows Arabic
windows-1257	Windows Baltic (for example, Latvian)
windows-1258	Windows Vietnamese

APPENDIX C

Scripts in UCS

Table C.1 lists all the different sections of UCS. The first column lists the name used in Unicode, the second column displays the character range in hexadecimal, and the third column includes notes.

For more details on UCS characters see the Unicode Web site at http://www.unicode.org.

TABLE C.1

Scripts in UCS

Name	Range	Notes
C0 Controls and Basic Latin	0000-007F	Same characters as ASCII
C1 Controls and Latin-1 Supplement	0080-00FF	Latin-1 extended characters
Latin Extended-A	0100-017F	
Latin Extended-B	0180-024F	
IPA Extensions	0250-02AF	
Spacing Modifier Letters	02B0-02FF	
Combining Diacritical Marks	0300-036F	
Greek and Coptic	0370-03FF	
Cyrillic	0400-04FF	Used for Russian, Ukrainian, Bulgarian, and many languages from Central Asia
Armenian	0530-058F	
Hebrew	0590-05FF	
Arabic	0600-06FF	Used for Arabic, Urdu, Farsi, and some Eastern languages
Syriac	0700-074F	

TABLE C.1 CONTINUED

Name	Range	Notes
Thanaa	0780-07BF	Used for Dhivehi (Maldives islands)
Devanagari	0900-097F	Used for Hindi, Marathi, Konkani, Jaipuri, and many other Indian languages
Bengali	0980-09FF	Used for Bengali, Assamese, and others
Gurmukhi	0A00-0A7F	Used for Punjabi
Gujarati	0A80-0AFF	Used for Gujarati
Oriya	0B00-0B7F	Used for Oriya, Khondi, Santali, and others
Tamil	0B80-0BFF	Used for Tamil, Badaga, and others
Tegulu	0C00-0C7F	Used for Tegulu, Gondi, Lambadi, and others
Kannada	0C80-0CFF	Used for Kanarese and Tulu
Malayalam	0D00-0D7F	Used for Malayalam
Sinhala	0D80-0DFF	Used for Sinhala, Pali, Sanskrit, and others
Thai	0E00-0E7F	Used for Thai, Kuy, Lavna, and Pali
Lao	0E80-0EFF	
Tibetan	0F00-0FFF	Used for Nepali, Dzongkha, and others
Myanmar	1000-1090	Used for Burmese, Shan, Mon, Pali, Sanskrit, and others
Georgian	10A0-10FF	
Hangul Jamos	1100-11FF	
Ethiopic	1200-137F	Used for Amharic, Tigrina, and others
Cherokee	13A0-13FF	
Unified Canadian Aboriginal Syllabics	1400-167F	Used for Inuktitut, Alonquian, and Athapascan languages
Ogham	1680-169F	Early form of Old Irish
Runic	16A0-16FF	Early Scandinavian script

TABLE C.1   CONTINUED

Name	Range	Notes
Khmer	1780-17FF	Cambodian
Mongolian	1800-18AF	Classical Mongolian
Latin Extended Additional	1E00-1EFF	
Greek Extended	1F00-1FFF	Precomposed polytonic Greek
General Punctuation	2000-2060	
Superscripts and Subscripts	2070-209F	Superscript and subscript decimal digits
Currency Symbols	20A0-20CF	
Combining Diacritical Marks for Symbols	20D0-20FF	
Letter-like Symbols	2100-214F	
Number Forms	2150-218F	
Arrows	2190-21FF	
Mathematical Operators	2200-22FF	
Miscellaneous Technical	2300-23FF	
Control Pictures	2400-243F	
Optical Character Recognition	2440-245F	
Enclosed Alphanumerics	2460-24FF	Alphanumeric characters in parentheses and circles
Box Drawings	2500-257F	
Block Elements	2580-259F	
Geometric Shapes	25A0-25FF	
Miscellaneous Symbols	2600-267F	
Dingbats	2700-27BF	Dingbats symbols
Braille Patterns	2800-28FF	
CJK Radicals Supplements	2E80-2EFF	
Kangxi Radicals	2F00-2FDF	
Ideographic Description Characters	2FF0-2FFF	
CJK Symbols and Punctuation	3000-303F	

TABLE C.1   CONTINUED

Name	Range	Notes
Hiragana	3040-309F	Japanese cursive syllabary
Katakana	30A0-30FF	Japanese non-cursive syllabary
Bopomofo	3100-312F	Chinese phonetic, especially for Mandarin
Hangul Compatibility Jamo	3130-318F	
Kanbun	3190-319F	Marks to indicate Japanese reading order of Classical Chinese text
Bopomofo Extended	31A0-31BF	Chinese phonetic
Enclosed CJK Letters and Months	3200-32FF	
CJK Compatibility	3300-33FF	
CJK Unified Ideographs Extension-A	3400-4DB0	
CJK Unified Ideographs	4E00-9FAF	
Yi Syllables	A000-A48F	
Yi Radicals	A490-A4CF	
Hangul Syllables	AC00-D7AF	
Surrogates Area	D800-DFFF	Area for surrogate pairs
Private Use Area	E000-F8FF	Area reserved for user- and corporate-defined characters
CJK Compatibility Ideographs	F900-FA5F	
Alphabetic Presentation Forms	FB00-FB4F	
Arabic Presentation Forms	FB50-FDFF	
Combining Half Marks	FE20-FE2F	
CJK Compatibility Forms-A	FE30-FE4F	
Small Form Variants	FE50-FE6F	Small form variations of some ASCII characters
Arabic Presentation Forms-B	FE70-FEFF	

TABLE C.1 CONTINUED

Name	Range	Notes
Halfwidth and Fullwidth Forms	FF80-FFEF	Fullwidth ASCII, halfwidth Katakana, and a few halfwidth Hangul characters
Specials	FFF0-FFFF	
Old Italic	10300-1032F	Historical alphabets of the Italian peninsula (Etruscan, Oscan, Umbrian, etc.)
Gothic	10330-1034F	Historical script for the East Germanic language
Deseret	10400-1044F	Historical phonemic alphabet used by the Mormons in the middle of the nineteen century
Byzantine Musical Symbols	1D000-1D0FF	Symbols for the Byzantine musical notation
Musical Symbols	1D100-1D1FF	Symbols for the Common musical notation of the Western world
Mathematical Alphanumeric Symbols	1D400-1D7FF	Letter-like symbols used in mathematic notation
CJK Unified Ideographs Extension B	20000-2A6D6	
CJK Compatibility Ideographs Supplement	2F800-2FA1F	
Tags	E0000-E007F	Language tagging for plain-text (The use of these characters is strongly discouraged)
Private Use Area	F0000-FFFFD	Area reserved for user- and corporate-defined characters
Private Use Area	100000-10FFFD	Area reserved for user- and corporate-defined characters

APPENDIX D

Language Codes

The majority of the language variant codes are built from the ISO 639 language codes and the ISO 3166 country codes. Table D.1 does not list all the possible combinations, but covers most of the variants you are likely to come across.

The table is ordered by the 4-letter codes (first column).

The second column shows the 2-letter code when the given variant is the default for the corresponding language in Windows LCIDs (Locale Identifiers). Note that in some cases the default variant is not the one from which the language originates. For example, `en-US` is the default for `en`, `pt-BR` is the default for `pt`, and so forth.

The third column displays the name of the language and the region (or variation). In some cases an alternative name for the language is shown between parentheses.

The fourth column lists the script for the given variant. Note that some languages can be written using different scripts.

The last column indicates one possible code set for the given variant. In many cases, you can use other code sets for that variant.

The end of the table includes several examples of user-defined language variants.

For the complete list of ISO language codes see `http://lcweb.loc.gov/ standards/iso639-2/langhome.html`, and for the ISO country codes see `http://www.din.de/gremien/nas/nabd/iso3166ma/codlstp1`.

TABLE D.1

Most Commonly Used Language Variant Codes

4-Letter Code	2-Letter Code	Description	Script	Code Set
aa-dj	aa	Afar, Djibouti	Roman	iso-8859-1
ab-ge	ab	Abkazian, Georgia	Cyrillic	iso-8859-5
af-za	af	Afrikaans, South Africa	Roman	iso-8859-1
am-et	am	Amharic, Ethiopia	Ethiopic	ucs-2
ar-ae		Arabic, United Emirates	Arabic	iso-8859-6
ar-bh		Arabic, Bahrain	Arabic	iso-8859-6
ar-dz		Arabic, Algeria	Arabic	iso-8859-6
ar-eg		Arabic, Egypt	Arabic	iso-8859-6
ar-iq		Arabic, Iraq	Arabic	iso-8859-6
ar-jo		Arabic, Jordan	Arabic	iso-8859-6
ar-kw		Arabic, Kuwait	Arabic	iso-8859-6
ar-lb		Arabic, Lebanon	Arabic	iso-8859-6
ar-ly		Arabic, Libya	Arabic	iso-8859-6
ar-mo		Arabic, Morocco	Arabic	iso-8859-6
ar-om		Arabic, Oman	Arabic	iso-8859-6
ar-qa		Arabic, Qatar	Arabic	iso-8859-6
ar-sa	ar	Arabic, Saudi Arabia	Arabic	iso-8859-6
ar-sy		Arabic, Syria	Arabic	iso-8859-6
ar-tn		Arabic, Tunisia	Arabic	iso-8859-6
ar-ye		Arabic, Yemen	Arabic	iso-8859-6
as-in	as	Assamese, India	Bengali	ucs-2
ay-bo	ay	Aymara, Bolivia	Roman	iso-8859-1
az-az	az	Azerbaijani, Azerbaijan	Roman	iso-8859-9
ba-ru	ba	Bashkir, Russia	Cyrillic	iso-8859-5
be-by	be	Belarusian, Belarus	Cyrillic	iso-8859-5
bg-bg	bg	Bulgarian, Bulgaria	Cyrillic	iso-8859-5
bh-in	bh	Bihari, India	Devanagari	ucs-2
bi-vu	bi	Bislama, Vanuatu	Roman	iso-8859-1
bn-bd	bn	Bengali, Bangladesh	Bengali	ucs-2
bo-zh	bo	Tibetan, Tibet	Tibetan	ucs-2
br-fr	br	Breton, France	Roman	iso-8859-1

TABLE D.1	CONTINUED			
4-Letter Code	*2-Letter Code*	*Description*	*Script*	*Code Set*
bs-ba	bs	Bosnian, Bosnia	Roman	iso-8859-2
ca-es	ca	Catalan, Spain	Roman	iso-8859-1
co-fr	co	Corsican, France	Roman	iso-8859-1
cs-cz	cs	Czech, Czech Republic	Roman	iso-8859-2
cy-gb	cy	Welsh, United Kingdom	Roman	iso-8859-8
da-dk	da	Danish, Denmark	Roman	iso-8859-1
de-at		German, Austria	Roman	iso-8859-1
de-ch		German, Switzerland	Roman	iso-8859-1
de-de	de	German, Germany	Roman	iso-8859-1
de-li		German, Liechtenstein	Roman	iso-8859-1
de-lu		German, Luxembourg	Roman	iso-8859-1
dz-bt	dz	Bhutani, Bhutan (Dzongkha)	Tibetan	ucs-2
el-gr	el	Greek, Greece	Greek	iso-8859-7
en-au		English, Australia	Roman	iso-8859-1
en-bz		English, Belize	Roman	iso-8859-1
en-ca		English, Canada	Roman	iso-8859-1
en-gb		English, United Kingdom	Roman	iso-8859-1
en-ie		English, Ireland	Roman	iso-8859-1
en-jm		English, Jamaica	Roman	iso-8859-1
en-nz		English, New Zealand	Roman	iso-8859-1
en-pg		English, Papua New Guinea	Roman	iso-8859-1
en-ph		English, Philippines	Roman	iso-8859-1
en-tt		English, Trinidad and Tobago	Roman	iso-8859-1
en-us	en	English, United States	Roman	iso-8859-1
en-za		English, South Africa	Roman	iso-8859-1
en-zw		English, Zimbabwe	Roman	iso-8859-1
eo	eo	Esperanto	Roman	iso-8859-3
es-ar		Spanish, Argentina	Roman	iso-8859-1
es-bo		Spanish, Bolivia	Roman	iso-8859-1
es-cl		Spanish, Chile	Roman	iso-8859-1

TABLE D.1	CONTINUED			
4-Letter Code	*2-Letter Code*	*Description*	*Script*	*Code Set*
es-co		Spanish, Colombia	Roman	iso-8859-1
es-cr		Spanish, Costa Rica	Roman	iso-8859-1
es-do		Spanish, Dominican Republic	Roman	iso-8859-1
es-ec		Spanish, Ecuador	Roman	iso-8859-1
es-es	es	Spanish, Spain (Iberian Spanish)	Roman	iso-8859-1
es-gt		Spanish, Guatemala	Roman	iso-8859-1
es-hn		Spanish, Honduras	Roman	iso-8859-1
es-mx		Spanish, Mexico	Roman	iso-8859-1
es-ni		Spanish, Nicaragua	Roman	iso-8859-1
es-pa		Spanish, Panama	Roman	iso-8859-1
es-pe		Spanish, Peru	Roman	iso-8859-1
es-pr		Spanish, Puerto Rico	Roman	iso-8859-1
es-py		Spanish, Paraguay	Roman	iso-8859-1
es-sv		Spanish, El Salvador	Roman	iso-8859-1
es-uy		Spanish, Uruguay	Roman	iso-8859-1
es-ve		Spanish, Venezuela	Roman	iso-8859-1
et-ee	et	Estonian, Estonia	Roman	iso-8859-4
eu-es	eu	Basque, Spain	Roman	iso-8859-1
fa-ir	fa	Farsi, Iran	Arabic	iso-8859-6
fi-fi	fi	Finnish, Finland	Roman	iso-8859-1
fj-fj	fj	Fijian, Fiji	Roman	iso-8859-1
fo-fo	fo	Faroese, Faroe Islands	Roman	iso-8859-1
fr-be		French, Belgium (Wallon)	Roman	iso-8859-1
fr-ca		French, Canada (Québécois)	Roman	iso-8859-1
fr-ch		French, Switzerland	Roman	iso-8859-1
fr-fr	fr	French, France	Roman	iso-8859-1
fr-lu		French, Luxembourg	Roman	iso-8859-1
fr-mc		French, Monaco	Roman	iso-8859-1
fy-nl	fy	Frisian, Netherlands	Roman	iso-8859-1
ga-ie	ga	Irish, Ireland	Roman	iso-8859-1

TABLE D.1	CONTINUED			
4-Letter Code	*2-Letter Code*	*Description*	*Script*	*Code Set*
gd-gb	gd	Scottish Gaelic, United Kingdom	Roman	iso-8859-1
gl-es	gl	Gallegan, Spain	Roman	iso-8859-1
gn-py	gn	Guarani, Paraguay	Roman	iso-8859-1
gu-in	gu	Gujarati, India	Gujarati	ucs-2
gv-gb	gv	Manx Gaelic, United Kingdom	Roman	iso-8859-1
ha-ng	ha	Hausa, Nigeria	Roman	iso-8859-1
he-il$_1$	he	Hebrew, Israel	Hebrew	iso-8859-8
hi-in	hi	Hindi, India	Devanagari	ucs-2
hr-hr	hr	Croatian, Croatia	Roman	iso-8859-2
hu-hu	hu	Hungarian, Hungary	Roman	iso-8859-2
hy-am	hy	Armenian, Armenia	Armenian	ucs-2
ia	ia	Interlingua	Roman	iso-8859-1
id-id$_2$	id	Indonesian, Indonesia	Roman	iso-8859-1
ie	ie	Interlingue	Roman	iso-8859-1
ik-us	ik	Inupiak, United States	Canadian Syllabary	ucs-2
is-is	is	Icelandic, Iceland	Roman	iso-8859-1
it-ch		Italian, Switzerland	Roman	iso-8859-1
it-it	it	Italian, Italy	Roman	iso-8859-1
iu-ca	iu	Inuktitut, Canada	Canadian Syllabary	ucs-2
ja-jp	ja	Japanese, Japan	Japanese	shift_jis
jw-id	jw	Javanese, Indonesian	Roman	iso-8859-1
ka-ge	ka	Georgian, Georgia	Georgian	ucs-2
kk-kz	kk	Kazakh, Kazakstan	Cyrillic	iso-8859-5
kl-gl	kl	Greenlandic, Greenland (Kalaallisut)	Canadian Syllabary	ucs-2
km-kh	km	Khmer, Cambodia (Cambodian)	Khmer	ucs-2
kn-in	kn	Kannada, India (Kanarese)	Kannada	ucs-2

TABLE D.1 CONTINUED

4-Letter Code	2-Letter Code	Description	Script	Code Set
ko-kr	ko	Korean, Korea	Korean	ks_c_5601-1987
kw-gb	kw	Cornish Gaelic, United Kingdom	Roman	iso-8859-10
ky-kg	ky	Kirghiz, Kyrgyzstan	Cyrillic	iso-8859-1
la-va	la	Latin, Vatican	Roman	iso-8859-1
lb-lu	lb	Letzenburgesch, Luxembourg (Luxembourgian)	Roman	iso-8859-1
ln-cd	ln	Lingala, People's Republic of the Congo	Roman	iso-8859-1
lo-la	lo	Lao, Laos	Lao	ucs-2
lt-lt	lt	Lithuanian, Lithuania	Roman	iso-8859-4
lv-lv	lv	Latvian, Latvia	Roman	iso-8859-4
mg-mg	mg	Malagasy, Madagascar	Roman	iso-8859-1
mi-nz	mi	Maori, New Zealand	Roman	iso-8859-1
mk-mk	mk	Macedonian, Macedonia	Cyrillic	iso-8859-5
ml-in	ml	Malayalam, India	Malayalam	ucs-2
mn-mn	mn	Mongolian, Mongolia	Cyrillic	iso-8859-5
mo-md	mo	Moldavian, Republic of Moldova	Roman	iso-8859-2
mr-in	mr	Marathi, India	Devanagari	ucs-2
ms-bn		Malay, Brunei Darussalam	Roman	iso-8859-1
ms-my	ms	Malay, Malaysia	Roman	iso-8859-1
mt-mt	mt	Maltese, Malta	Roman	iso-8859-3
my-mm	my	Burmese, Myanmar (Myanmar)	Myanmar	ucs-2
na-nr	na	Nauruan, Nauru	Roman	iso-8859-1
ne-in		Nepali, India	Devanagari	ucs-2
ne-np	ne	Nepali, Nepal	Devanagari	ucs-2
nl-be		Dutch, Belgium (Flemish)	Roman	iso-8859-1
nl-nl	nl	Dutch, Netherlands	Roman	iso-8859-1
nn-no	nn	Norwegian, Norway (Nynorsk)	Roman	iso-8859-1

TABLE D.1	CONTINUED			
4-Letter Code	*2-Letter Code*	*Description*	*Script*	*Code Set*
no-no$_3$	no	Norwegian, Norway (Bokmål)	Roman	iso-8859-1
nv-us	nv	Navajo, United States	Roman	iso-8859-1
oc-fr	oc	Occitan, France	Roman	iso-8859-1
om-et	om	Oromo, Ethiopia	Roman	iso-8859-1
or-in	or	Oriya, India	Oriya	ucs-2
pa-in	pa	Punjabi, India	Gurmukhi	ucs-2
pl-pl	pl	Polish, Poland	Roman	iso-8859-2
ps-af	ps	Pashto, Afghanistan	Arabic	iso-8859-6
pt-br	pt	Portuguese, Brazil	Roman	iso-8859-1
pt-pt		Portuguese, Portugal	Roman	iso-8859-1
qu-pe	qu	Quechua, Peru	Roman	iso-8859-1
rm-ch	rm	Raeto-romance, Switzerland	Roman	iso-8859-1
rn-bi	rn	Rundi, Burundi	Roman	iso-8859-1
ro-ro	ro	Romanian, Romania	Roman	iso-8859-2
ru-ru	ru	Russian, Russia	Cyrillic	iso-8859-5
rw-rw	rw	Kinyarwanda, Rwanda	Roman	iso-8859-1
sa-in	sa	Sanskrit	Sinhala	ucs-2
sd-pk	sd	Sindhi	Arabic	iso-8859-6
sg-cf	sg	Sango, Central African Republic	Roman	iso-8859-1
si-lk	si	Singhalese, Sri Lanka	Sinhala	ucs-2
sk-sk	sk	Slovak, Slovakia	Roman	iso-8859-2
sl-si	sl	Slovenian, Slovenia	Roman	iso-8859-2
sm-ws	sm	Samoan, Western Samoa	Roman	iso-8859-1
sn-zw	sn	Shona, Zimbabwe	Roman	iso-8859-1
so-so	so	Somali, Somalia	Roman	iso-8859-1
sq-al	sq	Albanian, Albania	Roman	iso-8859-1
sr-yu	sr	Serbian, Yugoslavia	Cyrillic	iso-8859-5
ss-sz	ss	Swati, Swaziland (Siswati)	Roman	iso-8859-1
st-ls	st	Sotho, Lesotho (Sesotho, Southern Sotho)	Roman	iso-8859-1
su-id	su	Sundanese, Indonesia	Roman	iso-8859-1

4-Letter Code	2-Letter Code	Description	Script	Code Set
TABLE D.1	**CONTINUED**			
sv-fi		Swedish, Finland	Roman	iso-8859-1
sv-se	sv	Swedish, Sweden	Roman	iso-8859-1
sw-ke	sw	Swahili, Kenya	Roman	iso-8859-1
ta-in	ta	Tamil, India	Tamil	ucs-2
te-in	te	Telugu	Telugu	ucs-2
tg-tj	tg	Tajik, Tajikistan	Cyrillic	iso-8859-1
th-th	th	Thai, Thailand	Thai	tis-620
ti-er	ti	Tigrinya, Eritrea	Ethiopic	ucs-2
tk-tm	tk	Turkmen, Turkmenistan	Cyrillic	iso-8859-5
tl-ph	tl	Tagalog, Philippines	Roman	iso-8859-1
tn-bw	tn	Tswana, Botswana (Setswana)	Roman	iso-8859-1
to-to	to	Tongan, Tonga	Roman	iso-8859-1
tr-tr	tr	Turkish, Turkey	Roman	iso-8859-9
ts-za	ts	Tsonga, South Africa	Roman	iso-8859-1
tt-ru	tt	Tatar, Russia	Cyrillic	ucs-2
tw-gh	tw	Twi, Ghana	Roman	iso-8859-1
ty-fr	ty	Tahitian, France	Roman	iso-8859-1
ug-kz	ug	Uighur, Kazakstan	Cyrillic	iso-8859-5
uk-ua	uk	Ukrainian, Ukraine	Cyrillic	iso-8859-5
ur-in		Urdu, India	Arabic	iso-8859-6
ur-pk	ur	Urdu, Pakistan	Arabic	iso-8859-6
uz-uz	uz	Uzbek, Uzbekistan	Roman	iso-8859-9
vi-vn	vi	Vietnamese, Vietnam	Roman	viscii
vo	vo	Volapuk	Roman	iso-8859-1
wo-sn	wo	Wolof, Senegal	Roman	iso-8859-1
xh-za	xh	Xosha, South Africa	Roman	iso-8859-1
yi-il$_4$	yi	Yiddish, Israel	Hebrew	iso-8859-8
zh-cn	zh	Chinese, China	Simplified Chinese	gb2312
zh-hk		Chinese, Hong Kong	Traditional Chinese	big5

TABLE D.1 CONTINUED

4-Letter Code	2-Letter Code	Description	Script	Code Set
zh-mo		Chinese, Macau	Simplified Chinese	gb2312
zh-sg		Chinese, Singapore	Simplified Chinese	gb2312
zh-tw		Chinese, Taiwan	Traditional Chinese	big5
zu-za	zu	Zulu, South Africa	Roman	iso-8859-1
x-az-Cyr		Azerbaijani, Cyrillic	Cyrillic	iso-8859-5
x-es-Intl		Spanish, International	Roman	iso-8859-1
x-es-LatAm		Spanish, Latin America	Roman	iso-8859-1
x-mn-Trad		Mongolian, Classical	Mongolian	ucs-2
x-uz-Cyr		Uzbek, Cyrillic	Cyrillic	iso-8859-5

1 The language code for Hebrew was originally IW. It has been changed to HE.

2 The language code for Indonesian was originally IN. It has been changed to ID.

3 An alternative language code for Norwegian Bokmål is NB, but NO is used more often.

4 The language code for Yiddish was originally JI. It has been changed to YI.

APPENDIX E

OpenTag Quick Reference

In This Appendix:

The OpenTag format is an XML document type designed to store text and other localizable data extracted from an arbitrary original format. This document type allows for the modification of the data and for merging of the changed data back into its original format. The non-extracted codes necessary to rebuild the original file are stored in a reference document.

General Remarks

An OpenTag document can be encoded in any valid encoding for XML. If the encoding is different from UTF-8 or UTF-16, a proper encoding declaration must be included in the XML initial processing instruction. As for any XML documents, element and attribute names are case sensitive (except the value of the lc attribute). If OpenTag elements are used within other types of XML documents, the namespace identifier for OpenTag (version 1.2) is urn:OpenTag:Version12.

Traditionally, OpenTag files have an .otf extension, whereas the reference files, generally called *skeleton files*, use an .skl extension.

OpenTag elements are separated into two main categories:

- **Structural and informative elements**—These elements provide a way to structure the extracted data into abstract groups and to attach relevant properties or notes to them.
- **Inline and delimiter elements**—Inline elements represent the original codes of the original file that were embedded within the extracted text. They appear

always within a `<p>` element. The delimiter elements are a special case of inline elements that do not represent original codes.

The OpenTag attributes use several standard types of values:

- **DateTime: Date and Time**—Valid time stamp in the format `YYYY-MM-DDThh:mm:ssZ` for Universal Coordinated Time (UTC) or `YYYY-MM-DDThh:mm:ss` for local time. For example, `2001-02-13T20:05:12Z` is February 13, 2001 at 20 hours, 5 minutes and 12 seconds.
- **LocaleID: Locale Identifier**—A code based on ISO-639 language codes and ISO-3166 country codes. For example, `en` is English, `fr-CA` is French Canadian, and `ZH-TW` is Chinese for Taiwan (Traditional Chinese). Locale identifier values are not case sensitive.
- **EncodingName: Encoding Identifier**—A standard name defined by the Internet Assigned Numbers Authority (IANA).
- **WhiteSpaceType: Type of Handling for White Spaces**—The values allowed are 0 for any consecutive white spaces that are reduced to an ASCII space; 1 for all white spaces that are preserved; and 2 for any consecutive white spaces, except tab characters, that are reduced to an ASCII space. Tabs are preserved.

Structural and Informative Elements

All elements above `<p>` are either structural or informative elements. Their relationships are shown in Figure E.1.

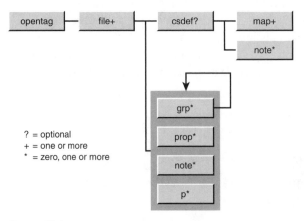

FIGURE E.1

The relationships of structural and informative elements.

Table E.1 shows all the structural and informative elements, as well as their respective attributes.

TABLE E.1

Structural and Informative Elements and Their Attributes

Elements and Attributes	Descriptions	
`<opentag>`	Document root.	
version	mandatory	Version of OpenTag the document. The current version is 1.2.
`<file>`	Encapsulating element for the data extracted from a single original file.	
tool	mandatory	Specifies the signature and version of the tool that created or modified the document. The value is tool specific.
datatype	mandatory	Specifies the kind of text contained in the element.
original	mandatory	Specifies the name of the original file from which the contents of the `<file>` element have been extracted.
lc	mandatory	Specifies the default locale of the text. The value must be in the LocaleID format.
reference	optional	Specifies the name of the reference file (skeleton file) that should be used to merge the content of the `<file>` element back into its original format.
date	optional	Indicates when the file was created or modified. The value must be in the DateTime format.
type	optional	Specifies the default context and the type of resource or style of the data.
ws	optional	Specifies the default way white spaces (ASCII spaces, tabs, and line breaks) should be treated. The value must be in the WhiteSpaceType format.
ts	optional	Short tool-specific properties that apply to this element.
`<csdef>`	Specifies user-defined code sets and characters.	
name	mandatory	Specifies the name of the user-defined code set.
base	mandatory	Specifies the encoding upon which the remapping of characters defined in the element is based. The value must be in the EncodingName format.

TABLE E.1   CONTINUED

Elements and Attributes		Descriptions
`<map/>`		Specifies the correspondence between a Unicode value and a code point of a user-defined code set.
code	mandatory	Specifies the user-defined code point.
ucode	mandatory	Specifies the Unicode code point.
ent	optional	Specifies the name of the character. The value must be in ASCII.
comp	optional	Specifies the possible base Unicode characters used to compose this character.
case	optional	Specifies the opposite case character of the given one. (For example, *A* is the case change for *a*.)
subst	optional	Specifies a possible substitute text when the character cannot be mapped to a target code set. The value must be in ASCII.
`<note>`		Used to attach comments and notes to specific parent or sibling elements.
lc	optional	Specifies the locale of the text in this element. The value must be in the LocaleID format.
rid	optional	Used to link this element with another.
`<prop>`		Allows you to specify non-standard information for a specified element.
type	mandatory	Specifies the context or the type of resource or style of the data for this element.
lc	optional	Specifies the locale of the text in this element. The value must be in the LocaleID format.
rid	optional	Used to link this element with another.
`<grp>`		Delimits a set of elements that should be processed together: all the items of a menu, several translations of the same paragraph, and so on. Note that a `<grp>` element can contain other `<grp>` elements.
tool	optional	Used to specify the signature and version of the tool that created or modified the element. The value is tool specific.
datatype	optional	Specifies the kind of text contained in this element.
id	optional	Unique reference to the construct corresponding to this element in the original file.
rid	optional	Used to link this element with another.

TABLE E.1	CONTINUED	
Elements and Attributes	*Descriptions*	
coord	optional	Specifies the x, y, cx, and cy coordinates of the text for this element. The cx and cy values must represent the width and the height. The extraction and merging tools must make the right corrections for the original formats that use a top-left/bottom-right coordinate system. The value is $x;y;cx;cy$, in that order and separated by semicolons.
font	optional	Specifies the font name and font size of the text for this element. The font attribute is generally used for resource-type data: change of font in document-type data can be marked with the <g> element. The value of font must be the name of the font and its size separated by a semicolon.
type	optional	Specifies the context or the type of resource or style of the data for this element.
lc	optional	Specifies the locale of the text in this element. The value must be in the LocaleID format.
ws	optional	Specifies the way white spaces (ASCII spaces, tabs and line breaks) should be treated. The value must be in the WhiteSpaceType format.
ts	optional	Short tool-specific properties that apply to this element.
cond	optional	Identifies an element corresponding to conditional text in the original format. You can use the <ct> element to set a condition for a given span of text.
var	optional	Allows you to identify the way this element has been generated.
<p>		Used to delimit a unit of text. A paragraph in OpenTag does not necessarily correspond to a paragraph in a word processor. It is a unit of text that could be a paragraph, a title, a menu item, or a caption.
tool	optional	Used to specify the signature and version of the tool that created or modified the element. The value is tool specific.
datatype	optional	Specifies the kind of text contained in this element.
id	optional	Unique reference to the construct corresponding to this element in the original file.

TABLE E.1   CONTINUED

Elements and Attributes		Descriptions
rid	optional	Used to link this element with another.
seg	optional	Identifier for a segment or specific translation unit.
coord	optional	Specifies the x, y, cx, and cy coordinates of the text for this element. The cx and cy values must represent the width and the height. The extraction and merging tools must make the right corrections for the original formats that use a top-left/bottom-right coordinate system. The value is x;y;cx;cy, in that order and separated by semicolons.
font	optional	Specifies the font name and font size of the text for this element. The font attribute is generally used for resource-type data: change of font in document-type data can be marked with the <g> element. The value of font must be the name of the font and its size separated by a semicolon.
type	optional	Specifies the context or the type of resource or style of the data for this element.
lc	optional	Specifies the locale of the text in this element. The value must be in the LocaleID format.
ws	optional	Specifies the way white spaces (ASCII spaces, tabs and line breaks) should be treated. The value must be in the WhiteSpaceType format.
ts	optional	Short tool-specific properties that apply to this element.
cond	optional	Identifies an element corresponding to conditional text in the original format. You can use the <ct> element to set a condition for a given span of text.
var	optional	Allows you to identify the way this element has been generated.

Inline and Delimiter Elements

All elements within <p> are either inline or delimiter elements. Their relationships are shown in Figure E.2.

Table E.2 shows all the inline and delimiter elements, as well as their respective attributes.

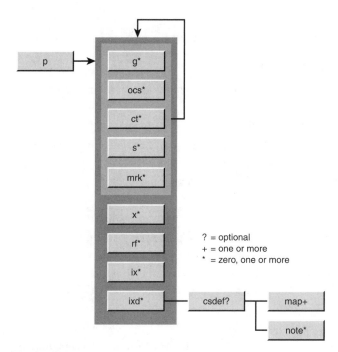

FIGURE E.2

The relationships of inline and delimiter elements.

TABLE E.2

Inline and Delimiter Elements and Their Attributes

Elements and Attributes	Descriptions	
`<g>`	Used to replace any inline code of the original document that has a beginning and an end, and can be moved within its parent element. When possible, the `type` attribute enables you to specify what kind of attribute the placeholder represents. Note that a `<g>` element can contain another `<g>` element. In this case, if the embedded group has an `id` attribute, it should never be moved outside of its parent group.	
`id`	optional	Unique reference to the construct corresponding to this element in the original file.
`type`	optional	Specifies the context or the type of resource or style of the data for this element.
`rid`	optional	Used to link this element with another.

The figure legend within the diagram reads:

? = optional
+ = one or more
* = zero, one or more

TABLE E.2 CONTINUED

Elements and Attributes	Descriptions	
ts	optional	Short tool-specific properties that apply to this element.
`<x/>`	Used to replace any inline code of the original document.	
id	optional	Unique reference to the construct corresponding to this element in the original file.
type	optional	Specifies the context or the type of resource or style of the data for this element.
rid	optional	Used to link this element with another.
ts	optional	Short tool-specific properties that apply to this element.
`<ix/>`	Specifies a reference to an index entry. The definition of the entry itself is done in the corresponding `<ixd>` element (both are linked by their `rid` attribute).	
rid	mandatory	Used to link this element with another.
id	optional	Unique reference to the construct corresponding to this element in the original file.
ts	optional	Short tool-specific properties that apply to this element.
`<ixd>`	Specifies the entry corresponding to one or more `<ix/>` elements. It does not have to be in the same `<p>` or even the same `<grp>` element. Markers and definitions do have to be in the same `<file>` element.	
rid	mandatory	Used to link this element with another.
id	optional	Unique reference to the construct corresponding to this element in the original file.
ts	optional	Specifies short property data understood by a specific tool.
`<lvl>`	Delimits the different levels of an index entry.	
id	optional	Unique reference to the construct corresponding to this element in the original file.
ts	optional	Short tool-specific properties that apply to this element.
seg	optional	Identifier for a segment or specific translation unit.

TABLE E.2	CONTINUED	
Elements and Attributes	**Descriptions**	
`<tx>`	Delimits the text of an index entry level.	
id	optional	Unique reference to the construct corresponding to this element in the original file.
ts	optional	Short tool-specific properties that apply to this element.
seg	optional	Identifier for a segment or specific translation unit.
`<so>`	Indicates the text that should be used to sort an index entry in the parent `<lvl>` element.	
id	optional	Unique reference to the construct corresponding to this element in the original file.
ts	optional	Short tool-specific properties that apply to this element.
`<rf/>`	Specifies a reference to any type of reference text (variable, pre-composed text, footnote, and so on). The definition of the reference text itself is done in one or more corresponding `<p>` elements (linked by their `rid` attribute).	
rid	mandatory	Used to link this element with another.
type	optional	Specifies the context or the type of resource or style of the data for this element.
id	optional	Unique reference to the construct corresponding to this element in the original file.
ts	optional	Specifies short property data understood by a specific tool.
`<ocs>`	Indicates the code set (encoding) of a part of the text that is different from the default code set. Note that `<ocs>` is only informative; in the OpenTag file the text within an `<ocs>` element is in the same code set as the surrounding text.	
cs	mandatory	Specifies the original encoding for this element. The value must be in the EncodingName format.
id	optional	Unique reference to the construct corresponding to this element in the original file.
ts	optional	Short tool-specific properties that apply to this element.
`<ct>`	Used to mark specific strings of the text for a given condition.	
cond	mandatory	Name that identifies the condition for this element.

TABLE E.2 CONTINUED		
Elements and Attributes	*Descriptions*	
`id`	optional	Unique reference to the construct corresponding to this element in the original file.
`ts`	optional	Short tool-specific properties that apply to this element.
`<s>`	Delimits a unit of text such as a sentence, title, menu item, or message. The `<s>` element is not part of the tags used to merge the OpenTag file back into its original format.	
`seg`	optional	Identifier for a segment or specific translation unit.
`id`	optional	Unique reference to the construct corresponding to this element in the original file.
`ts`	optional	Short tool-specific properties that apply to this element.
`type`	optional	Specifies the context or the type of resource or style of the data for this element.
`var`	optional	Allows you to identify the way this element has been generated.
`<mrk>`	Delimits a section of text that has special meaning, such as a terminology unit, a proper name, or an item that should not be modified. It can be used for various processing tasks, for example to indicate to a machine translation tool the proper names that should not be translated, and for terminology verification to mark suspect expressions after a grammar check. The `<mrk>` element is not part of the tags used to merge the OpenTag file back into its original format.	
`type`	mandatory	Specifies the context or the type of resource or style of the data for this element.
`id`	optional	Unique reference to the construct corresponding to this element in the original file.
`ts`	optional	Short tool-specific properties that apply to this element.

Sample File

Listing E.1 is an example of an OpenTag document composed of two `<file>` elements corresponding to the extraction of two different original files: an XML document in Polish and a compiled Windows resource file.

LISTING E.1

`Sample1.otf`—Simple OpenTag Document

```
<?xml version="1.0" ?>
<opentag version="1.2"
         xmlns="urn:OpenTag:Version12">


 <file lc="PL" tool="PrepToolv2" datatype="xml"
  original="dokument123.xml"
  reference="dokument123.skl">
  <p id="1" type="title">Aby zapamiętać Plik w Formacie XML.</p>
  <p id="2">Aby zapamiętać bieżący document w formacie XML wykonaj
➥poniższe czynności:</p>
  <p id="3">Wybierz komendę <g id='1'>Zapamiętaj Jako</g> w menu
➥<g id='2'>Plik</g>.</p>
  <p id="4">Wprowadź nazwę dokumentu XML. Jeśli plik z identyczną nazwą
➥już istnieje, to pojawi się okno dla potwierdzenia zapisania pliku
➥starszego poprzez dokument, który właśnie zapamiętujesz.</p>
  <p id="5">Wybierz opcję <g id='1'>Dokument XML</g> w polu dialogowym
➥<g id='2'>Format</g>.</p>
  <p id="6"><x id='1'/>Kliknij na przycisk <g id='2'>OK</g>.</p>
 </file>


 <file lc='EN-US' tool='LXExe.dll v1.00' datatype='winres' ws='1'
       original='c:\Project\Hobbit\WinApp.exe'>
  <grp id='144' coord='0;0;302;90' type='dialog' rid='124'
       font='MS Sans Serif;8'>
   <p id='0' type='caption'>Add Input Files</p>
   <p id='1' coord='4;4;294;44' type='groupbox'>&amp;Mask</p>
   <p id='2' coord='10;18;262;12' type='edit'></p>
   <p id='3' coord='276;18;16;12' type='button'>...</p>
   <p id='4' coord='10;34;97;10' type='check'>Include files in
&amp;sub-folders</p>
   <p id='5' coord='4;50;238;36' type='groupbox'></p>
   <p id='6' coord='12;59;20;20' type='icon'></p>
   <p id='7' coord='40;60;194;20' type='label'>To specify several masks,
➥simply separate them with a semicolon. (for example:
➥C:\\Project\\*.hpj;*.rtf;*.cnt)</p>
   <p id='8' coord='248;54;50;14' type='button'>OK</p>
   <p id='9' coord='248;72;50;14' type='button'>Cancel</p>
  </grp>
 </file>


</opentag>
```

DTD for OpenTag

Listing E.2 shows the document type definition for OpenTag.

LISTING E.2

`opentag.dtd`—DTD for OpenTag Version 1.2

```
<!ENTITY % groups "ocs|ct|g" >
<!ENTITY % groupsMinusOcs "ct|g" >
<!ENTITY % groupsMinusCt "ocs|g" >
<!ENTITY % delim "mrk|s" >
<!ENTITY % alones "x" >
<!ENTITY % markers "ix|rf" >
<!ENTITY % defs "ixd" >
<!ENTITY % allinline "#PCDATA|%groups;|%alones;|%markers;|%defs;" >
<!ENTITY % allinlineMinusOcs
➥"#PCDATA|%groupsMinusOcs;|%alones;|%markers;|%defs;" >
<!ENTITY % allinlineMinusCt
➥"#PCDATA|%groupsMinusCt;|%alones;|%markers;|%defs;" >


<!ENTITY   lt    "&#38;#60;" >
<!ENTITY   amp   "&#38;#38;" >
<!ENTITY   gt    "&#62;" >
<!ENTITY   apos  "&#39;" >
<!ENTITY   quot  "&#34;" >


<!-- Structural Elements -->

<!-- OpenTag -->
<!ELEMENT opentag     (file)+ >
<!ATTLIST opentag
     version          CDATA        #REQUIRED >

<!-- File -->
<!ELEMENT file        (csdef*, (note|prop|grp|p)*) >
<!ATTLIST file
     lc               CDATA        #REQUIRED
     tool             CDATA        #REQUIRED
     datatype         CDATA        #REQUIRED
     original         CDATA        #REQUIRED
     reference        CDATA        #IMPLIED
     date             CDATA        #IMPLIED
     ws               CDATA        #IMPLIED
```

```
            ts              CDATA       #IMPLIED
            type            CDATA       #IMPLIED >

<!-- Group -->
<!ELEMENT grp           (grp|p|note|prop)* >
<!ATTLIST grp
            lc              CDATA       #IMPLIED
            tool            CDATA       #IMPLIED
            datatype        CDATA       #IMPLIED
            id              CDATA       #IMPLIED
            rid             CDATA       #IMPLIED
            coord           CDATA       #IMPLIED
            font            CDATA       #IMPLIED
            type            CDATA       #IMPLIED
            ws              CDATA       #IMPLIED
            ts              CDATA       #IMPLIED
            var             CDATA       #IMPLIED
            cond            CDATA       #IMPLIED >

<!-- Note -->
<!ELEMENT note          (#PCDATA) >
<!ATTLIST note
            lc              CDATA       #IMPLIED
            rid             CDATA       #IMPLIED>

<!-- Property -->
<!ELEMENT prop          (#PCDATA) >
<!ATTLIST prop
            lc              CDATA       #IMPLIED
            type            CDATA       #REQUIRED
            rid             CDATA       #IMPLIED>

<!-- Code set definition -->
<!ELEMENT csdef         (note*, map+) >
<!ATTLIST csdef
            name            CDATA       #REQUIRED
            base            CDATA       #REQUIRED >

<!-- Character mapping -->
<!ELEMENT map           EMPTY >
<!ATTLIST map
            code            CDATA       #REQUIRED
```

```
        ucode          CDATA       #REQUIRED
        ent            CDATA       #IMPLIED
        subst          CDATA       #IMPLIED
        comp           CDATA       #IMPLIED
        case           CDATA       #IMPLIED >

<!-- Paragraph -->
<!ELEMENT p          (%allinline;|%delim;)* >
<!ATTLIST p
        lc             CDATA       #IMPLIED
        tool           CDATA       #IMPLIED
        datatype       CDATA       #IMPLIED
        id             CDATA       #IMPLIED
        rid            CDATA       #IMPLIED
        seg            CDATA       #IMPLIED
        coord          CDATA       #IMPLIED
        font           CDATA       #IMPLIED
        type           CDATA       #IMPLIED
        ws             CDATA       #IMPLIED
        ts             CDATA       #IMPLIED
        var            CDATA       #IMPLIED
        cond           CDATA       #IMPLIED >

<!-- In-Line Elements -->

<!-- Generic Group Place-Holder -->
<!ELEMENT g          (%allinline;|%delim;)* >
<!ATTLIST g
        id             CDATA       #IMPLIED
        type           CDATA       #IMPLIED
        rid            CDATA       #IMPLIED
        ts             CDATA       #IMPLIED >

<!-- Generic Place-Holder -->
<!ELEMENT x          EMPTY >
<!ATTLIST x
        id             CDATA       #IMPLIED
        type           CDATA       #IMPLIED
        rid            CDATA       #IMPLIED
        ts             CDATA       #IMPLIED >
```

LISTING E.2 **CONTINUED**

```
<!-- Index Marker -->
<!ELEMENT ix        EMPTY >
<!ATTLIST ix
        rid             CDATA       #REQUIRED
        ts              CDATA       #IMPLIED
        id              CDATA       #IMPLIED >


<!-- Index Definition -->
<!ELEMENT ixd       (lvl)+>
<!ATTLIST ixd
        rid             CDATA       #REQUIRED
        ts              CDATA       #IMPLIED
        id              CDATA       #IMPLIED >

<!-- Index Level Entry -->
<!ELEMENT lvl       (tx, so?)  >
<!ATTLIST lvl
        id              CDATA       #IMPLIED
        ts              CDATA       #IMPLIED
        seg             CDATA       #IMPLIED >

<!-- Index Level Entry Text -->
<!ELEMENT tx        (#PCDATA|%groups;|%delim;|%alones;|rf)* >
<!ATTLIST tx
        id              CDATA       #IMPLIED
        ts              CDATA       #IMPLIED
        seg             CDATA       #IMPLIED >

<!-- Index Sort Order Text -->
<!ELEMENT so        (#PCDATA) >
<!ATTLIST so
        id              CDATA       #IMPLIED
        ts              CDATA       #IMPLIED >

<!-- Reference Marker -->
<!ELEMENT rf        EMPTY >
<!ATTLIST rf
        rid             CDATA       #REQUIRED
        type            CDATA       #IMPLIED
        ts              CDATA       #IMPLIED
        id              CDATA       #IMPLIED >
```

LISTING E.2 CONTINUED

```
<!-- Original Code Set -->
<!ELEMENT ocs        (%allinlineMinusOcs;|%delim;)* >
<!ATTLIST ocs
      cs             CDATA      #REQUIRED
      ts             CDATA      #IMPLIED
      id             CDATA      #IMPLIED >


<!-- Conditional Text -->
<!ELEMENT ct         (%allinlineMinusCt;|%delim;)* >
<!ATTLIST ct
      cond           CDATA      #REQUIRED
      ts             CDATA      #IMPLIED
      id             CDATA      #IMPLIED >



<!-- Delimiter Elements -->

<!-- Segment Delimiter -->
<!ELEMENT s          (%allinline;|mrk)* >
<!ATTLIST s
      id             CDATA      #IMPLIED
      ts             CDATA      #IMPLIED
      var            CDATA      #IMPLIED
      type           CDATA      #IMPLIED
      seg            CDATA      #IMPLIED >

<!-- Marker Delimiter -->
<!ELEMENT mrk        (%allinline;|s)* >
<!ATTLIST mrk
      type           CDATA      #REQUIRED
      ts             CDATA      #IMPLIED
      id             CDATA      #IMPLIED >
```

APPENDIX F

TMX Quick Reference

In This Appendix:

The TMX (Translation Memory eXchange) format is an XML document type designed to store aligned translation units in any type of original format.

General Remarks

A TMX document must be encoded in UCS-2, UTF-8, or US-ASCII. Although TMX is an XML application, other encodings are not part of the specifications. As for any XML documents, element and attribute names are case sensitive (except the value of the lang attribute). If TMX elements are used within other types of XML documents, the namespace identifier for TMX is http://www.lisa.org/tmx.

TMX elements are separated into two categories: Container elements and Content elements. The first category provides the structure of the document and its administrative information; the second provides a way to mark up native codes inside a segment.

There are three levels of TMX documents depending on how inline codes are treated. For example, with the XHTML paragraph

```
<p>The cat is <b>black</b>.</p>
```

you can have the following cases:

- **Level 1**—Segments have no inline codes. There are no Content elements in the file.
  ```
  <seg>The cat is black.</seg>
  ```

Tools supporting only Level 1 TMX and dealing with paragraph-type data (rather than source code) lose all inline information.

- **Level 2**—Inline codes are marked by Content elements, but the code inside each Content element is not the original code in the native format. For example, it can be a placeholder generated by a translation tool.

```
<seg>The cat is <bpt i="1" type="bold">{1}</bpt>Black<ept
↪i="1">{2}</ept>.</seg>
```

The native code for bold is not stored, but the `<bpt>` and `<ept>` elements keep track of where the tags should be.

- **Level 3**—Inline codes are marked by Content elements, and the code inside each Content element is the original code in the native format.

```
<seg>The cat is <bpt i="1"
↪type="bold">&lt;b></bpt>Black<ept i="1">&lt;/b></ept>.</seg>
```

The original codes for bold are preserved, but they are also abstracted in `<bpt>` and `<ept>`.

The attributes of TMX use several standard types of values:

- **DateTime**: **Date and Time**—A valid time stamp in the format `YYYYMMDDThhmmssZ` in Universal Coordinated Time (UTC). For example, `20010213T200512Z` is February 13, 2001 at 20 hours, 5 minutes, and 12 seconds.
- **LocaleID**: **Locale Identifier**—A code based on ISO-639 language codes and ISO-3166 country codes. For example, `en` is English, `fr-CA` is French Canadian, and `ZH-TW` is Chinese for Taiwan (Traditional Chinese). Locale identifier values are not case sensitive.
- **EncodingName**: **Encoding Identifier**—A standard name defined by the Internet Assigned Numbers Authority (IANA).

Container Elements

All elements above `<seg>` are Container elements. Their relationships are shown in Figure F.1.

Table F.1 shows the Container elements and their respective attributes.

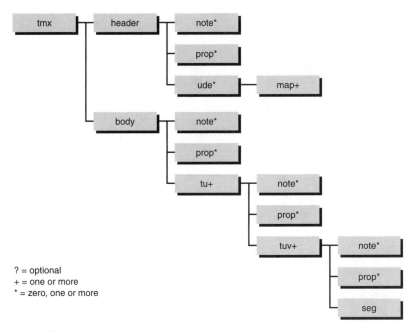

? = optional
+ = one or more
* = zero, one or more

FIGURE F.1

Container elements.

TABLE F.1

Container Elements and Their Attributes

Elements and Attributes	Descriptions	
`<tmx>`	Document root.	
`version`	mandatory	Version of TMX for the document. The current version is 1.2.
`<header>`	Encapsulating element for general document-level administrative information.	
`creationtool`	mandatory	Name of the tool that created the document. The value is tool specific.
`creationtoolversion`	mandatory	Version identifier of the creation tool. The value is tool specific.
`segtype`	mandatory	Default type of segmentation used in the file. (block, paragraph, sentence, or phrase). This can be overwritten at the `<tu>` level.

TABLE F.1   CONTINUED

Elements and Attributes	Descriptions	
o-tmf	mandatory	Identifier of the original TM format. The value is tool specific.
adminlang	mandatory	Language identifier for the text of the notes. The value must be in the LocaleID format.
srclang	mandatory	Language identifier for the source in the translation units. The value must be in the LocaleID format, or if all languages can be used as source, the value *all* is used.
datatype	mandatory	Type of data the <seg> element contains.
o-encoding	optional	Original encoding of the data. The value must be in the EncodingName format.
creationdate	optional	Date and time of the creation of the document. The value must be in the DateTime format.
creationid	optional	Identifier for the user who created the initial document.
changedate	optional	Date and time indicating when the document was last modified. The value must be in the DateTime format.
changeid	optional	Identifier for the user who last changed the document.
<prop>		Tool-specific properties.
type	mandatory	Type of property. The value is tool specific.
lang	optional	Language identifier of the property data. The value must be in the LocaleID format.
o-encoding	optional	Original encoding of the property data. The value must be in the EncodingName format.

TABLE F.1 CONTINUED		
Elements and Attributes	*Descriptions*	
`<note>`	Notes.	
lang	optional	Language identifier of the note. The value must be in the LocaleID format.
o-encoding	optional	Original encoding of the note. The value must be in the EncodingName format.
`<ude>`	User-defined encoding information. Container for `<map/>` elements.	
name	mandatory	Name of the set of user-defined characters.
base	mandatory if one `<map/>` element contains a `code` attribute	The base attribute specifies the code set on which the mapping of the user-defined characters is based. The value must be in the EncodingName format.
`<map/>`	Mapping of a user-defined character.	
unicode	mandatory	Unicode code point of the user-defined character. The value must be a valid UCS code point in the hexadecimal format `#xHHHH` (for example, `Unicode="#xF8FF"`).
code	optional	Code-point value in a given encoding corresponding to the user-defined character. The value must be in the hexadecimal format `#xHH` (for example, `code="#x9F"`).
ent	optional	Entity name of the user-defined character. The value must be in ASCII (for example, `ent="AppleSymbol"`).
subst	optional	Alternative string for the user-defined character. The value must be in ASCII (for example, `"(c)"` for the copyright sign.
`<body>`	Encapsulating element for the translation units.	

TABLE F.1   CONTINUED

Elements and Attributes		Descriptions
`<tu>`		Translation unit.
tuid	optional	Identifier for the translation unit. The value can be numeric, alphabetic, or alphanumeric. TMX does not enforce unique `tuid` within the same document (however, it is a recommendation).
usagecount	optional	Number of times the translation unit has been accessed.
lastusagedate	optional	Date and time when the translation unit was last accessed. The value must be in the DateTime format.
creationtool	optional	Name of the tool that created the translation unit. The value is tool specific.
creationtoolversion	optional	Version identifier of the creation tool. The value is tool specific.
segtype	optional	Default type of segmentation used in the translation unit (block, paragraph, sentence, or phrase).
o-tmf	optional	Identifier of the original TM format. The value is tool specific.
srclang	optional	Language identifier for the source in the translation units. The value must be in the LocaleID format, or if all languages can be used as source the value `*all*` is used.
datatype	optional	Type of data the `<seg>` element contains.
o-encoding	optional	Original encoding of the data. The value must be in the EncodingName format.
creationdate	optional	Date and time of the creation of the translation unit. The value must be in the DateTime format.
creationid	optional	Identifier for the user who created the initial translation unit.

TABLE F.1 CONTINUED

Elements and Attributes	Descriptions	
changedate	optional	Date and time indicating when the translation unit was last modified. The value must be in the DateTime format.
changeid	optional	Identifier for the user who last changed the translation unit.
<tuv>	Translation unit variant. Contains the segment of the translation unit in a given language.	
lang	mandatory	Language identifier of the translation unit variant. The value must be in the LocaleID format.
usagecount	optional	Number of times the translation unit variant has been accessed.
lastusagedate	optional	Date and time when the translation unit variant was last accessed. The value must be in the DateTime format.
creationtool	optional	Name of the tool that created the translation unit variant. The value is tool specific.
creationtoolversion	optional	Version identifier of the creation tool. The value is tool specific.
o-tmf	optional	Identifier of the original TM format. The value is tool specific.
datatype	optional	Type of data the <seg> element contains.
o-encoding	optional	Original encoding of the data. The value must be in the EncodingName format.
creationdate	optional	Date and time of the creation of the translation unit variant. The value must be in the DateTime format.
creationid	optional	Identifier for the user who created the initial translation unit variant.

TABLE F.1 CONTINUED		
Elements and Attributes	*Descriptions*	
changedate	optional	Date and time indicating when the translation unit variant was last modified. The value must be in the DateTime format.
changeid	optional	Identifier for the user who last changed the translation unit variant.
<seg>		Segment. Contains the text and inline codes of the translation unit variant.

Content Elements

All elements inside a <seg> are Content elements. Their relationships are shown in Figure F.2.

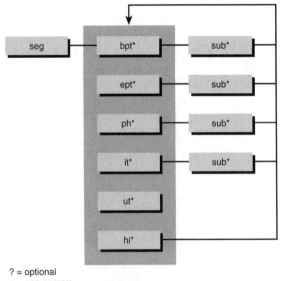

? = optional
+ = one or more
* = zero, one or more

FIGURE F.2

Content elements.

Note that the <sub> and <hi> elements lead to a recursive structure.

Table F.2 shows these Content elements and their respective attributes.

TABLE F.2

Content Elements and Their Attributes

Elements and Attributes		Descriptions
`<bpt>`		Begin paired tag. Encloses the start of code that has a corresponding ending part in the same segment.
`i`	mandatory	Internal matching identifier. Used to match the element with its corresponding `<ept>`.
`type`	optional	Type of inline code bracketed by the element. The value is tool specific.
`x`	optional	External matching identifier. Used to match the element across translation unit variants.
`<ept>`		End paired tag. Encloses the end of code that has a corresponding beginning part in the same segment.
`i`	mandatory	Internal matching identifier. Used to match the element with its corresponding `<bpt>`.
`<it>`		Isolated tag. Encloses the beginning or ending part of code that has no corresponding beginning or ending inside the same segment.
`pos`	mandatory	Position. Used to specify whether the element is the beginning or the end part of a paired code that has no correspondence in the segment. The value must be an empty string, begin, or end.
`type`	optional	Type of inline code bracketed by the element. The value is tool specific.
`x`	optional	External matching identifier. Used to match the element across translation unit variants.
`<ph>`		Placeholder. Encloses a run of codes that is self-contained.
`type`	optional	Type of inline code bracketed by the element. The value is tool specific.
`x`	optional	External matching identifier. Used to match the element across translation unit variants.
`assoc`	optional	Association indicator. Used to define whether a `<ph>` element is associated with the previous or the following text, or both. The value must be `p` (previous), `f` (following), or `b` (both).

TABLE **F.2**	**CONTINUED**	
Elements and Attributes	*Descriptions*	
`<ut>`	Unknown tag. Used to delimit a sequence of code about which the exporter tool has no information.	
x	optional	External matching identifier. Used to match the element across translation unit variants.
`<sub>`	Subflow. Delimits a run of text included inside a sequence of inline code: for example, the value of an attribute in a XHTML tag.	
type	optional	Type of inline code bracketed by the element. The value is tool specific.
datatype	optional	Type of data the element contains.
`<hi>`	Highlight. Used to delimit a portion of content for a tool-specific purpose.	
type	optional	Type of inline code bracketed by the element. The value is tool specific.
x	optional	External matching identifier. Used to match the element across translation unit variants.

Sample File

Listing F.1 is a sample TMX document. It contains a simple sentence in Simplified Chinese and English.

LISTING **F.1**

`Sample1.tmx`—Simple TMX Document

```
<?xml version="1.0" ?>
<tmx version="1.2">
 <header creationtool="ToolXyz" creationtoolversion="2.00"
  datatype="plaintext" segtype="sentence"
  adminlang="en-US" srclang="*all*" o-tmf="TMxyz">
 </header>
 <body>
  <tu tuid="1">
   <tuv lang="en-US">
    <seg>This is an example of horizontal text.</seg>
   </tuv>
   <tuv lang="zh-CN">
    <seg>这是一个横排版文字的例子。</seg>
```

LISTING F.1   CONTINUED

```
   </tuv>
  </tu>
 </body>
</tmx>
```

DTD for TMX

Listing F.2 is the Document Type Definition for TMX version 1.2. The online version is available at http://www.lisa.org/tmx/tmx12.dtd.

LISTING F.2

TMX.dtd—Document Type Definition for TMX Version 1.2

```
<!ENTITY   lt    "&#38;#60;" >
<!ENTITY   amp   "&#38;#38;" >
<!ENTITY   gt    "&#62;" >
<!ENTITY   apos  "&#39;" >
<!ENTITY   quot  "&#34;" >


<!ENTITY % segtypes     "block|paragraph|sentence|phrase" >


<!-- Container Markup ================================================ -->

<!-- Base Document Element -->
   <!ELEMENT tmx             (header, body) >
   <!ATTLIST tmx
        version              CDATA          #REQUIRED >

<!-- Header -->
   <!ELEMENT header          (note|prop|ude)* >
   <!ATTLIST header
        creationtool         CDATA          #REQUIRED
        creationtoolversion  CDATA          #REQUIRED
        segtype              (%segtypes;)   #REQUIRED
        o-tmf                CDATA          #REQUIRED
        adminlang            CDATA          #REQUIRED
        srclang              CDATA          #REQUIRED
        datatype             CDATA          #REQUIRED
        o-encoding           CDATA          #IMPLIED
```

```
        creationdate        CDATA           #IMPLIED
        creationid          CDATA           #IMPLIED
        changedate          CDATA           #IMPLIED
        changeid            CDATA           #IMPLIED >

<!-- Body -->
  <!ELEMENT body          (tu*) >
  <!-- No attributes          -->

<!-- Note -->
  <!ELEMENT note          (#PCDATA) >
  <!ATTLIST note
        o-encoding          CDATA           #IMPLIED
        xml:lang            CDATA           #IMPLIED >

<!-- User-defined Encoding -->
  <!ELEMENT ude           (map+) >
  <!ATTLIST ude
        name                CDATA           #REQUIRED
        base                CDATA           #IMPLIED >
<!-- Note: the base attribute is required if one or more <map>
     elements in the <ude> contain a code attribute. -->

<!-- Character mapping -->
  <!ELEMENT map           EMPTY >
  <!ATTLIST map
        unicode             CDATA           #REQUIRED
        code                CDATA           #IMPLIED
        ent                 CDATA           #IMPLIED
        subst               CDATA           #IMPLIED >

<!-- Property -->
  <!ELEMENT prop          (#PCDATA) >
  <!ATTLIST prop
        type                CDATA           #REQUIRED
        xml:lang            CDATA           #IMPLIED
        o-encoding          CDATA           #IMPLIED >

<!-- Translation Unit -->
  <!ELEMENT tu            ((note|prop)*, tuv+) >
```

LISTING F.2 CONTINUED

```
<!ATTLIST tu
      tuid                    CDATA          #IMPLIED
      o-encoding              CDATA          #IMPLIED
      datatype                CDATA          #IMPLIED
      usagecount              CDATA          #IMPLIED
      lastusagedate           CDATA          #IMPLIED
      creationtool            CDATA          #IMPLIED
      creationtoolversion     CDATA          #IMPLIED
      creationdate            CDATA          #IMPLIED
      creationid              CDATA          #IMPLIED
      changedate              CDATA          #IMPLIED
      segtype                 (%segtypes;)   #IMPLIED
      changeid                CDATA          #IMPLIED
      o-tmf                   CDATA          #IMPLIED
      srclang                 CDATA          #IMPLIED >

<!-- Translation Unit Variant -->
   <!ELEMENT tuv               ((note|prop)*, seg) >
   <!ATTLIST tuv
         xml:lang              CDATA          #REQUIRED
         o-encoding            CDATA          #IMPLIED
         datatype              CDATA          #IMPLIED
         usagecount            CDATA          #IMPLIED
         lastusagedate         CDATA          #IMPLIED
         creationtool          CDATA          #IMPLIED
         creationtoolversion   CDATA          #IMPLIED
         creationdate          CDATA          #IMPLIED
         creationid            CDATA          #IMPLIED
         changedate            CDATA          #IMPLIED
         o-tmf                 CDATA          #IMPLIED
         changeid              CDATA          #IMPLIED >

<!-- Text -->
   <!ELEMENT seg               (#PCDATA|bpt|ept|ph|ut|it|hi)* >


<!-- Content Markup ================================================== -->

   <!ELEMENT bpt               (#PCDATA|sub)* >
   <!ATTLIST bpt
        i                      CDATA          #REQUIRED
```

LISTING F.2   CONTINUED

```
        x                CDATA          #IMPLIED
        type             CDATA          #IMPLIED >

<!ELEMENT ept            (#PCDATA|sub)* >
<!ATTLIST ept
        i                CDATA          #REQUIRED >

<!ELEMENT sub            (#PCDATA|bpt|ept|it|ph|ut|hi)* >
<!ATTLIST sub
        datatype         CDATA          #IMPLIED
        type             CDATA          #IMPLIED >

<!ELEMENT it             (#PCDATA|sub)* >
<!ATTLIST it
        pos              (begin|end)    #REQUIRED
        x                CDATA          #IMPLIED
        type             CDATA          #IMPLIED >

<!ELEMENT ph             (#PCDATA|sub)* >
<!ATTLIST ph
        assoc            CDATA          #IMPLIED
        x                CDATA          #IMPLIED
        type             CDATA          #IMPLIED >

<!ELEMENT ut             (#PCDATA) >
<!ATTLIST ut
        x                CDATA          #IMPLIED >

<!ELEMENT hi             (#PCDATA|bpt|ept|it|ph|ut|hi)* >
<!ATTLIST hi
        type             CDATA          #IMPLIED
        x                CDATA          #IMPLIED >


<!-- End -->
```

INDEX

SYMBOLS

A